journalism in the mass media

NORMAN B. MOYES

DAVID MANNING WHITE

VIRGINIA WOODRING
Text Consultant

GINN AND COMPANY
A XEROX COMPANY

ABOUT THE AUTHORS

Dr. Norman B. Moyes, associate professor in the Division of Journalism, School of Public Communication, Boston University, has lectured and written extensively on high school journalism topics and has been a school newspaper and yearbook adviser. He has been a reporter and editor for the *Syracuse Post-Standard* and the *Boston Herald Traveler* and has also worked in the advertising and public relations fields. He was the executive director of the New York State Society of Newspaper Editors.

Dr. David Manning White, chairman of the Division of Journalism, School of Public Communication, Boston University, is well known throughout the country as a writer and lecturer in the field of mass communication. He is editor of *Television Quarterly* and author of a number of books. *Mass Culture*, one of his best-known books, is now in its 14th printing. Dr. White has had extensive experience on magazines, newspapers, and in radio and television.

Mrs. Virginia Woodring, Text Consultant, was named 1969 National High School Journalism Teacher of the Year by The Newspaper Fund, Inc. She is editor of the Journalism Education Association's publication *Communications: Journalism Education Today* and edits and advises Missouri State Department of Education publications. In addition to being a teacher and the journalism coordinator in the Springfield, Missouri, Public Schools, Mrs. Woodring is moderator and producer of "Teen-Talk," a televised panel program, which has earned three Freedom Foundation Awards and a Golden Mike Award.

PREFACE

Recently, millions of people all over the world watched on television the presentation of "Oscars" to the outstanding motion-picture actors and actresses of the year. Through the use of a communications satellite, excited viewers in America, Europe, and Asia learned who the winners of the awards were at precisely the same moment as those present at the ceremonies. This world-wide, "live" coverage demonstrated the great advances which have been made in communications. The next morning, the "Oscar" presentations were a front-page story in thousands of newspapers throughout the world.

Although the "Oscar" presentations cannot compare in consequence to a Presidential decision from the White House, or to troops moving from a Russian province to the Czechosolovak border, or to riots in Shanghai, or to man's first landing on the moon, this event does exemplify the advancement and potential of the mass communications media in the area of news.

At the beginning of this century there could not possibly have been such immediacy in communications, nor such an "event" to report, principally because there was no motion picture industry (and therefore were no "stars"), no television (or radio), and, of course, no communications satellite. Our world is, indeed, changing rapidly in many respects, and nowhere is the change more dramatic and important than in man's ability to communicate with his fellowman in every part of the world. Mass communication has come to fruition during the twentieth century, and it is hard to conceive how our grandfathers were able to get along without all of the technical wonders that we now take for granted each day.

This book proposes to tell you something about mass communications in its many forms, and hopefully it can help you think about a career in this ever-widening field. One of the best proving grounds for one who believes he has the aptitude and interest to pursue the professional goal of a career in communications is in school. By working on a school publication, whether it be the newspaper, yearbook, or literary magazine, you can get some feeling for the problems that face every communicator, whether he is the Editor of *The New York Times*, a commentator on network television, a top-notch copywriter for a New York advertising agency, or a photographer for *Life* Magazine. Every communicator must be able to describe with clarity, style, and accuracy that portion of contemporary life that is his current assignment —and must do this in a manner that will interest his reader or listener.

You probably have heard the adage that "writers are born, not made." Don't believe it. Writers, naturally, have more of an aptitude for communication than for designing bridges or for molecular biological research. But most of us begin with a small talent that flourishes because we work at it with all of our strength. Nothing is as satisfying as watching an embryonic talent grow into a full and powerful one, especially your own.

Many of you will begin your eventual life-work here at school. If you discover that nothing can quite equal the satisfaction of being a communicator, the next step will be further pre-professional study in communications.

Our hope in this volume is to stimulate your interest in the many-faceted world of mass communications and to invite you to become acquainted with the skills that will help you get started in this field.

David Manning White

INTRODUCTION

High school and college students, constantly exposed to and aware of the vast potential of the mass media of communications, are studying journalism in increasing numbers every year. Technological advances in communications have made possible immediate, and often simultaneous, news coverage of events anywhere in the world—even in space. More than ever before the future journalist will be not only a reporter and interpreter of events but, because of the influence of the mass media, will also play a role in the forming of public opinion and in the bringing about of democratic changes in society. The need for capable, responsible journalists and discriminating consumers of the mass media has never been greater. For these reasons this book was written to:

1. Give journalism students a comprehensive picture not only of the school media, but of the professional media as well, thus acquainting them with the roles of the mass media in a democratic society and creating a sound basis for the discriminating reading, listening, viewing, and intelligent use of the mass media.

2. Provide a supplement to the language arts program by presenting journalistic writing as a form of composition, thus enabling students to further develop their writing skills.

3. Develop in staff members of student publications a sense of responsibility for use of the printed word, thereby encouraging the improvement of student publications and the use of these publications as a laboratory for student writing.

4. Acquaint students with the possibilities of continuing their education in the field of communications.

To accomplish these goals, this book has been divided into three major parts. Part One, "The Roles of the Mass Media in a Democratic Society," offers students a comprehensive view of the professional mass media. This section develops a sound basis for discriminative reading, listening, and intelligent consumer use of the mass media. The section begins with a short history of the development of communication from its primitive beginnings to the complex communications satellite systems being developed today. Separate chapters about newspapers, magazines, the electronic media, public relations, and advertising present a brief history of each of these media, a description of their organization and operational procedures, and information for students interested in pursuing journalism in the mass media as a career. Part One concludes with a glimpse into the future of the mass media.

Part Two, "Basic Mass Media Writing Assignments," acquaints the student with journalistic writing as a form of composition. The section focuses on the structure and purpose of various types of news stories, dealing primarily with the newspaper—the first and basic conveyor of information. Included are chapters on newswriting (for both the print and electronic media), interviewing, speech and meeting coverage, feature writing, sports writing, editorial writing, and the social responsibility of journalists. Since the fundamentals of writing are the same for both school and professional journalism, the student will find these chapters helpful for preparing writing assignments for school publications.

Part Three, "The School Media," describes in detail how to produce the school newspaper, yearbook, and literary magazine. These chapters, dealing with the organization, writing, production, and finance of scholastic publications, outline the responsibilities of the various staff members and offer technical information on how to prepare these publications. The section also includes a chapter on photography in the school media.

The activities following each chapter take advantage of the fact that the student's world abounds in communications data he has seldom used in class. For example, he interrelates with his friends, he listens to the radio and watches television, and he notices signs and interprets signals. Based on his own environmental experience with communication, the activities lead the student to view the mass media of communications in a more meaningful relationship to himself, and to apply practical journalistic techniques in practical exercises.

The booklists presented at the end of each chapter offer the student an opportunity to explore further into the subject of journalism in the mass media.

The authors acknowledge with gratitude the many persons and organizations who have cooperated with the authors in the preparation of this textbook. Special thanks should go to the following persons and organizations: James Hamilton, Nimrod Press, Boston; S. Jack Weissberger and Edmund C. Arnold, both of Syracuse University; Roland D. Moyes, *Syracuse Herald-Journal;* Robert Smith, James Shen, Maurice Cullen, Robert Steele, Tim Cohane, Robert Baram, Elizabeth Bailey, Sue Cote, Elizabeth McGraw, Alexandra Holt, Robert S. Seeley, and Mark Wisen, all of Boston University; Taylor Publishing Co., Dallas, Texas; William Keller Co., Buffalo, New York; William Ward, University of Nevada; the *Boston Globe;* WBZ-TV, Boston; the *Emporia Gazette* (Kans.); the *St. Louis Post-Dispatch;* Time, Inc.; the *Reader's Digest;* Henry Selvitella, Medford High School, Medford, Mass.; Joseph M. Murphy, Columbia Scholastic Press Association; and Paul Swensson, Temple University, and consultant to The Newspaper Fund, Inc.

The cooperation of all schools that gave the authors permission to use excerpts from their publications is deeply appreciated.

Norman B. Moyes

Contents

PART ONE

THE ROLES OF MASS MEDIA
IN A DEMOCRATIC SOCIETY

CHAPTER 4   The Electronic Media   68

CHAPTER 5   Public Relations   92

CHAPTER 6   Advertising   108

PART TWO

BASIC MASS MEDIA
WRITING ASSIGNMENTS

cation Covers, 478; LITERARY PUBLICATION PRINTING METHODS, 479; Mimeographed Publications, 479; Low-cost Printing Methods, 479; FINANCING SCHOOL LITERARY PUBLICATIONS, 481; Advertising, 482; Circulation, 482; Promotion, 482; ACTIVITIES, 482; READING, 484.

PART ONE

The Roles of Mass Media in a Democratic Society

Chapter 1

Development of
Mass Communication

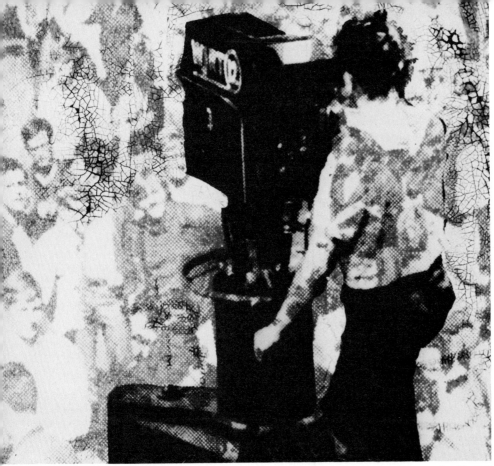

THE DYNAMICS OF COMMUNICATION

Almost every living thing communicates. Communication, which in its simplest form involves only two participants, began perhaps when some types of one-celled animals sent out chemical signals to other members of their species when the time was right for reproduction. Man, the highest form of living organism, has the most complex means of communicating. The art of communicating, a complicated process, implies both the ability to express and to understand. Early man gestured, made noises, and used elaborate systems of sound symbols to transmit his feelings and thoughts to other human beings. Today, man has developed a system of communicating which includes not only gestures and signs, but oral and written language as well. While there are several theories which attempt to explain the origin of human language, such theories are only speculative because there is no evidence about language before it was recorded in written form. We can be reasonably sure, however, that early man first communicated because he *had* to.

Man's Psychic Need

As civilization developed, man expanded his communicating processes and learned to express himself by organizing voice noises into what we call speech and by perfecting an ability to read and write what we call words and sentences. Because over the centuries he has evolved a written means for communicating, man has an advantage over other living things—his ability to leave behind a record of his experiences. Whether using smoke signals or sending television pictures over the communications satellite Intelsat, man's eagerness to communicate over increasingly larger areas and to make his communications permanent has always been the same in spirit—he seems to have a strong basic desire to transfer his thoughts to people he knows and to people he does not know and will never know. Roy E. Larson of Time, Inc., relates communication to learning:

> Man has a psychic need for communication—to communicate and to be communicated with, to express and to comprehend the expression of others. This is quite simple, when you stop to think of it: for all true education is communication, and all education is necessarily the consequence of communication.

The Four Elements of Communication

Communication involves four elements: a sender, a message, a medium, and a receiver. You (the sender) wish to transmit a joke (a message) by letter (the medium) to a friend (the receiver). Mass communication involves the same elements but the message is transmitted to a greater number of persons. The journalist (the sender) transmits the news (the message) by a newspaper (the medium) to thousands of readers (the receivers).

The Mass Media

Newspapers, magazines, radio, television, motion pictures, advertising, and public relations are considered the mass communication media because they are concerned with transmitting messages to great masses of people. These media were developed primarily as news media—methods by which information could be quickly and efficiently communicated to large audiences.

News and Journalism

News is a kind of timely information of interest to many people, usually concerning events that have just taken place or are about to take place. The collecting, writing, editing, and dissemination of news material is called jour-

4

nalism. The journalist selects the news which he considers most important to his audience, and he presents it in a manner that will stimulate thought as well as provide information. So that you will be a more informed, discriminating consumer of the mass media, this chapter briefly presents the development of the communications media, dealing primarily with the newspaper—the first and basic conveyor of information. By becoming familiar with the background of this printed medium and comparing early concepts of news with today's concepts, you will better understand the changing character of the mass media as a growing industry in a changing society. The remaining chapters in Unit I present the background and functions of the mass media in our society. Following is a summary outline of the common, or popular, media of news communication.

A SUMMARY OUTLINE OF THE COMMON, OR POPULAR, MEDIA OF NEWS COMMUNICATION

I. Informal
   1. Oral rumor, gossip, chatter
   2. Personal letters

II. Printed
   1. Newspapers
     a. Metropolitan dailies
     b. Suburban dailies
     c. Small-city dailies
     d. Country and community weeklies
     e. Ethnic and specialized newspapers

   2. Magazines, Periodicals, and Books
     a. Weekly news magazines
     b. Picture weeklies and bi-weeklies
     c. Journals of comment
     d. General, weekly, and monthly magazines
     e. Specialized periodicals
     f. "Confidential" reports
     g. Fiction
     h. Nonfiction

III. Broadcast
   1. Radio
     a. Networks
     b. Local programs
   2. Television
     a. Networks
     b. Local programs

IV. Projected
     a. Newsreels
     b. Documentary and educational films

FORERUNNERS OF THE MASS MEDIA

The modern mass media, generally conceded to be the gift of no one nation, had been in the process of development centuries before the first recorded distribution of the daily news in 60 B.C. At that time the pre-Christian Roman government issued handwritten news accounts called *Acta Diurna* (Day's Events) posting them in the Roman Forum. These newsletters containing official government announcements and some news of general public concern were established by Julius Caesar. The *Acta Diurna* were also sent to the Roman Legions then waging war in other countries. Many historians have suggested that this first recorded distribution of the daily news was done with the hope that the information contained therein would increase patriotism as well as create interest in public affairs. Handwritten handbills and posted newsletters carrying news to citizens appeared in other countries following the initial appearance of the *Acta Diurna*.

Development of Movable Type

Marco Polo, returning to Italy from China in 1295 A.D., told of having seen books that had apparently been printed using movable type. But the introduction of movable type to the Western World did not come about until the 1440's when Johannes Gutenberg used this method of printing, mainly to publish books. The introduction of movable type, ranking high among man's earliest achievements in the history of mass communications, freed him from the hours of tedious labor previously required for transcribing messages.

Development of the Newspaper

The newsbook and newsletter were among the earliest forerunners of our modern newspaper. The newsbook, issued by government initiative or approval, first appeared in Germany. Usually, the newsbook was the account of an event. One of the first English newsbooks, published by Queen Elizabeth's staff, was an account of the defeat of the Spanish Armada. In seventeenth century Europe newsletters became more numerous and were essential to merchants who were interested in international news.

In the mid 1500's the word "gazette" came into use in Italy where Italian citizens paid a gazetta, a small coin, for newsletters describing events in the Dalmation War. In the last half of the fifteenth century printing presses sprang up all over Europe, and the first press in North America was set up in Mexico in 1539. Fly sheets, as contrasted to established newspapers, first appeared on the European mainland in 1609 with Augsburg's *Avisa Relation oder Zeitung* and Strasbourg's *Relation*.

Development of Newspapers in England

In England, where William Caxton had begun that country's first printing press in 1476, printers lagged behind the rest of Europe in establishing newspapers. Despite the fact that the printing press liberated the printed word and eventually led to the widespread dissemination of ideas and information to masses of people, the first English newspapers of significance did not appear until the 1600's—some 160 years after Gutenberg introduced movable type to the Western World. Called *corantos*, these rudimentary prototypes of today's newspapers first appeared in the 1620's. Published irregularly by men interested in influencing public opinion, the corantos, like the earlier newsletters, were mainly concerned with European news of foreign events. Although few people at the time could read, the corantos soon gained enough interest to be produced in quantity. But it was not until 1624 that the corantos started to be identified by name, thus supplying some of the continuity required of true newspapers. The earliest-known coranto published by title was Thomas Archer's *The Continuation of Our Weekly Newes*, considered by many scholars to be the first genuine newspaper. The first daily domestic reports published in England can be traced to the publication of accounts of Parliamentary proceedings in 1628. Out of these accounts developed the *diurnals*, or daily reports of local events. The diurnals, true forerunners of today's dailies, are considered to be the oldest-known regularly published daily accounts of the news.

Milton's *Areopagitica*

The long-suppressed British public was clamoring for more freedom of expression, but the government, aware of the threat of the printed word, exercised close control and censorship over all early publications. In 1644 poet John Milton published his famous *Areopagitica*, probably the most perfect and eloquent expression of the idea of a free press. As a result, the censorship laws were considerably relaxed and a new era of journalism began, making way for the establishment in 1665 of *The Oxford Gazette*, the first periodical to meet all of the qualifications of a true newspaper. Milton's ideas, as expressed in *Areopagitica*, were picked up nearly a hundred years later all over the world, notably in America, where people were struggling to obtain an even greater freedom.

The First Daily Newspaper and the Essay Papers

On March 11, 1702, the *Daily Courant* appeared on the streets of London. It was the first daily newspaper printed in the English language, and set a new standard in journalism in that it was a *news* paper, not a rumor-mill.

The eighteenth century also brought about a high literary quality in English journalism, a quality evident in the *essay papers* still read today by students everywhere. The essay papers, the *Tatler* (1709–1711) and the *Spectator* (1711–1712, 1714), were the products of Richard Steele and Joseph Addison. Printed only on one side of a sheet of paper and costing a penny, this type of paper soon became extremely popular. The *Spectator* was issued daily and its literary form was widely imitated, especially in America where Colonial newspapers were influenced by their British predecessors.

Development of Newspapers in America

During the first part of the eighteenth century only five newspapers were established in Colonial America—three in Boston and one each in Philadelphia and New York. In America, newspaper reading did not spread among the masses until the early 1800's. The growth of the large American cities brought about the establishment of the newspaper as an important communication medium, and newspapers, in their presentation of news and advertising, soon became a true reflection of the American way of life. The history and the development of American newspapers is further described in Chapter 2, "Newspapers."

Technological Expansion

The nineteenth century brought with it the start of the greatest technological advances in the history of communications. Stereotyping came into use in 1805, followed by the first steam power press in 1814. Frenchman Louis Daguerre perfected his method of photography in 1839, and Samuel Morse transmitted the first telegraph message in 1844. The first transatlantic cable was laid in 1858, and photoengraving was developed in 1872. The world's first telephone message was sent by Alexander Graham Bell in 1876, and Thomas Alva Edison invented the phonograph in 1877. In 1886 the Mergenthaler Linotype was first used commercially by the *New York Tribune,* and in 1895 Guglielmo Marconi sent the first wireless messages. Motion-picture projectors were perfected in 1894, followed by the transmission of voice by radio in 1906.

Even greater technological advances in communication have been made in the twentieth century. The use of the computer in communications techniques and facsimile reproduction systems by publications became common practices. The invention of xerography, a process by which any printed or written material could be copied, presented countless new possibilities to the communications field. Television and radio transmission, newspaper and magazine publishing, book and film production—all made enormous strides as communications media.

8

This early American daguerreotype, made in 1850 by Daguerreotypist Fred Coombs, shows the corner of San Francisco's Clay and Montgomery Streets.

The twentieth century's greatest technological advance in telecommunications to date is, perhaps, the development of the International Tele-communications Satellite Consortium, known as *Intelsat,* which links sixty-three nations. In 1962 *Telstar I,* the first active experimental communications satellite, was launched by the Communications Satellite Corp. of the United States (*Comsat*), a member of *Intelsat.* This launching was followed by other communications satellites, notably *Early Bird* (the first commercial satellite) which linked North America and Europe with 250 two-way voice circuits. It is expected that by 1971 there will be an *Intelsat IV,* a proposed system of at least two communications satellites. Each satellite is planned to have 5,000 circuits. It is also planned that *Intelsat IV* will be followed by a direct-broadcast satellite that will bring pictures directly into home receivers.

The potential of communications links via satellites has only begun to be seen. Within a few years it will be possible to build a world-wide information network capable of transmitting man's accumulated knowledge throughout the globe. Until communications satellites came into use our information links with the rest of the world were limited. Overseas electronic circuits—such as telephone, teletype, and radio—were limited largely to the North

9

NASA AT&T

The Telstar photograph (left) is a composite showing the actual spacecraft in a space environment. The first TV transmission from Europe to the United States (right) via Telstar satellite featured French singer Yves Montand.

American area. There were no telecommunications links among Africa, South America, and Asia where approximately seventy percent of the world's population lived.

The new information network system will change this communications pattern dramatically. The high-flying communications satellites, able to transmit oral, visual, or printed information in any amount to any place, will be an integral part of the new information network system. The network, capable of processing high-speed transmissions, will be able to handle any kind of printed data, from the Wall Street stock quotations to entire books. Even as early as 1962 the "primitive" Telstar satellite handled data at the rate of one and one-half million words a minute—the equivalent of transmitting six entire books from the Bible every twenty-nine seconds.

Today, as in the past, mass communication has important social and political effects. And, as man's knowledge increases and he gains better understanding of his fellow man through mass communication, these effects will become even more important. The communications-conscious United States recognizes the importance of mass communications in helping to bring about this better understanding necessary for world peace. This idea was aptly expressed during the Johnson Administration when the President, in appointing a committee to study the nation's communications policy, said:

> Man's greatest hope for peace lies in understanding his fellow man. Nations, like individuals, fear what is strange and unfamiliar. The more we see and hear of those things which are common to all people, the less likely we are to fight over those issues which set us apart. So the challenge is to communicate.

MAJOR EVENTS IN THE HISTORY OF COMMUNICATIONS

Early man gestured and made sounds to communicate.

A pre-writing system was devised when early man drew pictograms on walls of caves.

Egyptians perfected a picture language called hieroglyphics in about 3300 B.C.

Around 1500 B.C. the Semites devised an alphabet.

In 1000 B.C. the Egyptians wrote on papyrus.

The Chinese wrote with ink on paper in 105 A.D.

Printing with separate and movable type characters was used in China about 1041.

Wang Chen employed nearly 60,000 movable type-characters to print a book on agriculture in 1314.

In 1403 a Korean emperor printed a large number of volumes from movable type.

Johannes Gutenberg introduced movable type to the Western World in the 1440's.

England's first printing press was established by William Caxton in 1476.

The first printing press in North America appeared in Mexico in 1539.

The first newspapers of significance appeared in Europe in 1609.

Ben Harris published *Publick Occurrences, Both Forreign and Domestick* in Boston in 1690.

In 1704 America's first continuous newspaper, the *Boston News-Letter,* was published.

Stereotyping was introduced in 1805.

The first steam-powered press was introduced in 1814.

In 1839 Louis Daguerre invented a type of photography.

Samuel Morse sent the first telegraph message in 1844.

Roger Fenton became the first war photographer when he covered the Crimean War in 1853.

The first transatlantic cable was laid in 1858.

Photoengraving was developed in 1872.

The telephone was invented by Alexander Graham Bell in 1876.

In 1877 Thomas Alva Edison invented the phonograph.

In 1886 the Mergenthaler Linotype was first used commercially by the *New York Tribune.*

George Eastman developed a practical photographic film in 1889.

In 1894 motion picture films were shown to the public.

The first wireless message was sent by Guglielmo Marconi in 1895.

Guglielmo Marconi invented the radio in 1896.

In 1923 pictures were televised between New York City and Philadelphia.

The first large, automatic digital computer was built at Harvard University in 1944.

The first artificial earth satellite, Russia's Sputnik I, sent information from space to earth in 1957.

In 1962 Telstar I, America's first active experimental communications satellite, was launched.

ACTIVITIES

1. Some scholars contend that early man wrote before he spoke. They claim that because no vocal signs existed to establish communication, early man probably had to resort to graphic symbols to convey his messages to others. How likely do you think this theory is? Compare and discuss your reasoning with your classmates.

2. Define the following: medium, message, journalism, news medium, Daguerreotype, xerography, communications satellite.

3. Discuss how social, economic, and political influences on communications have helped elevate journalism to its present status.

4. Throughout the history of communications ruling groups have attempted to control and censor the news and information given to the general public. Make a study of one of the following and report your findings to your class:
    a. Censorship of early European newspapers.
    b. Censorship of Colonial American newspapers.
    c. Government restrictions on access to news during the administration of an American President of your choice.
    d. Present-day postal censorship.
    e. Censorship of books, radio, television, and stage presentations in today's society.

5. Would it be possible for a country to function progressively in today's world if that country's citizenry were denied information about what is taking place elsewhere in the world? Discuss how or how not.

6. Would a dictatorship function more effectively if the flow of outside information were completely shut off, or, if the dissemination of selected items of information were allowed? Why?

7. From a recent issue of a local newspaper select those stories and pictures you think would be censored under the control of a dictator.

8. Some people claim that with recent technological advances and inventions of recording devices for the spoken word, the written word may be on its way out. Discuss whether or not you think this could be possible.

9. Assuming that life does exist on other planets, should our country continue its efforts to send signals into outer space? Explain your reasoning.

10. If we compare British and American English we find that many words sound the same but are spelled differently. Both the British and Americans use the Roman alphabet, but in some situations apply it differently.

a. Do you think that such differences in spelling could contribute to a breakdown in the basic communication and understanding between Englishmen and Americans reading the same material? If your answer is yes, explain how. If your answer is no, explain why.

b. Using as an example the translation of an important world news event from a foreign language into English, present an actual or imaginary situation that shows how a communications breakdown could come about.

c. Do you think that if all nations used a universal language world communications, knowledge, and understanding would increase or decrease? Explain how.

READING

BARNOUW, ERIK, *Mass Communication: Television, Radio, Film, and Press.* Holt, Rinehart & Winston, New York, 1956.

BERELSON, BERNARD, AND MORRIS JANOWITZ (Ed.), *Reader in Public Opinion and Communication.* Free Press, New York, 1966.

BROTHERTON, MANFRED, *Masers and Lasers, How They Work and What They Do.* McGraw-Hill, New York, 1964.

CHAFEE, ZECHARIAH, JR., *Government and Mass Communications: A Report from the Commission on Freedom of the Press.* Shoe String Press, Hamden, Conn., 1947.

CHRISTENSON, REO M., AND ROBERT O. McWILLIAMS, *Voice of the People: Readings in Public Opinion and Propaganda.* McGraw-Hill, New York, 1967.

DUNLAP, ORRIN E., JR., *Communications in Space: From Wireless to Satellite Relay.* Harper & Row, New York, 1964.

GOODMAN, EZRA, *The Fifty-Year Decline and Fall of Hollywood.* Simon and Schuster, New York, 1961.

HOVLAND, CARL, ET AL, *Experiments in Mass Communications.* Princeton University Press, Princeton, N.J., 1949. (PB)

KATZ, ELIHU, AND PAUL LAZARSFELD, *Personal Influence: The Part Played by People in the Flow of Mass Communications.* Free Press, New York, 1955.

McLUHAN, MARSHALL, *Understanding Media.* McGraw-Hill, New York, 1964.

McMURTRIE, DOUGLAS C., *The Book: The Story of Printing and Bookmaking.* Oxford University Press, New York, 1943.

NOSSITER, BERNARD, *The Mythmakers.* Beacon Press, Boston, 1964. (PB)

PETERSON, THEODORE, JAY W. JENSEN AND WILLIAM RIVERS, *The Mass Media and Modern Society.* Holt, Rinehart & Winston, New York, 1965.

SCHRAMM, WILBUR, *Mass Communications.* University of Illinois Press, Urbana, Ill., 1960.

WHITE, DAVID MANNING, AND LEWIS ANTHONY DEXTER, *People, Society, and Mass Communications.* Free Press, New York, 1964.

Chapter **2**

Newspapers

Ron MacNeil

THE NEWSPAPER IN OUR SOCIETY

A philosopher once prayed to be spared from living in a revolutionary age. His reason? If he lived in a revolutionary age, he would have to make decisions and take a stand. He knew that if he took a stand, he would be censured, and if he took *no* stand, he would be criticized.

Few professionals in America are required to make as many decisions as often as the men and women who write and edit for the news media. These people, whose decisions are disseminated throughout the world community, are as vital to the welfare of the United States as doctors, religious leaders, and educators are. They are faced with making major decisions daily, and, like the philosopher, they are often censured for the decisions they make— or they are criticized if they take *no* stand.

Associated Press General Manager Wes Gallagher once said:

If the reporter writes about drug addiction, he is charged

with making it attractive to nonusers; if he writes about Negro nationalists, he is accused of writing about a tiny minority; if he doesn't, he is told that he is not reporting the true militancy of the Negro. If he writes of a military victory in Vietnam, he is attacked by the doves; if he writes of the failure of the Vietnamese to clear their house of corruption, he is attacked by the hawks. If he reports that the Mets are strictly a dismal bunch of stumblebums, he is against the team; if he doesn't he is a publicity agent. And so it goes.

Today's journalist, by virtue of his role as a prime interpreter of society's happenings, not only has the freedom to express his own views, but also has the power to influence public decision. This is an awesome responsibility which imposes on the journalist a continual search for the elusive idea, truth. For since the journalist must write for the man who operates a lathe in a factory as well as for the Board Chairman of the company which runs the factory, he soon learns that what is truth for one man may seem like biased opinion to another. Moreover, while the journalist strives to be objective and truthful to all of his readers, he must also be true to his own perception of the world about him. Publisher Joseph Pulitzer emphasized the need for truth in American journalism when he warned:

> Nothing less than the highest ideals, the most scrupulous anxiety to do right, the most accurate knowledge of the problem it has to meet, and a sincere sense of moral responsibility will save journalism from a subservience to business interests, seeking selfish ends, antagonistic to public welfare.

EARLY AMERICAN NEWSPAPERS

Boston, the birthplace of the American newspaper, has often been referred to as "the cradle of American journalism." In the 1680's, Boston, famous as the intellectual capital of the New World, had all of the ingredients for the development of a newspaper—high literacy, self-government, interest in community affairs, prosperity, and cultural leadership.

However, no successful newspaper appeared there until the fourth generation of new settlers—possibly because any demand for news was satisfied by the English newspapers, often containing some Colonial news, arriving regularly on ships from the "homeland." When Colonial American newspapers (often called a "propaganda press") finally did appear, they were closely patterned after their British counterparts.

The First American Newspaper

Printer Benjamin Harris arrived in Boston in 1686, and was confronted by a situation seemingly made to order for the development of a newspaper. Harris, who had been arrested in London for the possession of seditious literature, had previously started a newspaper in London in 1679. After his arrest he had continued editing his newspaper from his cell. Early in 1686 his shop was again raided and, warned of the possibility of again being arrested, Harris fled to America with his family. In Boston in the fall of 1686 he opened a combined bookstore and coffee shop. The shop became a meeting place for some of the city's most prominent citizens, and Harris, having become a promoter of literary works, was soon publishing books for a distinguished clientele. His *Publick Occurrences, Both Forreign and Domestick,* called the first American newspaper by many authorities, was published in September, 1690. *Publick Occurrences* quickly ran into trouble with the British Governor and was suppressed after publication of the first issue.

Other Boston Newspapers

The first continuous Colonial American newspaper, the *Boston News-Letter,* appeared in Boston in 1704—fourteen years after *Publick Occurrences* had been suppressed. The postmaster of Boston, John Campbell, who had been sending out a newsletter to the governors of the New England colonies, decided to turn his newsletter enterprise into a profitable newspaper business by charging two-pence per copy (or nine shillings per year). The first edition of the newsletter as a newspaper stated in large type that the *Boston News-Letter* was "published by authority"—meaning that every word had been censored and approved by the Governor's licensor. The attitude of the English Colonial governors at that time was typified by Sir William Berkeley, governor of Virginia for thirty-eight years, who sent a report to the Crown stating:

> But thank God, we have no free schools nor printing, and I hope we shall not have these hundred years; for learning has brought disobedience and heresy and sects into the world; and printing has divulged them and libels against the best government. God keep us from them both.
>
> *Statutes at Large*
> *William Walter Hennings*

Because Campbell was a man the British Governor could trust to be discreet (all of Campbell's material was written by himself and his brother Duncan),

N. E.　　　　　　　　Numb. 2.

The Boston News-Letter.

Publiſhed by Authority.

From **Monday** April 24. to **Monday** May 1. 1704.

London Flying-Poſt, from *Decemb.* 23 to 25.

Warſaw, Decemb. 15.

Letters from great *Poland* ſay, That the King of *Poland* deſigns, If the republick will agree to it, to make an honourable Peace with the King of *Sweeden* in four Weeks time. The *Swediſh* general *Steinbock* is gone to *Daniſick* to demand 100000 crowns from that City; The *Sweeds* demand 300000 more crowns from *Elbing,* & 100000 from the diſtrict of *Ermelant,* The King of *Sweeden* is ſending 4000 *Saxon* Priſoners to *Sweeden* and demands Subſiſtance of the Country, by way of alms for thoſe poor People. The Diviſions in *Lithuania* increaſe daily.

Danrick, Dec. 19. The King of *Sweeden* has obliged the *Elbingers* to deliver all their Arms into the Town-houſe upon Oath, and promiſed to reſtore them when they have pa'd him 600000 Gilders Contribution. Six Companies of *Burghers* keep gaurd daily upon our Walls, for we are afraid that the *Sweeds* may Attack us during the Froſt.

Vienna, Dec. 14. Letters from *Turkey* ſay, the New *Sultan* is reſolved to maintain Peace with the Chriſtians, according to the Treaty of *Curlowitz.* Prince *Eugene* is doing all he can to ſuppreſs the Male Contents in *Hungary,* for which end he expects ſome thouſands of *Croats* and *Raſcians.* In the mean time our Troops are caſting Lines on the Rivers *Muravia* and *Leyta* to ſtop their progreſs. The Male Contents have lately Publiſh'd a large *Manifeſto* of 60 Articles, whereof the following 18 are the chief. 1. That they acknowledge the Emperor for their Soveraign, and are ready to ſpend their Lives and Eſtates for him, if he Treats them as a good Prince, and as they think him naturally oblig'd to do. 2. That they may be reſtor'd to the ſame liberty & freedom they enjoy'd when they were his Majeſties Subjects. 3. That he give them places to Worſhip God freely, according to the Dictates of their Conſcience, which the Blood of their Martyrs calls for. 4. That the Eſtates taken from their Conſiſtories, by the Jeſuites be reſtored. 5. That their Books and Archives be reſtored. 6. That they may be reſtored to their Poſts and Juriſdictions, as formerly. 7. That the Jeſuites be baniſhed from *Hungary* and *Tranſilvania,* inſtead of letting them enjoy the Eſtates of the Proteſtants. 8. That their Schools be reſtor'd, and their Rectors and Maſters be put in poſſeſſion of their Revenues. 9. That what has been altr'd by force in matters of Religion, may be ſet upon the former Footing. 10. That the Books and Manuſcripts of the Proteſtants, relating to their grievances of Religion, be reſtor'd. 11. That the gifts or conveyances of Eſtates of the Perſecuted Proteſtants to the Popiſh Clergy, be reſtor'd, for the ſubſiſtance of the Proteſtant Poor. 12. That all the Popiſh Clergy, except Natives, be baniſhed the Country. 13. That his Imperial Majeſty appoint Commiſſioners to treat with thoſe from Prince *Ragotski,* and his adherents in a place of Security; about a firm and durable Peace; And, in mean time grant a Ceſſation of Arms. 14. That ſome Great men be given up as Hoſtages, for the performance of what ſhall be agreed on. 15. That without being controlled by the Emperour, they may be at liberty to ſend ſuch Deputies to the *Diets* as they think fit, to take care of the Affairs of Religion. 16. That, To bury the memory of all Injuries done them they may have a freedom from all Impoſts for 15 years. 17. That there be no Tax laid on Import or Export, on Corn and Manufactures, to and from the Empire. 18. That they ſhall allow them free and uninterrupted Commerce with all but the Emperor's Enemies.

Frankfort, Decemb. 26. Letters from *Swiſſerland* ſay the Popiſh Cantons are much incens'd againſt *France* ſince the Duke of *Savoy's* Miniſter diſcovered to them, that *France* and *Spain* deſigned to Divide *Swiſſerland* betwixt them, and that they promis'd *Geneva* and the Country of *Gex* to his Maſter. They have already granted Levies to the Duke of *Savoy;* And the King of *France* pretended he would not break with the *Cantons,* has promiſed a Neutrality for the Dutchy of *Savoy,* provided *Piedmont* be included; but the Duke of *Savoy* will not agree to that. His Royal Highneſs has ſent 30000 Piſtoles to *Swiſſerland* to buy Horſes. The Duke of *Savoy* intercepted a Letter from the *French* King, to the Generals in *Italy,* to Seize old Prince *Vaudemont,* as ſoon as he ſhould hear of the new King of *Spain's* Arrival in *Portugal,* and that the Duke ſent this Letter to the Prince, who he thereupon poſſeſſed himſelf of *Mantua,* with 10000 men, which we wiſh may be confirmed. We have alſo Advice that 40000 *Spaniards* being on the Frontiers of *Portugal,* have Deſerted and Joyn'd the *Portugueſe.*

South-Carolina Via New-York.

An Account of what the Army from thence had done, under the Command of Colonel *Moore,* in his Expedition laſt Winter againſt the *Spaniards* and *Spaniſh* Indians. In a Letter from him to the Governour of *Carolina.* May it pleaſe Your Honour to accept of this ſhort Narrative of what I with the Army under my Command have been doing ſince my Departure from the *Ockmulgg* on the 19th. *December.* On the 14th. *January* we came to a Town, and ſtrong and almoſt regular Fort about Sun Riſing, call'd *Ayavalle,* at our firſt approach the Indians in it fired and ſhot Arrows at us briskly; from which we ſhelter'd our ſelves under the ſide of a great Mud-wall'd Houſe, till we could take a view of the Fort, and conſider of the beſt way of aſſaulting it: which we concluded to be by breaking the Church door, which made a part of the Fort, with Axes. I no ſooner propoſed this, but my men readily undertook it; ran up it briskly, (the Enemy at the ſame time ſhooting at them) were beaten off without effecting it, and fourteen white men wounded, two hours after th we thought fit to attempt the burning the Church; which

The first continuous Colonial American newspaper, the "Boston News-Letter," appeared in 1704—fourteen years after "Publick Occurrences, Both Forreign and Domestick," had been suppressed.

his "published by authority" newspaper was spared the fate of Harris' *Publick Occurrences. The Boston Gazette*—also "published by authority"—took a strong position against Colonial rule and became famous when editors John Gill and Benjamin Edes lashed out at the Colonial government.

The Power of the Press Grows

Public resentment of British authority was growing in the colonies, and in 1734, thirty years after the founding of America's first continuous newspaper, John Peter Zenger, a courageous New York printer, felt impelled to criticize in print a corrupt British governor. Tried for seditious libel, Zenger was defended by Andrew Hamilton who won the case on the point that "falsehood makes the libel," and—for the first time in any nation—truth was established as a defense in a libel action. The Colonial press began to openly criticize English authority and to promote the ideal of American independence. The short-lived *New England Courant,* published by James Franklin, conducted crusades and printed entertaining articles such as Benjamin Franklin's "Do-Good Papers." The Franklin brothers and their "Hell-Fire Club" of Couranteers have often been called the first school of propagandists for the American Revolution. Started at about the same time, *The Hartford Courant*, having been originally published as the *Connecticut Courant,* outlasted the Franklin publication. In 1837 this paper reverted to its original name, the *Connecticut Courant*, and became a daily. It is still printed today. The Colonial American press has often been termed "a propaganda press" and, as such, played an important role in stirring up opposition to Crown policies by publishing essays and letters under aliases by such leaders as John Adams and James Otis.

Small Papers and Small Circulations

Most of the Colonial American newspapers were weeklies, the remaining ones being semiweeklies. Page sizes were smaller than those of our modern tabloids, and each issue usually contained four pages: not until the 1760's did the more prosperous newspapers (Benjamin Franklin's *Pennsylvania Gazette,* for example) print as many as eight pages per issue. Because so few of the colonists could read and because efficient distribution was hampered by the crude roads and transportation facilities of the time, Colonial American newspapers had limited circulations.

Only twenty of the thirty-seven Colonial American newspapers published at the beginning of the American Revolution survived the war. Several others of minor importance came and went between the battles of Concord and Lexington and Cornwallis' surrender at Yorktown. Information about the Revolution was not covered methodically, and for their sources of news of the war Colonial American editors depended on chance information, clippings from other newspapers, and letters from friends, relatives, and business associates in other cities.

Even though our newspapers were founded on the belief that freedom of the press is the people's defense against tyranny, Colonial American statesmen could not agree on what amount of power should be delegated to the people. Alexander Hamilton felt that the public was a great beast and could not be trusted with the operation of the new society that was emerging as a result of the Revolutionary War. Thomas Jefferson, asserting that the only way to make a free society work was to have all the citizens participate, felt quite differently. If the citizens were well-enough informed and free to express their opinions, he maintained, they would make the right decisions most of the time. Jefferson won the argument. He insisted that if he had to choose between a government without newspapers or newspapers without a government, he would take the latter because he believed that the only way to make democracy work was to have a free flow of information and well-informed voters to make the decisions. As evidenced from their writings, later in life both Thomas Jefferson and Alexander Hamilton reversed their positions on a free press.

Freedom of the Press

Journalism acquired status with the "Freedom of the Press" clause which our founding fathers, recognizing the need for an informed electorate, wrote into the First Amendment of the Constitution:

> ARTICLE I
>
> Religion, Speech, Press, Assembly, Petition—Congress shall make no law respecting an establishment of religion, or prohibiting the free exercise thereof; or abridging the freedom of speech, or of the press; or the right of the people peaceably to assemble, and to petition the government for redress of grievances.

The Beginning of the Penny Press

Although early American newspaper circulations increased as the education of early Americans improved, it was not until the appearance of Benjamin Day's *New York Sun* in 1833 (the first penny newspaper) that newspaper reading spread among the mass of the population—a direct reflection of the increased awareness of early Americans.

Newspapers Move Westward

In 1824 the *Springfield Republican* was founded in Massachusetts by eighteen-year-old Samuel Bowles II. The *Republican* achieved renown through editorials denouncing the practice of slavery and the execution of John Brown. Despite the paper's name, the *Republican* supported the Whig political organization. In 1854 Bowles' son, having succeeded his father as publisher of the *Republican,* urged the formation of a new party "able to win the great contest to be fought in 1856 with the slave power in this country," thus making him one of the first publishers in the country to endorse the Republican Party and support the election of Abraham Lincoln.

Many persons credit Lincoln's election to the publisher of the *Chicago Tribune,* Joseph Medill, who purchased the paper in 1847. Today the *Tribune* claims to be "The World's Greatest Newspaper" (its radio station's call letters are WGN). The *Tribune* has always been strongly nationalistic in foreign policy and generally conservative in its politics.

The Era of the Giants

By the latter part of the nineteenth century the country's newspaper business was booming, and newspapers had gained an important place in their communities as the great cities grew. Newspapers, through their news and advertising, reflected the American way of life. This period was an era of growth for the journalistic giants in New York City, the most important of these giants being Horace Greeley's *Tribune,* James Gordon Bennett's *Herald,* Joseph Pulitzer's *World,* and Henry Raymond's *Times.* William Randolph Hearst and E. W. Scripps also established their great publishing enterprises during this period.

The American population was continuing to move westward when Horace Greeley, despite his "Go West, young man" advice, stayed in New York City to develop his penny newspaper into one of the country's largest—the *New York Tribune.* The transatlantic cable had been completed by this time and Greeley no longer had to send horseback riders to Boston to secure news of England from incoming ships. By 1861 the telegraph had reached the West Coast giving newspapers coast-to-coast access to international news. Greeley had competition from other newspaper publishers who, in order to increase circulations, had become concerned with reader interest and were "giving the readers what they wanted." Catering to the interests of his readers, publisher James Gordon Bennett, Jr., of the *New York Herald,* in one of the country's earliest examples of complete feature coverage, sent reporter Henry Stanley to Africa in search of the noted explorer David Livingstone. Henry Stanley is now perhaps best remembered for his famous statement, "Doctor Livingstone, I presume?"

In 1897 William Randolph Hearst's *New York Journal* was increasing its circulation by running sensational headlines like "Nearer Than Ever to War with Spain"—an attention-getting headline which was not followed by a story. Hearst, who was aware that news of wars helped sell newspapers, went so far as to send illustrator Frederick Remington to Cuba to draw war pictures. When Remington wrote back "There's no war here," Hearst is said to have replied: "You supply the pictures; I'll supply the war." The huge New York newspapers soon gained tremendous popularity and influence throughout the country despite the establishment of other newspapers in the west. James Rhodes, western correspondent for the *New York Tribune*, wrote: "Throughout the West, the *Tribune* ranks next to the *Bible*."

The *World* and Mr. Pulitzer

In 1880 Hungarian immigrant Joseph Pulitzer purchased the *New York World*, a newspaper with a circulation figure of about 15,000. While still in his twenties Pulitzer had founded an earlier newspaper that promised "to serve no party but the people." This newspaper later became known as the

The work of Richard Outcault, originator of the cartoon "The Yellow Kid," was duplicated by unethical publishers during the 1880's.

St. Louis Post-Dispatch. Using his earlier newspaper to crusade for improved social conditions and to attack corrupt politicians Pulitzer made a half-million dollars in about five years, thus enabling him to buy the *New York World*. He sold copies of the *New York World* for a penny an issue and instituted crusades that were similar to the ones that had been so successful in St. Louis. In the next three years he increased the circulation of the *New York World* to 250,000, making it that era's most widely read newspaper.

Yellow Journalism

One explanation of the origin of the term *yellow journalism* is that in the 1880's the term came about as a result of the unethical practices on the part of publishers concerning a cartoon strip titled "The Yellow Kid." Many publishers, using every possible means, tried to lure cartoonist Richard Outcault, originator of "The Yellow Kid," to their staffs. Unsuccessful in their attempts, they proceeded to have their own artists draw similar cartoon strips using the title "The Yellow Kid." The term "yellow journalism" has been used to describe the unethical practices and irresponsible journalism prevalent during that era. The term is often used today to describe unethical, sensational, and irresponsible journalism.

Despite the "yellow journalism" of the late 1800's, many journalistic advances were made during this period. The development of the engraving process meant that photographs could be used in newspapers. Comics and headlines in color became the vogue and more variety in the news was presented with coverage of sports, finance, and women's news events. Feature and human-interest stories were emphasized. The latter may have prompted Charles Dana of the *New York Sun* to give his classic definition: "If a dog bites a man, that's not news. But if a man bites a dog, that is news."

Founding of the *Times*

Another high point of this period was the founding by Henry Raymond of what is often regarded as the greatest newspaper in the world: *The New York Times*. Typifying the personal interest publishers took in their papers during this period, Raymond, although he was the publisher of the *Times*, also served as the paper's correspondent during the Civil War. Later, the *Times* was instrumental in exposing the politically corrupt Boss Tweed ring in New York City. In 1896 Adolph Ochs, owner of the *Chattanooga Times*, bought the faltering *Times* for about a million dollars. At that time the *Times* had the smallest circulation of any New York newspaper. Ochs' solid news reporting and intelligent editorials soon had their effect, and he developed the *Times* into one of the largest-selling newspapers in the country.

The Spokesman for "The New South"

Although the New York City dailies had gained considerable nationwide circulation, it was inevitable that other newspapers would be established elsewhere in the country. Contrary to popular belief, many of the great Southern editors advocated civil rights. The most influential of these was Henry W. Grady, managing editor of the *Atlanta Constitution*. By 1886 Grady was considered the outstanding spokesman of the South. In addition to speaking out on civil rights, he encouraged diversified agriculture and industrialization of the South. The South regained economic stability by following the points he advocated in a speech entitled "The New South." Upon Grady's death in 1889 the editorship of the *Atlanta Constitution* was assumed by writer Joel Chandler Harris.

Other Southern Newspapers

Both the North and South heeded the words of editor Henry Waterson of the *Louisville Courier-Journal*. Waterson's authoritative writing gained him the respect and admiration of his readers. In one of his most famous crusades he advocated the exchange of Negro rights for Southern political rights. Although a Democrat, Waterson supported the presidency of Abraham Lincoln. The *Atlanta Constitution* and the *Louisville Courier-Journal* have remained among the most influential papers in America to this day.

Although unpopular in some areas for his denunciation of the Ku Klux Klan, William Allen White of the *Emporia Gazette* in Kansas gained national recognition with an editorial entitled "What's the Matter with Kansas?" Americans in every walk of life were soon praising White for his short, simple, beautifully written editorials. One of his best-known writings is the obituary he wrote for the *Emporia Gazette* after the death of his daughter, Mary. Millions of high school students have read this obituary which epitomizes the love, understanding, and common bond between a father and his daughter. In 1877 another Kansas editor, Ed Howe, who at age twenty-two founded the *Atchison Globe*, became widely quoted when his opposition to religion and women's rights aroused a furor. Howe's witty sayings gained him fame as "The Sage of Potato Hill," and his column, entitled "Paragraphs," contained such remarks as: "Families with babies and families without babies feel sorry for each other," and "If you want to make a man really mad, get someone to pray for him."

In Missouri, millionaire William Rockhill Nelson had gone through three fortunes by 1880 when, with his last million, he founded the *Kansas City Star*. Nelson believed that the reporter was the backbone of a good newspaper and built up one of the best editorial staffs in the country. Charles E.

Rogers wrote of Nelson:

> Next to Nelson, but always through Nelson's triumphant
> spirit, it (the *Kansas City Star*) was the work of Nelson's
> editors and their staff of inspired reporters and editorial
> writers. Possibly Nelson's greatest genius lay in his ability to
> select editorial talent, to exploit it by giving it freedom, and
> to cherish its flowering, both by positive encouragement to
> expression and avoidance of negative rules of suppression.
> . . . By adhering to this policy, Nelson succeeded in exploit-
> ing the ablest men and gaining their loyalty. . . .

Nelson, concerned with the moral problems of his city, conducted crusades
against lotteries, gambling, and corrupt politicians. His campaigns also
helped give Kansas City one of the best systems of parks and playgrounds in
the country. Unlike most of the large newspapers in the country at that time,
the *Kansas City Star* was distributed in the afternoon, and under Nelson's influence the paper avoided sensationalism and remained independent from
political control.

The *Chicago Daily News*

Ambitious publisher Melville Stone founded the *Chicago Daily News* in
1876. Stone, the product both of Chicago journalism and the new, progressive national newspaper environment, helped to initiate the "99¢ sale" of merchandise in stores so that potential readers would have pennies with which
to buy his newspaper. Taking advantage of a circulation shortage of coins at
that time, Stone encouraged Chicago banks to import pennies from elsewhere in the country. At the same time he helped stores promote the sale of
merchandise for ninety-nine cents. Stone's policy as a publisher was that his
first responsibility was to print the news; his second responsibility was to
guide public opinion; and his third, to provide entertainment.

EMERGENCE OF THE MODERN NEWSPAPER

With the beginning of the twentieth century thousands of immigrants
poured into the United States where they first settled in the major seaboard
cities. They brought with them many printers who soon established newspapers for their own ethnic groups. As the immigrants pushed westward,
ethnic newspaper publishing moved with them and soon foreign-language

publications were being printed throughout the country. At about this time the forerunners of the country's Black American press were founded as some Black American communities, mostly in the Northeast, established newspapers of interest to their own residents when white publishers refused to print news about Black Americans.

Influential Newspapers Established

Many of today's most influential newspapers were established in the late 1800's and the early 1900's. Newspapers like the *Washington Post,* the *Washington Star,* the *Boston Globe,* the *Denver Post,* the *Portland Oregonian,* the *Los Angeles Times,* and the *San Francisco Chronicle* were founded during this era. In 1940 Marshall Field, one of the richest men in the world, became interested in newspaper publishing and helped to establish a daily called *PM* in New York City. *PM*'s policy was the expression of a liberal point of view through its news columns, a policy carried to such an extreme that the paper soon became a daily journal of opinion. When *PM* folded in 1941, Field, undiscouraged by the loss of seventeen million dollars, became interested in a Chicago tabloid called the *Sun.* He consolidated the *Sun* with the *Times,* and by 1950 had invested some twenty-five million dollars in the *Sun-Times.* By 1954 the profitable *Sun-Times,* having reached a circulation of 600,000, had returned Field's investment.

Other Developments

The editorial task of the modern newspaper was facilitated by the development of the wire services—the *Associated Press,* the *United Press, International News Service,* and the *Associated Negro Press*—and by the many emerging news feature syndicates that supply news, features, photographs, and short stories to client newspapers. Today, the wire services play a major role in the medium and small city dailies, and in the suburban press. In fact, the wire service men are still the most prestigious in the White House press corps because of their great reading audiences. A high percentage of American newspapers rely on the wire services for their national and world coverage. Before the establishment of the "Hot Line," the American and Soviet leaders used their respective wire services as an indirect means of communication when there was no time to wait for diplomatic protocol. Specialized newspapers such as the *Christian Science Monitor* and the *Wall Street Journal* were founded to meet the interests of specific-interest groups, and prosperous newspaper publishers like Hearst, Newhouse, Thompson, Gannett, Knight, Scripps, and Copley were buying up small newspapers and combining them with others to form today's great newspaper chains.

THE NEWSPAPER IN TODAY'S SOCIETY

Newspapers, along with books, were the first mass media—but despite the "age" of newspapers, the future of newspaper journalism in America has never looked so bright. The number of readers has increased each year since the first newspaper in the Colonies was established in 1690. In a recent twenty-year period, for example, total newspaper circulation rose more than twenty percent—from 50.9 million to 61.6 million. And in the same period, newspaper employment of 248,500 rose to 353,800—a gain of forty-two percent—while advertising volume in the country's 1,750 daily newspapers topped $4.4 billion, more than four times the rate twenty years before. Also, in the same period, the number of pages in daily newspapers has almost doubled. Today, more newspapers are sold daily than loaves of bread or bottles of milk: it would take a 3,000-car freight train to deliver all the newsprint a metropolitan daily uses in a year.

TYPES OF NEWSPAPERS

Newspapers can be placed into various categories according to their types. The major types are metropolitan, chain, country, association, trade, professional, weekly, school, and ethnic.

Metropolitan Dailies

Metropolitan dailies furnish written accounts of events that have happened or are about to happen. They report the facts about these events as accurately and in as much detail as time and space permit. Metropolitan dailies usually publish several editions each day, and offer the reader more complete coverage of news events than do radio and television broadcasts. Metropolitan dailies feature complete coverage of national and world-wide news as well as news from their own communities. They also carry sports, society, business, education, and entertainment news.

Chain Newspapers

In recent years a major trend in the newspaper industry has been the newspaper merger. Very few cities in the United States now have competing morning or evening newspapers. Even those few large cities still having one morning and one evening newspaper are finding it economically more practical to combine printing and circulation operations while retaining separate editorial policies.

When several newspapers combine, or merge, they become known as a "chain." Among the largest chain newspapers in our country are the Hearst Newspapers, the Scripps-Howard Newspapers, The Gannett Group, and the Newhouse Newspaper chain.

Country Newspapers

The country newspaper, like its city counterpart, prints news, editorials, interpretations of the news, practical information, entertainment news, and advertising. The bulk of the news content, however, is local news that is concerned with a particular rural area. Much of the information contained in a country newspaper is of an agricultural and home-living nature. Country newspapers are usually printed as weeklies, and this country's largest is *Capper's Farmer's Weekly*.

Association, Trade, and Professional Newspapers

Association, trade, and professional newspapers are usually published by organized groups like large industries, associations, societies, clubs, professions, and labor unions. The content of these publications usually consists of information that concerns limited or specific-interest groups, particular professions, or specific situations.

Weekly Newspapers

The main purpose of weekly newspapers is to cover the local news of the small town, community area within a city, or suburb that they represent. Weekly newspapers specialize in the one type of news not covered in detail by most metropolitan dailies: personal news, in detail, about people and events within the weekly's own community.

School Newspapers

School newspapers serve the interests of the schools they represent. Some are published monthly, while others are published bi-weekly, weekly, or in the case of some college newspapers, daily. They include news of school events, news and articles of interest to students and teachers, and advertisements of interest to students. Many school newspapers contain community news.

Black American and Other Ethnic Newspapers

The Black American press concerns itself with the world of the Black American. New York City's *Amsterdam News,* the country's best-selling Black American newspaper, presents news in the sensational style of New York's *Daily News.* It also covers daily racial gains, new fair housing rulings, and such general topics as job promotions. In contrast to the *Amsterdam News, The Pittsburgh Courier* favors society news and is geared to the world of the professional, well-to-do Black American.

Many of our larger cities now have Black American owned and operated newspapers representing the Black Americans in our society. Most of these papers are weeklies. Boston's *Bay State Banner,* for example, presents weekly news of particular interest to Black Americans in the Boston area.

New York City's *Irish Echo* is the country's leading Irish-American publication. Published as a weekly, the *Irish Echo* reflects the social, political, and religious thinking of Americans of Irish descent.

Other ethnic newspapers, usually printed as weeklies, are published in cities and areas where large concentrations of particular ethnic groups have

Most of this country's leading ethnic newspapers are published in cities and areas having large concentrations of particular ethnic groups.

Ron MacNeil

settled. Many of these newspapers are printed in the language of the ethnic group they represent. Following are some examples of this type of publication: the *Jewish Advocate* (Jewish), *La Notizia* (Italian), the *Hellenic Chronicle* (Greek), the *Polish American News* (Polish), the *German Courier* (German), the *Lithuanian Free Press* (Lithuanian), the *Scandinavian Tribune* (Swedish and Norwegian), the *Chinese World* (Chinese), and the *Portuguese Journal* (Portuguese).

MAJOR FUNCTIONS OF THE NEWSPAPER

What do you expect when you read a newspaper? What can you, as an informed, intelligent reader, have a right to expect? The major functions of a newspaper are to inform (news columns), to persuade (editorials), to entertain (feature articles), and to provide a means by which merchants can sell their wares (advertisements).

A good news column presents the background information and the news itself so that the reader will have no trouble reading and understanding it. A good news reporter needs to remember that although the primary function of news is to inform, not necessarily to entertain—he should keep his news presentation interesting as well as factual.

A good newsman knows which stories will interest the most readers. From over a million words of copy submitted to him daily, a metropolitan news editor selects some 100,000 words of what he thinks is the most important material. However, editors also base their news selection on what they think *should* interest readers.

The editorial section contains material written by the editors who express their newspaper's view (policy) on general issues and current problems. Theater and music sections provide news of entertainment, and particular columnists may write for the purpose of entertaining readers. Art Buchwald is an example of a celebrated columnist who enlivens a newspaper's pages with his satirical humor. Many persons consider the "comic" section to be the most "interesting." The sports and women's sections are both informative and entertaining. Sports news is heavily illustrated, and sports columns are usually written in more vivid, colorful language than the general news stories. In the women's section, society columns, advice columns, news from the fashion world, beauty tips, announcements of engagements, marriages, births, and helpful homemaking advice offer interesting reading. The well-organized classified advertising section provides a number of services to the reader. In this section are included such listings as job opportunities, lost-and-found, and products, services, and real estate for sale.

READING A NEWSPAPER

The average newspaper reader devotes approximately one-half hour of his day to reading a newspaper. Because a single issue of a typical daily contains much more than one-half hour's reading material, the average reader must be selective in his choice of reading matter. His selection is, of course, completely personal, and the procedure followed by most readers is to categorize material into that which can be read carefully, that which can be skimmed or read only in part, and that which can be ignored completely.

Most readers start with the front-page headlines, selecting from them news items to be read in depth. Good headlines facilitate choice of reading material by accurately outlining the contents of the news stories, thus helping the reader decide how much time, if any, he will devote to a given item. Many readers skim headlines only, getting the gist of the news stories from them. For other stories, many readers consider only the lead, which should contain the *who, what, when, where, why,* and *how* of the story. In long stories, the subheads will indicate which parts the reader may want to read.

The well-informed reader retains materials such as important names and dates, the basis for new and proposed laws, facts concerning the local, national, and world-wide situations, the national and world economies, etc. Such readers make daily newspaper reading a habit. They are discriminating in their choice of reading material and are able to distinguish between the significant and insignificant, slanted and straight news, fact and opinion.

Your Newspaper Reading Habits

You, as a discriminating reader, should be aware of and interested in developing your own reading habits. In order to determine how much time you spend reading newspapers, and how you might improve your reading habits, complete these activities:

1. Check your newspaper reading habits by keeping a daily log for one week, listing the types of materials and names of publications you read. After each listing, enter the time (rounded off to the nearest half-hour) you spent reading a particular type of material. Keep an accurate record. At the end of the week, tabulate the number of hours per week, and the average number of hours per day, that you spent reading.

2. From the results of your log, make a graph showing time spent reading different types of newspaper materials. The completed graph will show the variety or lack of variety in your newspaper reading habits. You may use the graph on the following page as a general guide in preparing one of your own.

3. Allowing for individual interests and schedules, compare and evaluate your daily and weekly reading habits with those of your classmates. Compile a total class average for time spent reading different types of news matter, and have an open discussion to determine class opinion of particular publications.

EXAMPLE:

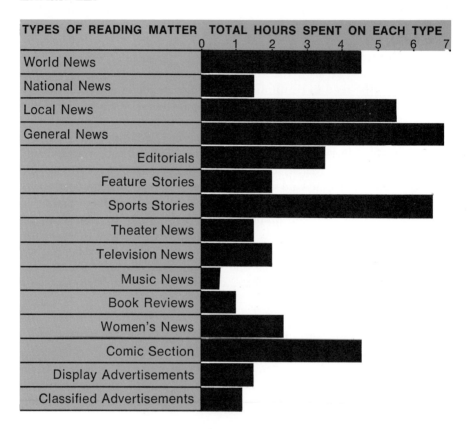

TYPES OF READING MATTER	TOTAL HOURS SPENT ON EACH TYPE
World News	
National News	
Local News	
General News	
Editorials	
Feature Stories	
Sports Stories	
Theater News	
Television News	
Music News	
Book Reviews	
Women's News	
Comic Section	
Display Advertisements	
Classified Advertisements	

MAJOR DIVISIONS OF THE AVERAGE DAILY

The major divisions of an average daily newspaper are the editorial, mechanical, and business management departments. Men and women employed in the editorial departments gather and prepare the news; the mechanical department is responsible for composition, printing, and production; business management supervises all business aspects of producing the newspaper, including advertising and circulation. Typical staff organization for a large metropolitan newspaper is shown on page 35.

The Editorial Department

Gathering and preparing the news is an art, not an exact science. A newspaper is the product not of scientific rules, but of the wisdom and conscience of responsible men and women; the end product reflects their judgment. There is an art to writing, to editing, to selecting the best stories, an art to the taking and cropping of photos, an art to the writing of bright headlines, and an art to combining all these elements into an attractive makeup ready for the printer before a given time (deadline).

The Editor-in-chief—Supervising the overall news operation is the editor-in-chief. In addition to overseeing the product from beginning to end, the editor-in-chief makes a number of policy decisions that guide the direction of the newspaper. Also, he and the managing editor usually collaborate in the hiring, firing, and promotion of all editorial department workers.

The Managing Editor—The managing editor supervises the combined news-gathering operation. The sports, society, feature, and women's page editors operate independently from the editor assigned to news beats (a listing of city-wide offices and topics to be covered for possible news stories), but all four are responsible to the managing editor. The managing editor ordinarily consults the news editor on the choice of national and world news stories. Editorial writers may also ask his advice on the newspaper's policy. Some managing editors decide how important each story is and determine where these stories are to be placed in the paper. After assessing each story, he marks the headline size at the top of the article's first page and gives the story to a copy reader who edits the story and writes a headline. The managing editor often lays out each page in the newspaper. This process may be compared to doing a jigsaw puzzle—each story, photo, and headline must fit into a given amount of space. Major news is placed at the top of the page with large headlines; minor news appears at the bottom of the page with smaller headlines. Most managing editors are consulted on top story decisions.

The City Editor—The city editor makes certain that the news beats are covered and that additional stories are supplied as news events warrant. If the President of the United States were to speak in a community, a number of reporters and photographers would be assigned by the city editor to cover all phases of the visit. One reporter might be assigned to the airport to do a sidebar (a minor feature story) on how the crowd reacted, what security measures had been taken, and what the President did. If anything out-of-the-ordinary were to occur, such as a demonstration, there might be another sidebar. If the President were to be accompanied by the First Lady, a reporter would do still another sidebar on what the First Lady did during the visit. A background story on other presidential visits to the community and an article describing the crowd lining the parade route would be appropriate. The main story, of course, would be the coverage of the President's speech. The city editor also sees that stories are turned in on time and that they do not overlap.

The News Editor—Selecting the comparatively few of the hundreds of stories filed daily by the wire services subscribed to by his newspaper is the job of the news editor (sometimes called the telegraph editor) and his staff. The news editor consults with the managing editor on the final choice of such stories. The gathering and compiling of news from all over the world (too costly an operation for individual newspapers) is a service performed by the wire services, newsgathering agencies originally formed when a group of large newspapers, in order to defray expenses, banded together to form a cooperative world-wide newsgathering effort. The *New York Associated Press,* forerunner of the present *Associated Press,* was founded in 1848. The *Associated Press* was followed by two similar agencies, the *United Press* and the *International News Service.* In order to meet the pressure of competition, the latter two merged in 1958 into what is presently *United Press International.* The *Associated Press* (*AP*), and *United Press International* (*UPI*), are this country's largest wire services, and *Associated Negro Press* (*ANP*) is this country's leading Black American wire service. *Reuters* is the British counterpart of the American wire services.

The Reporter—The backbone of any publication is the reporter, many of whom are assigned regular news beats. Editors attempt to assign this beat in light of the reporter's background and interests. For example, if the new reporter took a number of education courses in college, he might well be asked to cover the superintendent of schools' office, the school board meetings, and the various schools in the community. His stories would deal with such topics as school budgets, bond issues, appointments and elections, modern techniques in education, construction of new facilities, or any other matters relating to and affecting the education of the community's population.

Should the education reporter work on a large, metropolitan daily, he would be assigned to the education editor's desk where the stories to be covered are divided with other reporters who work under an education editor. This type of large daily would also have editors and staffs in government, crime, courts, entertainment, social welfare, and business and finance.

Other major desks depend on the type of economic development in the area. Metropolitan dailies in the Midwest, for instance, would naturally have a staff that is familiar with local agriculture to cover agricultural news. (A

TYPICAL STAFF ORGANIZATION FOR A LARGE METROPOLITAN NEWSPAPER

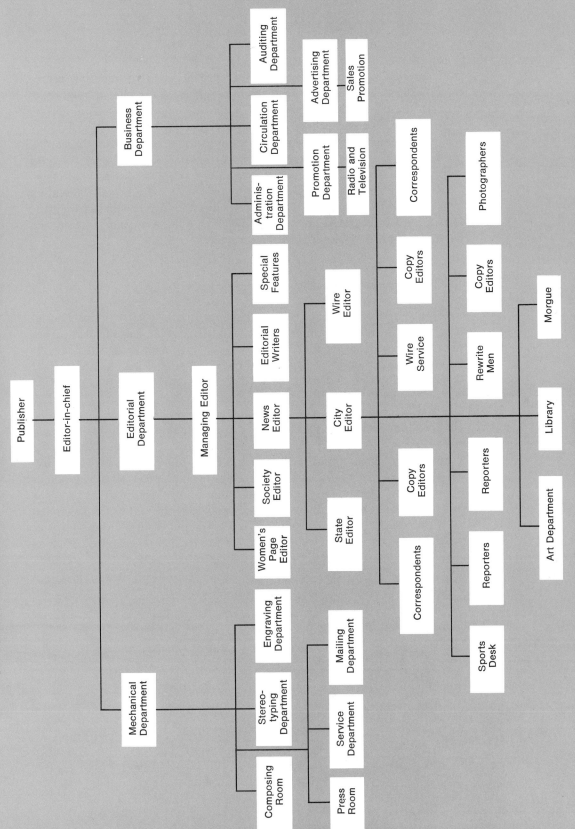

Midwestern newspaper editor tells of an instance when a reporter from a large Eastern city was rewriting a story and changed the phrase "seed corn" to "corn seed" throughout his article. Fortunately, the mistake was caught by copy editors who had a good laugh at the new reporter's mistake.) Many news beats call for highly specialized training and knowledge on the part of the reporter. General assignment reporters—reporters who cover a variety of subject matters from day to day—must also have wide background knowledge.

If a reporter—general assignment or otherwise—does his job well, presenting facts objectively and clearly to allow the reader to judge for himself what the facts signify, he gains the satisfaction of knowing he has contributed to and has a stake in the well-being of his community.

The Mechanical Department

The major cost of putting out a newspaper is entailed by the mechanical department; in fact, one publisher estimates that two-thirds of all expenses stem from this department. The four areas in this department are: engraving, composing, stereotype, and pressroom. Engravers make a negative of the photo being used in the paper and etch the negative into a zinc plate that will reproduce the original. Compositors in the composing room, using linotype machines, retype the reporter's edited stories. The linotype machine sets the story into metal strips called slugs, each slug making one column-width line in the finished paper. When the compositor finishes setting the story, the type is proofread, corrected, and taken to a makeup man who, following a small diagram of the page that has been planned by the news editor, places the engravings, type, and headlines into their specified positions in a page form. Once a page is finished (or "locked up"), the form is rolled to the stereotype department where a full-size replica is produced on a lead plate that will fit on a high-speed printing press. This process, called letter-

As a result of recent technological advances, many publications have replaced hand composition and page makeup with computer and film operations.

Ron MacNeil

press printing, is used by the majority of large newspapers. Many modern presses print, collate, fold, count, and bind more than a thousand copies of the completed newspaper in a minute's time. Conveyor belts carry the bundled newspapers to delivery trucks that distribute the paper throughout the circulation area.

Many smaller newspapers—weeklies, house organs, and trade publications —are produced by another process called offset printing, a newer and less expensive procedure. In offset printing (also called photo-offset), the news stories are typed, usually on a Justowriter, Varityper, or IBM Executive typewriter, and attached to a master-dummy page (flat) that is the same size as the actual newspaper page. The headlines, which have been set separately, are added and photos are indicated by dark paper windows. Photographs (halftones) are photographed separately and the negatives are later stripped into the film negative of the flat, replacing the dark paper windows. Advertisements which are usually supplied by the advertiser in the form of reproduction proofs (an exact reproduction of the actual advertisement) are also placed in position on the plate. The entire page is photographed, and a lightweight aluminum engraving plate is made from the resulting negative. The printing is done from this plate.

Business Management

The publisher, general manager, business manager, and treasurer supervise the business aspects of publishing a newspaper. They oversee the entire operation, and they keep the paper financially sound—newspapers must make money or go out of business. Occasionally newspapers are criticized for having too many advertisements in proportion to news content; however, if the ratio doesn't stay about sixty percent advertising to forty percent news, the paper will lose money. Commercial pressures from unethical advertisers, political pressures from the power structure, criminal pressures from the underworld, all have been a thorn in the side of the publishers since the earliest days of the press, and probably will continue to be. However, such pressures are a minor factor, contrary to Grade B movies that show the average publisher juggling the Mafia in one hand and a weak mayoral candidate in the other. A financially sound newspaper need fear no pressures; its independence is its seal.

The Circulation Department

The newspaper's two main sources of revenue are circulation and advertising. Circulation is important because no advertiser would want to pay money to put an advertisement in a limited-circulation publication that only a few readers might see. The advertising costs are usually based on the number of readers a publication has.

The Circulation Manager—Each newspaper has a circulation manager whose job is to sell more papers. He supervises distribution and collections through district managers and private distributors, plans promotional campaigns to increase circulation, and sponsors contests among delivery boys. His paper may well succeed or fail in proportion to his efforts.

The Advertising Department

The advertising department of a newspaper is usually divided into three sections: local, national, and classified. The local advertising salesmen contact potential advertisers and advertising agencies in the areas of distribution. In addition to attempting to convince advertisers of the need to place advertising on a regular basis, these men sell space in special editions (such as home-buying guide supplements) and on special pages (such as church pages). Advertising rates are usually based on a circulation number which is verified by an agency like the *Audit Bureau of Circulations* (ABC). For example, a one-column, one-inch deep ad in a relatively small paper in Washington, Pa., would cost about two dollars; the same-size ad in the largest newspaper in Washington, D.C., would cost about twenty dollars.

The national advertising manager usually has no staff because the majority of national advertisements are placed by agencies located in New York City. However, he must keep these agencies informed about his paper's circulation figures and about plans for special editions.

The classified department accounts for a large percentage of advertising revenue. The classified advertising manager supervises advertising rates and manages the office staff which receives ads. He also promotes placement of classified ads by writing promotional blurbs that are usually printed in the classified section.

A NEWSPAPER CAREER

School is a good place to begin training for the journalism profession. A journalism student might gain experience by working on school publications or by working during the summer on his community newspaper. As a copy boy, for instance, he would go on errands, deliver copy from one department to another and become familiar with newspaper environment and procedure.

In setting up his college program of studies a student should remember that, in addition to journalism, an area of specialization would increase his job opportunities. If the college he is attending requires selection of a major field, he might consider a double major—journalism and economics, art, or education, for example. In college, he should work on the campus newspaper and gain additional experience on other newspapers—again, during summer vacations. With a college education, a good journalism background, and experience in the field, he would be good hiring material for any newspaper.

ACTIVITIES

1. Discuss what you, as an enlightened, informed, free citizen, have the right to expect from a newspaper. What newspapers do you read and why do you read them?

2. Make arrangements to have several reporters and feature writers visit your class as an informal panel. Before the meeting, prepare a list of good questions to ask them.

3. Discuss the differences between the words "interesting" and "entertaining." Are they mutually exclusive words? Examine some newspapers to determine whether their news presentation is primarily "interesting" or "entertaining." If you were drawing up editorial policy for a newspaper, what stand would you take on this issue? What would be some of the determining factors in your decision?

4. Plan a class visit to a local newspaper where you will be able to see the mechanical department at peak operation. Then, for presentation as an assignment, prepare a brief news story on the visit.

5. Study the major sections of a daily newspaper. Do a critique on which sections you think are given too much space.

6. Compare the style and content of the average story on page one of a weekly newspaper with the average page-one story on a metropolitan daily. Write a three-paragraph statement concerning the differences between the two.

7. Write an informative, readable, and interesting news article on a subject of your choice. Specify the newspaper or kind of newspaper you are writing for, and the section in which your article should appear.

8. To best qualify you as an applicant for a job in professional journalism present, in outline form, what your plans for employment and education (through college) might be.

READING

Alsop, Joseph and Stewart, *The Reporter's Trade*. Reynal, New York, 1958.

Ault, Phillip H., *News Around the Clock*. Dodd, Mead, New York, 1960.

Canham, Erwin D., *Commitment to Freedom: The Story of the Christian Science Monitor*. Houghton Mifflin, Boston, 1958.

Clark, Thomas, *The Rural Press and the New South*. Louisiana State University Press, Baton Rouge, La., 1948.

———, *Southern Country Editor*. Peter Smith Publishers, Magnolia, Mass., 1964.

Cooper, Kent, *Kent Cooper and the Associated Press*. Random House, New York, 1959.

Detweiler, Frederick G., *The Negro Press in the United States*. McGrath Publishing Co., College Park, Md., 1968.

Emery, Edwin H., *The Press and America*. Prentice-Hall, Englewood Cliffs, N.J., 1962.

——— (Ed.), *The Story of America—As Reported by Its Newspapers, 1960–1965*. Simon and Schuster, New York, 1969.

———, and Phillip H. Ault, *Reporting the News*. Dodd, Mead, New York, 1960.

———, and Edwin H. Ford, *Highlights in the History of the American Press*. University of Minnesota Press, Minneapolis, Minn., 1954.

Hohenberg, John, *The News Media: A Journalist Looks at His Profession*. Holt, Rinehart & Winston, New York, 1968.

———, *The Professional Journalist*. Holt, Rinehart & Winston, New York, 1960.

Hough, Henry Beetle, *Country Editor*. Doubleday, New York, 1940.

Janowitz, Morris, *The Community Press in an Urban Setting*. University of Chicago Press, Chicago, Ill., 1967. (PB)

Kobre, Sidney, *Development of American Journalism*. Wm. C. Brown, Dubuque, Iowa, 1968.

Lent, John A., *Newhouse, Newspapers, Nusiances*. Exposition Press, New York, 1967.

Liebling, A. J., *The Press*. Ballantine Books, New York, 1964. (PB)

MacDougall, Curtis D., *Newsroom Problems and Policies*. Dover Publications, New York, 1941. (PB)

Morris, J. A., *Deadline Every Minute: Story of the United Press*. Little, Brown, Boston, 1957.

Mott, Frank Luther, *American Journalism*. Macmillan, New York, 1962.

———, *News in America*. Harvard University Press, Cambridge, Mass., 1952.

Noble, Iris, *Joseph Pulitzer*. Messner, New York, 1957.

Quill and Scroll Society, *Daily Newspapers, Weekly Newspapers, Wire Services*. State University of Iowa, Iowa City, Iowa, 1963.

Reston, James, *The Artillery of the Press: Its Influence on Foreign Policy*. Harper & Row, New York, 1966.

Riesman, David, *The Lonely Crowd*. Yale University Press, New Haven, Conn., 1950. (PB)

RIESMAN, DAVID, *Process and Effects of Mass Communications.* University of Illinois Press, Urbana, Ill., 1954.

——, *The Science of Human Communication.* Basic Books, New York, 1963.

RIVERS, WILLIAM L., *The News Media: Reporting, Writing, Editing.* Harper & Row, New York, 1964.

RUCKER, FRANK W., AND HERBERT L. WILLIAMS, *Newspaper Organization and Management.* Iowa State University Press, Ames, Iowa, 1969.

RYAN, LEONARD EAMES, AND BERNARD RYAN, JR., *So You Want to Go into Journalism.* Harper & Row, New York, 1963.

SCHETTLER, CLARENCE, *Public Opinion in American Society.* Harper & Row, New York, 1960.

SIM, JOHN C., *The Grass Roots Press: America's Community Newspapers.* Iowa State University Press, Ames, Iowa, 1969.

STEFFENS, LINCOLN, *The Autobiography of Lincoln Steffens.* Harcourt, Brace & World, New York, 1936.

STEWART, KENNETH, AND JOHN TEBBEL, *Makers of Modern Journalism.* Prentice-Hall, Englewood Cliffs, N.J., 1952.

SWANBERG, W. A., *Citizen Hearst.* Scribner's, New York, 1961.

TALESE, GUY, *The New York Times: The Kingdom and the Power.* World Publishing, Cleveland, Ohio, 1969.

TEBBEL, JOHN, *The Compact History of the American Newspaper.* Hawthorn Books, New York, 1963.

——, *Life and Times of William Randolph Hearst.* Dutton, New York, 1952.

——, *The Marshall Fields: A Study in Wealth.* Dutton, New York, 1947.

UNESCO, *Space Communication and the Mass Media.* UNESCO, United Nations, New York, 1963.

WEISBERGER, BERNARD A., *The American Newspaperman.* University of Chicago Press, Chicago, Ill., 1961.

WHITE, DAVID M., AND ROBERT H. ABEL, *The Funnies: An American Idiom.* Macmillan, New York, 1963.

WOLSELEY, ROLAND E., *The Journalist's Bookshelf.* Chilton Book Co., Philadelphia, Pa., 1961.

WOODS, ALLAN, *Modern Newspaper Production.* Harper & Row, New York, 1963.

Chapter 3

Magazines, Books, and Specialized Periodicals

THE JOURNALISTIC POTENTIAL OF MAGAZINES

"Don't go up in the plane—and if you do, don't tell me!," an apprehensive *Life* Magazine editor warned one of his young reporters assigned to cover a girl's parachute club. When the reporter confidently strapped herself into a parachute and hopped a plane, everything went well until she jumped and landed "off-target," in a tree.

The producers of the more than five billion copies of magazines distributed yearly in this country have to be more "on-target" than this reporter was. Magazine readers want articles that interest them; if magazines miss their "reader-interest target," readers will desert the publications. Magazine editors, like newspaper editors, are faced with the constant "on-target" problem of getting people to read, and keep reading, their publications.

Today, magazine publishing—a field which includes more than just those types of magazines found on newsstands—is one of the broadest fields of mass communication. Magazines employ thousands of persons as reporters, authors, writers, editors, artists, and photographers, and concern themselves

43

with almost every area of human interest or endeavor. Special magazines serve industry, ethnic groups, education, science, religion, management, and labor. In activities related to magazine publishing such as advertising, circulation, research, and printing, thousands of other persons are employed.

Magazines, like newspapers, exist to inform, entertain, and influence readers. The major difference between magazines and newspapers is that many magazines are more concerned with reaching special-interest groups while newspapers try to include stories of interest to every reader within their communities. Because magazines print information and entertainment written for specific groups or for particular geographic areas, they are a more desirable medium for national advertisers. Also, they are more durable than newspapers. The quality papers on which magazines are usually printed display to better advantage the advertiser's message. For example, advertisements printed in color appear more effective when printed in magazines than they do when printed on newsprint in newspapers. Published less frequently than daily newspapers (usually weekly, bi-monthly, or monthly), magazines can. offer their readers more detailed analyses of news events and more inter-

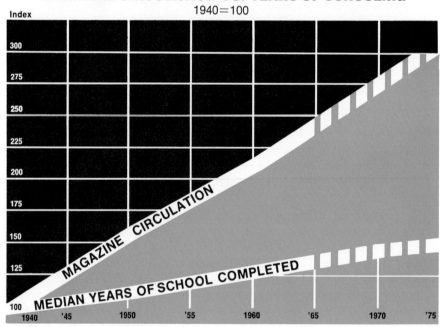

MAGAZINE CIRCULATION VS. YEARS OF SCHOOLING
1940=100

Source: U. S. Department of Commerce Audit Bureau of Circulation/with Projection

Chart A

AVERAGE ANNUAL EXPENDITURES FOR MAGAZINES
by Education of Household Head

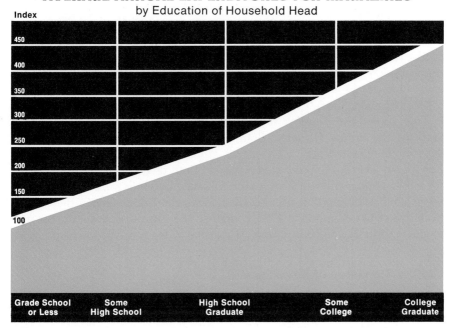

Index

450
400
350
300
250
200
150
100

| Grade School or Less | Some High School | High School Graduate | Some College | College Graduate |

Source: National Industrial Conference Board and Bureau of Labor Statistics (1961-62) 1965

Chart B

pretations of trends and ideas—and they can allow writers and editors more time for research and rewriting.

Since the number of highly educated Americans has increased, the growth in magazine circulations, magazine reading, and magazine effectiveness as a communications medium have accelerated. The growth rate of magazine circulations in this country is much larger than the national growth rate of higher education (see Chart A, page 44). The effect of a better-educated reading public on overall magazine sales is indicated by the annual spending of purchasers who represent various levels of educational attainment (see Chart B, page 45).

The National Industrial Conference Board reports that family spending for for magazines increases sharply as the education of heads of households increases—college-graduate parents spend four and one-half times as much on magazines as other parents. The expansion of magazine circulations, a direct reflection of the rapid growth of education in the United States, has increased the ability of magazines to help advertisers sell their merchandise, thus helping to boost the country's economy.

GROWTH OF THE MAGAZINE

Early publishers may well have chosen the word "magazine" when they combined the best qualities of successful newspapers into a more durable format and presented readers with a "storehouse" of material. The first publication known to have used the word "magazine" in its title was *The Gentleman's Magazine,* founded in London in 1731.

The first magazine in Colonial America was founded by William Bradford in 1741. Called the *American Magazine, or a Monthly View of the Political State of the British Colonies,* Bradford's publication was followed within days by Benjamin Franklin's *General Magazine and Historical Chronicle, For All the British Plantations in America.* Both of these publications lasted for a few months only, and were soon followed by other magazines that, because of circulation problems, also lasted but a short time. One of these short-lived magazines, founded in 1778, contained the suggested name for the new nation in its title: *The United States Magazine.*

Literary Standards of Magazines

Following the American Revolution magazines in this country experienced the start of their major period of growth with the birth of several newcomers, some of which were destined to prosper over the years: *American Museum* (1787), *Port Folio* (1801), *The Monthly Anthology* (1803), *Salmagundi* (1807), *The North American Review* (1815), *The Saturday Evening Post* (1821), *Genesee Farmer, or Country Gentleman* (1831), *The Knickerbocker Magazine* (1833), *The Atlantic Monthly* (1850), and *Harper's* (1850). Because literary groups owned and operated many of them, magazines were considered the most favorable medium in which to develop and publish native American literature. Magazines could carry more lengthy articles than newspapers, and they were easier to circulate and less expensive to publish than books. Many of these magazines reflected high literary standards and were responsible for determining the literary taste of their particular periods. Like newspapers, magazines of the post-Revolutionary era were free to print controversial articles such as the bitter denunciation of George Washington that was written by Benjamin Franklin's grandson. Magazine editors were well aware of their power, and editorial policy during the period was often marked by blind partisanship.

An Early Crusader

In 1865 Edwin L. Godkin, one of the country's most influential newspapermen and successor to William Cullen Bryant as editor of the *New York Post,*

46

joined the ranks of magazine publishers. Having decided that the country needed a quality journal of opinion and literary criticism, Godkin founded *The Nation*. Godkin geared the contents of his magazine to the interests of intellectuals. His editorials advocating "peace, entrenchment, and reform" are considered to be among the best ever written on these subjects, and Godkin soon had readers from coast to coast. In *The Nation* he stressed the importance of education and sought to better conditions for Black Americans. Although he crusaded against governmental intervention in economic matters, Godkin felt that government should take action in social welfare areas. Philosopher William James wrote of Godkin:

> His was certainly the towering influence in all thought concerning public affairs, and indirectly his influence has assuredly been more pervasive than that of any other writer of the generation.

Trend Toward Specialization

Many magazines soon developed into more specialized types of periodicals. By 1900 the *Ladies' Home Journal,* selling for ten cents a copy, had reached a circulation of one million. The *Journal's* publisher, Cyrus H. K. Curtis, who founded the magazine in 1883, purchased *The Saturday Evening Post* in 1897 for one thousand dollars. Curtis soon developed the *Post* into a leader in the weekly magazine field. Curtis, who was not a writer, had begun his career as an advertising man and, because he knew what the public was interested in, his publications soon became a profitable publishing venture called the Curtis Publishing Company. Curtis, whose career has often been called "The Great American Success Story," hired George Horace Lorimer as his managing editor. Lorimer further increased the popularity of the Curtis publications by hiring such well-known writers as Rudyard Kipling, Bret Harte, and Mark Twain; Lorimer even had the country's Presidents writing articles for the *Post. The Saturday Evening Post* ended its career as a leader in the weekly magazine field when it ceased publication on February 8, 1969.

The popularity of magazines increased with the beginning of the twentieth century, and circulation figures rose as magazines launched crusades. "Muckraking" (a word popularized by Theodore Roosevelt), which means public exposure of apparent misconduct on the part of prominent individuals or organizations, became a fad in magazine journalism during Roosevelt's presidency. The reading public, however, soon tired of this type of journalism, and magazines started experimenting with pictures to attract readers and further increase circulation figures.

The News in Brief

During the post-World War I magazine publishing boom, Yale student Henry R. Luce, realizing the power of the press in shaping the thinking of readers, solicited from Yale alumni contributions totaling some $86,000 with which to start a magazine. The new weekly publication would give readers capsule versions of the news in such areas as national affairs, foreign news, science, religion, business, education, and books. After making an informal survey that showed that the word "time" was often on the minds of Americans, Luce and *Time* Magazine co-founder Briton Haden chose this word as the title for their magazine. In the first issue of *Time* Magazine in March of 1923 the editors announced:

> People are uninformed because no publication has adapted itself to the time which busy men are able to spend on simply keeping informed.

The editors of *Time* Magazine presented the weekly news in a light, human-interest style that used narrative leads. They also initiated a system for researching the background of each story. The story background was then interwoven with the actual news account, the result being that most sentences came to be written in a unique inverted word order. This type of presentation prompted one critic to comment: "Backwards ran sentences until reeled the mind." In 1930, the year that many magazines went out of business because of the stock market crash and subsequent depression, the undaunted Luce launched a lavish business magazine titled *Fortune*. *Fortune* prospered and six years later Luce brought out *Life,* a magazine geared to the interests of increasingly picture-conscious readers. *Life* was an overnight success and Time, Inc., the name of Luce's combined publishing interests, soon became a giant in the field of magazine publishing. Luce began another magazine before his death in 1967: *Sports Illustrated*. Despite a rough start, *Sports Illustrated* became a successful publishing venture and is currently one of the country's most widely read sports magazines.

The Pocket-Size Magazine

Another magazine success story resulted from the efforts of newspaperman DeWitt Wallace and his wife. They began clipping stories from uncopyrighted magazines, compiling the clippings, and then presented them to readers as the pocket-sized *Reader's Digest*. The first issue of the *Reader's Digest* appeared in 1922 and was an overnight sensation. By printing condensed versions of entertaining and informative articles, the Wallaces built the *Digest's* circulation into the largest magazine circulation in the world.

Growth Continues

Magazine authority Dr. Roland E. Wolseley estimates that today there are about twenty thousand different magazines in the United States. While many of these magazines are special-interest publications, the majority are consumer-oriented. With the recent advances in printing techniques and photography, magazines have become an integral part of the mass media. This country's magazine circulation growth during a recent twenty-five year period is shown on Chart C, below.

MAGAZINE CIRCULATION GROWTH 1942-1967

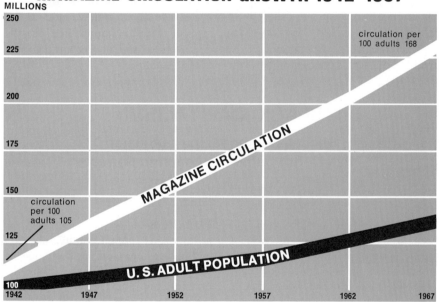

MILLIONS

circulation per 100 adults 168

MAGAZINE CIRCULATION

circulation per 100 adults 105

U. S. ADULT POPULATION

250 · 225 · 200 · 175 · 150 · 125 · 100

1942 · 1947 · 1952 · 1957 · 1962 · 1967

Sources: Circulation - ABC General and Farm Magazines, averages per issue for the second six months of year, U. S. Adult Population (15 years of age and over) - Bureau of Census, U. S. Department of Commerce
Magazine Advertising Bureau of Magazine Publishers Association, inc.

Chart C

Types of Magazines

To appeal to the greatest number of readers, most magazines must be national—rather than local—in scope. The circulation leader among magazines is the *Reader's Digest*, which has a total domestic and foreign circulation of more than twenty-eight million. *TV Guide* holds the second largest magazine circulation figure (more than twelve million)—an indication of the popular-

49

ity of television in our country. *Life* Magazine sells more than seven million copies a week, because it appeals to readers in all parts of the country.

Ethnic Magazines

Ethnic magazines represent a large portion of the magazine publishing industry. They are devoted to expressing the culture of races or groups whose members share common traits and customs within our society. *Ebony*, which has a circulation of over one million, represents the country's major Black American magazine. In format and content *Ebony* Magazine resembles *Life* Magazine. *Ebony* appeals to an upper middle-class reading audience, and tries to accentuate the positive aspects about the position of Black Americans in American society. The following feature article about a newcomer to the ethnic-magazine field—*Tuesday* Magazine—reflects the importance of this type of publication in our society. Read it carefully and be prepared to answer the questions concerning it at the end of this chapter.

BLACK CAPITALISM*

Successful magazine publisher
ties Negro gains to economic power

By Guy Halverson
Staff correspondent of The Christian Science Monitor

Chicago: "My faith in the system has been justified," the patrician, conservatively attired publisher quietly says, lounging back in his padded office chair.

By all standards, the assessment of W. Leonard Evans, Jr., would seem accurate. At a time when the publishing field is littered with the debris of press failures—from mass-circulation dailies like the *New York Mirror* and the *New York Herald Tribune,* to glossy magazines like *The Reporter* and *Collier's*—Mr. Evan's predominantly Black oriented *Tuesday* magazine has soared into national prominence in the short space of three years.

And as the magazine's circulation has steadily risen—from 1.4 million in 1965 to 2 million today—so has the influence and voice of Mr. Evans within the American publishing field.

Soft-spoken but articulate and intense, this black publisher-businessman believes that:

• To make tangible social and economic gains, Black America must increasingly own its own business enterprises.

• Blacks must be allowed greater influence in the "investment and financial system."

- Black economic power must be achieved within the larger context of a genuinely integrated society.
- Black universities and colleges, now basically oriented toward the "liberal arts," must establish business programs.
- Political or social separatism by Blacks would be "foolhardy," "defeatist," and "unnecessary."

Like another Chicago-based Black magazine—*Ebony*—*Tuesday* magazine is geared to the increasingly mobile and affluent Negro middle class. Issued as a Sunday supplement each month by 16 newspapers, the magazine spotlights Black history, Black family life and cultural trends, as well as the type of "general interest" story that might be carried by *Life* or *Look*. The staff—numbering some 16 full-time employees and 50 free-lance writers—is integrated.

"When I was with a Chicago advertising agency in the late 1950's I saw quite clearly that the spectrum of magazines for the American Negro was just totally insufficient," Mr. Evans says. "I was concerned about the image that my children—Black children living in a white-led society—would form of themselves. I decided that I just had to do something about this gap.

"Most major Black publications—like the *Chicago Defender*—were first founded as protest sheets. We want to go beyond mere protest. We want to affirm the positive, the enduring, the constructive in Negro life. The mass-circulation daily press focuses on the negatives—sit-ins, wrongdoers, militants, and political activists. But what about Black social and family life? How do white Americans—or even Negroes who read only the white press—know what goes on in Black homes, churches,

businesses? We want to show the richness of Black life."

Mr. Evans says that although the monthly lost money the first three years, it finally turned a profit with the May, 1968, issue. In the first seven months of this year, advertising reached $1.2 million. A net profit—somewhere in "six figures"—is expected for the entire year.

With $90,000 in personal funds and an additional $850,000 raised from friends and a bank loan. Mr. Evans first published *Tuesday* as a supplement to 10 papers in 1965. Advertising for the first year reached a touchy $560,000, Mr. Evans chuckles. Since then, national advertisers have been scrambling for space, partly because of *Tuesday* findings that some 80 percent of all Blacks shop outside inner-city areas. In the first seven months of 1968 alone, advertising revenue reached $1.2 million.

"Negotiations are under way to crack Southern metropolises (St. Louis, Houston, Dallas, Atlanta, and Kansas City, Mo.) as well as eventually to convert to a semimonthly."

Staffers optimistic

Tuesday staffers remain optimistic about the future. The magazine (named after the day of the week when most Black protest sheets were published during the 19th century) is currently distributed by only one Southern or border-state newspaper, the *Louisville Courier-Journal and Times*. But plans are under way to crack Southern metropolises, and eventually to convert to a semimonthly.

It is also hoped that white readership can be expanded (currently put at about 20 percent of the total) and that the company will eventually branch into book publishing.

Tuesday management officers foresee almost limitless circulation possibilities within Black inner-city areas. Though there are some 150 newspapers and two dozen magazines directed primarily to Blacks, studies show that five sixths of all Blacks still depend on the "general" press for their basic reading.

Mr. Evans, who was graduated from the University of Illinois School of Commerce in 1935, and subsequently undertook training at Kent College of Law, argues that the Black community must be built up through "Black economic power."

Money flows away

"If you look at Black America as a whole," he says, "we're a wealthy people. In fact, in dollar statistics, the 10th richest nation in the world, with a wealth of about $32 billion. Yet Blacks control less than 1 percent of American industry.

"Unfortunately, capitalism just isn't functioning in the ghetto today. What's functioning there is a sort of 'welfare socialism.' Federal and state relief continues to be all too necessary. Workers must settle for inferior local jobs or travel great distances to the suburbs where industry is relocating. And all the while, Black money keeps flowing out of black areas. We've got to start up our own businesses—creating products and services that whites as well as Blacks can use. That way money will flow back to the inner city, and we'll all be enriched."

Can the black man build a successful enterprise in the face of lavishly financed and stiff competition from white-led firms?

"My experience shows that it can be done," he says emphatically. "I had an idea, and I had the preparation and experience to make it work. My creditors evaluated me on the basis of integrity and purpose, not just on the fact that I'm a Negro. I conducted myself in a manner that won their confidence and trust, and that paid off in capitalization and backing and eventually success for *Tuesday.*

"Yes, the system does indeed work," W. Leonard Evans, Jr. adds as an afterthought. "If I could do it, so can other Negroes."

Other Types of Magazines

The general field of magazines can be arbitrarily broken down into categories such as Consumer (*Better Homes and Gardens, Ebony, Life*), News (*U.S. News & World Report, Time, Newsweek*), General Editorial (*Look, Reader's Digest, Cosmopolitan*), Literary Quality Magazines (*Harper's, The Atlantic Monthly, Esquire, Saturday Review, The New Yorker*), Business (*Barron's, Fortune, Business Week*), Women's Magazines (*Bazaar, Vogue, Good Housekeeping, McCall's, Woman's Day, Ladies' Home Journal*), Men's Magazines (*True, Argosy, Field and Stream*), Religious (*Catholic Digest, Together*), Technical (*Electromechanical Design, Popular Science*), Medical (*New England Journal of Medicine, American Medical Association Journal*), Specialized (*The Rotarian, Medical Economics*), Ethnic (*Tuesday,*

Sepia), and House Publications (*Ford Times, Bell Telephone News*). Many other magazines exist solely for the purpose of entertaining the reader (*Photoplay, Mad, Playboy*), while others are concerned with investigative reporting of current problems (the Kiplinger Service's *Changing Times*).

A comparative newcomer to the magazine publishing field is the Sunday magazine newspaper supplement. Even experienced newspaper and magazine publishers find it difficult to classify these supplements as either newspapers or magazines. Sunday supplements are publications assembled and delivered with the thick weekend newspapers. There is little doubt that the Sunday supplement makes the newspaper more appealing to its readers, although some newsmen feel that it takes the reader's attention away from the newspaper itself.

The three largest Sunday supplements in the United States are *Family Weekly, Parade,* and the *Sunday Magazine Group* (Metropolitan Sunday Newspapers). *Parade,* the second oldest, was first published in 1941. Its editor, Jess Gorkin, who came to *Parade* from *Look,* says he tries to make his publication provocative and "gutsy." *Family Weekly* is distributed by ninety-four newspapers in small and medium-sized towns and cities throughout the country. Most unique of the three Sunday supplements is the *Sunday Magazine Group* which does not send out a complete supplement to member newspapers. Instead, the *Sunday Magazine Group* sends selected articles, picture stories, and photographs to some twenty-five newspapers nationally. The need for this type of publication increased when the independently edited Sunday newspaper magazine supplements became successful, profitable, and large.

The three largest Sunday supplements in the United States are "Family Weekly," the "Sunday Magazine Group," and "Parade."

Parade

Similar to magazines in that they present more in-depth feature-type material than the newspapers they are a part of, the Sunday supplements still must conform to deadlines—deadlines that are only slightly less rigid than those imposed on their parent newspapers. Editors on Sunday magazine supplements begin their work approximately eight weeks prior to the parent newspaper's deadline.

The original supplement was started by Morris Goddard in the 1890's as a part of only one newspaper, William Randolph Hearst's *American.* Joseph Pulitzer, impressed with the possibilities offered by the supplement, followed Hearst and used the supplement as a run-of-the-paper operation. The Sunday supplements held their own until World War II when Hearst expanded them, realizing their value as profitable media for advertisers. *Parade, Family Weekly,* and the *Sunday Magazine Group,* with their combined circulation of fifty million copies, represent one of the country's broadest fields of reader interest; each one has shown a continued yearly increase in growth and advertising potential.

Magazine Writing

There is little difference between good magazine writing and good newspaper writing, as shown in the following two leads—one from a magazine article, the other from a newspaper article.

EXAMPLE:

> A few miles from where you live there is a part of America nobody wants. It may be a group of ramshackle farm houses or the gray, weatherworn tenements of a city street. Row on row they shelter the culls of society whose togetherness is marked by frayed collars and the musty smell of the poor.
>
> *Harper's Magazine*

EXAMPLE:

The windows of Dr. Irving Sklar's reception room at 2 Fifth Avenue in New York City look out across Washington Square. A patient waiting uneasily for the dentist's drill can watch the pigeons circling Standford White's dignified Washington Arch, the children playing hopscotch on the square's wide walkways and the students walking hand in hand beneath the American elms.

The New York Times
© 1967 by The New York Times Company.
Reprinted by permission.

The first lead, from a *Harper's* Magazine article "A Way Out of the Welfare Mess," was written by Edgar May, a Pulitzer Prize-winning reporter for the *Buffalo Evening News*. Since *Harper's* is a nationally distributed magazine, May's article deals with problems existing in cities throughout the country. But earlier, when he wrote the story as a part of a series for the *Evening News,* his focus centered on Buffalo's unique problems. In the complete magazine story he gives the *why* of the problem and offers solutions. While the majority of newspaper stories give only the *who, what, when,* and *where* of the story, magazines often add the two that are, in many cases, the most important: the *how* and the *why*.

The second lead, written as a newspaper article by *New York Times* reporter J. Anthony Lukas, is from the 1967 Pulitzer Prize-winning story entitled "The Two Worlds of Linda Fitzpatrick." This story of a murdered 18-year-old girl who lived one kind of life in Greenwich, Connecticut, and a completely different kind of life in Greenwich Village, New York, begins with the local angle. Although the second story was written for New Yorkers, it achieved national significance because it dealt with teenagers everywhere.

Freelance Writers

While the majority of newspaper articles are written by staff personnel, magazines often assign freelance writers to do specific stories. In this way magazines can use articles by top authorities in desired fields. If the *Saturday Review* wanted an article on the Cuban missile crisis, for example, the editors could hire a famous historian to write it.

Many magazines purchase unsolicited manuscripts from freelance writers. Unknown writers often break into print this way, like the journalism student who, having attended a concert, became interested in electronic music. After checking through the *Reader's Guide to Periodical Literature* in his school library, he read a number of magazine articles related to electronic music and then wrote a 700-word article for submission to a music magazine. The editor liked the story and bought it. A large Midwestern newspaper's music editor read the article and offered to pay the student for permission to reprint parts of it. Then, the editor of a musical instrument company's trade magazine asked the student to write still another story on the same topic. The enterprising journalism student received over $150 from the publications represented by the three editors.

While many professional freelancers prefer, for the sake of variety, to write about a number of different subjects, others prefer to write articles on specialized subject areas. Most magazine editors request that freelance writers submit what is called a letter of query prior to submitting their actual manuscript. This query may be either a letter detailing exactly what the article is about, or an actual outline of the article. Following is an example of this type of query, written by a student:

EXAMPLE:

April 17, 19—
114 Smull Ave.
Trenton, New Jersey 07006

Nonfiction Editor
Argosy Magazine
205 E. 42nd St.
New York, N.Y. 10017

Dear Mr. Mechlin,

    The number of books and magazine articles written about the life of Lincoln in recent years, and especially during the current Civil War Centennial, has indeed been overwhelming. Why the "Lincoln Boom"? Simply, because the market beckons. However, these manuscripts tend to pursue the same theme—the romantic portrayal of Lincoln, and his "rags to riches" success story that destined him to become the leading figure of the Civil War, a hero of the American people for generations to come.
    Opposed to this romantic picture of Lincoln's rise to fame, I have taken a realistic look at his life, his violent death. Very few people know the true story behind Lincoln's assassination. John Wilkes Booth was a mere puppet!
    Knowing of Argosy's style and format from the standpoint of a regular reader, I have attempted to write this manuscript with a flavor of mystery, intrigue, and an aura of much previously forgotten historical evidence which lends itself admirably to your requirements and your readers' tastes.

My story has been authenticated as factually true and "very enlightening" by the Civil War and Lincolnian expert of the Maxwell School at Syracuse University, the celebrated author, Dr. O. T. Bark.

I have access to many previously unpublished photos of the assassination, conspirators, excellent photos of the fake reward posters Stanton had printed, and with the "go ahead" from you, will procure them for the story.

I am anxiously awaiting your reply. Thank you for your consideration.

Yours truly,
William T. Critchley

As this query shows, the writer has thoroughly researched his subject and has prepared his article for a specific reading audience—*Argosy* Magazine. The steps he used in writing the actual article were similar to those he'd use in writing a newspaper feature story or an English composition. Such articles must have an introduction (called a lead), a middle, and a conclusion. The lengths of the lead and the conclusion should be in proportion to the length of the entire story. A rule-of-thumb is to have each of these two portions approximately one-eighth the length of the entire article. To achieve variety, magazine editors often suggest that articles contain anecdotes, case histories, and other human-interest devices. Most magazine articles contain a great deal of descriptive detail and some figurative language—similes, metaphors, hyperboles, and personification.

The Short

Many beginners write shorts (material used as page filler, and material used to relieve solid editorial content) and have them accepted by magazines. Shorts usually run from one paragraph to some two hundred words in length. Some are humorous and some are of the "how-to-do-it" variety. The "Life in These United States" section of the *Reader's Digest* is an example of the humorous type of short, and contains material that deals with incidents happening to average people. The popular "how-to-do-it" short appears mostly in magazines like *Mechanics Illustrated*. The topic areas of shorts are usually related to the magazine's subject area. For example, "How to start your power mower," and "How to repair a TV antenna" are types of shorts *Mechanics Illustrated* would be apt to use.

Steps in Writing For Magazines

The following steps, used by a well-known freelance writer, may be used as a general guide in preparing a magazine article:

1. Get the main idea or theme for the article. This can come from attending a concert or art show, hearing a lecture or sermon, talking with someone who has an opinion to offer, or reading an article or book.

2. Work the idea over in your mind and think of specific magazines that might be interested in an article related to it. Send a query to the editors of these magazines.

3. Do research on your chosen subject. Write letters to authorities, interview specialists, read background articles, and either secure pictures or make suggestions for pictures to accompany the story. File any possible related ideas for future reference. These ideas can serve as a basis for organizing the article.

4. Set up a logical outline to prevent "topsy-turvy" writing.

5. Write the beginning and ending of the article. Include in the beginning the thesis statement, a statement telling what the article is about.

6. Write the first draft of the article. From the first draft, rewrite until you are satisfied with the finished product.

7. Put the article aside for about a week. When the material is no longer fresh in your mind, reread and edit it.

8. Forward the finished article to an interested magazine editor.

MAJOR DIVISIONS OF A LARGE MAGAZINE

The major divisions of an average large magazine are: management, editorial, advertising, and circulation. Management supervises the business aspects of producing the magazine, editorial is responsible for the magazine's editorial content or viewpoints, the advertising department contracts for and sells advertising space, and the circulation department is responsible for subscriptions and distribution. A typical staff organization chart for a large magazine is shown on page 60.

Few magazine publishers own the plant in which their magazines are printed. The high-quality printing equipment needed by the major magazines represents a huge financial investment and requires the full-time use of specialists in the printing process. Most magazine publishers job shop their printing to printing plants that specialize in magazine publishing. Many of these printers handle several different magazines. At the printing plant the articles and headlines are set in type, and engravings are made of the illustrations. These elements are placed in page forms and printed on high-speed color presses. Then, the pages are collated and bound.

The Editor-in-chief—The editor-in-chief is in charge of the editorial staff and decides what articles and artwork are to be published. His decisions are based on his best knowledge .of what the magazine's readers want. The editor-in-chief also supervises the production of each issue. Ordinarily, he does not write the articles. He may, however, write editorials or special reports. The editor-in-chief must combine executive and creative duties. Some editors-in-chief spend a great deal of time revising and correcting articles, selecting the illustrations, and planning the layouts for each page. Other editors-in-chief delegate this work to subordinates and devote their own time to general supervision, policy determination, and administrative duties. The editor-in-chief reports to the publisher, as do the heads of all other departments. On larger publications, magazine publishers may have separate staffs of their own, often including an executive assistant, business manager, a public relations man, and other specialized executives.

Department Editors—On large magazines department editors may confer and work with the editor-in-chief on each issue. They also direct the editorial work of departments such as sports, theater, arts, fashion, and fiction.

Editorial Assistants—Magazine editorial assistants spend most of their time doing library research to aid the writers. Facts in the finished story are double-checked by these assistants who also retype copy, answer letters, interview callers, and do other routine office work.

Copyreaders—Finished manuscripts are checked by copyreaders for length, style, grammar, spelling, punctuation, organization, technical accuracy, and for readability.

The Advertising Director—The advertising director is responsible for managing the sale of advertising space. He may also have a group of district sales offices throughout the country to manage. Some magazines have sales staffs numbering more than fifty persons.

The Circulation Department—Magazine circulation departments are often divided into two departments: subscription sales and newsstand sales. The subscription division obtains new subscribers by mail or from outside sales agencies, while the newsstand division is concerned with single-copy sales

TYPICAL STAFF ORGANIZATION FOR A LARGE MAGAZINE

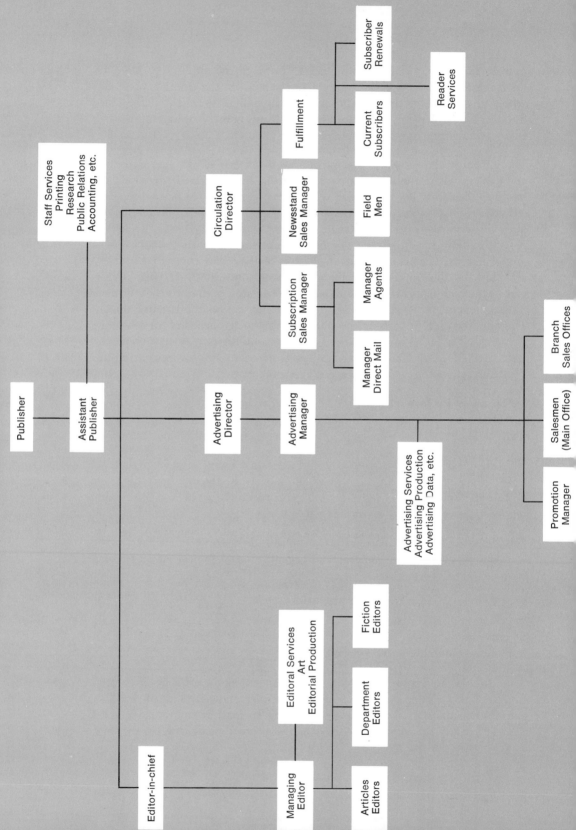

at newsstands. Other members of the circulation department handle subscription billing, subscription renewals, and distribution.

Advertising Production—The advertising production department is concerned with the handling and processing of engravings sent by advertisers, with advertising makeup, and with advertising layout. The advertising production department also serves as a liaison between the advertising department and the printer.

THE FUTURE OF MAGAZINES

Our country's education explosion (see Chart A, page 44) has given new impetus to the magazine market. This market already represents fifty-three percent of the total adult population, and will probably grow to fifty-nine percent (or about three-fifths of America's potential adult buyers) by 1975. By then there should be approximately eighty-five million high school and college graduates—and at least forty million of these graduates should be heavy magazine readers.

A Magazine Career

A student interested in entering magazine journalism should begin his preparation now. He should get a good background in English, literature, foreign languages, science, and the social sciences. In college, he should take journalism and liberal arts courses. Both in high school and in college he should read far beyond the course requirements—the better informed he is, the greater will be his ability to cover a variety of assignments. Knowing how to type and knowing shorthand or speedwriting would be valuable assets for many magazine writing assignments.

Although there is no general rule, most magazines seem to prefer writers who have had experience on a newspaper prior to joining their staffs. Specialized magazines often require a background in their specific fields. For example, the journalism student who hopes to work on *High Fidelity* Magazine should take courses in music. But the major requirement is that the applicant know how to write. Hedley Donovan, editor-in-chief of Time, Inc., tells of the background needed by writers for *Fortune* Magazine:

> A background in business is of course valuable. However, we can teach this person all that he'll need to know about the field in a few months.

Opportunities in the Profession

The curious, enthusiastic, self-reliant, and well-trained person will find a number of opportunities in magazine journalism. Jobs are available not only for writers, but also for photographers, designers, artists, clerical workers, and editors. Because there are more magazines today than ever before, and because new magazines are appearing frequently, there are more magazine jobs available. And, as in the newspaper field, there is no job discrimination against women. In fact, over half of all magazine journalists are women, and many major magazines employ women as editors. A good way for a young woman to break into the magazine business is to begin as a secretary. Once she has her foot in the door, she often finds it much easier to move into an editorial post.

The earnings of magazine employees vary depending on the size and geographical location of the magazine, and of course, different job levels affect the salary scale. General editorial salaries range from $5,000 to $20,000 a year, while some top-flight editors earn as much as $100,000 a year.

SPECIALIZED PERIODICALS

Specialized periodicals are aimed at readers who share a particular occupation or interest. These periodicals are dependent on subscription, not on newsstand sales. Many are not available on newsstands. It has been estimated that specialized periodicals represent more than sixty-five percent of all magazines published in this country. Some specialized periodicals do have general public appeal but are limited to specific groups. For example, *National Geographic* has a general-public reader appeal, but is only sent to members of the *National Geographic Society*.

The largest group of specialized publications are those published by business and industry, including house organs and other similar types of company publications. Specialized publications are important media for influencing opinion and disseminating business news.

BOOKS

Our growing population reads more than ever before. More leisure time in which to read, more financial ability with which to buy books, availability of expensive editions in paperback form, all contribute to the success of book publishing in this country.

Wesley Williams, Jr.

The rapidly expanding field of magazine journalism offers career opportunities for writers, editors, photographers, designers, artists, and clerical workers.

In the 1830's the appearance of the dime novel heralded the first paperbacks, and political tracts and almanacs began to appear. Our current paperback boom began one hundred years later—in the late 1930's. Most recently, the paperback has entered the classroom on primary, secondary, and college levels.

Textbook publishing, a major part of the book publishing industry, accounts for more than one-third of the total publishing figure for books printed in this country. The rise in importance of textbooks in the book-publishing industry can be attributed to our education explosion.

The book publishing boom directly reflects the rising cultural level of the American public. The public's increased interest in public events accounts for still another trend in book publishing. With technical advances in printing, many publishers can print books about major news events just a few weeks after the event occurs. These books offer the reader timeliness with their detailed and in-depth coverage of news events, and cause and effect analyses. In the tragic assassinations of President John F. Kennedy, his brother Robert F. Kennedy, and Dr. Martin Luther King, Jr., books on these events were published in less than a month after the actual happening.

ACTIVITIES

1. Without rereading the feature story "Black Capitalism," which you read earlier in this chapter under "TYPES OF MAGAZINES," test your recall by answering the following questions:

a. State, in your own words the assessment of the magazine publishing field as given by *Tuesday* Magazine publisher W. Leonard Evans, Jr., in the feature story.

b. What is the socio-economic background of the readers of *Tuesday* Magazine?

c. According to the editorial, to what other Black American magazine is *Tuesday* compared? Why?

d. What is the editorial content of *Tuesday* Magazine?

e. Paraphrase Mr. Leonard Evans, Jr.'s statement concerning the aim of his magazine.

f. What percentage of the total reading audience of *Tuesday* Magazine is white?

g. Does Mr. Evans think that Black Americans can build successful enterprises despite the competition offered by highly financed white-led firms? Explain how.

2. From the following list, select one subject as the basis for a research paper to be written and presented orally to the class. Use the resource materials available in your school and local library.

Digests	Professional Journals
Picture Magazines	Literary Magazines
Pulp Magazines	Weekly News Magazines
Science Magazines	Trade Magazines
Business House Organs	Comic Magazines

3. Study four or more issues of one magazine of your choice. Prepare a written report, analyzing the magazine for content, reader appeal, advertising appeal, and writing style. In your report, determine the socio-economic group for which the magazine is written.

4. Choose a familiar weekly or monthly news magazine for analysis. After studying it carefully, answer the following questions:
   a. What is the significance of its name?
   b. What is the purpose of its cover?
   c. What type of magazine is it?
   d. What is its editorial policy?
   e. What kinds of reading materials are included in it?
   f. What is its general order of content? Why?
   g. Why do you think it is the size it is?
   h. What kind of people do you think subscribe to it?
   i. What do you think is the general age level and background of the magazine's subscribers?
   j. Do you think the magazine's subscription price is reasonable for value received? Why?
   k. What types of merchandise are advertised in it? Why?

5. Poll the members of your class and prepare a brief, informal magazine-reading survey for oral presentation to the class. You may use the following questions as a guide in preparing your poll. After completing the poll, you may wish to compile your results with those found by your classmates into a master magazine-reading survey.
   a. What magazine do you most often read?
   b. Why do you read this particular magazine?
   c. What is the editorial policy of this magazine?
   d. Who publishes this magazine?
   e. How much time do you spend each week reading this magazine?
   f. What are some of the names of the leading contributors to your favorite magazine?
   g. Are you familiar with the backgrounds of these contributors?
   h. Which features do you find the most appealing? Why?

6. Bring copies of three different specialized periodicals to class. Analyze them for treatment of articles, similarities in content, format, and audience appeal. Compare the articles with those found in the magazine of your choice selected in question 3 for *a*) similarities, and *b*) differences.

7. The class will be divided into three groups. Each group will read one of the leading news magazines for a particular week. The groups will compare the magazines for treatment of stories, writing style, and similarity of content. Results of the comparisons will be discussed in class.

8. Make a study of one issue of a news magazine. Prepare an oral report on the magazine's coverage of a specific social issue such as urban renewal, civil rights, student protest, or public welfare.

READING

BAIRD, RUSSELL N., AND ARTHUR T. TURNBULL, *Industrial and Business Journalism.* Chilton Book Co., Philadelphia, Pa., 1961.

BIRD, GEORGE, *Modern Article Writing.* Wm. C. Brown, Dubuque, Iowa, 1967.

CASSIRER, ERNST, *An Essay on Man.* Yale University Press, New Haven, Conn., 1944. (PB)

CATER, DOUGLASS, *The Fourth Branch of Government.* Houghton Mifflin, Boston, 1959.

FERGUSON, ROWENA, *Editing the Small Magazine.* Columbia University Press, New York, 1958. (PB)

GOULDEN, JOSEPH C., *The Curtis Caper.* Putnam, New York, 1965.

GRANNIS, CHANDLER (Ed.), *What Happens in Book Publishing.* Columbia University Press, New York, 1967.

KOBLER, JOHN, *Luce: His Time, Life and Fortune.* Doubleday, New York, 1968.

LEHMANN-HAUPT, HELLMUT, LAWRENCE C. WROTH AND ROLLO G. SILVER, *The Book in America: A History of the Making and Selling of Books in the United States.* Bowker, New York, 1961.

MAGAZINE PUBLISHERS ASSOCIATION, *Magazines in America.* Magazine Publishers Association, Skokie, Ill.

MODERN LANGUAGE ASSOCIATION, *The Little Magazine and Contemporary Literature.* Modern Language Association, New York, 1966. (PB)

MOTT, FRANK LUTHER, *Golden Multitudes.* Bowker, New York, 1947.

———, *A History of American Magazines,* 5 vols. Harvard University Press, Cambridge, Mass., 1957.

MUMBY, FRANK A., *Publishing and Bookselling: A History from the Earliest Times to the Present.* Bowker, New York, 1956.

PATTERSON, HELEN M., *Writing and Selling Feature Articles.* Prentice-Hall, Englewood Cliffs, New Jersey, 1956.

PETERSON, THEODORE, *Magazines in the Twentieth Century.* University of Illinois Press, Urbana, Ill., 1964.

QUILL AND SCROLL SOCIETY, *Magazines and Books* (from the *Careers in Journalism Series*). State University of Iowa, Iowa City, Iowa, 1963.

ROOT, ROBERT, *Modern Magazine Editing.* Wm. C. Brown, Dubuque, Iowa, 1966.

SINGLETON, M. K., *H. L. Mencken and the American Mercury.* Duke University Press, Durham, N. C., 1962.

UNWIN, SIR STANLEY, *The Truth About Publishing.* Bowker, New York, 1960.

WALKER, GERALD (Ed.), *Best Magazine Articles,* (*1966–1968*). Crown, New York, 1968.

WHITTEMORE, REED, *Little Magazines.* University of Minnesota Press, Minneapolis, Minn., 1963. (PB)

WOLSELEY, ROLAND E., *Understanding Magazines,* Second Edition. Iowa State University Press, Ames, Iowa, 1969.

WOOD, JAMES PLAYSTED, *Magazines in the United States.* Ronald, New York, 1956.

WOODWARD, HELEN, *The Lady Persuaders.* Ivan Obolensky, New York, 1960.

Chapter 4

The Electronic Media

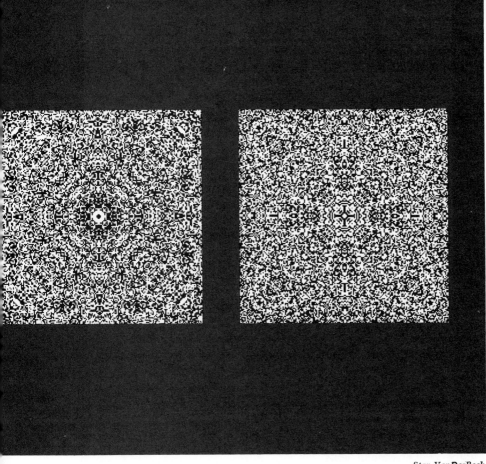

THE EMERGENCE OF THE ELECTRONIC MEDIA

In the early days of our country professional journalism was restricted to the print media alone—newspapers, magazines, specialized periodicals, and books. Today, due to the inventive genius of men like Morse, Bell, Marconi, and Edison, we have such additional communications media as the telephone, teletype, wirephoto, radio, motion pictures, television, facsimile, and the satellite.

In 1876 Alexander Graham Bell paved the way for the development of the telephone when he used Morse's idea of communicating by wire to transmit the human voice. The telephone, with its intimate, personal communications appeal, soon became one of the most important means of communication in the country.

Guglielmo Marconi's wireless telegraphy invention in 1896 was the forerunner for the development of the radio. With its ability to reach masses of the population instantaneously, the radio became a major source of information and entertainment. Because listening audiences could be reached immediately, the radio soon became one of the most important mediums for dissemination of the news.

Thomas Alva Edison developed the Kinetoscope in 1893, a camera which projected pictures taken from rolls of celluloid film onto a screen. The Kinetoscope, forerunner of the modern motion-picture camera, projected separate stills which, when run off rapidly in sequence, appeared as a series of continuous actions.

The Kinetoscope was the beginning of today's motion-picture industry which began its development early in the twentieth century with productions like *The Great Train Robbery* (1903). In 1927 sound was incorporated with film, and the first "talking" motion picture, *The Jazz Singer*, was produced. Today, many motion-picture producers are concentrating their efforts on preparing films for television production.

In 1926 a working television receiver was produced, as scientists and media engineers gained further understanding of the new developments and techniques in photoelectronics. From the early developments of the image dissector tube and the iconoscope emerged the image orthicon tube which is now used in most television studios. Color has added an even more exciting dimension to a medium that has not, as yet, reached its full potential in providing information to the public. How important television can be to the average man's knowledge of the world about him was dramatically seen on July 20, 1969, when "live" television transmission permitted millions of viewers to witness the first moon walk.

Facsimile reproduction, a means by which a "living-room newspaper" may one day be supplied to consumers, is the electronic transmission of printed or photographed material from a transmitter to a receiver. With facsimile reproduction, proof of a newspaper page can be put on a transmitter, allowing the consumer to receive a copy of the page on his facsimile set at home. Facsimile, a method that could revolutionize the newspaper industry, is presently too costly an operation to make installation in homes practical. Several preliminary attempts have been made to combine facsimile transmission and reception with telephone, radio, and television facilities in order to bring costs down by reaching the consumer through the use of these other, much less-expensive media.

Our electronic age is a global age. Speed and frequency of intercontinental transportation combined with electronic technology of communications have made us neighbors in time and space to people who live on the other side of the globe. Satellites are further revolutionizing telecommunications technology. One of the most recent developments in communications, the satellite, has enabled viewers to have on-the-scene experience of events that take place thousands of miles away.

One of the most recent developments in communications, the communications satellite, enabled TV viewers to see man's first moon landing in July, 1969.

THE ELECTRONIC MEDIA AND TODAY'S JOURNALISM STUDENT

The rapid growth of the electronic media has brought about a communications revolution in our society. Information is now relayed more quickly to more places than ever before, thus enabling people everywhere to be far better informed than was possible forty years ago. Since today's journalism student finds himself in the midst of this communications revolution, he is, necessarily, more concerned than was the student of forty years ago with the latest media developments and their application to journalism. To better acquaint you with the more important of the electronic mass media, this chapter deals primarily with their backgrounds and functions as news communicators in our society.

Telephone

In 1968 ninety percent of all American households—some one hundred million in all—had telephones. The number of households having telephones, which has been growing at the rate of from four to five million annually, has increased by fifty percent since the end of World War II.

The telephone, an indispensible part of the news media since its inception, is used as a basic conveyor of information, as a primary source for gaining information, and as a quick means for securing and checking facts. Telephone lines are used by teletype and telephoto operations to transmit information and pictures to and from news agencies and newspapers all over the world.

It has been predicted that in the near future satellites will make it possible for a person to telephone anywhere in the world for only a small cost. Telephone rates, which now vary according to the distance of the call, will become constant because the speed and space coverage of satellite communications will virtually eliminate distance as a factor in accounting cost.

Teletype

Teletype machines are used to transmit and receive thousands of words of news copy daily. The news copy is transmitted by an operator using a teletype machine with a keyboard similar to that of a typewriter. As the operator types, each character is simultaneously perforated onto a paper tape in an accompanying machine. The accompanying machine, called a teletypesetter, converts the perforations into sound signals and transmits them over telephone lines to other teletype machines which, in turn, reconvert them back onto perforated tapes. These tapes are then fed into newspaper composing room typesetting machines that automatically set the copy from the tapes. Newspapers using teletype equipment save a great deal of time and money.

Wirephoto

Wirephoto (also called telephoto and radiophoto) machines transmit copies of pictorial material and photographs to newspapers and news agencies throughout the world in a matter of minutes. Photoelectric cells, scanning the surfaces of materials to be transmitted, send out sound signals on radio waves and telephone lines to client news agencies and newspapers where similar photoelectric machines expose the signals onto sensitized photographic paper. Strong sound signals are reproduced as dark areas on the facsimile print, while weaker ones are reproduced as light areas. Pictorial materials can be both transmitted and received on wirephoto machines.

The Emergence of Radio

Many Americans, with radio and television almost always at their fingertips, often find it difficult to imagine living in an age without these comparatively new media. Early events leading up to the invention of the radio began in 1558 when Giovanni Battista della Porta proposed a message-sending device that utilized magnetism—a phenomenon which had been known since ancient times. Early experimenters were hampered by their lack of knowledge of physics, and further progress wasn't made until the nineteenth century. Samuel Morse, in 1844, invented the electromagnetic telegraph and sent the first message by wire ("What hath God wrought?") from Washington to Baltimore. In America overhead wires pushed across the country with the railroads and, by 1876, Alexander Graham Bell had discovered that wires could carry human speech as well as dots and dashes.

Scientists the world over, intrigued with these developments, began to make further progress in electronics. A year after Bell's telephone was invented, Thomas Alva Edison fastened a needle to a telephone mouthpiece and found that he could permanently record the sound vibrations on wax.

Invaluable Uses

In 1896, Guglielmo Marconi, at the age of twenty-two, determined that sound could be transmitted without the aid of wires and cables. The invaluable uses of wireless—or radio—were seen by people in all countries. The new invention was used by ships to ensure greater safety, by large companies to communicate with far-flung clients, and by the armed forces in World War I to transmit and receive vital intelligence information.

Uses of the device as an entertainment and journalistic medium were yet to be developed. It took the foresight of David Sarnoff, who later became chairman of the board of the Radio Corporation of America, to envision possibilities for future use. In 1916 Sarnoff wrote:

> I have in mind a plan of development which would make radio a household utility. . . . The idea is to bring music into the home by wireless. . . . The receiver can be designed in the form of a simple "Radio Music Box" and arranged for several different wavelengths, which should be changeable with the throwing of a single switch or the pressing of a single button. . . . The same principle can be extended to numerous other fields, as for example receiving lectures at home, which would be perfectly audible; also events of national importance can be simultaneously announced and received. Baseball scores can be transmitted in the air. . . .

The First Disc Jockey

Thousands of Americans soon became interested in the possibilities presented by the wireless. Many listened with amazement to the messages being transmitted and, in 1920, a young scientist named Frank Conrad talked, read aloud, and played records for wireless transmission from his garage in Pittsburgh. Conrad began receiving post cards from listeners who asked him to play their favorite records. In order to test the range of his transmitter, he complied with their requests and thus became the country's first disc jockey. To the astonishment of the Westinghouse Corporation for whom Conrad worked, a department store advertised receivers "for those who want to tune in the Westinghouse station." Taking advantage of the situation, Westinghouse, late in 1920, set up one of the country's first radio stations, Station KDKA in Pittsburgh, and broadcast the results of the Harding-Cox presidential election.

The Emergence of Networks

Many more radio stations were soon established and receivers were being purchased to hear, among other events, the 1921 heavyweight championship fight between Jack Dempsey and Georges Charpentier. Radio stations were soon hooked up with others, thus forming the national radio networks that better provided listeners with news of national events. The National Broadcasting Company was formed in 1926, the Columbia Broadcasting System a year later, and the American Broadcasting Company in 1941. The Rose Bowl football game of 1927 was the country's first program to be broadcast from coast-to-coast. To give listeners even more and better news coverage, radio stations began subscribing to the wire services of the Associated Press, United Press, and International News Service. By World War II radio networks had built up their own vast newsgathering agencies, and Americans got their news—from President Roosevelt's declaration of war to the Japanese surrender on the Battleship Missouri—from the radio. The names of radio news commentators such as Lowell Thomas, Walter Winchell, and war correspondents such as Eric Sevareid, Edward R. Murrow, and Walter Cronkite soon became well-known names in most American households.

Propaganda Uses

Between the two World Wars, governments began to recognize the value of radio as a propaganda medium. In 1942 the United States government established a radio broadcast called the "Voice of America" to serve as a psychological warfare weapon and as a means of transmitting American news to allied and neutral countries. Presently, "Voice of America" is the radio division of the United States Information Agency, and its purpose, as established by the 80th Congress, is to "promote the better understanding of the United States among the people of the world and to strengthen cooperative international relations." "Voice of America," which consists of news, news analy-

74

sis and commentary, drama, and music, is broadcast to countries throughout the world including Russia and other Eastern countries. Similar in purpose to "Voice of America," "Radio Free Europe," a privately owned network of five radio stations supported by voluntary contributions, also broadcasts programs, but to countries in Eastern Europe only. "Radio Moscow" and "Radio Peking" broadcast almost as much propaganda as "Voice of America."

Millions of Listeners

A recent survey sponsored by the broadcasting industry states that 19,100,000 people are tuned-in on our country's radio stations during the average quarter hour, and that nearly 140 million people twelve years of age and older (or ninety-five percent of the population) listen to the radio in the average week. This same survey found that three out of every four adults and four out of every five teenagers listen to the radio during the average day. It has been estimated that there are currently more than 270,000,000 radio sets in the United States. The number of radio receivers in our country is substantially more than the total population.

Program Formats Change

With the advent of television, many media experts erroneously predicted that this newer medium would bring about the near death of radio. Though radio has survived, television has had major effects on the medium. Listening habits have changed: many people now listen to the radio only during the day and watch television at night. Program format has changed dramatically: recorded music punctuated with newscasts has replaced, for the most part, the variety programming and dramatic shows that were popular twenty years ago. Radio stations no longer broadcast as many network shows as they did in pre-television days, and variety of radio programming has decreased sharply—most programming today is news and public opinion. Many networks specialize in weekend and special programs, while the smaller, independent radio stations broadcast their own programs. These small radio stations and the increasing popularity of the transistor radio account for a major part of the growth in today's radio industry.

Motion Pictures

Motion-picture attendance in the United States was seriously affected by massive television viewing beginning in the mid-forties. The huge, palacelike cinemas which dominated the national scene during the twenties have been closing throughout the country. In their place we have a burgeoning of small cinemas seating from three to five hundred, theaters in suburban shopping centers, and outdoor cinemas.

While television ended the movies' newsreel productions, television's dependence upon feature films for its programming has resulted in there being insufficient films to meet market needs. Making films for television has become an important part of Hollywood film production. In an attempt to compete with television filmviewing, Hollywood produced spectaculars—but the market for these films has declined. The multimillion-dollar productions of the sixties have had to compete with low-budget films made in Europe by independent producers in the United States. These low-budget films, often having good stories and characters but no "stars," have outgrossed extravaganzas and caused their decline.

Educational and nontheatrical films, an exploding field in motion pictures, include films produced for government and for business, medical, educational, and religious groups. Both the amount of money spent on making educational films and the number of titles produced yearly have shown a marked increase during the past decade.

The influence of European films upon American films and the increased opportunity of American films to present adult themes as a result of relaxed censorship codes have given films a conditional protection and freedom. On November 1, 1968, the Motion Picture Association of America launched a rating and classification system for feature films to try to stave off the threatened federal, state, and municipal film censorship. The M.P.A.A. endeavor is a voluntary one.

Studios Merge

In the late 1960's many of the major film studios either merged with other corporations or changed hands completely. United Artists, for example, became a wholly owned subsidiary of TransAmerica Corporation, a giant holding company. Paramount became a part of Gulf and Western Industries, Inc., while Cinerama merged with the American Broadcasting Company. The Columbia Broadcasting Company set up its own studios for the production of feature films on what had been the Republic Pictures lot.

Facsimile Reproduction

The country's first regularly produced facsimile newspaper was *The Wall Street Journal*. The operation of the *Journal's* San Francisco plant includes making a proof of the pages of its *Pacific Coast Edition* for facsimile transmission to its Riverside, California plant. A transmitted negative of the San Francisco edition is sent to Riverside where it is developed onto a positive, placed on a zinc plate, and then run off on printing presses.

The *Daily Mirror* between Scotland and Ireland, the *Australian*, and

France Soir are all committed in one way or another to experimenting with facsimile. Facsimile has great potential for the future of the print media. At present its greatest use is for newspicture transmission to newspapers and television stations, and for transmission of entire pages of newspapers from one printing plant to another.

Television

The public depends upon the electronic media for its immediacy as a source of information and entertainment. Many claim that TV is our greatest single source of information and entertainment. The television industry can claim a major advantage over the print media in the news broadcasting field—it is faster. And by offering a combination of sight, sound, and motion, it is able to dramatize the news of the day. A U.S. Navy study showed that audience retention is far greater when the viewer is exposed to both sight and sound (television) than when he is exposed to sight (newspapers) or sound (radio) alone. Since television is such a powerful medium, it necessarily has obligations to the public for responsible broadcasting.

The telecast "On Being Black" is an example of the television industry's attempt to present informative programs in the public's interest.

Conrad White

Important Source of News

Despite the fact that newspapers, with their dependence on the wire services, are considered by many publishers as the major source of news, the radio industry claims that it is "the dominant source of news" during the day for the average American. This lead is yielded to television after six in the evening, but radio maintains that it still outranks newspapers during that time period. However, as newscaster Walter Cronkite has remarked, radio and television can provide merely a quick headline service, whereas newspapers provide the depth of coverage that can give the "why" behind the headlines. Along these same lines, Charles Kuralt of Columbia Broadcasting System comments:

> We can take you there and show you, but we haven't done much to explain the WHY of the news. Television is not a medium dedicated to news anyway. It's more like running the comics on page one.

Years of Viewing

A recent survey revealed that Americans own more than ninety million television sets and there are more than 800 television stations currently in operation. Another survey found that more than 54 million families have one or more television sets. This same survey also revealed that each day these families spend some 300 million viewing hours before their sets, and that the average person watches television more than two hours a day. In 1969 the National Commission on the Causes and Prevention of Violence headed by Dr. Milton Eisenhower disclosed the following facts: the average American between his second and sixty-fifth year spends 3000 entire days (almost nine years of his life) watching television; by the time a five-year-old child enters kindergarten he has spent more time learning about life from the family television set than the average student in a liberal arts program spends in a classroom in his four years of college attendance; based on a recent average week of television programming, an incident of violence is enacted every fourteen minutes and a killing every forty-five minutes.

Effects of Violence

Such viewing habits and programming would seem to have far-reaching effects, especially for children, although concerned viewers often differ in their analyses. Most viewers agree, however, that children are disturbed by the excessive violence depicted and that many children can thus come to believe that violence is an accepted response to a difficult situation. Some viewers also feel that many television commercials place too much emphasis on materialism. The attractive actors shown in such commercials are usually seen living in expensive surroundings where their every wish is fulfilled. Young viewers—especially those living in poverty areas—often cannot understand why they, also, don't enjoy similar luxuries, a result being that they might grow up resenting their parents and society.

A recent British study of television-viewing habits titled *Television and the Child** made the following conclusions:

1. Children's interests can be extended by what they see, and their receptiveness to new ideas and their understanding of situations and people outside their immediate experience broadened. But by the same token, if the values portrayed on television are slick and materialistic and give a stereotyped and one-sided view of societies and groups, these values too will be absorbed.

2. Such effects on outlook and values are cumulative; each play and each program makes only a small effect, but the sum total is considerable.

3. Children are not so much frightened by the amount of violence shown and the physical seriousness of its consequences, as by the context in which it occurs and the way in which it is presented; some programs disturb not so much through the violence or aggression they contain, as through the picture they give of adult relationships which (in the case of an adolescent, for instance) may heighten the child's concern about the difficulties of adult life. We have evidence that girls particularly suffer from this adverse effect.

Developments in Television

Television suffered a great many growing pains. The device had been in the experimental stage as early as the 1920's. Telecasts, for testing purposes, were begun as early as 1936, and a regular schedule of programs was begun in 1939. Ten commercial stations were then on the air but only six continued after the beginning of World War II. Because of the scientific and technological advances brought about by the war, the medium entered a period of tremendous growth. The light-sensitive orthicon tube was developed by RCA in 1945, and low-temperature lights were developed for use by television studios. The war prosperity enabled Americans to purchase television sets and, following World War II, electronics companies quickly converted from producing war materials to making television equipment. Advertisers

---

*From *Television and the Child*—An Empirical Study of the Effect of Television on the Young—by Hilde T. Himmelweit, A. N. Oppenheim, and Pamela Vince, published by the Oxford University Press under the auspices of the Nuffield Foundation.

flocked to the new medium to promote their products. The 1948 political conventions were covered live, and President Truman became the first President whose inauguration was televised. A coast-to-coast link of coaxial cable and microwave relay was completed in 1951, thus making possible instantaneous transmission between widely separated stations that formerly had to rely on "canned" material from distant originating stations. More than one hundred stations in sixty cities were on the air in the early 1950's.

By the late 1950's the television networks had organized extensive news organizations, and in 1958 the Columbia Broadcasting System pitted Walter Cronkite against National Broadcasting System's Chet Huntley and David Brinkley. Fred Friendly and Edward R. Murrow converted their imaginative radio show, "Hear It Now," to television. The show, retitled "See It Now," had much impact and led to the socially significant television documentary program "CBS Reports," a program that exposed many of America's social ills. President John Kennedy's live television press conferences and the Kennedy-Nixon televised debates had a major effect on both American journalism and on the American Democratic Political System by showing how political leaders can go over the heads of the press and negative newspaper editorials. They also showed the remarkable quality of the television medium when it comes to direct relations between the public and its public men. Eric Sevareid became one of television's outstanding news interpreters, and the civil rights crisis of 1963, which pointed up the tremendous power of television news, prompted Sevareid to comment:

> The Civil Rights Bill would not have been passed by the Congress when it was had it not been for television.

Harry Truman was the first President whose inauguration was televised.

Later, Sevareid commented on television's role in a larger context:

> The nation has come to think automatically in terms of social progress, of a better life for all. Television may well have been a critical prod to America's conscience and the spur of Congressional action. . . . Civil rights, employment, poverty and ignorance, . . . people are ready for these actions by government, and one reason may well be fifteen years of a new kind of mass communication, the intimate impact of television.
>
> W. A. Wood
> *Electronic Journalism*

Television Processes

Technologically, television has advanced far beyond Thomas Edison's Kinetoscope. Today's television camera observes the scene to be transmitted, changing light values into electrical signals. In this complex process, an electronic beam moves across the image stored on a rectangular signal plate, scanning the complete picture in one-thirtieth of a second. The process of converting the visual scene into an electrical signal is called video (sight). The other portion of the television process, audio (sound), is similar to radio transmission in that in order to be carried over great distances, the sound must be converted into electrical impulses (sound waves). A thin diaphragm within a microphone, vibrating at the same frequency as the sound waves passing through it, converts the sound into electric currents. These electric currents pass through wires to a modulator where they are converted into a radio frequency that goes to television transmitters which, in turn, transmit them on specific frequencies capable of being received on your television set. The television tuner and associated circuits in your set reverse this procedure and reconvert the electric currents back into sound waves that you can hear, just as the electronic "video" signal is reconverted into light waves on the face of the television receiving screen.

Educational Potential

Although there are over 800 television stations and millions of viewers in the United States, the medium has yet to realize its full potential. For example, television can be a great educational force in our society. Many schools and colleges have been experimenting with educational television. Often, teachers ask students to watch certain television programs, such as news coverage of specialized events or televised chemistry lab courses, which supplement regular classroom sessions. Students confined to their homes or living in remote areas can "attend classes" by tuning in on special channels programmed for educational purposes. It has been claimed that students absorb the information they view on television more rapidly than that which they read in the print media.

Your Television-viewing Habits

You, in order to become a better-informed and more discriminating television viewer, should be fully aware of your viewing habits. To determine what your viewing habits are, complete the following activities:

1. Make a list, in order of preference, of the types of television programs you watch. Possible headings could include such categories as news broadcasts, situation comedy, drama, westerns, documentaries, variety shows, musicals, and movies.

2. Keep a daily log, for one week, listing the time you spent viewing a particular type of show. Keep an accurate record.

3. At the end of the week, tabulate the number of hours per day and the number of hours for the week that you spent viewing the different types of shows.

4. From the results of your log, make a graph similar to the one shown in Chapter 2 (page 32), by charting your television-viewing habits. The completed graph will show the variety and preference of your television-viewing habits. Compare and discuss your results with those of your classmates.

'Little pig, little pig, let me in or I'll huff and I'll puff . . .

Communications by Satellite

The first successful communications satellite, *Echo I,* was launched in 1960. Its purpose was to relay microwave telephone conversation and facsimile photographs between Pasadena, California and the Bell Laboratories at Homdel, New Jersey. *Echo,* a "passive" satellite, was a huge aluminum balloon which reflected (or bounced) signals off its surface; it contained no electronic equipment. But it was the success of the communications satellite *Early Bird,* orbited in 1965 and carrying a capacity for 250 simultaneous telephone conversations, that demonstrated the feasibility of the communications satellite idea. Since 1965 telecommunications research has produced plans for satellites whose capacity is twenty-five times greater than that of *Early Bird.* A single satellite put in orbit in September, 1968, provides 1,200 overseas circuits—approximately the same number as are available from all other technologies for transmission of telephone, telegraph, and data from the United States to the rest of the world. This single satellite is the first in a system of four *Intelsat III* satellites that will improve upon the relay systems of *Early Bird, Atlantic 2,* and *Pacific 1* and *2.* The *Intelsat* system includes participants from the many countries to be linked with the system's four satellites, thus providing world-wide communications coverage for the first time. The *Intelsat* satellites will be launched into higher orbits and, like other synchronous satellites, will appear to be stationary since their orbits will be synchronized with the earth's rotation.

Satellite Use

Network television will probably be one of the most immediate beneficiaries of communications satellite research. The cost of television transmission could be reduced, the range of television networks increased, and coverage of events vastly improved. The dramatic possibilities of education for masses of people in underdeveloped countries and for spreading technological knowledge should lead to increased consideration of global social responsibility. R. L. Shayon, in an article in the *Saturday Review,* stressed the importance of vision in our country's satellite program:

> What America needs in communications is a long vision —perhaps a communications Marshall Plan for Asia, Africa, and Latin America. As plans go now, satellite television, commercially used, will spread the image of this rich nation's consumership around the globe. We have seen, in the riots and lootings in our black ghettos, the consequences of such imagery on our own have-nots. If we don't use satel-

lites to help lift the mental horizons of the dispossessed who inhabit the backroads of modern communications, we may be risking the fate of the Roman Empire, that failed to share consumership with its colonials, and was eventually looted.

The more technologically advanced a country is, the more influence it can extend throughout the global mass media. In 1967 President Johnson pledged the support of the United States to *Intelsat* and urged the Soviet Union to join it. The U.S.S.R., however, is more interested in developing its own system of communication satellites than in supporting *Intelsat*. Perhaps Russia's attitude can be attributed to the fact that an American company owns about fifty percent of *Intelsat*. At any rate, Russia has in its four *Molniya* satellites the first domestic system in the world, and plans to tie it in with an international system for use in its European bloc countries.

Technology and Environment

Canadian communications expert Marshall McLuhan has publicized the idea that technology shapes our total environment. Some telecommunications technicians foresee a takeover of the print media by the electronic media. Newspapers might be broadcast into the home, for instance, and students involved with research might find themselves sitting in front of a screen and pressing a series of buttons instead of wandering in the library stacks to collect a pile of printed material.

WORK AREAS IN THE ELECTRONIC MEDIA

In addition to the large number of engineers and technicians required to bring television and radio signals into your home, there are many other specialists working behind-the-scenes on each program. The major areas of work in both radio and television stations are news, programming, sales, engineering, and general administration. The number of personnel in these divisions varies, of course, depending upon the size and purpose of the station.

News—The news director is in charge of the assigning and editing of news stories. Working with him are a number of news, sports, and weather reporters who cover and report on the major events occurring in their assigned areas. Photographers accompany the reporters to newsworthy events and photograph the events on motion-picture film. The larger stations also employ writers and editors who prepare stories and news material for the station's announcers. Writers may also prepare editorials to be presented on the air by station executives. To enable stations to cover events in outlying areas, many stations have a number of film correspondents. These cameramen-reporters live in the communities throughout the station's coverage area and do stories of interest to the entire area.

Another function of the radio or television station news department is to prepare or supervise public affairs and community service programs. Some examples of the types of shows in this category are as follows: the school system might be asked to provide teachers and students for a panel discussion on the activities and needs of the community's schools; colleges in the area might provide students to discuss careers available to graduates; another show might give information in the areas of medicine, space, jobs, welfare, religion, and community problems.

Programming—Unlike the print media, radio and television must be licensed by the federal government for, without such regulation, airwaves would be jammed with an overabundance of broadcasting stations. Thus, the Federal Communications Commission (FCC) regulates which stations will be licensed (including amateur or "Ham" stations), how much transmitting power each station can have, and how many hours during the day each station can broadcast. The federal government has also tried to provide guidelines concerning the nature of programming and has suggested that stations should devote a percentage of time to programs in "the public interest." The FCC also regulates the time allowed for commercials.

The programs to be used on radio and television stations are determined by the programming department. Local programs are conceived, produced, and scheduled by the programming department staff. Another type of programming is supplied by independent program producers and syndicated companies. This type of programming service may supply feature films in such areas as drama, comedy, games, sports, or documentary. The third—and most important—source of programming originates from one of the major networks: American Broadcasting Company (ABC), Columbia Broadcasting System (CBS), or National Broadcasting Company (NBC). These three networks service both television and radio stations, while a fourth network, Mutual Broadcasting Company, provides programs only for radio stations. A station affiliated with one of the national networks, while not necessarily owned by the network, has a contractual arrangement by which it agrees to carry programs supplied during part of the broadcast day. Since the average station is on the air at least eighteen hours a day, seven days a week, it would be almost impossible for the station's own staff to write and produce the number of programs required. Network affiliation offers a definite advantage. Because many network shows are too elaborate and expensive for an individual station to produce, the network produces and sells such programs to advertisers and shares the revenues with the local stations that carry them.

Programming policies are worked out by the program director in collaboration with the general manager and sales manager. The program director works with the producer-directors, broadcasting talent, and other members of the programming department in planning the most effective program schedule for the station. He also develops news programs, improves old programs, works out all aspects of publishing the station's "program guide," and participates in decisions involving the purchase of programs supplied by outside sources. Each day he supervises activities of personnel in his department on such matters as work assignments and schedules, budgetary concerns, and the problems of production.

The producer-director plans and supervises the production of a program. This includes selection of material and performers, the general planning of the sets, lights, and properties, and the selection of the sequence and angles of camera shots. In addition, he coordinates various elements such as selection of film, scripts, and music, and also maintains budgetary controls. The producer-director's job involves a sense of dramatics combined with the ability to weld together the talents of the performers into a smooth and artistic production. He is the person most responsible for the success or failure of any program.

Another basic job in any radio or television station is that of the staff announcer who reads commercial copy, introduces live or filmed programs, gives station identification and time signals, and makes promotional and public-service announcements. On some radio stations he is called a "disc jockey" and reads news briefs or announces the names of musical selections to be played.

In television stations there are several other jobs connected with the production of programs. The film director handles the screening and preparation of all film. Under his supervision film editors cut, splice, and clean film. The floor manager (unit manager) directs the performers on the studio floor in accordance with the director's instructions, while a program assistant coordinates the various portions of the show by assisting the producer-director. The program assistant may also arrange for props, makeup, and for cue cards. Most stations have their own artist who plans set designs, paints backdrops, and handles lettering and artwork.

Sales—In the sales division the sales manager is responsible for setting up the general sales policy of the station as well as for supervising the daily activities of his salesmen. He develops sales plans and packages which will appeal to sponsors, sets up seasonal sales campaigns, plans special programs publicizing the station, and promotes special events. He encourages his salesmen to sell and has charge of hiring and training. He works with the program director in developing salable programs. His salesmen sell radio or television time in the form of programs, portions of programs, or commercial announcements to advertising agencies or to individual advertisers. His most important asset is his ability to sell. He must often be imaginative in order to develop advertising approaches which will appeal to a particular client.

The traffic manager prepares daily logs of the station's program activities using information collected from the sales, programming, and engineering departments to prepare periodical reports for the Federal Communications Commission.

Engineering—Heading up the technical work in the engineering division is the chief engineer. On a radio station he may have only a few subordinates but on a television station he may have as many as forty technicians working for him. His work involves planning and coordinating the engineering requirements of his station's programs as well as scheduling the work of the technicians. The chief engineer is also responsible for supervising the maintenance of equipment. The technicians are concerned with the operation and maintenance of all technical equipment. They may also operate projection equipment and handle lighting.

General Administration—The two main positions in the general administration divisions of a radio or television station are general manager and business manager. The responsibilities of the general manager include handling of the daily problems of station operation in consultation with the news director, program manager, sales manager, and chief engineer. The general manager determines the general policies guiding the station's operation. He also supervises the carrying out of these policies. On a radio station, for example, the general manager will decide whether his station will have a popular or classical music format or whether it will broadcast solely news. A business manager oversees the station's financial transactions and prepares the necessary financial reports for the Federal Communications Commission.

WRITING FOR THE ELECTRONIC MEDIA

Writing for radio or television is different from writing for a newspaper or magazine. An audio-visual writer must learn to simplify his ideas, thoughts, words, language, sentences, and punctuation. It has been said that the ideal radio or television writer directs his words simultaneously at three age groups. First, to the grandparents. This helps him select the words that are easy to hear. Second, to the grade school student. This helps the writer use words and expressions that are easy to understand. Third, to the forty-year-old executive. This ensures that the writer sounds intelligent and doesn't sound condescending.

The writer for radio is faced with the reality that the public is trained to observe with its eyes but not with its ears. Both the eye and ear must transmit signals to the brain. But the ear must transmit them the first time it hears words from a radio. The ear cannot go back and re-hear, as the eye can go back and reread written composition. When writing for the ear the writer must do so in a fashion that will assure the highest probability of accurate reception and transmission of his signals to the listener's brain.

In writing for the ear simplicity is of the essence. For example, try reading a newspaper aloud to a friend. He will probably miss much of what you are saying because, unlike reading the newspaper where he has a chance to re-read, he doesn't have the chance to relisten to unfamiliar words. Rewrite the same story in simple, everyday language and your friend will absorb much more of it. For example, the following is a high school newspaper lead:

EXAMPLE:

A Work Experience Program for 10th, 11th, and 12th grade students will be offered for the first time next year in Ohio County schools.

A student telling of this same program might say, "This program certainly presents a great opportunity to our students." So for radio, modify the newspaper lead in this way:

EXAMPLE:

A new, opportunity-filled program is coming next year to Ohio County students. Special tutoring will be available to sophomore, junior, and senior students under a new Work Experience Program...

Many Techniques Available

Writing for television is similar to writing for radio in that simplicity is essential. The television writer, however, is able to maintain viewer interest more easily because he has a larger variety of techniques at his disposal. While the radio writer is limited to the use of such techniques as sound effects, music, and a limited number of announcers, the television writer can maintain interest by the use of these same effects plus film, props, lighting, color, and various camera angles.

Writers must keep in mind that radio and television are guests in the homes of millions of persons. The announcers and actors, speaking the words written by newswriters, will be heard and seen by perhaps millions of people. Therefore, common sense and good taste in the preparation and presentation of news copy must be maintained at all times.

Preparing for a Career in the Electronic Media

The student interested in the electronic media should have qualities such as enthusiasm, reliability, sensitivity, and creativity. If he is interested in radio or television engineering he should consider attending an electronics school. Business training is almost essential for those considering sales department work, and the student planning a career in programming might attend a specialized radio and television school. If the student would like to work in news broadcasting he should consider a college with a good journalism school. Many colleges offer excellent training in broadcasting as part of their communications program. Newspaper work, following graduation from college, is ideal training for electronic media newswriters. In fact, one major network requires that its news-department personnel have newspaper experience before being considered as applicants.

A CENTURY OF PROGRESS

Immense strides have been taken since the electronic media had their beginnings. The next hundred years will see even more remarkable feats performed in this area of mass communication. Many of these prospects for the future will be taken up in Chapter 7, "The Future of the Mass Media."

ACTIVITIES

1. Consider what features you look for in determining what is good, bad, or mediocre when you listen to the radio, watch a motion picture, and watch a television show. Then list the criteria you use for judging each.

2. As the program director for a local radio station, you have been asked to prepare an effective program schedule for an eight-hour daytime listening audience. In preparing your list, consider the criteria established in Activity 1. You may schedule your programs for fifteen-minute, half-hour, and one-hour periods. Do not base your programming on personal likes and dislikes—in establishing time lengths, consider your listening audience, advertising sponsor, and consider possible use of "public-interest" type material.

3. Conduct an informal survey among your classmates to determine what one television program viewed by the majority in the past two weeks they are most in agreement on as being "an insult to their intelligence." Discuss their reasoning. List conclusions, drawn from your classmates' reactions, that might justify the presentation of such a program.

4. As a news source, do you prefer newspapers, radio, or television? Defend your choice in a three-paragraph statement which compares the three media. Consider such factors as which of the three gives more "in-depth" coverage, which is the easiest to accept, and which do you see or hear most often.

5. List, in order of importance to you, the value of radio, motion pictures, and television as entertainment media. Beside each listening give a brief explanation for your choice.

6. Why must radio and television stations be licensed with the Federal Communications Commission? Do you think it advisable that a similar regulation be imposed on newspapers? Explain your reasoning.

7. Evaluate the educational films you have seen for their effectiveness, comparing them to textbooks. Prepare a list of suggestions for possible types of educational films you would like to see during the school year.

8. The Motion Picture Association of America requires that theaters display for the public the letter rating of the film shown. Bring to class the entertainment section of your local paper and discuss the merits of a rating system. Does it encourage or discourage your going to the movie? Do you think that the Association should try to define "maturity"? Do you think the system for rating movies should be abandoned? If so, why?

9. Prepare a research paper, using as your theme "The Growing Use of Educational Television in School Systems." Use the facilities available at your school and local library in researching your subject. Back issues of news magazines like *Time* and *Newsweek* are excellent sources for information concerning current developments in educational television.

READING

ABBOTT, WALDO, AND RICHARD L. RIDER, *Handbook of Broadcasting.* McGraw-Hill, New York, 1957.

BARNOUW, ERIK, *The Golden Web: A History of Broadcasting in the United States,* Volume 2: 1933–1953. Oxford University Press, New York, 1968.

BLEUM, WILLIAM A., *Documentary in American Television.* Hastings House, New York, 1964.

BOGART, LEO, *The Age of Television.* Frederick Ungar, New York, 1968.

BOND, F. FRASER, *An Introduction to Journalism*. Macmillan, New York, 1961.

BRETZ, RUDY, *The Techniques of Television Production*. McGraw-Hill, New York, 1962.

CHESTER, GIRAUD, GARNET R. GARRISON AND EDGAR WILLS, *Television and Radio*. Appleton-Century-Crofts, New York, 1963.

COLUMBIA BROADCASTING SYSTEM, *News Reporting*. Columbia Broadcasting System, New York.

COONS, JOHN E. (Ed.), *Freedom and Responsibility in Broadcasting*. Northwestern University Press, Evanston, Ill., 1961.

CURRAN, CHARLES W., *Screen Writing and Production Techniques*. Hastings House, New York, 1958.

FANG, IRVING E., *Television News*. Hastings House, New York, 1968. (PB)

GASKILL, ARTHUR L., AND DAVID A. ENGLANDER, *How to Shoot a Movie Story*. Morgan & Morgan, Hastings-on-Hudson, New York, 1968. (PB)

GORDON, GEORGE N., AND IRVING A. FALK, *On-the-Spot Reporting: Radio Records History*. Messner, New York, 1967.

GOWDY, CURT, WITH AL HIRSHBERG, *Cowboy at the Mike*. Doubleday, New York, 1966.

HILLIARD, ROBERT L. (Ed.), *Understanding Television: An Introduction to Broadcasting*. Hastings House, New York, 1964. (PB)

HIMMELWEIT, HILDE T., ET AL, *Television and the Child*. Oxford University Press, New York, 1958.

KAEL, PAULINE, *I Lost It at the Movies*. Little, Brown, New York, 1965.

KNIGHT, ARTHUR, *The Liveliest Art*. Mentor Books, New York, 1959. (PB)

NATIONAL ASSOCIATION OF BROADCASTERS, *Broadcasting the News*. National Association of Broadcasters, Washington, D.C.

ORWELL, GEORGE, *1984*. Harcourt, Brace & World, New York, 1949. (PB)

RAMSAYE, TERRY, *A Million and One Nights. A History of the Motion Picture*. Simon and Schuster, New York, 1964.

ROSENBERG, BERNARD, AND DAVID MANNING WHITE (Ed.), *Mass Culture: The Popular Arts in America*. Free Press, New York, 1957.

ROTHA, PAUL, SINCLAIR ROAD AND RICHARD GRIFFITH, *The Documentary Film*. Hastings House, New York, 1964.

SCHICKEL, RICHARD, *Movies: The History of an Art and an Institution*. Basic Books, New York, 1964.

SCHRAMM, WILBUR, ET AL, *Television in the Lives of Our Children*. Stanford University Press, Stanford, Cal., 1961. (PB)

SELDES, GILBERT, *The Seven Lively Arts*. A. S. Barnes, Cranbury, N.J., 1962. (PB)

SEVAREID, ERIC, *Not So Wild a Dream*. Knopf, New York, 1946.

STEINER, GARY, *The People Look at Television: A Study of Audience Attitudes*. Knopf, New York, 1963.

WIMER, ARTHUR, AND DALE BRIX (Ed.), *Workbook for Radio and-Television News Editing and Writing*. Wm. C. Brown, Dubuque, Iowa, 1966.

WITTICH, WALTER ARNO, AND CHARLES FRANCIS SCHULLER, *Audio-Visual Materials*. Harper & Row, New York, 1967.

Chapter **5**

Public Relations

Ron MacNeil

PUBLIC RELATIONS AND THE JOURNALISM STUDENT

Ask an average journalism student how he rates his school in comparison with other schools and he will most likely base his answer on his views concerning his fellow students, athletics, school spirit, classes, teachers, and student government.

But how can the general public evaluate a school? The public often bases its evaluation of a school on the quality of the school's student publications. From impressions gained from these publications, persons outside the school form opinions and are often impressed—or unimpressed—with the school. As a line of communication between students and community, student publications have a definite responsibility to each group. By its attitudes and policies, a school publication can play a constructive role in the community by representing the school to the people of the community. Thus, student publications serve the schools they represent as an important public relations medium.

93

Student editors often feel that their fellow students are the only "public" for their publications. There are, however, several other "publics" that should be considered—"publics" whose awareness of the school and its problems benefit the students. Some of these "publics" are:

Parents—Parents want their children to have the best possible education in an environment that will ensure ideal conditions for mental and moral growth. School publications are a direct reflection of a school's environment.

Teachers—Teachers are concerned with the image of their school as presented in school publications. Such publications often reflect the results of the quality of instruction offered at the school.

Alumni—Alumni who remain interested in their alma mater like to be kept informed of their school's activities and often wish to compare the education they received with the educational opportunities offered to today's student. One of the best ways to keep such alumni informed is through the school's publications.

Board of Education—The Board of Education is often influenced in its thinking about curriculum considerations and budget appropriations by what its members read in a school's publications. These men and women are responsible for the kind and quality of education within the school system.

Taxpayers—Taxpayers, because they are paying for public education and want to be assured that their money is not being wasted, often keep informed of educational trends in the schools within their communities through school publications.

Companies Many companies in the community are interested in the future of students. Naturally, the better the quality of the school's graduates, the better the quality of the employees the company will have the opportunity to hire. A company may even donate equipment to a chemistry lab or typewriters to a journalism class in a school where outstanding programs have been written up in school publications.

Because the future of educational institutions is so dependent upon the public, many school systems are becoming more aware of the need for good public relations. Recently, a large private school retained a public relations agency to deal with two major problems: 1) the school was getting a reputation as a football school, more interested in athletics than in education, and 2) the school, which planned to expand, needed more financial contributions from its alumni.

The public relations agency did several research studies and came to the conclusion that the best way to ensure donations from the school's alumni was to continue to win football games. The agency found a direct correlation between the size of alumni donations and the number of games won; in fact, more contributions were made during a year the team won national recognition than in any other year. The solution advanced by the public relations agency was that while the school's football team should continue trying to win games, the school's news bureau should cut down on the amount of publicity releases written about the games. It was suggested that more publicity be devoted to academic news such as the school's educational contributions to the community.

DEVELOPMENT OF PUBLIC RELATIONS

Since the beginning of recorded history public opinion has played a powerful role in the influencing of human affairs—a role that has developed in complexity and sophistication throughout the centuries. Proponents of the earliest-known religions used to their advantage the arts of writing and speaking. Knowing the importance of having the support of the masses, early Roman authorities printed "S.P.Q.R." (meaning Senate and the Roman people) on shields and buildings. Greek and Roman orators, having carefully studied the opinions held by various segments of the public, valued such opinions and used them to influence the masses.

In the seventeenth century the Roman Catholic Church, in order to propagate its faith, set up an information agency called the College of Propaganda. Russia's Catherine the Great, considering the importance of favorably impressing her subjects, is said to have been extremely careful to release only information about herself that she considered beneficial to her image.

Colonial Beginnings

Public relations played an important role in Colonial America as early as 1641 when Harvard College sent a group of ministers to England to solicit funds. In England, discovering the need for a brochure describing the college, the ministers wrote and published the first public relations pamphlet of its type in Colonial America, titling it "New England's First Fruits." Our earliest recorded public relations news release was sent in 1758 to New York newspapers by what is now Columbia University.

Because there was more freedom of expression in America than there had been in Europe, the opinions of the masses were held in greater regard and soon showed an influence on political events. Statements such as "Give me liberty or give me death," and "We shall all hang together or we shall all hang separately" did much to unify the divergent factions in the Colonies. The writers of the Declaration of Independence said that the Declaration was written "out of a decent respect for the opinions of mankind," and Samuel Adams devoted much of his energy to the task of formulating public opinion in favor of the Revolution.

Amos Kendall

In the 1820's a former Kentucky newspaper editor named Amos Kendall became one of America's first public relations men when, working from behind the scenes, he served President Andrew Jackson as a pollster, ghost writer, and publicist.

Although his official title was Fourth Auditor of the Treasury, Amos Kendall spent most of his time while in government service advising President Andrew Jackson, and writing speeches, pamphlets, and news releases for the Jackson administration. For this reason Amos Kendall came to be known as "the mouthpiece of the Jacksonian Administration."

Ivy Lee

Public relations gained recognition as a legitimate field of endeavor early in the 1900's when business interests were threatened by a period of union organizing, striking, and rioting. These events threatened the security of businessmen who, previously having cared little about the rights and working conditions of employees, now came to realize the necessity for more favorable relationships between industry and the public.

During this era Ivy Lee, known as "The Father of Public Relations," left the *New York World* to help improve the public images of John D. Rockefeller, Jr., and several other prominent businessmen. Lee, who believed in an informed citizenry, felt that the public had a right to be informed about what business was doing, and is said to have told clients:

> I believe in telling your story to the people. If you go direct to the people and get them to agree with you, everybody else must give way in your favor.

Lee accomplished a great deal when he humanized businessmen in the eyes of the public by putting "Big Business" in the best possible light. He served many clients from 1919 to 1934.

Edward Bernays

During World War I the government established a public relations committee called the Committee on Public Information. The committee, headed by George Creel, came to be called the Creel Committee. This committee demonstrated the power of mass publicity techniques in influencing public opinion. Edward L. Bernays, having worked with the Creel Committee, went on to become one of the country's most articulate advocates of public relations. After World War I Bernays commented:

> It was the war which opened the eyes of the intelligent few in all departments of life to the possibilities of regimenting the public mind.

Bernays, in his book *Crystallizing Public Opinion,* first coined the phrase "public relations counsel."

The techniques used by the Creel Committee were soon being applied to fund drives for colleges, hospitals, foundations, and research institutions. Private industry began hiring full-time public relations men to help formulate company policy and then tell the world about it.

In 1923 the first course in public relations was offered at New York University. The Depression of the 1930's gave the greatest impetus to business public relations when large industry fought for survival against social critics. Following the Depression, progressive politicians such as Franklin Delano Roosevelt realized the importance of swaying public opinion in order to pave the way for the introduction of radical reforms. For instance, without the aid of public relations men, Roosevelt could never have been able to say, "Private business is a public trust."

Office of War Information

During World War II an office similar to the World War I Creel Committee was set up by Elmer Davis. Called the Office of War Information, it was primarily concerned with promoting the sale of War Bonds, promoting government rationing, encouraging the use of Victory Gardens, and raising the morale of employees contributing to the war effort.

The Total Function

Following World War II the emphasis in public relations developed into an awareness of *total* public relations, meaning that because of their effect on the public, everything from the voice of a company's switchboard operator to the quality of the company's end-product came under the scrutiny of public relations departments. More universities began offering degrees in public relations, and public relations emerged as a profession as the public became more aware of the value of public relations functions. Jobs in the field of public relations, such as presidential press secretary, are constantly being created. Presidential press secretaries James Haggerty, Pierre Salinger, Bill Moyers, and Ronald Ziegler (each one a top public relations expert), played important roles in informing the nation about what the government was doing and why.

Today, the public relations man or woman uses the spoken word, the mass media, staged events, and audio-visual materials to achieve his objective of keeping the public informed. Most organizations, from P.T.A.'s to the nation's largest industries, employ people to handle their public relations. Thirty years ago there were about one thousand persons in the United States working in public relations, and it has been estimated that today there are well over one hundred thousand.

TYPES OF WORK IN PUBLIC RELATIONS

The primary concern of the public relations man or agency is to win good will for clients. An important part of public relations work is supplying for publication materials that promote good will about the public or private enterprise represented by the public relations man or agency. Most public relations practitioners in our society are employed either on administrative staffs in industry, business, government, or educational institutions, or in the entertainment field.

Good public relations bases its operations on the principle, "Do something good, and then tell the world." In order to "tell the world," public relations people research and write extensively, work with community organizations, and work directly with the news media.

For example, several kinds of public relations activities were used by a public relations firm whose client was a private corporation that had hired a nationally known marine biology expert:

News and Feature Stories—First, the public relations firm prepared a straight news release announcing the appointment of the marine biologist (see the following EXAMPLE). Then, follow-up feature stories discussing government research, as opposed to private-industry research projects, were submitted to newspapers. The marine biologist was asked to participate in special press interviews as important news events fell within the general area of his specialization.

MARINE BIOLOGY EXPERT APPOINTED
AT SOUTHWEST LABS

World famous marine biology expert Raymond Hughes has been named by Robert Feinman, president of the Southwest Marine Laboratory in Los Angeles, to set up a research project to study the possibility of growing edible vegetable life under the ocean.

Feinman announced that Dr. Hughes will bring together and supervise a staff of experts to investigate using marine facilities to increase the world's food supply. He stated that if the research project shows that such an idea is feasible, the research staff will plant and harvest crops in underwater farms. Feinman estimated that the project will take five years.

Dr. Hughes, a native of Coos Bay, Oregon, is married and has two children. He is a graduate of Oregon State University and holds master's and doctorate degrees from the California Institute of Technology.

Dr. Hughes, formerly Director of Underwater Experimentation for the U.S. Department of Agriculture in Washington, D.C., is the author of a textbook on marine biology.

Television and Radio Scripts—After publication of the actual news event, the public relations firm followed up the news releases by informing radio and television stations that the marine biologist was available for interviews. Plans were made with several of these stations to present documentary and panel-type shows. The marine biologist was asked to be the host, the interviewee, or the guest speaker on the shows.

Speeches—The marine biologist, with other employees from the private corporation, increased public awareness of the corporation's activities by speaking to various community groups. The speakers addressed men's service organizations and civic groups, conservation groups, women's guilds, and student clubs. The public relations firm set up a speaker's bureau to handle requests and arrangements for speakers and the public relations people even wrote some of the speeches.

Advertising—In order to better publicize their client, the public relations firm worked directly with the corporation's advertising department. An advertisement attempting to lure other prominent scientists to the corporation contained a quoted statement by the marine biologist and showed a photograph of him at work (see the EXAMPLE on next page).

EXAMPLE:

"join me as an underwater pioneer"

David Doubilet

Employee Publications—The corporation's publication, designed to influence the thinking of customers, stockholders, and employees, and to inform them of the corporation's policy and products, was supplied with articles concerning the marine biologist. A published interview with the marine biologist introduced the newcomer and his credentials.

Photographs—All news items supplied to newspapers, magazines, radio and television stations were accompanied by high-quality photographs and film clips. The public relations firm had found that news and publicity releases that were accompanied by photographs and film clips had a better chance of being used.

Community Involvement—The private corporation, in the community interest, made the marine biologist's and other executive talents available to help various organizations within the community.

In addition to informing the public about their client organization, the public relations office has other functions. One important function is to keep a client's executives aware of their organization's public image. The public relations office also helps determine what kinds of activities are the most effective public relations for client organizations.

Types of Public Relations Writing

There is not a great deal of difference between writing general news items for newspapers and writing publicity releases for a public relations client. Public relations practitioners have found that they have a better chance of having material accepted for publication if the stories are written for a particular newspaper using the newspaper's own style. One basic difference between general news items and the preparation of publicity releases, however, is timing. Public relations employees usually must clear their stories through a number of company executives in order to ensure against duplication of effort, inaccuracies, and premature release of information. Since newspapers want to know what happened today—not last week—the story, unless it gets immediate clearance, may not be published.

Following are examples of the opening paragraphs from two general news stories about the same event. The first account of the event appeared on the front page of the morning edition of a daily newspaper. The second story, another version of the same event, appeared in later editions of papers throughout the country. Compare the two examples. Then answer the questions that follow them.

EXAMPLE:

Star's Temper Tantrum
Disrupts Film's Premiere

Members of the audience at the downtown Heldon Theater's world premiere of "Where Love Goes" were noisily disrupted last night when the guest of honor and star of the film, Lana Jo Woodman, screamed and leaped from her seat throwing the contents of her pocketbook at Mrs. Carlton Smith, occupant of the next seat.

Miss Woodman reportedly stated that she couldn't hear the movie over Mrs. Smith's loud criticisms of the film, and that while she couldn't repeat exactly what was said, found the complaints so annoying that she couldn't stand them any longer.

EXAMPLE:

New Woodman Flick Assured
Success at World Premiere

The success of last night's world premiere of the smash hit "Where Love Goes," held at New York City's Heldon Theater, was assured when the film's glamorous leading lady, Jana Jo Woodman, told reporters that she became so fascinated with the film's plot that she absentmindedly dumped the contents of her pocketbook onto her lap. The resulting noise of items slipping to the floor surprised her, causing her to jump from her seat and accidentally spill other items onto the lap of the occupant of the next seat, Mrs. Carlton Smith, wife of Miss Woodman's press agent and a long-time friend of the star.

Miss Woodman explained that the resulting apologies were hardly heard by an appreciative audience which was so absorbed by the film spectacular that even an air raid wouldn't have distracted them.

1. What are the basic differences between the two examples?

2. Which one of the examples do you consider to be the more accurate interpretation of the actual event? Why?

3. Which example do you think was supplied by a public relations person or agency? Why?

4. What are the key words in the public relations version that make it different from the general news item? How do these words accomplish this difference?

5. Would the person or agency who supplied the public relations account most likely have as a client the Heldon Theater, the star, the film maker or the press agent's wife? Why?

Problems in Public Relations

Because public relations is a relatively new medium, most public relations jobs are as yet not clearly defined. Many of these jobs may include anything from writing two-paragraph news releases and arranging testimonial dinners to creating favorable images for clients on a national or world-wide basis. Often, successful public relations persons are creative in enlarging the scope of their particular jobs. One common problem in this comparatively new field is that there is no proven way to test or evaluate the effectiveness of the various public relations programs. While some corporation executives make full use of their public relations departments, others are skeptical about investing money in indeterminate methods that cannot be proven effective. Public relations does, however, offer the attraction of costing less than a comparable advertising operation which usually involves general-circulation publication fees.

Lack of Training

In many companies public relations functions are delegated to persons who have no special training in the field but whose jobs involve dealings with the public. Many personnel directors handle public relations functions for smaller companies, as do vice-presidents, advertising managers, and heads of sales departments in even smaller companies. Other companies, realizing the value of good public relations but being too small to staff a public relations department of their own, assign their public relations functions to outside agencies or to individual professionals.

Lack of Newsworthy Material

What does a public relations firm do when there is nothing essentially newsworthy about a client's product? The answer, usually dependent on the ingenuity and creativeness of the individual handling the client's account, is to make the product seem newsworthy. One public relations agency solved such a problem when it introduced a new fire starter by hosting a party for newsmen on the roof of a Manhattan hotel. Five beauty contestants had been invited to the party where they were asked to participate in a fire-starting contest. The judges were five Boy Scouts! This publicity stunt made such amusing reading that the invited newsmen gave the story prime space in their publications. The story, picked up and used by other newspapers, magazines, and radio and television stations across the country, received nation-wide exposure.

The One-man Shop Versus the Large P. R. Agency

A one-man public relations agency is mainly interested in the individual handling of only one aspect of a client's publicity, while a large agency can offer a variety of more complex services (such as consulting) and can handle all facets of a client's publicity. In a one-man agency, the owner-operator often writes his own news stories, feature stories, and publicity releases for newspapers, radio stations, television stations, and magazines. He could also write and edit a company publication (house organ) for a small company, might handle the writing and designing of advertising brochures, make photography assignments, and secure television and radio coverage for clients.

In a large public relations agency the person who handles each individual client is called an account executive. The account executive serves as a liaison person between his agency and the client and makes sure that the client's wishes are followed. Account representatives work with the agency's account executive and often become involved with helping to carry out the plans set up by the agency or the account executive.

THE PUBLIC RELATIONS PROFESSION TODAY

Public relations is one of the fastest-growing professions in the United States. The Public Relations Society of America estimates that, not counting the public relations personnel engaged in government service, there are more than 100,000 persons currently employed in this field. About sixty percent of these people are on the staffs of industrial and business firms, some thirty percent are with independent public relations companies, and the remaining ten percent are employed by non-profit organizations such as educational television stations, schools and universities, social concern organizations, and cultural arts institutions. It is estimated that there will be a total of over 200,000 persons employed in the field of public relations by 1975. While the number of persons involved with public relations has been increasing, budgets for many public relations departments have also been increasing. A few years ago, for example, a large broadcasting company reportedly included in its budget $100,000 to fly a planeload of mass media people to London as part of a promotion for an all-news program being planned by two of its stations. Yearly, the Chamber of Commerce for a large midwestern state publicizes the most lucrative part of that state's tourist program, the opening of the fishing season, by taking prominent sports and vacation editors to a deluxe fishing lodge. The sponsors hope that when the newsmen return to their papers, they will write glowing reports about the pleasures and excitement of fishing.

Public relations and the news media have been termed "interdependent" fields—public relations agencies are often dependent on the news media as a means to publicize their efforts, and the news media often depend on the public relations agencies for newsworthy information and ideas. Because the two media are dependent on each other they function well together, especially when they are both acting in the public interest. The future of public relations in our society is directly related to and dependent upon the expansion of the news media.

A PUBLIC RELATIONS CAREER

Positions in public relations agencies vary depending on the size of the organization and the number of accounts handled. Among the qualifications most sought for by employers in this field are poise and a good personal appearance, the ability to express oneself orally, and a good writing background. The majority of persons in the field are college graduates who have majored in journalism, advertising, public relations, psychology, or sociology. A few of the larger universities offer courses in public relations which place major emphasis on training in special fields like television script writing, public speaking, the mass media, and liberal arts courses.

Many people presently employed in public relations have had newspaper or other types of journalism backgrounds. In a recent survey conducted by the National Research Committee of the Public Relations Society of America it was found that fifty-three percent of the country's public relations practitioners began their careers on newspapers.

Public relations has come to be recognized almost universally as a powerful force. Its first concern must be to serve the public interest. If skillfully used, the profession can do much to bring understanding, harmony, peace, and prosperity to the nation and the world.

ACTIVITIES

1. Obtain several different student publications from your school library or write a form letter to several schools requesting such publications. Evaluate the schools represented in these publications by choosing news items that would be of special interest to parents, alumni, the Board of Education, taxpayers, the large companies. Prepare a brief written report explaining your evaluation. Present the report in class.

2. Telephone several large companies in your area whose products interest you, asking for the public relations office or for the company's public relations representative. Explain that as a journalism student studying public relations you are interested in their method of operation and in their views on current problems in public relations. Note carefully how the public relations office handles you, a member of the public. Ask if it would be possible for a member of your class to conduct an interview with one of the members of their public relations staff. Accept alternate suggestions. Prepare an oral report of the experience for presentation to your class. Include an analysis of the effectiveness of the public relations person who handled your call.

3. By telephoning your local Chamber of Commerce, discover what companies in your community make their executives or their company facilities available to community organizations. Look into the effectiveness of some of these programs and try to locate press releases about them. Use this information as the basis for inviting a speaker to your class.

4. Bring newspapers to class and make a bulletin board display of the types of news and feature stories that probably originated as public relations releases. Then choose a topic—an organization, an institution, or an individual—and write your own news or feature story as a publicity release for submission to a particular newspaper. Compare and discuss your release with the releases prepared by your classmates.

5. Choose one member of your class who has a particularly interesting background or hobby. Write a straight-news publicity release about him, similar in outline to the first example in this chapter. Submit the article to your teacher for approval, and then to your school newspaper for publication.

6. Do a study of propaganda techniques as related to public relations. From the study prepare, for presentation in class, a brief public relations release advocating public relations.

READING

ASSOCIATION OF NATIONAL ADVERTISERS, *How Public Relations and Advertising Are Working Together to Meet Company Objectives.* Association of National Advertisers, New York.

BAIRD, RUSSEL, AND ARTHUR T. TURNBULL, *Industrial and Business Journalism.* Chilton Book Co., Philadelphia, Pa., 1961.

BERNAYS, EDWARD L., *Biography of an Idea.* Simon and Schuster, New York, 1965.

———, *Crystallizing Public Opinion.* Liveright, New York, 1961.

———, *Public Relations.* University of Oklahoma Press, Norman, Okla., 1957.

———, *Your Future in Public Relations.* Richards Rosen Press, New York, 1968.

BOND, FRASER, *An Introduction to Journalism.* Macmillan, New York, 1961.

BRINK, EDWARD L., AND WILLIAM T. KELLEY, *The Management of Promotion: Consumer Behavior and Demand Stimulation*. Prentice-Hall, Englewood Cliffs, N.J., 1963.

CANFIELD, BERTRAND R., *Public Relations: Principles, Cases, and Problems*. Richard D. Irwin, Homewood, Ill., 1964.

CATER, DOUGLASS, AND MARQUIS CHILDS, *Ethics in a Business Society*. Mentor Books, New York, 1954. (PB)

CUTLIP, SCOTT M., *A Public Relations Bibliography*. University of Wisconsin Press, Madison, Wis., 1965.

——, AND ALLEN H. CENTER, *Effective Public Relations*. Prentice-Hall, Englewood Cliffs, N.J., 1964.

DONOHUE, JODY, *Your Career in Public Relations*. Messner, New York, 1967.

HALL, BABETTE, *The Right Angles*. Doubleday, New York, 1965.

HARLAN, E. H., AND ALAN SCOTT, *Contemporary Public Relations*. Prentice-Hall, Englewood Cliffs, N.J., 1955.

HILL, JOHN W., *The Making of a Public Relations Man*. McKay, New York, 1963.

HOVLAND, CARL, IRVING JANIS AND HAROLD H. KELLEY, *Communication and Persuasion*. Yale University Press, New Haven, Conn., 1963. (PB)

KELLEY, STANLEY, JR., *Professional Public Relations and Political Power*. Johns Hopkins Press, Baltimore, Md., 1956. (PB)

KOBRE, SIDNEY J., *The Dynamic Force of Public Relations Today*. Wm. C. Brown, Dubuque, Iowa, 1964.

LERBINGER, OTTO, AND ALBERT J. SULLIVAN (Ed.), *Information, Influence, and Communication: A Reader in Public Relations*. Basic Books, New York, 1964.

LESLY, PHILLIP (Ed.), *Public Relations Handbook*. Prentice-Hall, Englewood Cliffs, N.J., 1967.

MARSTON, JOHN E., *The Nature of Public Relations*. McGraw-Hill, New York, 1963.

PUBLIC RELATIONS SOCIETY OF AMERICA, *Let's Consider Public Relations*. Public Relations Society of America, New York.

QUILL AND SCROLL SOCIETY, *Public Relations* (from the *Careers in Journalism Series*). State University of Iowa, Iowa City, Iowa, 1963.

SCHOENFELD, CLARENCE A., *Publicity Media and Methods*. Macmillan, New York, 1963.

SIMON, RAYMOND (Ed.), *Perspectives in Public Relations*. University of Oklahoma Press, Norman, Okla., 1966.

STEINBERG, CHARLES S. (Ed.), *Mass Media and Communication*. Hastings House, New York, 1965. (PB)

STEPHENSON, HOWARD, *Handbook of Public Relations*. McGraw-Hill, New York, 1960.

TELEVISION INFORMATION OFFICE, *ABCs of Radio and Television*. Television Information Office, New York.

——, *The Television Station Manager*, Television Information Office, New York.

MAKE AMERICA A BETTER PLACE.

LEAVE THE COUNTRY.

Of all the ways America can grow, one way is by learning from others.

There are things you can learn in the Peace Corps you can't learn anywhere else.

You could start an irrigation program. And find that crabgrass and front lawns look a little ridiculous. When there isn't enough wheat to go around in Nepal.

You could be the outsider who helps bring a Jamaican fishing village to life, for the first time in three hundred years. And you could wonder if your country has outsiders enough. In Watts. In Detroit. In Appalachia. On its Indian reservations.

Last year, for the first time, Peace Corps alumni outnumbered Volunteers who are now out at work overseas.

By 1980, 200,000 Peace Corps alumni will be living their lives in every part of America.

There are those who think you can't change the world in the Peace Corps.

On the other hand, maybe it's not just what you do in the Peace Corps that counts.

But what you do when you get back.

The Peace Corps, Washington, D.C. 20525.

"The Peace Corps ruined my Bernie's life."

"I just don't know. We had such plans for him. When he graduated he was interviewed by all the big companies. What offers he had. He and Barbara were going to get married and live in the Monte Carlo Gardens with the rest of their friends. His father and I had all the furniture picked out. It was only two blocks away from here. We could have had coffee and played Scrabble and watched TV every night. But no. Not Bernie. He had to run off half cocked and, live in a shack ten thousand miles away. He works in a hospital of all places. And with a degree in Ac It wouldn't be so bad for a but two years. These kids ne I just don't know. The Pea Washington, D. C. 20525.

ADVERTISING CONTRIBUTED FOR THE PUBLIC G

Chapter **6**

Advertising

If you told these people The Peace Corps is hypocritical extension of an imperialistic [esta]blishment's military industrial complex, they [wou]ld think you were crazy.

And you would be.

YOU, THE CONSUMER

What is advertising, and how does it influence our society? Is it an unscrupulous business which uses the techniques of persuasion to create a longing in consumers for products they probably don't need, or is it a means by which business can better serve society? Or is it both? And what is its influence on you, the individual, as a consumer?

You, as a consumer, are the continual target of advertising. You are constantly surrounded by the advertising messages contained in the newspapers and magazines you read, on the television shows you watch, and on the radio programs you listen to. Advertising, with its basic intent to inform, persuade, and sell, is, to William D. Patterson, former Vice President of the *Saturday Review:*

> . . . the indispensable handmaiden of abundance, and of the steadily rising standard of living that is the cherished American goal.

Others have claimed that advertising "enslaves" our society. In order to be an informed, intelligent consumer, you should critically examine the advertising that surrounds you—and then decide how that advertising might improve or damage the quality of your life. As you read or listen to advertising information, you, as an intelligent consumer, should ask: Who is the source of this advertising information? Why is this advertising information important? What does this advertising information mean to me? The informed consumer understands all of the mass media's functions and can tell when the media are reporting facts and when they are expressing opinions.

What Is Advertising?

Advertising is a kind of propaganda. At its best, propaganda is the spreading of ideas for the promotion of a cause; at its worst it is the controlling of men's minds for the promotion of a cause. Political propaganda works if it is distributed anonymously; advertising does not. In advertising the consumer knows who is spreading the information and what the advertisers want him to do. Political propagandists can operate more insidiously.

Professional advertising men claim that when they distribute information about their products, thus creating a market, they are giving the consumer an opportunity to improve his life. These professionals also claim that by creating a market for America's eight hundred billion dollar annual output of goods and services, the advertising profession serves the public as well as its clients. Not all advertising, however, is aimed at publicizing worthwhile causes or supplying useful and important information to the general public.

Critics of advertising object to the profession's over-emphasis on the material values which undermine the quality of life in a society. Advertising, despite being an important public medium capable of benefiting the economy, does have some negative effects on our lives. Billboards which blot out the landscape and television commercials which splinter a film into many parts are just two examples of how advertising can detract from the quality of our environment. Still, as consumers we do have freedom of access to open country, freedom to turn off the television and pursue other interests, and freedom to influence the advertising profession by criticizing its practices. You, the consumer, can help put advertising on a higher plane by refusing to patronize advertisers whose methods you find objectionable.

Truth in Advertising

In 1911 *Printers' Ink* Magazine formulated an advertising code, the "Model Statute for Truth in Advertising," that placed the responsibility for deception upon the advertiser, dealt with the importance of expressing facts rather than just opinion in advertising, and designated the making of untruthful, deceptive, or misleading statements a misdemeanor. Since 1911, the majority of our country's states have passed laws based on the *Printers' Ink* advertising code. The American Association of Advertising Agencies (AAAA) regularly requests its members to report objectionable advertising to its national headquarters. Other advertising groups request that their members do the same. Thus, the agencies themselves support efforts for advertising which is honest and in good taste. Today, many newspapers, magazines, and radio and television stations have high standards that advertising copy must meet before it is accepted for publication or broadcasting. What these media lose in advertising revenue is gained in increased customer confidence.

THE GROWTH OF ADVERTISING

Experts disagree when advertising as a business venture actually began. Many claim that primitive cavemen could well have been the first advertising men, their stone tablets possibly having served as advertisements for the barter of goods and services. Even the Dead Sea Scrolls can be said to have been, in a sense, advertisements for the religion of the day. It is known that in early Rome events scheduled to take place in the Roman Circus were publicized. And in our own Colonial American society, the town criers can be said to have been this country's first living, walking advertisements.

In London in 1702 Samuel Buckley's *Daily Courant,* the first daily newspaper to be printed in the English language, contained advertisements. Consisting of one sheet of paper, the *Daily Courant* carried editorial material and news on the front of the sheet and advertisements on the back. Although many of Buckley's advertisements were unethical, the revenue he obtained from them helped him to keep his newspaper financially sound despite the tax the Crown placed on all advertising.

The first advertisement to appear in a Colonial American newspaper was printed in John Campbell's *Boston News-Letter* in 1704. The advertisement was the type we now call a house ad; that is, any advertisement placed in a publication, by the owner of the publication, that makes promotional claims for that publication.

The First Advertising Agency

What is often referred to as the first advertising agency in the country was established by Volney B. Palmer in Philadelphia in 1841. Because Palmer's agency was successful, he was able to establish other offices in New York, Boston, and Baltimore. These branch offices were set up to find advertisers for the newspapers represented by Palmer. Other advertising agencies were soon established, many of them unethical and unscrupulous in their practices. Advertisers, having no means for checking on the price of the news-paper advertising space sold to them (often no prices had been established), had to depend on the word of advertising agency representatives. This problem was remedied in 1869 when George P. Rowell (who later founded the magazine *Printers' Ink*) published the *American Newspaper Directory*, the country's first accurate listing of newspaper advertising rates.

Era of Rapid Growth

In 1897 Commodore J. Walter Thompson purchased the Carlton & Smith Agency. This agency soon gained control of the advertising in what Thompson called his "List of Thirty Publications." Most of the advertising in the publications listed by Thompson was directed toward women. Today, the agency founded by Thompson is the world's largest. Newspaper and magazine advertising revenue continued to grow, and in the first part of the twentieth century, while many ethical national advertising campaigns were begun by such firms as Eastman Kodak, Wrigley's, Royal Baking Company, and Procter and Gamble, the leading advertisers of the period continued to be patent medicine manufacturers. Few of the era's publishers exerted any form of censorship over unethical advertising.

Newer, more advanced advertising techniques such as use of direct mail, billboards, and car-cards came to be used in the early 1900's. Manufacturers and business firms found that the more they advertised, the greater their profits. In the 1920's business firms helped advertising and radio to become allies. The first radio stations, having been set up by organizations such as Westinghouse Corporation, large department stores, and automobile dealers, did not carry commercials as we know them today. Listeners tuned in to the radio station of, for example, the Jones Department Store which operated the station to create a feeling of good will. Many businessmen, fascinated by the possibilities of hearing the spoken word over the airwaves, wondered if there could be a profitable application. Since it was impossible to make listeners pay to listen to a news event or to a musical selection, businessmen became concerned about who would pay for the production costs involved. The obvious answer was the advertisers. Millions of radio receiving sets were being used everywhere in the country, and in 1922 Station WEAF in New York City became the first radio station to sell time for commercial messages. By 1930 advertisers throughout the country were spending $60,000,000 yearly to advertise their wares over the nation's airwaves.

Advertisers Flock to Television

As a result of the advances being made in television following World War II, advertisers flocked to this newer medium because of the possibilities for visual advertising appeals. The number and cost of commercials skyrocketed. For example, in 1950 an advertiser could buy all the commercial time on a half-hour television show for $60,000; by 1968 he was paying almost three times as much for a one-minute commercial in prime time.

The total advertising sales figure has currently reached $8,000,000,000 annually. The advertising profession and the mass media have become inseparable; neither can survive without the other. And without advertising, industrial and business growth would slow down considerably—and could, conceivably, come to a complete halt.

THE FUNCTION OF ADVERTISING

The main function of advertising is to bring the buyer and seller together. This function was established before the age of printing when early man discovered there was a market for his goods and services and advertised them by inscribing messages on stone tablets. The first printed newspaper advertisements, having appeared in seventeenth-century London, were followed in America in the 1750's by American newspaper publishers who used advertising as a source for additional revenue in order to meet expanding pro-

Young & Rubicam, Inc.

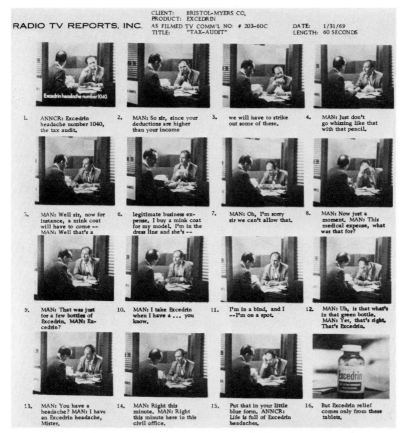

duction costs and to gain further profits. Merchants found that they also could realize even greater profits by advertising their goods in newspapers. Today, advertising provides more than sixty percent of the income of magazines and newspapers and nearly all of the income of radio and television stations. In figures prepared by the *Publisher's Information Bureau—Leading National Advertisers*, each of the first ten of the country's top hundred advertisers in four media during the first half of 1968 showed advertising expenditures totalling well over $20,000,000 (see Chart A, below).

TOP ADVERTISERS IN FOUR MEDIA
1ST HALF OF 1968

Source: PIB-Leading National Advertisers

COMPANY	TOTAL EXPENDITURE	MAGAZINES	NEWSPAPER SUPPLEMENTS	NETWORK TELEVISION	SPOT TELEVISION
1. Procter & Gamble Co.	$98,699,377	$ 6,711,063	$ 170,914	$52,288,500	$39,528,900
2. General Foods Corp.	53,158,573	* 2,439,000	1,202,733	23,088,800	26,428,000
3. Bristol-Myers Co.	52,952,582	12,854,249	441,733	25,585,100	14,071,500
4. General Motors Corp.	52,851,066	23,310,493	1,556,573	20,610,500	7,373,500
5. Colgate-Palmolive Co.	41,929,581	5,414,615	189,566	20,689,100	15,636,300
6. American Home Products Corp.	34,381,888	3,165,177	101,511	22,950,700	8,164,500
7. R. J. Reynolds Tobacco Co.	32,707,467	4,376,532	76,435	22,498,800	5,755,700
8. American Tobacco Co.	32,210,530	6,269,394	28,336	14,191,000	11,721,800
9. Sterling Drug, Inc.	27,998,485	3,827,956	545,229	18,806,700	4,818,600
10. Lever Brothers Co.	26,775,698	1,932,440	95,258	14,784,90	9,963,100

Advertising Age, Sept. 23, 1968

Chart A

THE ADVERTISING PROCESS

Because practically every business and non-profit organization within our society is concerned with some type of advertising, advertising departments and agencies—groups of specialists involved in the creating of advertising and in the planning of the marketing programs of which advertising is a part—were formed to help solve sales problems and to coordinate the efforts of sales staffs with advertising programs.

Advertising departments and agencies vary in size from "one-man agencies" handling few accounts to huge agencies handling hundreds of accounts and having thousands of employees in branch offices all over the world. A typical advertising agency's organization by functions is shown on page 115.

114

A TYPICAL ADVERTISING AGENCY
ORGANIZATION CHART
BY FUNCTIONS

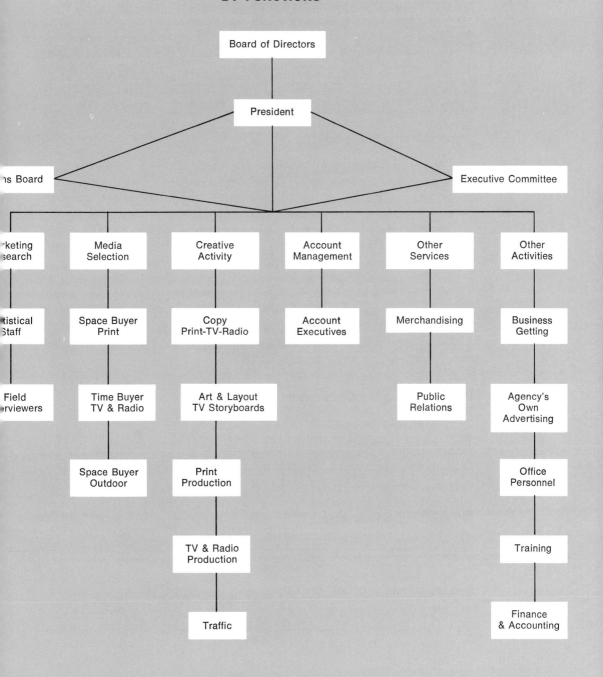

Source: American Association of Advertising Agencies, Inc.
200 Park Avenue, New York, N.Y. 10017
(From Career Opportunities in Advertising) © 1967

RESEARCH

Amateurs occasionally try their hand at setting up advertisements. When they come up with something they feel looks presentable and possibly clever, they assume that the preparation and writing of advertisements is a simple matter. However, an advertising client must have concrete evidence that an advertisement will be successful, usually in terms of increased profit, before he is willing to invest large sums of money for a piece of paper that merely looks good and contains clever words.

Understanding the Product

Prior to preparing an advertisement extensive research is done on the product, on the consumer, and on the competition. The advertiser must fully understand the product to be advertised. The more complex the product, the more time needed for the study. For instance, when one automobile manufacturer developed a new car the advertising agency personnel assigned to the account were given a thorough course in the automotive business before they began preparing any advertisements. For each product to be advertised, advertisers need to find answers to questions like: Is this product an impulse item or a considered purchase? Is it a low-cost item or a large investment? Is it a frequently or seldomly purchased product? How will the client, stockholders, employees, and lawmakers react to the advertisement? And most important, how will the *typical consumer*, the buyer the product is intended to reach, react to the advertisement?

Understanding the Consumer

The typical consumer is the person who, in the final analysis, will have to spend his hard-earned money for the advertised product. The advertiser, by using methods of psychology, must find the best way to appeal to the typical consumer. Before beginning preparation of an advertisement, the advertiser attempts to understand the consumer as well as he does a close friend or relative, and to find the answers to these questions: What sex is the consumer? What education has he had? What is his economic level? What are his likes and dislikes? What are his hobbies? What are his fears and aspirations? What are his everyday problems?

Understanding the Competition

Advertisers must also study the competition's product—and the competition's advertising. An advertiser needs to know how his product is different from other products. He also needs to know what segment of the total audience his competition is attempting to reach. Breakfast cereal, for example, is a product that can be consumed by all age groups. The fact that one breakfast cereal advertiser is gearing an advertising campaign to mothers of grade school children might be the reason why a competing advertiser would decide to gear a campaign to mothers of high school students.

The "Unique Selling Proposition"

A well-planned research program should reveal what many men and women employed in advertising refer to as a "Unique Selling Proposition" (USP). A USP has three necessary qualities. First, a "unique" claim is essential—one which the opposition cannot or does not offer. Second, the unique proposition must help to "sell" the product. And third, a definite "proposition" is necessary: "Buy *this* product and you get *this* particular benefit." An example of a unique proposition by a toothpaste manufacturer advertising a multi-colored toothpaste was: "It comes out like a rainbow and looks good on your toothbrush." The toothpaste didn't sell. An advertising agency proposed: "Tastes good while it whitens your teeth." Because no one had ever suggested as "unique" a "proposition" as taste in a toothpaste, the product "sold" and the manufacturer gained a large percentage of the market.

Media Selection

Advertising departments and agencies have at their disposal thousands of daily newspapers throughout the country in which to advertise, hundreds of consumer magazines, thousands of business and professional publications, thousands of radio and television stations, unlimited outdoor advertising and transportation facilities, and millions of indoor signs and displays in every town and city.

The choice of which of the mass media will be the most effective in a particular case entails a careful analysis of territories in which the product will be sold, a careful study of the living and buying habits of the consumer for whom the product is intended, and an analysis of the reading and listening habits of the consumer audience to be reached. Based on careful consideration of all of these factors, the media director of the advertising department or agency makes his selection, always keeping in mind as first choice the medium which will give the best return for the most reasonable investment.

Basic Copy Appeals

How can the advertiser convince the consumer that a product will be good for him? After completing a research program on the uniqueness of the product, on the typical consumer, on the competition, and on choice of medium, the advertising man plans different possible copy appeals for approaching and appealing to the basic human needs of the consumer he intends to reach. Semantics plays the most important part in all of the copy-appeal methods used to reach the consumer. Semantics, the branch of language study that deals with the meaning of words and their effect on people, is important because many words have the power to create positive, pleasant feelings while others can create negative, unpleasant feelings. Some of the most commonly used basic copy appeals are:

Mastery—Milk producers in a large Eastern state decided to set up their advertising without the help of an advertising agency. Throughout the state signs were put up saying, "Help your State Milk Producers. Drink Milk." But consumers did not rush out to buy more milk as a result of seeing this advertisement. Milk sales went down, and the next year an advertising agency was hired. Their appeal? A movie star, pictured with the headline, "I owe my complexion to X Brand Milk." Sales went up—the campaign had worked. Most advertising tries to make people believe they will somehow be more successful if they buy the advertised product. Personal vanity and a desire for recognition or prestige contribute to making most people vulnerable to the mastery appeal.

Hunger and Thirst—A flour manufacturer once ran an advertisement for a new Danish-pastry mix. The headline in the advertisement read, "Almond Danish! Almond Danish, Almond Danish, Almond Danish!" The phrase was repeated for emphasis. An excellent-quality photograph showed an appetizing slice of the pastry. The body copy was comparatively short: "In, and on, and all around the Danish—rich, chunky almonds! Tomorrow, during coffee-break, have a homemade Almond Danish." Advertisers know that hunger is one of the three basic drives. Hunger-appeal advertisements are emotional; all they have to do is remind the reader how satisfying good food is.

Sex Appeal—An advertisement for a wool manufacturer pictured a college man looking admiringly at a coed. Both were wearing coats made of a famous brand of wool. The typical consumer was led to believe that if he wore a coat made of the advertised wool, he would become more attractive to the opposite sex. The sex-appeal approach was especially suitable for this manufacturer because his product was manufactured for both men and women.

Parental Instinct—Parents get vicarious pleasure from the happiness of their children; the health, safety, and well-being of their children is of utmost importance to them. Most advertising men try, however, to be wary of unethical appeals which might psychologically damage a child. Imagine the effect on a sensitive child of the television advertisement which says, "Mothers who love their children serve them brand X cereal." Consider the reaction of the child whose mother does not serve him brand X cereal.

Security—An advertisement for a life insurance company pictured a young, cleancut looking couple. In the picture the wife was shown knitting a baby's sweater as the husband asked, "Do you think we'll have a boy?" The headline read, "Get full coverage with family-packaged life insurance policy . . . only $14 a month." To many persons, financial security is as important as food, clothing, and shelter; for peace of mind, many people purchase products they might not need. Manufacturers of car batteries, tires, and fire-protection equipment sometimes promote their products on the basis of the security such products can offer.

Health—The average person usually doesn't mind spending money for health benefits. For example, look in your family medicine cabinet. Sometimes advertisers fabricate health benefits if the competition is using the other possible appeals. For years advertisers have been trying to make the public believe that mouthwash is a necessity. Various agencies have applied the mastery, sex, and security appeals to mouthwash advertising. Several agencies have utilized the health claim that their clients' mouthwashes have germ-killing abilities.

Comfort—Airline and automobile advertisements often appeal to the modern American's love of comfort. While one airline might emphasize the quiet ride available on its flights, another airline might advertise softer seats. Automobile manufacturing advertisers often feature "wall-to-wall carpeting" and "reclining seats" in their advertisements. Many razor-blade manufacturers play up the comfort angle of their product. For example, a television advertisement might show a man grimacing with pain while he is shaving with razor X, then smiling and humming a catchy tune while he is using the advertiser's product.

Sociability—Most people don't like to be alone. They feel that if they have a brand-name soft drink in the refrigerator they'll have company—they'll be part of the "in" group. Advertising of an unethical nature plays up the fear of loneliness, of not having friends. Advertisers often insinuate that "If you don't buy our deodorant (mouthwash, cosmetics, toothpaste, hair sprays, etc., etc., etc., etc.,), you'll be a wallflower." The intelligent consumer critically examines advertising claims like: "Whether a person is likable or undesirable depends upon whether or not he uses brand X soap," an obviously

Experience The Now Generation

Embroidered Velvet Vest, **$40.00**
Matching Velvet Pants, **$30.00**
Experience Clothes available in sizes
3 to 13 at all better department stores.

Nancy Trigg

*What is the basic copy appeal in
this advertisement?*

unsound statement. A lonesome person, however, might be strongly affected by this kind of advertising. But if that person were to follow the advertisement's superficial prescription, how much better off would he actually be?

Beauty—A radio and phonograph manufacturer stresses the beauty of the console as well as the sound production, and a carpet company advertises its product as "handsome" as well as "tough." Most people like to be surrounded by beauty. Advertisers stress modern design in advertisements for furniture and other household accessories; in fact, the implication in many advertisements is that "modern" means "beautiful." Some companies, however, make a point of recognizing individualism in their advertising. A silverware company advertisement, for example, pictures three different types of women and makes the claim that the company knows Sara, Lucille, and Anne are different. The company claims that it designs its products to suit a variety of individual tastes.

Economy—Everyone wants to save money, and at the same time not be associated with anything that can be labeled as "cheap." Advertising writers must be extremely tactful in their presentation of economy appeals. Because the "cheap-but-not-too-cheap" attitude is usually a by-product of "status-seeking," advertisers have found that it pays to give a brand a first-class ticket. Many people don't like to be seen consuming a product their friends might regard as third-class. For example, the public was led to believe the idea that a new, low-priced automobile was cheaply made. It took a gigantic advertising campaign to correct this misconception.

Convenience—If an advertiser manufactures a quick-drying paint that doesn't run, the advertising would probably emphasize the convenience of the product. Many automobile manufacturers use the "convenience" appeal —for an air-cooled motor, for instance. When advertising a new, automatic car starter, one company's advertisement read, "A great new starter that takes the guesswork out of driving."

You've undoubtedly noticed ads which combine two or more of these appeals. While some advertisers feel that an advertisement is more effective if its approach is limited to only one appeal, others argue that in simplifying the approach an advertisement will reach only a limited audience.

Writing Advertising Copy

Advertising copy is the written part of an advertisement: it consists of the headlines and the detailed written material. The goal of most advertising copy is to gain consumer interest, desire, conviction, and action.

Attention—The headlines in advertising copy should attract the attention of the consumer audience the product is intended for, and should interest the consumer enough to make him want to read the body of the copy. An advertisement for tomato sauce containing the headline "We hate to see a woman cry," for example, would have a strong emotional appeal for many women. Such a headline could make the average woman wonder what the connection is between crying and tomato sauce. The reader finds, after reading the copy, that this is an advertisement for "Tomato Sauce with Onions."

Interest and Desire—In the body the writer enlarges on the statement made in the headline. The body should be written in an interesting manner and, at the same time, should create a desire for the product. The advertising copywriter often uses language devices to make the product sound appealing. "Balmybath beautifies the body—"bubbles," "buoys," and "bathes," (body copy for a bath oil advertisement) is an example both of alliteration and onomatopoeia. The popping of the "b" sound is like the popping of bubbles and the implied sensuousness of the "bubbles," "buoys," and "bathes" appeals to a woman's love of luxury. Careful choice of words and tone which will appeal to a business executive characterizes an advertisement for an office furniture manufacturer: "Make an executive decision now! Choose a

Thoron Desk for your office. Thoron is tough! Aggressive! Competitive!"
What other language device was used in the opening sentence of this ad?

Conviction—The advertising copy tries to convince the typical consumer
that he should purchase the product because it is the best available. An advertisement for a piece of mechanical equipment would probably make a
rational appeal to the consumer. A stereo system, for instance, might be presented as a machine offering certain superior features such as an ellipitical
stylus, a hysterisis motor, and acoustical suspension speakers. If the product
is not mechanical, the body copy will have to use more subtle persuaders.
Repetition of a key phrase is a common advertising device. One sixty-second
television commercial for a soft drink mentioned the name of the product
seventeen times. Repetition implants the name of the product in the consumer's mind and makes it difficult for him not to respond to the product
when he sees it. A shopper wheeling her cart down a grocery store aisle
usually reaches for a brand-name soup because she has not seen or heard
the names of other soups.

Action—The final step in preparing the body copy is to inspire the consumer
to go out and buy the advertised product as soon as possible; if he waits too
long, he may see a competitor's advertisement and decide that instead of the
original product, he prefers the competition's. Copywriters make it as easy
as possible for the consumer to purchase a product. They usually tell the
consumer where to buy the product and how much the product will cost. In
their copy they try to provide the consumer with the incentive to act as soon
as possible. Often, they prepare copy that offers bonuses to the first buyers
—or they lower the prices for a limited amount of time. Coupons offering
bargains are another device used by copywriters to encourage consumers to
go out and buy a product. Such "convenience" coupons are built into the
advertisement itself. Many are of the "no-money-now-we'll-bill-you-later"
type and require only that the consumer fill in his name, address, size of order, and signature on a postage-paid form. Many publications use these
coupons to solicit new and renewal subscriptions.

Basic Visual Appeals

Art Copy—Art copy is the pictorial part of an advertisement. Many advertisers claim that art copy is the most important element in a good advertisement because it "catches" the eye, thus gaining the reader's interest and
leading him into the body copy. Successful art copy can direct the eye to the
focal point of the advertisement, the name of the product. Pictures, combined with the written copy, help excite the reader's interest in a product.

122

Color—While many black and white advertisements can prove effective, it has been found that the discriminating use of color can make an advertisement even more effective. Color is used in advertisements to affect the reader's feelings—not just to enhance the advertisement's appearance. For example, green and blue are "cool" colors while red and yellow are "warm" colors. The choice of appropriate colors in advertisements is one of the most important considerations for gaining visual appeal. Subconsciously the consumer responds to color. The impact of an advertisement for a cooling iced drink would be defeated if portrayed only in warm reds, oranges, and yellows.

Other Basic Appeals

Recently, many advertisers have been using newer, more innovative appeals than sight to gain consumer interest. An advertisement for one perfume advertiser contained a perfumed paper strip which released the scent of the advertised perfume when scratched. Another advertiser for a new paper towel included a sheet of the new product, on which was printed an advertising message, bound into a magazine. The reader could tear out and use the paper towel, thus allowing him to test it and feel its texture. Still another advertiser had his "message" printed on plastic stock and bound into a magazine. The plastic material, containing a recording, could be removed from the magazine and played on a record player by the consumer.

The use of these innovative appeals in advertising, as well as the traditional use of basic copy and visual appeals, is likely to be successful if the advertiser has an understanding of the psychology behind the consumer's reasons for buying a particular product.

ADVERTISING AS A CAREER

The mass media are interested in the sale of their advertising space or of their broadcast time for financial gain. Media advertising men are the salesmen for the mass media, and each medium has its own policy and program for training beginners for its sales department.

In many companies, new product development and product research are areas in which men and women work to create or design products and services better than those of their competitors. Once such a product or service is ready for the public, the company will want to notify as many prospective users as possible. The way to tell the greatest number of people about a product or service in the shortest time at the lowest cost per message has been found to be advertising.

Significant to a student selecting a field for his life's work is the great rate of expansion in the use of advertising. The money invested in advertising today—over seven billion dollars a year by national advertisers alone—is more than double the amount spent ten years ago.

Students interested in joining the advertising profession should have good business sense and writing ability. They should take courses in business, English, and journalism. A college degree is usually necessary. In a recent issue of *Advertising Age* Magazine, William A. Marsteller, chairman of the Marsteller, Inc. advertising firm, recommended a major in advertising at a recognized school of journalism because:

> It is not enough to simply attain general standards of morality and taste. It is important to be subjected to the deliberate considerations of *advertising* morality and taste, just as it is important for the law student to be exposed to the careful examination of the ethical concepts of the law.

Marsteller added that courses in economics, sociology, and psychology serve as a good base if they can be applied to the specifics of advertising.

Without the proper background, the advertising industry is one of the most difficult fields in which to succeed. Initiative and creative abilities are important assets, as exemplified by one applicant who having waited in vain several times to see an agency personnel director, left a carrier pigeon with the secretary. "When he can see me, please have him release the pigeon," the young man said. The agency was impressed with the applicant's resourcefulness and offered him a job.

John Crichton, president of The American Association of Advertising Agencies, feels that there are three qualities particularly important in a successful advertising career:

> The first is a *belief in advertising*. It is a fact in advertising, as in most business, that it is extremely hard to work contentedly if you don't have a basic belief in what you are doing, that it is worthwhile and important.
>
> The second is the ability to *transmit ideas*. It is essential that the advertising man be able to communicate two ways —from buyer to seller, from seller to buyer—and the translation must be accurate.
>
> The third is the ability to *remain a student,* life long. Ours is a society which never stands still; advertising is the ally of change; the advertising man or woman must keep abreast of change.

from *Education for Advertising Careers*
AAAA Pamphlet

ACTIVITIES

1. Try to increase your awareness of various kinds of propaganda that surround you. Pay attention to news reports on propaganda. Write an evaluation of them indicating whether they are beneficial, harmful, or innocuous.

2. Make a collection of newspapers and magazine advertisements. If possible, use a tape recorder to obtain radio and television examples. Choose two of your best examples to bring to class for analysis and rating. Categorize your examples according to the basic copy appeals you learned about in this chapter. Then, rate them according to the personal appeals they have to you, the consumer.

3. Offer your services to school organizations that need poster advertisements of activities or projects. Experiment with different appeals. You might first consider the "typical consumer" concept as it applies to students you know.

4. How ingenious can you be at thinking up original ways to promote either school or extra-curricular activities? You might try doing a tape, for instance, then hooking it up to an amplifier. List any other promotional possibilities that you can think of.

5. How flooded is the market with unethical advertising? Find some subtle examples of advertisements that threaten social punishment to the person who does not buy the advertised product. Write some letters to the American Association of Advertising Agencies to express your views. Write to one of your state representatives and ask about your state's law on advertising practices.

6. In connection with Activity 5, read Vance Packard's *The Hidden Persuaders* and organize a class discussion on the effects of advertising on the individual and on society.

7. For each of the following common terms (*a–f*) name at least one euphemism, or "more pleasant" term. Then, list what type of advertisements your chosen euphemisms would most likely appear in. For example,
> *pimples: euphemism = blemishes; advertisement = skin cream*

a. sweat c. gin mill e. old maid
b. false teeth d. fat person f. underwear

8. Select an article of apparel necessary to all members of your class, and prepare a complete research study of the article to find out all of the information about it necessary to plan an effective advertisement. Decide which medium you would like to advertise your article in and present your complete plans for an advertisement aimed at that medium.

9. A large company has asked you to plan an advertising campaign for its newest product, a frozen breakfast food. Plan your campaign by completing the following steps:

a. Invent an appealing brand name for your product. In choosing the brand name, consider the "basic appeals" you learned about earlier in this chapter.

b. Write a headline and body copy for your advertisement. You may want to include a catchy slogan. Use basic, simple appeals in preparing the copy.

c. Plan and sketch a magazine advertisement for your copy. For more effective visual appeal, keep your sketch simple and uncluttered.

d. Write a two-minute radio commercial for your product, preparing your copy for a station that mainly features classical-music programs.

e. Sketch a plan for a highway billboard advertisement, keeping in mind simplicity and brevity of copy. Remember that billboards primarily reach people who travel by too quickly to read too many words.

f. Plan and write a two-minute television commercial for your product. Include camera directions you think might capture the viewer's attention. Also, consider inclusion in your dialog of the slogan you prepared in *b.*

g. Suggest any other advisable methods for promoting and publicizing your new product.

10. Discuss with your classmates what you think the mass media should do for you and what you must do for the mass media in order to be informed, intelligent consumers.

READING

AMERICAN ASSOCIATION OF ADVERTISING AGENCIES, *Career Opportunities in Advertising.* American Association of Advertising Agencies, New York.

———, *Education for Advertising Careers.* American Association of Advertising Agencies, New York.

———, *What Advertising Agencies Are—What They Do and How They Do It.* American Association of Advertisers, New York.

BARTON, ROGER, *Advertising Agency Operations and Management.* McGraw-Hill, New York, 1955.

———, *Media in Advertising.* McGraw-Hill, New York, 1964.

BEDELL, CLYDE, *How to Write Advertising That Sells.* McGraw-Hill, New York, 1952.

BOGART, LEO, *Strategy in Advertising.* Harcourt, Brace & World, New York, 1967.

BORDEN, NEIL H., AND MARTIN V. MARSHALL, *Advertising Management: Text and Cases.* Richard D. Irwin, New York, 1959.

BRIDGE, HARRY P., *Practical Advertising*. Holt, Rinehart & Winston, New York, 1949.

BROWN, RUSSEL A., AND CHARLES H. EDWARDS, JR., *Retail Advertising and Sales Promotion*. Prentice-Hall, Englewood Cliffs, N.J., 1957.

BURTON, PHILLIP WARD, *Principles of Advertising*. Prentice-Hall, Englewood Cliffs, N.J., 1958.

———, AND BOWMAN KREER, *Advertising Copywriting*. Prentice-Hall, Englewood Cliffs, N.J., 1961.

DEVOE, MERRIL, *Effective Advertising Copy*. Macmillan, New York, 1956.

DUNN, S. WATSON, *Advertising Copy and Communication*. McGraw-Hill, New York, 1956.

———, *Advertising: Its Role in Modern Marketing*. Holt, Rinehart & Winston, New York, 1969.

FREY, ALBERT W., *Advertising*. Ronald, New York, 1961.

GRAHAM, IRVIN, *Encyclopedia of Advertising*. Fairchild Publications, New York, 1968.

HEPNER, HARRY W., *Advertising: Creative Communication with Consumers*. McGraw-Hill, New York, 1964.

JOHNSON, GEORGE, *Your Career in Advertising*. Messner, New York, 1966.

KIRKPATRICK, C. A., *Advertising*. Houghton Mifflin, Boston, 1969.

KLEPPNER, OTTO, *Advertising Procedure*. Prentice-Hall, Englewood Cliffs, N.J., 1966.

LUCAS, DARRELL BLAINE, AND STEUART HENDERSON BRITT, *Advertising Psychology and Research*. McGraw-Hill, New York, 1950.

———, *Measuring Advertising Effectiveness*. McGraw-Hill, New York, 1963.

MAYER, MARTIN, *Madison Avenue, USA*. Harper & Row, New York, 1958. (PB)

McCLURE, LESLIE W., *Newspaper Advertising and Promotion*. Macmillan, New York, 1950.

MESSNER, FREDERICK R., *Industrial Advertising*. McGraw-Hill, New York, 1963.

MULHOLLAND, JOHN, AND GEORGE N. GORDON, *The Magical Mind*. Hastings House, New York, 1966.

OGILVY, DAVID, *Confessions of an Advertising Man*. Atheneum, New York, 1963.

PACKARD, VANCE, *The Hidden Persuaders*. Pocket Books, New York, 1957. (PB)

———, *The Waste Makers*. Pocket Books, New York, 1963. (PB)

SANDAGE, CHARLES H., AND VERNON FRYBERGER, *Advertising Theory and Practice*. Richard D. Irwin, Homewood, Ill., 1967.

——— (Ed.), *The Role of Advertising: A Book of Readings*. Richard D. Irwin, Homewood, Ill., 1960.

SEEHAFER, EUGENE F., AND JACK W. LAERMMAR, *Successful Television and Radio Advertising*. McGraw-Hill, New York, 1959.

WAINWRIGHT, CHARLES ANTHONY, *The Television Copywriter: How to Create Successful Television Commercials*. Hastings House, New York, 1965.

WOOD, JAMES PLAYSTED, *The Story of Advertising*. Ronald, New York, 1958.

WRIGHT, JOHN S., AND DANIEL S. WARNER, *Advertising*. McGraw-Hill, New York, 1966.

Chapter 7

The Future of Journalism in the Mass Media

JOURNALISM IN A CHANGING SOCIETY

The craft of the journalist is changing radically, almost daily, as are most crafts in our constantly changing society. Many changes in the craft of today's journalist have been caused by the newer techniques for gathering and presenting the news, by the demands of the more mobile and educated audiences for whom this news is intended, by the major technological advances in communications equipment, and by the everchanging business procedures necessary to more profitably organize and operate a mass communications medium. As these changes continue, newer problems, challenges, and responsibilities affecting today's journalists continue to emerge.

While it would be impossible to project exactly how journalists of the future will go about reporting news, it is possible, by taking past and present developments into consideration, to predict probable trends in the future organization and production procedures of the present members of our mass media. Such trends and their probable effect on the future of journalism are outlined in this chapter.

129

NEWSPAPERS

In 1969 *The American Press*, a trade publication for editors and publishers, estimated that from 34 to 39 percent of the American population lived in the suburbs, 30 percent lived in urban areas, and the remainder lived in rural areas. The suburban and urban population, with an average age of under 30, consisted of 60 million students, with 8 million of them attending college. In the homes of these students television sets were used, helping to contribute to making them more aware members of our society. Both the increased education and awareness of these members of our population has influenced, and should continue to influence, the editing, producing, and administrating of America's ever-changing newspaper publishing industry.

Newspaper Content

Because the other mass media are attempting to gain the interest of a better educated and more informed public, the content of newspapers should continue to change. To meet this competition daily newspapers having circulations over 100,000 have grown in size from an average of 27 pages in 1946 to an average of 53 pages in 1966—and are continuing to grow. During this same period newspaper editorial and news page content almost doubled, and advertising content more than doubled. While many factors have contributed to these changes, one major factor has been what media experts term an "information explosion"—a demand made by consumers who require more information to control and improve their lives.

In-depth Coverage

In contrast to newspapers, radio and television are able to deliver "on-the-spot" news immediately following a news event and, in cases such as a presidential inauguration, simultaneously with the news event. A newspaper's presentation of a similar event is slower, for newspapers must take the time to convert an account of the news event into print. Newspapers, which by 1969 were employing thousands of journalists to gather, write, and edit the news, have not overlooked the impact on news coverage offered by the competing radio and television media. Realizing that they cannot compete with the timeliness of the news coverage as presented in the electronic media, newspapers have become increasingly more aware that what they can provide is a service not designed for radio or television: a more "in-depth" type of journalism—information and editorials which enable readers to understand more fully the scope and deeper significance of important news events. For example, while the electronic media can report that there is a disturbance at a large university and television can show a film on the conflict, a newspaper can favorably compete by presenting an "in-depth" account by a writer or reporter familiar enough with educational problems to be able to analyze and clarify the issues involved. Newspapers can also devote space to "in-depth" reporting in order to clarify issues for the public.

Specialists Needed

To help meet the current demand for "in-depth" journalism, newspapers now seek personnel who are specialists in particular facets of news reporting. Newspaper editors, in evaluating the effects of the increasing education of readers on newspaper content, will continue to emphasize this need for expertise in specialized areas when hiring journalists in the future.

Newspaper publishers claim that print is here to stay because of the length and depth limitations imposed on news presentations in the electronic media, and that the print journalist will, of necessity, have to continue to serve the increasing special interests of the public. *The Wall Street Journal,* an example of a newspaper for people involved in business, is written by journalists thoroughly knowledgeable in the working of finance. The *Journal* has steadily increased its circulation since its beginning, and in 1968 had a circulation of over one million. The *National Observer* and the *Christian Science Monitor,* also examples of newspapers appealing to special-interest readers, both rely on "in-depth" news presentations. Many newspaper publishers further claim that another advantage newspapers have over the competing electronic media is their "permanence"—a printed news account can always be reread.

Another aspect in the developing "in-depth" type of newspaper coverage will be increased reporting of local news, a service which television and radio networks cannot at present provide. The growth of suburbia will add interest to the local news. As John Tilton, associate publisher of Minneapolis based *Suburban Papers, Inc.,* has indicated:

> There are new communities developing every day that will, of necessity, have to have their own newspaper. In the next 20 years someone will start another 2000 suburban newspapers.

Meeting the Needs of the Community

The managing editors of these new suburban newspapers, in allocating space for worthwhile news stories, will take into account the special needs of the community while continuing to leave room for wire service and other national and international news. This interest in community matters is creating the need for journalists who are well informed on problems specific to a community. For instance, future stories dealing with the Black community may conceivably be covered exclusively by Afro-American journalists who have a background in urban affairs. Daily, weekly, semi-weekly, and tri-weekly newspapers, in order to appeal to readers, will probably have to closely identify with their reading audiences as well as present their readers with the information they need to intelligently participate in the affairs of the community, city, state, or nation.

Technology

In 1904 a German physicist named Arthur Korn developed facsimile, the process which transmits photographs and printed material over thousands of miles. Expanding on the process, The Radio Corporation of America in 1947 built the Ultrafax, a facsimile machine capable of transmitting a 50,000-word novel over a distance of 3000 miles in one minute. By 1968 facsimile was sufficiently advanced technically for newspapers to be transmitted from the composing room to the living room—in fact, facsimile could now reproduce all of a newspaper's copy and advertising that would normally have to be set and printed. Due to the enormous expenses involved in producing facsimile equipment, however, its full-scale use to produce newspapers remains something for the distant future. Meanwhile, other advances in the composing and printing of newspapers are being implemented in newspaper plants. Publishers, in trying to produce high-quality newspapers efficiently and inexpensively, cannot overlook the technology of the computer, the satellite, the laser, and the many other electronic paraphernalia which science has developed. In 1967 alone, American and Canadian dailies spent more than 147 million dollars for newspaper plant expansion and modernization, and estimates by trade analysts predict that this figure will rise annually.

The Computer Age

The computer has entered newspaper production in the form of a photo-typesetting machine which is capable of setting up to 6000 characters per second. The benefits of this *Fototron, VideoComp, CRT* or *Linotron*—as each respective company calls its machine—are enormous, and many publishers involved in setting up new plants or modernizing old ones will probably employ this new process.

Printing Techniques

For the printing of newspapers, photo-offset lithography will continue to take the place of letterpress printing because of the former's flexibility in use

132

of color and its very rapid rate of printing. One such press, the *Harris Lithotronic 78*, can print 7500 sheets per hour. This printing press has a built-in computer digital logic system which can automatically regulate the processes formerly controlled by a pressman.

Employee Relations

New machines and equipment, as they have become necessary in the increasing automation of newspaper plants, have caused serious labor-management problems. Union demands have also played an important role in newspaper labor-management disputes. Many newspapers claim to have folded because of unrealistic demands by unions. How much such demands contribute to actual newspaper failure is uncertain, although unions have often had, and still have, a major effect on the financial status of newspapers. For example, New York City, which had seven newspapers in 1953, found itself with only three in 1967. Five newspaper strikes—10 days in 1953, 19 days in 1958, 114 days in 1962–63, 25 days in 1965, and 140 days in 1966—undoubtedly contributed to the financial difficulties of the four newspapers that went out of business. Newspaper management, which has to bargain with as many as sixteen different unions composed of lithographers, typographers, photoengravers, pressmen, journalists, and other craft unions, often claims that meeting union considerations can contribute to putting newspapers out of business. The unions, however, feel that it is poor management which ultimately hurts a newspaper. But management and labor are in agreement that automation is inevitable, and the International Typographers Union (ITU), in its trade magazine, has admitted that automation is an unavoidable trend.

> The wedding of the computer to high-speed photo composition is a fact. The hot metal linecasting machine, traditional standby for composing rooms the last 70 years, will go out of business in the foreseeable future. It will soon be an antique, comparable to future printing machinery as a Model T Ford compares to a modern jet aircraft.
>
> *The Bulletin*
> The American Society of Newspaper Editors

Management

The major role of the newspaper publisher is to see that the newspaper serves the public and continues to make a profit by publishing accurate and interesting information as rapidly and efficiently as possible, and at the same time seeing that circulation and advertising revenues do not decrease. It is impossible to foretell how much these responsibilities in newspaper publishing will contribute to the expansion or failure of newspapers of the future. Publishers have cited the following reasons for the collapse of many of our nation's newspapers:

1. The growth of newspaper chains that consolidate competing newspapers in the same city or that buy up newspapers in an area in order to clear the market for their own papers.

2. The loss of advertising revenue to television and radio.

3. Falling circulations.

4. Spiralling costs of production and conflicts with labor unions.

5. The effects the electronic media have had on the reading habits of the newspaper-reading public.

In addition to these difficulties, newspaper publishers are also beset with an increasing involvement by the government in the structure and function of the newspaper business.

The Increase of "Chain" Newspapers

During the 1960's newspaper chains increased their growth by buying either established but floundering newspapers, or by founding new newspapers in suburban areas. Unaffiliated single ownership newspapers became less common, and twenty-five percent of all of the daily newspapers were controlled by the seven large newspaper chains. By 1968 more than 700 dailies were owned by some 160 group enterprises, and these dailies comprised the majority of newspapers sold daily in the United States. The consolidation of smaller newspapers with large chains has made concerned citizens and the government aware of the dangers of newspaper monopolies if such a trend continues unrestrictedly. Some newspapers have bought radio and television stations, claiming that they cannot survive without the added revenue from another medium. By 1968 some 381 AM stations, 191 FM stations, and 183 TV stations were owned by newspapers and/or magazines, thus causing further concern about monopoly control of the communications media. The government, sensing a danger, has become more involved in the communications media. The Federal Communications Commission, the courts, and the Congress are frequently concerning themselves with newspaper mergers and media control. Intervention by the government in communications matters is seen by many publishers as a violation of the First Amendment guarantee of freedom of the press. These publishers argue that government involvement might lead to government regulation, and perhaps to eventual government suppression.

Government Relations

The relationship between newspapers and the government is constantly changing, with newspapers sometimes accusing the government of managing the news by withholding information. During the Presidency of Lyndon B. Johnson, this conflict came to be known as the "credibility gap" because reporters felt they couldn't believe the President, and the President wasn't sure he could trust the communications media. In a democratic society in which the public has a right to be informed, the friction between the press and various branches of government will probably continue. The government will continue to put pressure on the press, and the press will continue to put pressure on the government. The public will probably remain somewhere between the two. Publishers of the future will inherit the responsibility of ensuring that accurate news coverage and responsible opinion reach the public.

MAGAZINES

In the future, magazines, like newspapers, will also take into account the impact of a younger, more educated and informed urban population that is greatly influenced by the electronic media. Never-ending changes in fashions and the popular arts, attitudes and behavior, leisure time, recreation, and entertainment have influenced the form and content of the modern magazine and should continue to do so. A good example of the changes a magazine must undergo in its fight for survival is the now defunct, but once thriving, *Saturday Evening Post*. According to the president of the Curtis Publishing Company which controlled the *Post*, the magazine which once published stories by such well-known writers as Ernest Hemingway and William Faulkner, failed because:

> Apparently there is just not the need for our product in
> today's scheme of living.

In the last years of the *Post*, as the cover illustrations on page 136 show, the magazine tried to suit itself to the changing times by giving itself a more "youthful" image. Such editorial changes did not save the *Post* because it lost much-needed advertising revenue both to other magazines and to the electronic media.

All magazines try to conform to the changes in our evolving society. In the future, as in the past, new magazines will arise as enterprising publishers sense that the public is interested in buying a new magazine, and that advertisers are interested enough to advertise in it. Older magazines will die, of course, when they no longer stimulate public interest.

1822

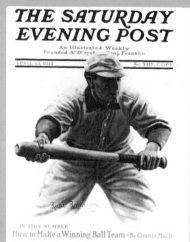

1912

1925

1936

1944

1955

1964

1968

1969

TELEVISION AND RADIO

The electronic media will not remain static in the future. As society changes, the comparatively young radio and the even younger television media, both having become integral parts of our society, will no doubt reflect and respond to an ever-changing environment. Further major modifications in the technology and programming of both media can be anticipated, as witnessed to date by the recent modifications imposed by community antenna television and satellites.

Technology

Television offers immediacy: it can instantaneously bring distant events into your home. This immediacy—and intimacy—is what has propelled television as a mass communications medium. In the future further technological advances which can increase viewer involvement in world events will be used by television. Space satellite systems such as *Intelsat;* Community Antenna Television (CATV), a means of relaying TV programs into remote areas by cable; Ultra High Frequency Broadcasting (UHF), which opens 1400 additional channels beyond the channels presently available; color television, which by 1968 served over 14 million homes; and the use of television tapes are already increasing the range and flexibility of television.

The development of the laser beam, a method of focusing and harnessing light energy, is also creating new possibilities for the mass media, particularly television. In 1969, the U.S. Air Force, interested in transmitting reconnaissance photos from a war zone to the Pentagon within minutes, developed a laser-beam scanning unit. This unit is capable of picking out the tiniest variations of a picture's light values and converting them into electronic impulses. The impulses can then be sent via satellite, and within seconds they are received by a companion laser unit and reconverted back into the original photograph—without any loss of detail or clarity. This process, if adapted by television and the other media, could transmit and develop perhaps thirty high-quality pictures taken anywhere on the globe within ten seconds. The laser beam scanning unit, which would also allow transmission of film and live programming over thousands of miles within minutes, should further intensify audience involvement in the news.

Radio, once the sole electronic medium for reaching a mass audience, has continued to grow despite the rise of television. The development of the transistor has permitted radio to travel with a listener wherever he goes. In 1922 only 100,000 radios were manufactured; by 1968 over 270 million automobile, portable, and house radios were in operation, and no end to large-scale manufacture of radios is foreseen. The American public does not seem to be losing interest in its radio stations, and in 1968 the nation's radio stations netted nearly a billion dollars in advertising revenue.

Programming

In 1963, minutes after President Kennedy was assassinated, the three major television networks interrupted their scheduled programming to cover the tragic event. From November 22, the day of the assassination, to November 25, the day of Kennedy's burial, ABC, NBC, and CBS suspended most of their programming for continual coverage of the assassination's aftermath. The national television and radio audience, stunned by the tragedy, turned to the electronic media for information about the future of their country—and they accidentally became witness to the murder of Lee Harvey Oswald, the accused assassin of President Kennedy.

Television coverage of the events following the Kennedy assassination is indicative of the opportunities and difficulties which will concern the television industry in the decades ahead. As television becomes closer to news events, in some cases broadcasting them simultaneously with their occurrence, the television audience can witness man's future triumphs, such as exploration of other planets. In other cases like the Oswald murder, complicated legal and constitutional questions arise about the possibility of a fair trial when millions of people are witness to a crime. Questions of good taste further complicate the selection of suitable television programming. There are no simple solutions to these problems and the industry is continually looking for ways to better serve the public without violating its trust. The government, having concerned itself with the content of programming and advertising in the electronic media, is also seeking some further, overall type of government regulation of the entire media and, like the print media, the electronic media are wary about government intervention. The future, hopefully, will see a clarification of the relationship between government and the mass media.

Educational Television

One facet of the electronic media which the government wishes to expand is noncommercial, educational or "public" television. The Federal Communications Commission in 1952 assigned UHF and VHF channels to 242 communities for exclusive use as noncommercial stations. Since 1952, educational television has received financial support from the Department of Health, Education, and Welfare, the Ford Foundation, and other groups interested in the development of educational television. Some schools have become deeply involved in educational radio and television, and others operate stations of their own. In 1967 the Public Broadcasting Act, based on recommendations of the Carnegie Commission, provided for the founding of The Corporation for Public Broadcasting (CPB), a nonprofit public corporation created to raise the quality of noncommercial television by granting funds to public service broadcasters. This represented the beginning of a federally subsidized public television system. With a 10 million dollar grant from the Ford Foundation, a test program, *Public Broadcast Laboratory* (*PBL*) was established in 1967 as a unit of the National Educational Television network (NET) to demonstrate the possibilities of public television. Educational television should continue to grow if the number of people willing to support a nonprofit educational enterprise also grows.

Many noncommercial television facilities gain financial help by conducting "Auctions," the proceeds of which go to the broadcasting facility.

Richard Wolfe

ADVERTISING

When a New York advertising executive was asked whether he thought advertising made people buy products they didn't need, he replied:

> If you don't think people need deodorants, you are at liberty to criticize advertising for having persuaded 87 percent of American women and 66 percent of American men to use them. If you don't think people need beer, you are right for criticizing advertising for having persuaded 58 percent of the adult population to drink it. If you disapprove of social mobility, creature comforts, and foreign travel, you are right for blaming advertising for encouraging such wickedness. If you dislike affluent society, you are right to blame advertising for inciting the masses to pursue it.
>
> David Ogilvy
> *Confessions of an Advertising Man*

As pointed out in the preceding quotation the future of advertising depends on the nation's continued economic growth. When the economy of a nation falters, a complex series of events often occurs which eventually affects all media—perhaps advertising most of all. But, barring any economic depression, the future of advertising looks bright, as shown in the Advertising Expenditures Chart on page 141.

Code of Ethics Needed

Critics of advertising, in their claims that many advertisements and commercials are annoying, offensive, exaggerated, and misleading, often further claim that advertising doesn't even provide the necessary information needed for a consumer to make an intelligent choice of the products offered. In the future, Government agencies like the Federal Trade Commission (FCC) and the Postmaster General, which have in the past questioned the honesty and good taste of much advertising, may seek to further regulate the profession. The advertising business, in response to this challenge, may try to regulate itself through three of the industry's largest advertising groups: the American Association of Advertising Agencies (AAAA), the Association of National Advertisers (ANA), and the Advertising Council. A code of ethics similar to the National Association of Broadcasters' Code of Ethics could possibly be the result of the advertising industry's concern for responsibility in advertising.

140

ESTIMATED ANNUAL
U.S. ADVERTISING EXPENDITURES: 1955–1968

(In Millions of Dollars)

SOURCES

Year	Total	Agriculture, Forestry, and Fisheries	Mining	Construction	Manufacturing	Transportation, Commun., Other Public Utilities	Wholesale Trade	Retail Trade	Trade Not Allocable	Finance, Insurance, Real Estate	Services	Business Not Allocable
1955	8,997	142	20	141	3,842	194	715	2,407	195	586	748	7
1956	9,674	138	20	149	4,151	212	782	2,548	201	626	838	9
1957	10,313	123	22	166	4,555	244	854	2,592	166	674	903	14
1958	10,414	117	20	158	4,623	261	834	2,550	171	720	949	11
1959	11,358	112	22	201	5,067	284	915	2,707	217	787	1,031	15
1960	11,900	132	27	184	5,322	318	935	2,875	165	892	1,039	11
1961	12,048	137	28	192	5,355	323	950	2,835	125	960	1,130	13
1962	12,919	146	30	209	5,734	379	985	3,070	123	1,041	1,192	10
1963	13,639	148	29	210	6,080	409	950	3,298	103	1,083	1,320	9
1964	14,571	148	30	220	6,490	438	1,040	3,515	100	1,172	1,410	8
1965	15,570	152	30	225	6,970	460	1,110	3,780	100	1,230	1,505	8
1966R	16,985	170	32	248	7,595	515	1,230	4,180	95	1,320	1,590	10
1967R	17,380	167	33	245	7,730	575	1,190	4,285	85	1,380	1,680	10
1968P	18,350	171	34	265	8,185	605	1,255	4,520	70	1,475	1,760	10

ALLOCATIONS

Year	Total	Newspapers	Magazines	Business Publications	Farm Publications	Television	Radio	Direct Mail	Outdoor	Point of Purchase Displays	Agency Income	Other Expenditures
1955	8,997	2,320	668	250	50	745	453	1,229	176	311	597	2,198
1956	9,674	2,476	680	275	53	897	480	1,308	189	345	675	2,296
1957	10,313	2,510	695	319	56	943	517	1,324	201	318	737	2,693
1958	10,414	2,459	652	302	55	1,030	523	1,419	219	344	757	2,654
1959	11,358	2,705	718	354	58	1,164	560	1,597	221	362	815	2,804
1960	11,900	2,821	769	383	55	1,269	598	1,658	239	387	859	2,862
1961	12,048	2,818	774	384	53	1,318	591	1,687	209	405	870	2,939
1962	12,919	2,930	797	378	50	1,486	636	1,758	203	416	955	3,310
1963	13,639	3,087	832	413	47	1,597	681	1,760	202	490	1,005	3,525
1964	14,571	3,350	873	451	47	1,793	732	1,873	207	554	1,075	3,616
1965	15,570	3,541	924	475	53	1,965	793	1,998	215	574	1,172	3,860
1966R	16,985	3,907	997	540	54	2,203	853	2,166	225	597	1,270	4,173
1967R	17,380	3,945	990	558	52	2,273	877	2,144	222	639	1,282	4,398
1968P	18,350	4,182	1,020	582	52	2,500	956	2,232	246	677	1,346	4,557

RRevised   PPreliminary

"If you want bread go to the bakery."

Harbaugh in the Christian Science Monitor © TCSPS

The Generation Gap

PUBLIC RELATIONS

If the Canadian communications media expert Marshall McLuhan is correct, people who were born before the advent of the electronic media and computer are very different from those born after it. This difference, or so called "generation gap," is, according to media experts, one of the results of the advances made possible by electronics in science, industry, and business. Many public relations men believe that public relations functions will help to bridge future generation gaps by communicating new changes to the various segments of the public. Informing businessmen about new and efficient techniques of organization, consulting industries on new and profitable means of production, and speaking to minority groups about increasing opportunities at colleges and universities are but some of the possible tasks for the public relations man of the future.

THE SCHOOL MEDIA

Changes in the communications media occurring outside the school should produce changes within the school. A generation of students which is made increasingly aware of its surroundings by the electronic media will probably seek to communicate its feelings and knowledge through its school publications. In the future, student involvement with problems of direct concern to students will be reflected in school publications. Recently, for example, a student in Florida used his school publication to launch a campaign

The growth of underground student publications reflects today's student awareness and concern with current problems.

Bruce Pendleton

against obscenity. Another student in New York City, unable to have printed in a school publication material he felt was relevant to fellow students, organized an underground newspaper which published folk-rock record reviews, advertisements for modern clothing, and notes on civil rights activities. In 1969 a Supreme Court decision on the free speech rights of high school students raised many questions about high school newspaper censorship and its consequent development, the growing number of student underground publications. Noted writer Fred Graham, in a *New York Times* article, noted that:

> . . . the free speech right extended by the Supreme Court to students permits school authorities to curb student rights of expression whenever there is reason to believe it would cause disorder or invade the rights of others—a restrictive standard that will give school personnel power to limit students' speech under many, and perhaps most circumstances.

In a later *Times* article, Nicholas Pileggi observed that:

> While the Court emphasized that the ruling was limited to the student's right of free speech and was limited to non-disruptive conduct only, many attorneys feel that it will make it far more difficult for school officials to censor student publications. . . .

A JOURNALIST'S EDUCATION

To train journalism students to meet the high standards set by the mass communications media, schools of public communication may well become the training grounds for future Pulitzer Prize winners. The increasing knowledge needed by editors, reporters, and newswriters, coupled with the never-ending advances in the techniques of gathering and presenting the news, will make an education at one of the many schools of journalism an indispensable requirement for aspiring journalists. Schools of journalism will provide the setting where students can discuss the technical and ethical problems they will face when they assume the responsibility of informing the public. The following statement, made in 1920 by noted political commentator and Pulitzer Prize winner Walter Lippman, becomes more significant each year:

> It is altogether unthinkable that a society like ours should remain forever dependent on untrained accidental witnesses—the better course is to send out into reporting a generation of men who will, by sheer superiority, drive the incompetents out of the business.

ACTIVITIES

1. As a class project, develop a journalism library that contains professional magazines, newspapers, and other publications relating to information about the field of journalism. *Editor and Publisher, Publisher's Weekly,* the *Public Relations Journal,* and *Printing* Magazine are some periodicals that should be considered for inclusion. If possible, have the school library subscribe to these publications. Valuable information on how to plan a future in journalism will result from diligent reading of such professional publications.

2. Contact the Newspaper Fund, Inc., of Princeton, New Jersey, to request that your name be added to their mailing list. This organization, financed by *The Wall Street Journal,* will supply free of charge a number of booklets, articles, newsletters, and scholarship information to students who desire to enter the communications field.

3. Establish a number of student teams to visit the various printing and publishing shops in your area. For example, one team could visit a small hand-press printing shop while a second team could visit a letterpress plant. A third team could observe the operations of a modern offset printing company. Planning the details for the trips should be done well in advance. Bring back samples (most companies will be happy to provide these) of printed materials, type, plates, and negatives. Have each team plan and prepare a report on its field trip. Create a display on the results of the trips for "P.T.A. Night" or "Newspaper Week."

4. Consult the appendices at the end of this book for the *Canons of Journalism,* the *Radio Code,* and the *Television Code.* Prepare a written report on whether or not you think these rules impose too strict censorship and are being followed by all members of the mass media.

5. Prepare a television commercial for the year 1999. Your teacher will divide the class into groups so that some students can draw stills, some can plan special effects, and others can prepare copy. You might wish to present your commercial as a skit. In an open class discussion, compare the final commercial with present-day TV commercials. Discuss the major changes between the two.

6. Briefly comment on each of the following:
  a. What is a specialist reporter's function today?
  b. How have labor problems caused changes in printing techniques?
  c. What news printing developments have been created in the past decade?
  d. Discuss the role and advancement of women in journalism today.
  e. How have format changes helped or hurt the reading audience?

7. Obtain copies of old issues of newspapers and magazines. Compare their content and design, advertising and editorials, with modern newspapers and magazines. Discuss the changing trends shown by the comparison, and determine the reasons for these changes.

READING

ANGEL, JUVENAL L., *Careers in Television and Radio.* World Trade Academy, New York.

BRUCKER, HERBERT, *Journalist: Eyewitness to History.* Macmillan, New York, 1962.

BRYSON, LYMAN (Ed.), *The Communication of Ideas.* Cooper Square Publishers, New York, 1964.

CLARK, WESLEY C. (Ed.), *Journalism Tomorrow.* Syracuse University Press, Syracuse, N.Y., 1958.

CLARKE, ARTHUR C., *Voices from the Sky: Previews of the Coming Space Age.* Harper & Row, New York, 1965.

GEMMIL, HENRY, AND BERNARD KILGORE (Ed.), *Do You Belong in Journalism?* Appleton-Century-Crofts, New York, 1959.

KLAPPER, JOSEPH T., *The Effects of Mass Communications.* Free Press, New York, 1960.

MUELLER, GEORGE E., AND E. R. SPANGER, *Communication Satellites.* Wiley, New York, 1964.

PARADIS, ADRIAN, *For Immediate Release: Careers in Public Relations.* McKay, New York, 1955.

SCHRAMM, WILBUR, *Communication Satellites for Education, Science and Culture.* UNESCO, United Nations, New York, 1968.

SMITH, ROGER (Ed.), *The American Reading Public: A Symposium.* Bowker, New York, 1964.

STASHEFF, GARY, *The People Look at Television: Its Direction and Production.* Hill & Wang, New York, 1968. (PB)

PART TWO

BASIC MASS MEDIA WRITING ASSIGNMENTS

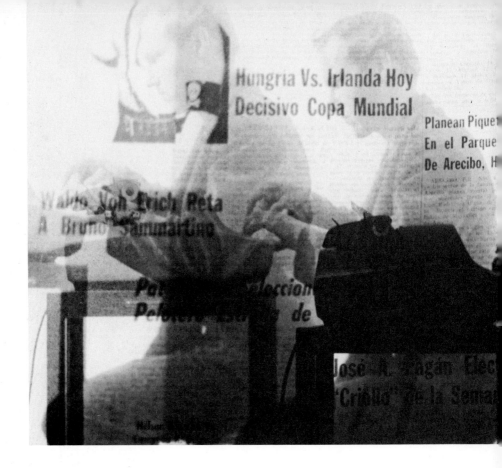

Chapter **8**

Newswriting

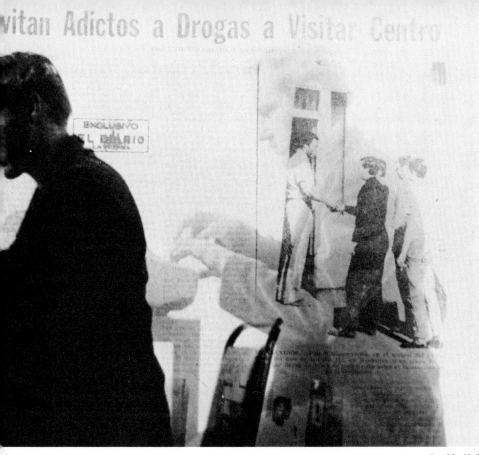

WHAT IS NEWSWRITING?

In American newspapers there is a distinct difference between news stories and editorials. Skilled newswriters, those reporters, editors, and other journalists who present the news in written form, should be careful to maintain the distinction between fact and opinion, news stories and editorials. News stories are news items, short or long, free from comment and opinion by writers and editors, that contain an accounting of the facts connected with an event. This accounting of facts attempts to explain the details of a news event, usually the *who, what, when, where, why,* and *how* of the event. Newswriting deals primarily with the written communication of such facts. Opinion (never the writer's) may appear in a news story only if it does so in the form of direct or indirect quotations and is attributed to persons either named or implied, or if the story is by-lined to indicate the opinion of the author. When a news story reflects even one opinion, no matter how indirectly, the story is said to be slanted. An editorial is any newsworthy article which attempts to interpret the news and therefore express either the writer's opinion or, in many

149

cases, his newspaper's, his publisher's, or his school's opinion. Editorials usually appear on the editorial page or are labeled as such.

News stories vary in news value, or appeal. News stories having the most news value are those that appeal to the largest number of consumers. In order to do this, newswriters capitalize on stories that contain at least one of the following news value ingredients: persons of both sexes and of all ages (especially the very young and the very old), timeliness, animals, amusement, personal appeal, adventure, love, sympathy, unusualness, progress, names, statistics, conflict, and suspense.

While most news stories present fact, not opinion, and most news values are determined by what interests the largest audience, there are other considerations beyond reader interest that should be taken into account by newswriters, reporters, and editors. Because the influence of newswriting means much in the progress of a community, a newswriter should not be content to offer only what he thinks interests the reader at the moment. He should go further and should think of matters of social concern and of the public welfare. A good newswriter should have a strong sense of obligation to arouse interest in significant news even if it is apparent that the average reader lacks such concern. Above all, a good newswriter should be a skillful questioner—an alert, thorough researcher of facts.

Skilled newswriters, in order to maintain the distinction between fact and opinion, must constantly research and verify facts.

Ron MacNeil

THE ELEMENTS OF A NEWS STORY

Newswriters, in order to present straight news stories that are relevant to the reader, take into consideration the following news elements when preparing their material.

Human Interest—Stories dealing with the basic human needs—food, clothing, and shelter—have great interest value to readers. The majority of human interest stories concern emotion. The word "emotion" covers the gamut of human responses ranging from base instincts to the highest spiritual satisfactions. Human interest stories often deal with romance, ambition, humor, sympathy, love, hate, fear, jealousy, vanity, and generosity. For example, you would have a good human-interest story—a story that would interest and involve many readers because of its timeliness and relevancy—if a reknown physician in your community believed that persons who begin smoking in high school live five years less than non-smokers.

Immediacy—News is perishable; old news lacks the interest of current news. The fresher the news, the more apt it is to capture reader interest. Newspapers that are published weekly or monthly often present, as news, information that is not timely. Many newspaper editors avoid publishing untimely news by becoming informed in advance about events planned to take place when the paper is published. For instance, background articles are often presented about films scheduled to begin when the paper comes out. Important stories that break after a paper's deadline are usually given feature treatment in later editions.

Proximity—A newswriter should write about personalities and issues relevant to the interests of his reading audience; readers are usually more interested in news about themselves and about problems directly related to themselves, their families, and their friends than they are in reading about unfamiliar people and unfamiliar situations.

Prominence—Articles about celebrities make good copy—readers enjoy news about well-known people. Human behavior is harder to interpret than fact, and readers respond to news about people in a more emotional way than they respond to news about events. In writing straight news stories about people, good newswriters remain objective and guard against showing personal feelings and prejudices in their articles. Editors are constantly on guard against news items concerning prominent people that contain innuendo, gossip, or slander. Often, background material on prominent people can be obtained by researching magazines, books, or the electronic media.

If you should have the opportunity to interview a celebrity, use quotations from the interview—quotations tell much about what a person is like, and many of the more famous performing artists and politicians often owe a part of their popularity to their colorful use of the English language. Prominent citizens in the community often have much to say that is relevant, important, and of interest to the general population.

Conflict—A news story of a conflict between two persons sparks reader interest. If a conflict story involves verbal confrontation, the persons involved should be accurately quoted. If one party mangles phrases and misplaces modifiers, don't try to cover up such mistakes—use direct quotations. For background material on the conflict, thoroughly research your sources for reliability and accuracy of facts. In any controversy, newswriters try to be as objective as possible by presenting the *what* approach to both sides of the situation and, with careful handling, taking the *why* approach to both the situation and the participant's arguments. Objectivity, always important in unbiased news reporting, is especially important when covering news events that contain the element of conflict.

Emotion—Good newswriting, while neither sentimental nor melodramatic, may often be emotional. Newswriters can stimulate readers by arousing their emotions. For example, an "emotion" story could deal with the plight of the high school dropout. In preparing such a story, the newswriter could ask several dropouts whether or not they would be willing to let him use their names. He would find out what they have been doing since they left school, who their friends are now, whether or not they regret having dropped out, how much money they earn, and what their advice is to students who are thinking of leaving school. The writer could ask employment counselors for advice for potential dropouts. He could present information about how much money a high school graduate can expect to make in a lifetime compared to expected earnings for dropouts, and explain the differences between the jobs that are available to high school and college graduates as compared to jobs available for nongraduates.

Consequence—It is important that newswriters become concerned and informed about the social problems and public welfare matters that make a difference in the lives of their readers. Noted columnist Bob Considine has said that, second only to the clergy, newsmen have the opportunity to help their community formulate a sense of values. By facing such relevant issues as the draft system or racial discrimination, and by dealing with subjects of consequence to members of the community and to the world-at-large—such as peace or the population problem—your school newspaper can help its readers decide the direction they want their lives to take.

GATHERING THE NEWS

While it can be said that news is wherever we see it, most media news-writers do not randomly pick up all kinds of general, unrelated facts expecting that such material will make good copy. The job of gathering usable news for any of the mass media calls for a general awareness of news values, a well-developed sense of selectivity in choosing human-interest angles, an awareness of what is considered good taste, and an ability to organize thoughts and facts. The newswriter is further guided in his choice of news by using material which generally falls into either of the following two categories: 1) specific news beat or other assignments given to him by an editor, and 2) unassigned stories seen or covered by the newswriter on his own.

Newswriters, constant researchers of facts, must be thorough in their organization and presentation of such facts. Organized newswriting involves both incidents and contacts with people in general that are often interesting enough to make news. Such incidents and contacts are a part of the newswriter's news sources. Newswriting for a school newspaper is, in many ways, similar to mass media newswriting: constant contact with administrators, teachers, fellow students, student body leaders, activity supervisors, coaches, and other such responsible persons must be maintained. The news sources developed by newswriters are their most important sources of information.

Printable and Unprintable News

Basically, printable news concerns ideas, events, and people. Stories about these ideas, events, and people should be presented as interestingly as possible in order to interest as many readers as possible. If this presentation is well thought out, a great many readers may be attracted to a story that might otherwise be boring. If the definition of "new" is followed, there is no such thing as "unprintable news." However, there *is* such a thing as unprintable rumor, unprintable libel, unprintable falsehood, and unprintable maliciousness. Student and professional reporters and editors have the responsibility to ignore stories that are inaccurate, unfair, one-sided, and in poor taste. Journalism is no place for any person who is foul-mouthed, malicious, irresponsible, or inaccurate. More on this subject will be dealt with in Chapter 14, "Social Responsibility of Journalists."

WRITING THE NEWS

Read the following straight news story, carefully noting the placement of facts in each paragraph:

EXAMPLE:

TENNIS LESSONS SCHEDULED FOR SATURDAYS

Youngsters from ages eight to fourteen wishing to learn how to play tennis will be given free lessons supervised by Coach LeRoy H. Smith from 9 to 11 a.m. on Saturdays at the L. J. Brooks Building, West 4th Street, South End, beginning on June 10th, announced Parks and Recreation Director Donald M. Johns.

The program, conducted by City Tennis Club Coach LeRoy H. Smith, former Olympic tennis coach, will be held in cooperation with the Park Department.

The instruction is intended for city children interested in learning and developing tennis skills. Funds from Project Inner-City have been set aside for equipment and facilities.

Coach Smith advised interested participants to register early. A large turnout is expected.

Had the preceding straight news story appeared in a metropolitan daily the average reader would probably have read only the first paragraph, which contains most of the important facts of the story. The opening paragraph tells *who* is concerned in the story—"youngsters from ages eight to fourteen." It tells *what* the story is about—"free tennis lessons." It tells *when*—"from 9 to 11 a.m. on Saturdays beginning on June 10th." The *where* is answered by the words "at the L. J. Brooks Building, West 4th Street, South End," and the *why* is explained by "wishing to learn to play tennis." The reader will understand the *how* from "supervised by Coach LeRoy H. Smith." The *who, what, when, where, why,* and *how* are summarized in the first paragraph. This first section is called the lead—the introduction. On a short news story the lead generally appears in the first paragraph, while in longer news stories it is often contained in the first two or three paragraphs.

Having completed the first paragraph, the reader probably has many unanswered questions concerning the facts given in the lead. The second paragraph in the EXAMPLE expands the *who* of the story by giving facts about Coach Smith, while the third and fourth paragraphs extend the *what* by giving details about the fund and more information about the tennis lessons. The *where* is obvious and needs no explanation. If the newswriter had wished to make the news story longer he might have expanded on the *why* by giving further details concerning the need for tennis lessons and maybe supplying a quotation by Coach Smith.

From the EXAMPLE we see that the body of the story is developed logically through the addition of more details about points connected with or mentioned in the lead. The paragraphs are arranged in order of importance of details. The following Checklist notes the essential characteristics of the straight news story form, whether the story is a routine editorial asssignment for the newswriter or a resourceful discovery of his own.

154

CHECKLIST FOR MAJOR ELEMENTS IN A STRAIGHT NEWS STORY

1. In a straight news story all of the important facts are summarized in the first section, or lead. The lead is often presented in only one sentence or paragraph.

2. The body of the story consists of facts that amplify or add to the statements in the lead. Usually these facts answer questions that come naturally to the reader's mind after he has read the lead.

3. Within the body of the news story the facts are arranged in descending order of importance, the least important facts coming last.

The typical straight news story, then, has an inverted pyramid form, with the most important facts appearing first and the least important appearing last (see EXAMPLE of the inverted pyramid form, page 158.) Straight news stories which conform to the inverted pyramid form, the most conventional arrangement for all news stories, do so for the following reasons: they are easier to shorten since material can be deleted from the end; hurried readers can "get the facts" by just reading the lead; the inverted pyramid tells the story in a "natural" way; the inverted pyramid reflects our modern society —a society that is concerned with getting the basic facts as quickly as possible rather than being concerned with details.

Writing the Lead

The most important part of the straight news story is a clear, concise statement that presents the basic facts of the story. This statement is called the lead. If the lead is weak or fails to present the basic facts of the story, the story usually fails in encouraging the reader to read the rest of the story.

Types of Leads

The three types of news story leads are the major idea lead, the summary lead, and a combination of the two. In deciding which lead to use, the writer first weighs each of the facts he has secured for his story. Then, he asks himself: "Which of the facts constitutes the most important 'maker of news'?"

Each of the makers of news is analyzed from the standpoint of reader interest, and the writer's personal opinion is relatively unimportant. After weighing the makers of news, the writer then asks himself a second question: "Which of the five W's and the H is most important to the reader?"

The Major Idea Lead—If, of all the facts secured for a story, one fact seems far more important than the others, the writer should use this fact in his lead. The others will be used later in the story, or discarded if unimportant.

EXAMPLE:

> The Student Council voted Monday to charge a $5 student fee.

The Summary Lead—If several facts are of about equal value, the writer should briefly combine these facts in his lead.

EXAMPLE:

> The Student Council proposed Monday a $5 student fee, the establishment of a History Club, and a change in the name of the school newspaper.

The Combination (or Features Summary) Lead—On occasion, the reporter may start his first sentence with the major idea, and then elaborate on the other facts in the rest of the sentence.

EXAMPLE:

> Students will have to pay a $5 student fee as a result of Monday's action by the Student Council, which also proposed formation of a History Club and a change in the school newspaper's name from *The Record* to *The Jacksonian*.

From the following EXAMPLE, determine what is the lead and explain its purpose. Is it an example of a major idea lead, a summary lead, or a combination lead? Then, read the rest of the article and be prepared to answer the questions that follow it.

156

EXAMPLE:

CITY SHUTTING ITS HIPPIE CENTER, WHICH OFFERED YOUTH "FREEDOM"

By Peter Kihss

The city is closing its Operation Hippie Free Store, which has been open since June at 14 Cooper Square to aid what the store director called "voluntary dropouts from society."

From a peak attendance of 300 on weekdays and 450 on Saturdays last summer, the hippies dropping in have dwindled in recent days to 18. A $40,000 city allocation had been budgeted for four months, but the sum was stretched to carry on until Nov. 15.

In a report to the staff of the Human Resources Administration, Mitchell I. Ginsberg, the Administrator, said the Free Store had "sought to serve as a bridge between society and these young people." He said every effort should be made to reopen such a project next summer.

A "Freedom" Available

The Free Store had a washing machine, two showers, a record player and a television set, and it served as an exchange where people could leave old clothes that the hippies could take free.

"We let the youngsters have a freedom they were unable to find in other youth centers," said Herbert Moore, 38-year-old director for the Youth Services Agency. "They drew pictures on the wall, wrote poems. They came in to write books and letters."

Mr. Moore said the store program had helped reunite 25 or 30 youths with their families, out of some 200 for whom parents were searching.

"I thought it was a very positive operation," he said. "The Lower East Side is a very volatile community. We were able to find youngsters jobs, keep them off the streets where a lot of crime was being committed."

Mr. Moore estimated that the number of "mainstay hippies" in the East Village might still be as high as last spring—"as a wild guess, 1,000 to 2,000," a figure that he said had multiplied five to eight times during the summer.

"When we went down there," he said, "youngsters were sleeping in the streets, on rooftops, in hallways. They were coming in from all over—California and Idaho. When we first opened, we found it was unreasonable to close. We were open 24 hours a day up to about the middle of August."

Mr. Moore said the store staff had consisted of one other Youth Services Agency member in addition to himself and eight hippies recruited from the neighborhood. In addition about 20 Neighborhood Youth Corps enrollees were used during the summer, and the store channeled 20 to 25 other corps youths to churches and non-profit groups, he said.

The operation's best-known aide was Abbie Hoffman, a leader of the Yippies Youth International Party. A Human Resources Administration spokesman said Mr. Hoffman worked 17 days between July 15 and Sept. 20 as a consultant who provided "insights" at $40 a day.

157

How much of the article did you have to read to find out its basic news content? Look at the article again, and determine which paragraphs answer the *who, what, when, where, why,* and *how* questions. What are the implications of the last paragraph? Do you consider the article an example of slanted news? If so, how is it slanted? If not, why not?

The Inverted Pyramid Style

While many professional newspapers require that their news stories be written in the inverted pyramid style, others allow for a more liberal structure. The inverted pyramid writing style is illustated in the following straight news story:

EXAMPLE:

The Lead—a summary of all important facts.

Leonard Schwartz, noted authority on teenage crime, will be the guest speaker at Thursday's all-student assembly in Hickman Auditorium.

The Body—details of secondary importance in descending order of importance.

In his talk Mr. Schwartz, author of "Teenage Crime in Our Cities," will compare American teenagers with European teenagers.

Recently returned from Europe, Mr. Schwartz has been making a speaking tour of the country's leading schools and colleges.

There will be a brief question-and-answer period following Mr. Schwartz's talk.

Newswriting Mechanics

Most newswriters use the following general procedures when preparing news material:

1. Use 8½ by 11 unlined paper leaving a one-inch margin on both sides, top, and bottom.

2. Type your name and a slug line (story identification, usually a word or two summarizing the story) at the top left-hand corner of the page.

3. Type the name of the proposed publication under this information.

EXAMPLE:

Jones, Charles
Student Proposal
Wendona Journal

4. Begin the body copy for the first page about one-third of the way down from the top of the page. The editor will later use this space for the story headlines and for printer's instructions.

5. Double or triple-space your body copy so that there will be room to edit between the lines.

6. If the story takes more than one page, type the word "more" at the bottom of the first page, centered. At the top left-hand corner of page two repeat the slug line, the name of the publication, and add the manuscript page number "2," or "page 2 of two pages," or the word "add." If the story runs longer than two pages repeat this procedure (changing the page numbers) at the bottom and top of each of the following pages.

7. Indicate the end of the article by typing the word "end," or by using symbols such as "–0–0–0–," or "#####," or "30," on a separate line.

Elements of Style in Newswriting

The written word is the newswriter's medium. Because the newswriter's basic intent is to communicate, the newswriter must be proficient in writing. Most newswriters develop a style which is simple, concise, and lucid. Which of the following two sentences "gets the message across" more effectively? Which of the preceding elements of style makes it better news copy?

1. Each of the teachers shall endeavor to notify all of the student violators that they are to consider themselves suspended until they receive a signal of clearance from the principal's office.

2. Teachers should inform students that if they are suspended, they should not return to school until they have been notified by the principal.

Sometimes newswriters inadvertently write something they do not mean. Results may be humorous or disastrous. What errors in structure cause confusion in the following sentences? How would you correct these errors?

1. They worked with a shovel in one hand, and a gun in the other, and a Bible in the other.

2. John Larson said he found France a wonderful country, especially the museums. When he stood in the Louvre he had really thought he was in paradise until he turned and saw his wife standing by his side.

3. It won't be real Irish stew unless you put your heart into it.

4. No one can take anything from the bookshelves except a librarian.

5. The new reporter wanted to write very badly.

Improving Your Newswriting

Beginning newswriters often make errors, even when trying to write simply. After observing the most common writing infractions made by new reporters, several newspaper editors, magazine editors, and writing teachers compiled the following checklist:

Spelling—Spelling was not standardized in America until *Webster's Dictionary* was first published in 1806. Readers, assuming that the spelling used by newspapers was correct, used them as a guide for spelling. English spelling is often difficult because some words sound different than they look. The pronunciation of *ough*, for instance, is different in *tough, though* and *through* but the sounds are written the same way. The vowel sounds for *ouch* and *owl*, however, are the same but the letter combinations are different. Errors in spelling often change the meaning of a sentence, as:

> Miss Davenport wore her great-grandmother's bridle out
> fit and the groom was attired in mourning dress.

Spelling mistakes can confuse meaning, distract the reader, and hamper reading speed. Spelling errors often result from carelessness, reluctance to check a dictionary, and not proofreading copy thoroughly. Writing is a skill and good newswriting is the result of a discipline which has no room for carelessness. If you have difficulty spelling words such as *questionnaire, occurred,* and *accommodate,* you should make an effort to memorize the proper spellings. You may want to make a list of problem words from which you can study correct spellings.

Hyphenation of Compound Words—Modern newswriters hyphenate two or more words when used in combination as one word or as a unit modifier:

> The pilot of the twin-engine plane seemed to lose control
> following loss of radio contact.

Twin-engine is hyphenated because both words are used together as a single adjective to modify *plane*. The aircraft is neither a *twin plane* nor an *engine plane*. Many words, through accepted usage, have been combined as one word, and it is often difficult to determine if you're dealing with one or two words. *Teenage*, for example, is sometimes hyphenated, sometimes not. It is always wise, of course, to consult a dictionary when problems arise. To avoid inconsistencies, most publications have their own style sheet, a listing of the publication's usage preference for problem words and terms.

Punctuation of Nonrestrictive Clauses—You might want to substitute the word *not* for *non* and the word *essential* for *restrictive* when referring to nonrestrictive and restrictive clauses. Use commas to punctuate a clause that is not essential to the meaning of a sentence, if the sentence makes sense without the clause. Do not use commas if the clause is necessary to the meaning of the sentence. Following are examples of sentences containing nonrestrictive and restrictive clauses:

> The reporter, who is the backbone of the newspaper staff,
> has a responsibility to the community.

Because *who is the backbone of the newspaper staff* is not essential to the meaning of the sentence, commas should be used. But commas should not be used in the following sentence:

> The reporter who cannot type is at a disadvantage.

Deleting the restrictive clause *who cannot type* leaves *The reporter is at a disadvantage,* changing the original meaning of the sentence by stating that every reporter (as opposed to the reporter who cannot type) is at a disadvantage.

Spelling of the Possessive Case—To form the singular possessive, add an apostrophe and an *s:*

> She does her homework on her brother's new typewriter.

When a singular or plural pronoun already ends in *s* most grammarians suggest adding the apostrophe after the final *s:*

> It was Lars' typewriter, not her sister Bess', that she used.

To form the plural possessive of nouns ending in *s*, add the apostrophe after the *s:*

> The officers' names on the artists' petitions were submitted
> at the engineers' ball.

Many journalism students have trouble with the indefinite pronoun *it.* Because the word is vague and, therefore, weak, the student should avoid using *it* whenever possible. The possessive form of *it* is *its*—without the apostrophe. The only time the apostrophe and *s* are used with *it* is to indicate the contraction for *it is* or *it has:*

> It's time for its first issue to hit the newsstands.

Agreement Between Subject and Verb—A plural subject must have a plural verb. But for many newswriters confusion arises when compound subjects are used:

> The old news clipping and the photograph that Emily found in the attic were musty and faded with age.

A careless writer might change *were* to *was*. Why would he be mistaken? A similar problem often occurs with the word *none:*

> None of the lettermen was at the banquet sponsored by local newswriters.

When the meaning is "not one," the word *none* is singular—even when it is followed by a prepositional phrase that ends in a plural noun.

Punctuation of Direct Quotations—Enclose direct quotations within quotation marks. The end-of-sentence punctuation precedes the final quotation mark:

> "Tom is the editor," the advisor said, "and policy decisions are up to him."

To punctuate one quotation within another, use single punctuation marks for the internal quotation and double quotation marks for the overall quotation:

> John lamented, "The editor told me, 'We've missed the deadline.'"

Why is the punctuation in the next sentence different from the punctuation in the first example in this paragraph?

> The advisor said that because Tom was the editor policy decisions were up to him.

Agreement Between Pronoun and Antecedent—Every pronoun must refer to an antecedent. If the pronoun refers to the wrong antecedent or to no apparent antecedent, the meaning becomes obscure. In the following sentence the word *his* refers to the singular noun *senior:*

> Any senior who has not cleared his library card will not receive his diploma.

162

Use the masculine pronoun when you are referring to both males and females; do not write *his and her*. . . . The repetition of *his and her* is tedious. Use a plural verb and the plural pronoun when using a collective noun to refer to a group of individuals:

> The team are adjusting their helmets.

Dangling Participles and Misplaced Modifiers—What is the difference in meaning between these two sentences?

> I saw the monkey hanging from the chandelier.
> Hanging from the chandelier I saw the monkey.

What in the word order determines who the reader will think is doing the hanging from the chandelier? To avoid confusion of meaning, place the modfiier (adjective, adverb, verbal, or phrase) immediately before or after the word it modifies.

Fragments—Why does the following clause leave you with a sense of incompleteness?

> While at the same time proposing long-range reforms to improve housing, health, civil rights, and to curb the rising crime rate throughout the country.

This fragment can be changed into a main clause or complete sentence by taking out one word, adding one word, and changing one verb ending.

> At the same time Congress proposes long-range reforms to improve housing, health, civil rights, and to curb the rising crime rate throughout the country.

Conciseness—Do not use a phrase if a single word conveys the same idea. For example, instead of writing "tendered his resignation," write "resigned." What phrase in the following sentence could be expressed by one word?

> The couple was united in holy matrimony yesterday.

A complete sentence should contain a subject and a main verb. In modern journalism, however, sentence fragments are often used effectively in the writing of news headlines, summary leads, and fiction.

The following list was compiled by a journalism student as a reminder of the types of writing infractions he hoped to avoid. Read the list carefully. Then, rewrite it in concise, lucid terms.

1. In my opinion, I think that as a writer when I am writing I shouldn't get into the habit of making use of too many unnecessary words that I don't really need in order to get my message across to the reader who is reading my writing.
2. Each pronoun agrees with their antecedent.
3. Watch out for irregular verbs which has creeped into our language.
4. About sentence fragments.
5. Verbs has to agree with their subjects.
6. It's trouble was that I didn't use apostrophes' right.
7. When dangling, don't use participles in sentences.
8. A clause, which is needed for the meaning of a sentence, should not be set off by commas.

GUIDELINES FOR REWRITING

In the preparation of any article for a newspaper or magazine, or in preparing copy for an advertisement or public relations brochure, the average writer usually does at least two rewrites before submitting his story to the editor. After conferring with the editor about his article, the writer may wish to do still another rewrite. In rewriting, the writer should correct any mistakes in spelling, grammar, and punctuation. Tim Cohane, professional writer, gives his students the following nine guidelines for rewriting:

1. Eliminate every word not necessary for clarity and grace. This, in itself, is quite a task. The best pro who ever lived, or ever will, couldn't escape it. It is even possible that the authors of the *Old* and *New Testaments* had to rewrite to eliminate verbosity.
2. Check all verb forms to make certain that you have used the active voice as often as possible.
3. If the situation calls for the passive, the verb "to be," or the participle, O.K. —then use it. But first, examine it carefully.
4. Check your paragraphs carefully to see if they are in the proper order. Does paragraph 6 belong up between paragraphs 2 and 3? Perhaps paragraph 8 will make a stronger lead than the lead you have. If so, don't hesitate to change it. Whenever paragraph sequence poses a major problem, consider scissoring each paragraph, and then rearranging them on the table like blocks.
5. Check the sentences within each paragraph to make sure the thoughts are in the proper sequence. Numbering the sentences can prove helpful.

6. Check every sentence closely to see if it can be invigorated by placing the main thought at the end.

7. Check transitions between sentences and paragraphs. Are they as smooth and as immediate as you can make them? Transition probably contributes more to smoothness than any other single factor.

8. Never hesitate to strive for the off-beat, the unorthodox, the picturesque. No matter how many times you fall on your face reaching, pick yourself up and try again. First, however, get it clearly in mind what you want to bring off. Get a true picture of the picture, and see if it is going to work. Your chances of bringing off the picturesque are much better once you have become acquainted with form—and the best way to learn form is to first learn how to put things clearly and simply.

9. Be conscious of the value of parallel forms, but don't overuse them. Don't overuse anything. Writing is nothing without variety. Without variety, the sound of writing becomes a dull thumping.

NEWS BRIEFS

Since names make news, editors often use a number of news briefs that include names. Such news briefs are usually one or two sentences long and are often used to fill news columns. Many editors use news briefs to relieve the monotony of long news stories.

EXAMPLE:

A sophomore beat out the upperclassmen in MAA math competition as Dave LeMaster earned the top score of 58.25. Senior Bill Lipp finished second.

The Lancer
Arlington High School, Indianapolis, Indiana

WRITING CAPTIONS

Captions (sometimes called cutlines) are the identifying lines of print accompanying photographs and illustrations. If an illustration is used without an accompanying article, the story must be briefly told in the caption using the five *W*'s and the *H*. The reporter assigned to write captions must be careful with identifications and the spelling of names. He should always double-check to make sure the right name has been used, and that it is spelled correctly.

165

EXAMPLE:

EXAMPLE:

Student Council officers for next year were installed at a ceremony May 14 in the auditorium. The new officers are, l. to r.: Tom L. Jurkowski, treasurer; Marilee Wilson, secretary; Barbara Marie Fingaldo, vice-president; and Martin J. McGee, president.

NEWSWRITING FOR THE ELECTRONIC MEDIA

The major difference between writing for the electronic media and the print media is the length of the story. After covering a major story for a newspaper, a reporter may write 1000 words or more while the newscaster may use but a dozen sentences to summarize the same event. The newswriter must write with the listener and viewer in mind and must, therefore, use simple, direct terms. The writer for the electronic media usually does not place the most important facts at the beginning of his story, but places them later to be sure to catch the listener's attention.

Radio—The radio newsman arriving at the scene of the event, like the newspaper reporter, must first secure the answers to the five *W*'s and the *H*. He then might tape record the voices of those involved in the event, attempting to have these people tell the story in their own words. Next, he writes a "lead-in" as an introduction to the story, summarizing the main points. In his conclusion the radio newsman again summarizes the major events, but in more detail, and adds any additional details or developments necessary for a complete presentation of facts.

Huntley-Brinkley newscast showing Brinkley on monitor in background.

NBC News

Television—Writing for television news programs is similar to writing for radio news programs. There is, however, a difference in coverage. Instead of using a tape recorder, the television reporter uses a camera. Often, he has a cameraman film the entire scene, and then has the witnesses filmed as they tell the story. The television newscaster writes his news story in the same way the radio newsman does. The television newscaster may be "on-camera" for but a few seconds, usually during the story lead and possibly again at the story's conclusion. As the newscaster tells the story, the viewer will see the scenes being described. Then, the eyewitnesses tell their stories and, finally, the newscaster appears to give the conclusion, or "wrap-up."

ACTIVITIES

1. Bring to class one example of a straight news story representing *fact* and one example of a brief editorial representing *opinion*. Be prepared to read your examples aloud in class, explaining the differences between fact and opinion.

2. Check several newspaper articles which demonstrate the different news value appeals. Choose the best examples of each type of appeal and bring them to class. Combine and catalog them with examples collected by your classmates and, as a combined effort with your classmates, select the one article that uses the most news value appeals.

3. From newspapers and magazines select one news story that best demonstrates the inverted pyramid structure. Cut out each paragraph of the story. On the back of each piece number its order of importance in the story, starting with *1, 2,* etc. Scramble the paragraphs and bring them to class for other class members to arrange in the correct order of importance.

4. Compile a list of subject areas and topics you think your school newspaper should deal with. Then, conduct an informal survey to find out what topics other students want to read about in the school newspaper. From this combined information compile a master list of topics and issues you can submit to your school newspaper editor.

5. Discuss the student relevance of each topic and the possible methods of fact-finding for each topic contained in the master list prepared for Activity *4.* Choose the one topic that most interests you and carry out a fact-finding mission, checking for the possibility of any previously published source material. Bring your notes to class and discuss any problems you might have encountered.

6. Using the topic chosen for Activity 5 as the basis, prepare an outline for a straight news story. Remember to place your most important facts first and your least important facts last.

7. Using the outline you prepared in Activity 6, expand your material into an inverted pyramid style straight news story.

8. Look at the news pictures on pages 168 and 169. Write brief, appropriate newspicture captions for each of the pictures.

READING

BARNOUW, ERIK, *The Television Writer*. Hill & Wang, New York, 1962.
———, *Tower of Babel: A History of Broadcasting in the United States, Volume 1: to 1933*. Oxford University Press, New York, 1964. (PB)
BECK, ARNOLD H. W., *Words and Waves: An Introduction to Electrical Communications*. McGraw-Hill, New York, 1967. (PB)
BERNSTEIN, THEODORE, *The Careful Writer*. Atheneum, New York, 1965.
———, *Watch Your Language*. Crown, New York, 1958.
BRIER, WARREN J., AND HOWARD C. HEYN, *Writing for Newspapers and News Services*. Funk & Wagnalls, New York, 1969.
BUSH, CHILTON A., *Newswriting and Reporting Public Affairs*. Chilton Book Co., Philadelphia, Pa., 1965.
CAIN, THOMAS H., *Common Sense About Writing*. Prentice-Hall, Englewood Cliffs, N.J., 1967.
CAMPBELL, LAURENCE R., AND ROLAND E. WOLSELEY, *How to Report and Write the News*. Prentice-Hall, Englewood Cliffs, N.J., 1961.
CHARNLEY, MITCHELL V., *Reporting*. Holt, Rinehart & Winston, New York, 1966.
COPPLE, NEALE, *Depth Reporting*. Prentice-Hall, Englewood Cliffs, N.J., 1964.
DICKSON, FRANK A. (Ed.), *Writer's Digest Handbook of Article Writing*. Holt, Rinehart & Winston, New York, 1967.
ENGLISH, EARL, AND CLARENCE HACH, *Scholastic Journalism*, 4th Ed., Iowa State Universtiy Press, Ames, Iowa. (PB)
FLESCH, RUDOLF, *The Art of Readable Writing*. Collier, New York, 1949. (PB)
FOLLETT, WILSON, *Modern American Usage*. Hill & Wang, New York, 1966.
GROSS, GERALD (Ed.), *Editors on Editing*. Grosset & Dunlap, New York, 1962.
HALL, EDWARD T., *The Silent Language*. Doubleday, New York, 1959. (PB)
HANSEN, CARL, ET AL, *Handbook for Young Writers*. Prentice-Hall, Englewood Cliffs, N.J., 1965.
JOHNSON, STANLEY P., *The Complete Reporter*. Macmillan, New York, 1965.
MacDOUGALL, CURTIS D., *Interpretive Reporting*. Macmillan, New York, 1968.
———, *Understanding Public Opinion*. Wm. D. Brown, Dubuque, Iowa, 1966.

MOTT, GEORGE F. (Ed.), *New Survey of Journalism*. Barnes & Noble, New York, 1961. (PB)

NEAL, ROBERT M., *News Gathering and News Writing*. Prentice-Hall, Englewood Cliffs, N.J., 1949.

NORWOOD, J. E., *Concerning Words and Phrasing*. Prentice-Hall, Englewood Cliffs, N.J., 1956. (PB)

RUCKER, BRYCE W., *Twentieth Century Reporting at Its Best*. Iowa State University Press, Ames, Iowa, 1964.

STRUNK, WILLIAM, JR., AND E. B. WHITE, *The Elements of Style*. Macmillan, New York, 1965. (PB)

VAN LAAN, THOMAS V., AND ROBERT B. LYONS (Ed.), *Language and the Newsstand*. Scribner, New York, 1968. (PB)

WARREN, CARL N., *Modern News Reporting*. Harper & Row, New York, 1959.

WICKER, TOM, *JFK and LBJ: The Influence of Personality on Politics*. Morrow, New York, 1968.

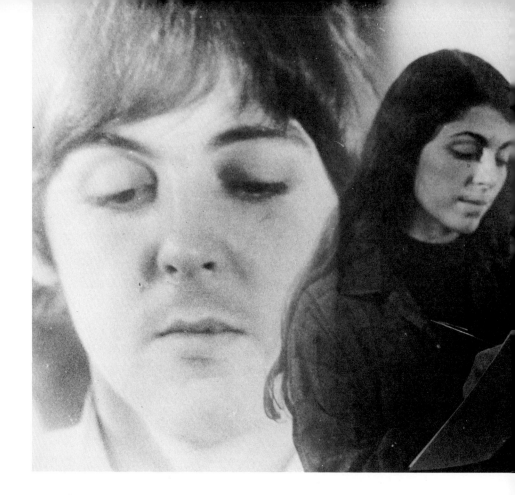

Chapter **9**

Interviewing

WHERE IT ALL BEGAN

Human beings have always been inquisitive by nature. Since the beginning of mankind they have attempted to satisfy their curiosities by questioning—or interviewing. In the *Bible*, the first woman can be said to have been interviewed in the Garden of Eden when the serpent asked Eve:

"Did God say, 'You shall not eat of any tree of the garden'?"

Purpose of Interview Stories

Mass media interviews are conducted mainly to gather all possible newsworthy information and facts concerning news situations of reader interest, and to present such information as news. Most mass media news stories are based on news and information obtained from questions asked by interviewers or newswriters. Because straight news stories often leave many of the detailed questions of a news event unanswered, many consumers of the mass media—not having access to those people who could answer their questions—rely on newswriters to supply additional information with more in-depth interview stories. Many mass media interview stories, in order to answer any further questions consumers may have, are presented as sidebars to the factual accounts contained in straight news presentations. The major portion of most interview stories concerns what the person being interviewed has to say.

TYPES OF INTERVIEW STORIES

Interview stories can be categorized under any of the following general classifications: the fact interview, the man-in-the-street interview, the question-and-answer interview, the biographical interview, the historical interview story, the descriptive interview story, the personality interview story, and the composite interview story.

The Fact Interview—The writer's purpose in conducting a fact interview is to obtain the facts connected with a news story, or to obtain any additional facts about a news event that might be of general interest to readers, thereby possibly shedding new light on a situation. To obtain the facts concerning a news event such as an accident, the reporter should interview victims (when possible), hospital attendants, policemen, witnesses, and any other persons involved. The more facts the reporter can obtain, the better his story will be. Unless a story is based on clearly defined facts obtained from interviews, it will lose its interest and validity. For example, a beginning reporter, assigned to do a fact-interview story about a woman whose car had been struck by a train while she was driving across a railroad crossing, submitted a story to his editor before he had conducted thorough interviews. The editor, questioning the article, asked the reporter the questions an average reader might ask: "Where was the woman going?" "Where was the woman coming from?" "Did the woman drive across the tracks often?" The reporter continued his interviewing and discovered that the woman had been enroute from home to her work in a charity hospital and that, because once before she had almost been struck by a train, she feared having to drive across railroad tracks.

The additional facts learned by the reporter during these further interviews paid off. He included them in his rewritten story, and presented the editor with a more interesting news preparation.

The Man-in-the-Street Interview—Beginning reporters usually consider the man-in-the-street interview to be the easiest type of interview assignment to prepare. Usually, the reporter conducts this type of interview by asking the same question of several randomly selected people. Some newspapers stand-
174

ardize the man-in-the-street interview by using a basic form similar to the one in the following EXAMPLE:

EXAMPLE:

> *The Question*—What do you think of the proposed busing policy?
> *The Answer*—Harold Wilson, senior: "It's good up to a point. However, . . ."

The Question-and-Answer Interview—Many readers, feeling that straight news presentations are often slanted, prefer to "judge for themselves" from the straight-forward presentations contained in question-and-answer interviews. The success of these interviews is dependent on the choice of questions asked, and the reporter must put considerable thought into his preparation for conducting such an interview. If the questions are not interesting, the interview will probably be dull. Usually, this type of interview involves the questioning of a prominent person, and the background for these stories is often contained in an Editor's Note preceding the transcript of the actual interview. Many reporters use tape recorders during these interviews.

EXAMPLE:

> *EDITOR'S NOTE:* A report issued last week points out that Mountainview High School spent $836 per pupil last year. *The Record* interviewed Principal Hagan on this subject. What follows is the unedited transcript of the interview.
> *Record*—We're interested in how the $836 per pupil spent at Mountainview compares with that spent per pupil by other high schools in the state.
> *Hagan*—This figure compares most favorably. In fact, as far as expenditures per pupil, we're in the top ten percent of all high schools in the state. . . .

The Biographical Interview—When the story emphasis is based on the life of the interviewee, the story is termed a biographical interview story. Such stories present many facts concerning the interviewee's background.

EXAMPLE:

> Father Humberto Galizar gave up a fascinating career in Hollywood 10 years ago to join the priesthood and come to teach at Christian High School—but there's still a lot of actor left in the padre. . . . (The account goes on to contrast the priest's two lives by presenting and comparing facts from the priest's past life with his present life.)

The Historical Interview Story—Reporters often consider doing an historical interview story when they wish to bring the reader up-to-date on an event that happened a number of years ago. One way to make an "old" story timely is to use the following approach. The example was prepared by a student reporter who interviewed a chemistry teacher regarding a serious chemistry laboratory explosion that had taken place fifteen years ago.

EXAMPLE:

> Fifteen years ago today an explosion in the Weirton High School chemistry lab resulted in serious injury to five students. The tragedy was recalled last week by Mr. J. B. Haskins, who was in the lab at the time. . . .

The Descriptive Interview Story—If either the physical appearance of the interviewee or the locale of the interview is more important than what the interviewee has to say, the reporter might want to handle the interview as a descriptive interview story. For example, an interview with an engineer at the Cape Kennedy launching pad site could emphasize the sights and sounds seen and heard by the reporter. Similarly, an interview with a 400-pound circus sideshow performer could stress the performer's appearance. The following interview, conducted with a waitress at a youth recreation center, stresses the mood, atmosphere, and decor of the center.

EXAMPLE:

> In a quiet, dark booth at the Center, with syncopated musical beats forming the background, you can sit and talk with a date any night of the week. The whole atmosphere is familiar to you: the fake brown leather seats, the green plastic plants on the pink window-sills, the partly emptied bottles of Coke — and Esther. . . .

The Personality Interview Story—Because names make news, interviews with well-known persons usually make interesting stories. Interview stories concerning celebrities and other prominent persons in the public limelight have high reader interest. The reporter's purpose in writing personality interview stories is to give the reader a "close-up" of the celebrity. The story emphasis should concern the interviewee's life, mannerisms, personality, and achievements. However, since many well-known persons have a great many facts at their disposal, the reporter may consider writing a combination fact-celebrity interview story. In the following EXAMPLE, reporter-novelist Jimmy Breslin tells of his feelings about the journalism profession.

EXAMPLE:

"The worst thing in life is older people who answer 'no!' to every idea that seems even remotely new," reporter Jimmy Breslin commented yesterday. "When you have your enthusiasm taken from you it's the worst thing that can happen," he continued.

Breslin opened a pack of Pall Mall cigarettes and sat back in a chair in the *Herald-Traveler* city room. He had just completed a night's work as nationally syndicated columnist. His curly hair drooped on his forehead and a navy-and-white striped tie hung loosely from his neck.

"You know why I write? It's all I ever wanted to do. I get to pick my own stories to cover and write the way I want." Breslin paused to light a cigarette. "Journalism is a great field. You're performing a great service."

"Editorials, comment columns like the one I write, and the news background stories are the places that you take your stand. Just don't editorialize in news columns. It defeats your whole purpose," Breslin said.

He paused for a moment to reflect on his own life. "You know I never graduated from high school. My job on the *New York Herald Tribune* was as good as college," Breslin commented. He lit another cigarette before saying thoughtfully. "I see value in every day at school. I'd give my right arm to go to college."

"Writing is all I can do," he continued. "I think it's fun. Some people make it torture. Oh yeah, four hours at a typewriter can wash you out pretty good. But then, it beats opening oysters," he said without cracking a smile.

Breslin flicked ashes into an ashtray before adding, "The thing that makes me really sick is people that think writing is a simple way to earn lotsa money. I tell them to go out and rob a bank or to invest in Campbell's Pork and Beans or something. You can be awfully unhappy with money. Write for satisfaction; that's what I see as the only way."

Breslin clicked the ballpoint pen he held in his left hand. "The main thing is hard work," he concluded. "There's even good work for a girl despite what you hear. You'll never be a dope in the kitchen if you can write."

Joan Hanley
School of Public Communications
Boston University

The Composite Interview Story—While single-interview stories are usually short, the composite interview story (multi-interview story or symposium story) is often longer because it contains much more detail and is the result of interviews with more than one person. Often, the composite interview story can run to one thousand or more words in length. Although one of the commandments of journalism is to "Keep it short!" many of the truly fresh, significant stories of our times cannot be compressed. Today's events are often too complicated to be adequately covered in a relatively short story. As the education of the news-consuming public increases, the demand for news stories based on comprehensive interviews increases. Today, daily as well as Sunday newspapers and magazines often present longer, more comprehensive stories. Many composite interview stories contain two or more elements from the types of interview stories previously mentioned. For example, a reporter assigned to do a story on a controversial subject might feel that in order to thoroughly cover the story he should interview several persons. In planning the interviews he should be careful to select persons having opposing viewpoints, thus being fair to all sides. By doing this, he would be including another maker of news in his story—conflict. The writer might also choose to combine the elements of the biographical interview story with those of the personality and descriptive interview stories in order to more adequately present a detailed composite interview report.

Elements of the Interview Story

After determining the type of interview best suited for his presentation, the interview writer must concern himself with such elements as determining the lead and organizing the parts of his story. The parts of the interview story should be presented in order of importance, the amount of space allotted to each part being determined by its importance to the overall story. Like all other mass media news presentations, the interview story has three parts: the *lead,* the *body,* and the *conclusion.*

WRITING THE INTERVIEW STORY

Once the subject of the interview story has been thoroughly researched, the writer should concern himself with the actual interview situation. Because the interviewee is often a person of importance with many demands on his time, the writer should, in the relatively short time he is usually allotted, make every question count. Since the interview situation is usually a face-to-face, extremely personal confrontation, the interviewer should attempt to put the interviewee at ease. Many successful interviewers accomplish this by chatting informally for a few minutes preceding the actual interview. Then, the interviewer gradually begins asking more specific questions directly related to the reason for the interview. For example, an interviewer would not be apt to ask a general question like, "What do you think of foreign aid?" Instead, he might ask, "Why do you advocate cutting one million dollars from the budget for aid to India?" One question should lead to another in an informal, conversational manner. The interviewer does his best to help the interviewee from wandering from the subject. The interviewer should keep personal opinions to himself, leading the conversation and not monopolizing it. In most cases interviewers are granted a specific amount of time in which to conduct the interview, and must keep an eye on the time in order to conclude the session when specified. Then, the interviewee should be thanked for his time, and asked if he can be called upon to double-check facts. Most interviewees are happy to cooperate on this point because they do not want to be misquoted.

Advance Preparation for Writing the Interview Story

Interview story assignments require thorough advance preparation. The interviewer should equip himself with any obtainable information about the interviewee and should check publications that might contain further information, such as *Who's Who* and the *Readers' Guide to Periodical Literature*. He might also search the newspaper's morgue for background stories that contain information about the interviewee. (Other research materials can be found in libraries.) The more complex the interview assignment, the more research that must be done. Biographer William Manchester, before writing *The Death of a President*, gathered 45 volumes of tapes, notes, and documents on the last few days in the life of President John F. Kennedy. Manchester spent as many as 15 hours a day for 21 months interviewing some 500 persons. In Dallas he retraced, on foot, the route of the Kennedy motorcade. He watched the film of the actual assassination no fewer than 75 times. Thorough research enables the reporter to learn much about the interviewee's achievements, failures, hobbies, likes, and dislikes. The interviewer can then ask himself, "What would the average reader want to ask this person?" Among other things, readers would probably want answers to ques-

Comedian and civil rights leader Dick Gregory being interviewed on TV.

WTTW News, Chicago

Ron MacN

tions of direct concern to themselves. The interviewer tries to prepare questions that will elicit more than mere "yes" and "no" answers.

Taking Notes—Many beginners assigned to doing interviews worry about how they should take notes. Often, if the interviewer has been thorough in his research, he won't have to write down everything said by the interviewee, and he will remember much of what was said. Usually, he will only have to take notes concerning important statements and specific facts, such as dates and figures. When an interviewer feels he must write down many statements, he should make his notetaking as inconspicuous as possible. Many interviewees, when confronted by a huge notebook, think that every word they say will be used in the story and become overly cautious. To avoid frightening the interviewee in this way, the interviewer should hold a small notepad low in his lap and try to prevent his writing from becoming too conspicuous. Some interviewers use tape recorders, a device having both advantages and disadvantages. By using a tape recorder, the reporter is certain to get accurate information. Experienced reporters rarely use tape recorders because writing a story from recorded material is often more time-consuming than writing a story from notes. Also, tape-recording equipment (other than cassettes) is usually cumbersome and often tends to upset interviewees who might suffer from "mike-fright."

Organizing the Material—After completing his interview the writer often discovers he has amassed a great deal of unorganized information which, in order to be properly presented, must be put into a logical sequence. To do this the writer must consult his notes, first segregating all material dealing with the same major point. He then skeletonizes the material by discarding all information not pertaining to the most significant points of the interview. The remaining material, which he places in order of importance, results in an outline which he uses as the basis for writing the actual interview story.

THE INTERVIEW STORY LEAD

The type of lead chosen for an interview story is, of course, dependent upon the type of interview conducted and the information learned as a result of the interview. Usually, if new, significant, or timely material is disclosed in an interview, the writer will use either a summary lead or a salient idea lead, both of which are described in the following paragraphs. Some of the more common leads for interview stories can be categorized as follows.

The Summary Lead—The summary lead summarizes the major points learned from the interview.

EXAMPLE:

> Ideal qualifications for foreign correspondents were cited by UPI reporter Joseph Taylor today. Last week he was given the George Polk Award "for courage and enterprise" in reporting an attempted coup in Latin America.

The Salient Idea Lead—The salient idea lead is a lead statement containing the main idea emphasized during the interview.

EXAMPLE:

> "Be interested in what you are doing." This was the basic qualification of a correspondent, as stated today by award-winning, UPI reporter Joseph Taylor.

The Feature Lead—The feature lead, usually presented in narrative style, is used to gain reader interest by supplying a background for the main idea of the interview.

EXAMPLE:

> It is from the troubled Caribbean that the storm clouds come with hurricane winds and driving rain. It is from the troubled Caribbean that revolutions spring overnight and governments fall. And it is from this troubled Caribbean scene that UPI's Joseph Taylor reported, and won an award: the George Polk Award for courage and enterprise in journalism.

The Word-picture Lead—The word-picture lead is usually chosen when the interviewee is either well known or if his personal characteristics are particularly striking. This type of lead presents a colorful visual image of the interviewee. To use this type of lead effectively, the interviewer should watch as well as listen during the interview. The interviewee's mannerisms, dress, and distinctive habits can often make interesting lead material which, when properly presented, can enable the reader to "see" as well as to "hear." A former governor of a large state became upset when a *Newsweek* Magazine reporter wrote that the governor ate peas with his knife. The reporter's answer was that the statement was the truth, and that by including this fact

182

in his story he had helped readers get a true picture of the governor. Description in a lead, while it can often add to a story, should not be out of proportion to the rest of the story. The following EXAMPLE of a word-picture lead, prepared by a student journalist, emphasizes the personal characteristics of the interviewee.

EXAMPLE:

John Kenneth Galbraith sat sipping tomato soup from the bowl in a small dining room at Harvard's Winthrop House. He had gone through the cafeteria line to get his lunch just as the undergraduates had done.

"I get no privileges," he said. "This is a participatory democracy."

Galbraith, at 60, has a long face consistent with his six-foot, eight-inch frame. His high forehead, hook nose, and long but not quite jowly cheeks are reminiscent of a 13th-Century Byzantine icon. . . .

Sandra Banisky
School of Public Communications
Boston University

The Figure of Speech Lead—In order to make a comparison, or analogy, the writer of the interview story often considers using the figure of speech lead. In this type of lead, the writer tries to present a clever, thought-provoking twist.

EXAMPLE:

Interviewing a veteran reporter is like dancing with an Amazon — it's debatable who's leading whom. . . .

The Thought-provoking Question Lead—Many interview stories, in order to gain reader interest, start with a thought-provoking question.

EXAMPLE:

"Would I wear a mini-skirt?" said diminutive blonde Pearl Oswald.

"No, never."

"Why not?"

"I'm too old."

Pearl is 19.

The mini-skirt—for those who haven't been listening to the latest from London—is a fashion that stops anywhere (depending on the state of your legs, not to mention your nerve) from three to 12 inches above the knee. . . .

Rose DeWolf,

The Philadelphia Inquirer

When mini-skirts first became popular, several journalism students were assigned to do a man-in-the-street interview using a question similar to the one in the preceding EXAMPLE. The students turned in the following leads.

EXAMPLES:

Boys, would you date a girl who was wearing a mini-skirt? "Well, I would—but I wouldn't take her home to mother," Bob Combs, a junior, answered. . . .

To what heights will the American girl rise to get a man interested in her? . . .

What's up on the Denver High scene? The mini-skirt. It starts at the waist and goes all the way down to about twelve to two inches above the knee. To find out what students thought of this war of the shifting front, we asked the following questions: . . .

There's a revolution going on. And this time the English are winning. They have swapped their red coats for paisley, polka dots, and frills. Led by General Mary Quant, the crusading faithful have disembarked from Carnaby Street and Soho Square, and now march characteristically out-of-step along Main Street and Washington Square. . . .

Composite Interview Story Leads

While any of the preceding types of leads may be used for interview stories (as long as they are accurate and lure the reader into the story), composite interview stories use only one of the following three types of leads.

184

The Comprehensive Lead—The most common lead for the composite interview story is the comprehensive paragraph in which the writer reduces the important ideas from the interview into a single, summarizing unit. This type lead is used when each idea from the interview is of about equal value.

EXAMPLE:

> Four area clergymen yesterday denounced the movement launched by the County Racing Association to permit pari-mutuel betting under a bill pending before the State legislature. . . .

The Main Idea Lead—The composite interview story writer usually uses the comprehensive lead when the interrelationship between the interviews is the outstanding news factor. However, when one quotation is superior to the others, the reporter may want to single out and play it up in the lead.

EXAMPLE:

> Mayor Francis P. Adams today termed the proposed pari-mutuel betting bill "a violation of the state's laws on gambling and an invaluable aid to the Syndicate." . . .

The Combination Lead—The third type of composite interview story lead is a combination of the two previous types. One main idea is used, and other minor points are briefly summarized.

EXAMPLE:

> While proponents of pari-mutuel betting garnered support from State Legislators, Mayor Francis P. Adams opposed the bill saying, "Enactment of this measure would be a violation of the state's laws on gambling and an invaluable aid to the Syndicate." . . .

The Body of the Interview Story

When the writer has determined his type of interview story and has decided on a lead that introduces the topics to be covered in the story, he should develop the body of the story, usually limited to a few major topics, by writing each paragraph so that it logically follows the preceding paragraph in thought development. The body of the interview story should be presented in a smooth, coherent style. This can best be accomplished by segregating the most important quotations under each topic discussed in the body. Each topic should be thoroughly discussed before the writer proceeds to the next topic to ensure that there are no unanswered questions left in the reader's mind. To achieve variety, the writer can consider alternating direct quotations with indirect quotations. If the interviewee made an especially forceful or controversial statement, or if he used colorful language, the writer might consider using only direct questions. Indirect quotations are often used as transitional devices or for summarizing passages.

EXAMPLE:

Body

> . . . The strains of an old ragtime tune were drowned out by the scream of an early-model diesel train.
>
> The physics teacher, Dr. Walter Smudski, dismissed the strange mixture of sounds. "The kids are playing," he said with a smile.
>
> He said the kids often played in the lab.
>
> The "kids" were two seniors, Harry Pander, "my electronic expert," and Mary Riebling, "sort of a jill-of-all-trades."
>
> Actually, they were studying the pitch of each of several sounds. . . .

The use of transitions is even more important in the composite interview story than it is in shorter interview stories. A few transitions that can easily be adapted for use in composite interview stories are "Another development in the story . . . ," "At the same time . . . ," and "Earlier in the day. . . ."

The Conclusion of the Interview Story

The final paragraph of the interview story, the conclusion, should give the entire story an air of finality and should summarize the purpose of the story. The writer may wish to use a summarizing statement in direct quotation preceded by a statement such as, "In conclusion, he said, . . . ," or "He concluded with, . . ." Another commonly used type of conclusion for interview stories is often referred to as the "picture-frame device." This type of conclusion refers the reader back to the lead by repeating the thought contained in the lead, thus indicating that the interview is over. The conclusion to the interview story should not editorialize, and it should avoid wordy, complicated sentences like the one shown in the following example. On a separate piece of paper, rewrite the sentence as a brief, clear, concluding statement.

186

EXAMPLE:

> All of the members of the faculty and the members of the senior class student body wish to thank Mr. Smith for his efforts in their behalf as well as to extend all of their best wishes to him for success in all of his future endeavors.

The conclusion for the composite interview story, also, must have an air of finality. All of the reader's questions should have been answered in the body of the story, and there should be no loose ends left hanging. The writer usually tries to present some sort of summary when bringing the composite interview story to a close.

CONDUCTING SUCCESSFUL INTERVIEWS

Beginning reporters sometimes have difficulty in handling interview assignments. Following are several of the most common errors that should be

The late Dr. Martin Luther King, Jr., with Dr. Ralph Abernathy, during an interview with members of the news media.

avoided by reporters in order to conduct successful interviews.

Lack of Proper Preparation—It is essential that the interviewer know the background of the person being interviewed. Ideally, the interviewee will think, "Here is a reporter who knows what I'm talking about." For example, a student reporter assigned to interview a prominent scientist doing government research on infrared rays hadn't done his research "homework." The student's interview story was written and published and, not realizing how inaccurate it was, a news reporter forwarded it to a news agency. When the article had been distributed to papers all over the country, the scientist began to receive irate letters—some from government officials. One congressman demanded an investigation to probe the waste of taxpayers' money, leaving the scientist in the position of having to deny the facts contained in the story. Thereafter, the scientist refused to grant interviews to students.

Misinterpretation—During an interview, United Press International foreign correspondent Joseph Taylor emphasized certain words, winked while using hyperbole, and laughed after tripping over one word. Near the end of the interview session, Taylor said that he had recently finished writing a book about Latin America. Being modest, he jokingly added, "It will put you to sleep." In writing about this, the interviewer unthinkingly included the following sentence in his article:

> He has recently finished a book on the Caribbean that, in his words, "will put you to sleep."

While it is true that Taylor made the statement, he didn't intend it for publication. Often, some quotations are best deleted and, without elaboration, many quotations become inaccurate.

Misunderstanding—Beginning writers frequently aren't careful to phrase the question so that the interviewee understands it. Interviewees, not wanting to seem unsure of themselves, often give the interviewer answers to what they think was asked. Consequently, the reporter takes down, and his paper publishes, the answer to the wrong question. Questions should be well planned and carefully thought out. They should be short, clear, and to-the-point. When the answer is given, the interviewer, if he has any doubts about the intended meaning, should repeat both the question and the answer. For example, an interviewer asked a senator, "Do you favor a ten percent tax increase?" The senator answered, "Yes." To double-check this, the reporter repeated, "You're saying you're in favor of a tax *increase*?" The senator exclaimed, "Heavens, no! I thought you said *decrease*!"

188

Attribution—For each quotation given in the interview story the speaker must be correctly identified so that there will be no doubt in the reader's mind to whom to attribute the statement. Although there are a great many synonyms for the verb "to say," most editors feel that the use of this verb is suitable in most cases. They reason that readers aren't conscious of the verb except when they want to be sure of the source of a statement. This attribution can come at the beginning, the middle, or at the end of the sentence:

EXAMPLES:

He said, "The President has granted no pardons except on the recommendation of the attorney general."

"The President has granted no pardons," he said, "except on the recommendation of the attorney general."

"The President has granted no pardons except on the recommendation of the attorney general," he said.

Use of the First Person Singular—Many interviewers make the mistake of revealing their own feelings in a story by overusing the first person singular. These writers don't realize that the average reader cares little about what the writer thinks. Awkward word order can often result from use of the first person singular.

EXAMPLE:

I asked him what he thought of the Letterman's Club. He answered that . . .

If the writer merely gives the answers that the interviewee gave, he'll have a much smoother story. The line could better read:

Concerning the Letterman's Club, he said, . . .

A WINDOW ON THE WORLD

A frequent theme in student English compositions is "How I'm Suffocated by My Environment." Regardless of the part of the country in which students live, they often feel that "the grass is greener on the other side of the fence." Many students in New York City and Los Angeles dislike city living and wish they could move to the country, while students living in rural communities often dream of what they think is the glamorous life of the city. Many students living in the North would gladly exchange their climate with students living in the South, and vice versa. These students can be compared to the "consumers of the mass media" mentioned at the beginning of this chapter. The average consumer often feels shut off from the "outside" world, or trapped by the four walls of his office or living room. The interview story writer can give such a person a "window on the world"—a window that gives the reader an insight into human emotions, failures, and accomplishments.

ACTIVITIES

1. Prepare a 15-minute skit that illustrates "What To Do During an Interview." Present the skit to your classmates. At the end of the skit your teacher will conduct a class discussion on what was done wrong during the interview shown in the skit. Be prepared to offer suggestions on how to remedy any of the mistakes mentioned in the discussion.

2. To gain experience with the various types of interview leads, write five short opening leads for an imaginary interview, using as the interviewee a celebrity of your choice. Choose the lead you prefer and discuss your choice with your classmates.

3. List the preliminary steps a journalist should take before conducting a successful interview.

4. List several steps that should be followed after the completion of an interview in preparation for writing an interview story.

5. Choose an inanimate object and write an imaginary story based on an interview with this "non-talking" interviewee. For example you could interview the door of the main entrance to your school. Ask specific questions which will require factual answers. The interviewee's "comments" could result in an unusual story about present and past students who have passed through the entrance to the school.

6. Make arrangements to spend one or more class periods interviewing your teacher on school-related issues. In conducting the interview keep in mind techniques of interviewing discussed in this chapter.

    a. Be prepared in advance to ask specific questions about the issue or issues being discussed.

    b. Try to have the questions follow one another in an easy, sequential, and informal manner.

    c. Keep in mind that the interviewee may have demands on his time—

try to make every question count.

d. Try to keep note-taking as inconspicuous as possible. Consider using a tape recorder, if available.

e. Try to avoid expressing your own personal opinions about the issue or issues being discussed.

f. If you have any doubt about the meaning of an answer, repeat both the question and the answer.

READING

BUSH, CHILTON R., *Newswriting and Reporting of Public Affairs.* Chilton Book Co., Philadelphia, Pa., 1965.

HARRAL, STEWART, *Keys to Successful Interviewing.* University of Oklahoma Press, Norman, Okla., 1954.

HIEBERT, RAY E. (Ed.), *The Press in Washington.* Dodd, Mead, New York, 1966.

HILLIARD, R. L., *Writing for Television and Radio.* Hastings House, New York, 1967.

McGAFFIN, WILLIAM, AND ERWIN KNOLL, *Anything but the Truth: The Credibility Gap—How the News Is Managed in Washington.* Putnam, New York, 1968.

MURROW, EDWARD R., AND FRED W. FRIENDLY (Ed.), *See It Now.* Simon and Schuster, New York, 1955.

OVERSEAS PRESS CLUB OF AMERICA, *How I Got That Story,* edited by David Brown and Richard Bruner. Dutton, New York, 1967.

POWELL, NORMAN, *Anatomy of Public Opinion.* Prentice-Hall, Englewood Cliffs, N.J., 1951.

PRESSON, HAZEL, *The Student Journalist and Interviewing.* Richards Rosen Press, New York, 1966.

WALLACE, MIKE, *Mike Wallace Asks.* Simon and Schuster, New York, 1958. (PB)

WOLSELEY, ROLAND E., AND LAURENCE R. CAMPBELL, *Exploring Journalism.* Prentice-Hall, Englewood Cliffs, N.J., 1957.

Chapter **10**

Speeches, Meetings,
Panel Discussions,
and Published Reports

SPEECH REPORTING

For reporters and television commentators in Washington, D.C., it was a routine assignment to cover a speech by President Lyndon B. Johnson. Armed with advance copies of the President's speech, the newsmen had already decided on their leads. Simply as a matter of course, they were politely listening. But then came the bombshell. The President had finished his prepared text and, with the satisfied look of having finally outwitted the reporters, he made a statement that was of the utmost significance: "Under no circumstances will I be a candidate for re-election." The President left the podium and television networks switched back to their studios for the "usual" commentary. Millions of viewers witnessed a most disorganized scene. The commentators were dumbfounded, confused, and tongue-tied. What the President had said in his 45-minute-long speech now seemed insignificant. His final statement was all that mattered.

No amount of advance preparation would have alerted newswriters and commentators to this unexpected eventuality: covering a speech can be as challenging and unpredictable an assignment as covering other, seemingly more exciting, news events.

Purpose of Speech Stories

Since the average person isn't able to attend every significant speech, he must rely on the news media to keep him informed about important speeches. The purpose of news stories about speeches is, like that of other straight news stories, to inform the reader by answering the questions *who, what, when, where, why,* and *how.* Writing stories about speeches is often more challenging than writing straight news stories. The writer, in addition to informing the reader about an event which has taken place, must also report on what was *said.* This requires that the writer be an attentive listener as well as a careful observer. The writer must be able to select from a speech, which may have been lengthy or poorly organized, the most important ideas that were expressed and then organize them into a coherent news story. In addition to accurately reporting the content of a speech, the writer must be careful to retain the spirit in which the speaker made his remarks. If it is important to the meaning of the story, the writer should give background information about the speaker and about the setting of the speech.

Advance Preparation for the Speech Story

As soon as the reporter is assigned to cover a specific speech, he should begin his preparation by researching all available source materials to obtain as much background information as possible about the speaker. This background information should include the speaker's complete name, biographical data about him, his views on various issues, and causes and activities with which he has been involved. The reporter should also obtain in advance as much information as possible about the speech—the correct title, the subject matter, and the time and location of the speaking event. Since many speeches are followed by question-and-answer periods, the reporter should try to think of questions that his readers would have asked if they had been given the chance.

Arriving at the scene of the speaking event about a half hour before the speech is scheduled to begin is a good policy. This gives the reporter time to register at the Press Table to secure the necessary credentials sometimes required by sponsors of speeches. The reporter will also have time to obtain an advance copy of the speech (mimeographed or printed copies are often made available to members of the press), if one is available, and to discuss any questions he has with the sponsors of the speech. By arriving early, the reporter will also be able to take a seat where he will be able to see and hear the speaker without difficulty.

Elements of a Speech Story

In his preparation for the writing of a speech story, the speech story writer should keep three elements in mind: the speaker, the audience, and the speech itself.

The Speaker—As in the interview story, the writer, when writing a speech story, should inform the reader of the speaker's full name and credentials and answer the reader's question, "Why should I pay attention to what this person has to say?" In addition to identifying the speaker and making clear why his statements are worth quoting, the writer might also consider describing the speaker's appearance and manner of speaking. By reporting *how* the speech was delivered as well as *what* was said, the writer preparing a story for the print media can describe the speaker and audience to the reader and re-create a visual picture of the event. For instance, did the speaker jab his index finger in the direction of the audience? Did he pound his fist on the lectern? Did he raise his voice to a shout when he made his main points? The inclusion of these details will help enliven the speech story.

UPI

Mayor Charles Evers, the first member of his race to head a biracial town in Mississippi, shown during a press interview shortly after his election in Fayette, Mississippi.

The Audience—The size of the audience, what interest-groups or prominent persons were in attendance, and the audience reaction to the speaker's remarks are often important elements in a speech story.

1. In approximating the size of the audience, the writer should be as specific as possible and avoid using such vague expressions as "full house," "near-capacity crowd," or "standing-room-only crowd," which mean little to the reader unless he is familiar with the size of the auditorium. By adding a phrase such as "at the 500-seat capacity auditorium" to these expressions, the writer can make his approximation more meaningful to the reader.

2. If it is important to the story, the writer might want to indicate what groups of people were represented in the audience. Were they taxpayers, union members, teachers, students, or bankers? If any prominent persons were in the audience, the writer might want to mention them in his story.

3. Finally, the writer might want to incorporate into his story the reaction of the audience to the speech. Did the audience applaud or cheer enthusiastically any particular statements made by the speaker? Did any people walk out of the auditorium at a certain point in the speech? In general was the audience warm or hostile?

The Speech—The final—and usually the most important—element in a speech story is the content of the speech itself. The writer should answer the reader's question, "What did the speaker say?" Since it may not be possible for a student reporter to obtain an advance copy of a speech, he will usually write his story from notes taken during the speech. In order to take well-organized notes from which he will be able to write a good speech story, the writer should first try to determine the main idea of the speech. Having established the speaker's main theme, the writer will then listen for supporting arguments. Since he will not be able to write down everything the speaker said, the writer should separate important statements from unimportant ones. He will summarize some statements, and will also listen for significant quotations which he will be able to use in his story, making sure to quote the speaker exactly.

WRITING THE SPEECH STORY

The reporter should begin writing his story as soon as possible after the speech, while he still has a strong impression of the speaker's remarks and other aspects of the occasion in his mind. Before beginning to write, he should read his notes and be sure that he understands the speaker's main theme and supporting ideas.

The Speech Story Lead

In addition to information such as the speaker's name, the subject of the talk, and the occasion of the speaking event, the speech story lead will often contain some important element from the speech. The lead will usually be contained in one paragraph. However, if the writer chooses to lead with a lengthy or two-sentence quotation he may wish to place the strictly factual information (*who, what, where, when*) in a second paragraph.

The most important element of a speech story is not always the content of the speech itself. Sometimes beginning with an element such as the speaker's name (if he is particularly well known), circumstances surrounding the event, or an unusual or striking title, may be a more appropriate way of leading into a speech story. In most cases, however, the reporter will begin the speech story in one of the following ways:

1. By summarizing the main ideas or general theme of the speech.

EXAMPLE:

> In a speech sponsored by the Drama Club, Burton Samson, playwright and actor, last week discussed the modern playwright and the theater.

2. By directly quoting a significant statement made by the speaker which effectively expresses the theme of the speech.

EXAMPLE:

> "The theater is an arena, an intellectual and emotional sporting event where the actors are sportsmen," philosophized Burton Samson, noted playwright, last week at Wheeling High School.

3. By quoting the speaker indirectly.

EXAMPLE:

> Playwright Burton Samson, speaking at Wheeling High School last week, said that attending the theater was like going through customs.

4. By using an interest-arousing quotation from the speech to lure the reader into the story. (If the reporter begins the story in this way, he should summarize the entire speech in the second or third paragraph of the story so that the speaker's intentions will not be misrepresented. When using a quotation from the speech in the lead, care should be taken against producing the wrong emphasis for the remainder of the story.)

EXAMPLES:

> "The theater is like going through customs when you're asked what you have to declare," said Burton Samson before a crowd of 400 students at Wheeling High School last week.

> "The most mysterious thing I have ever come across is an audience," said Burton Samson as he spoke at Wheeling High School last week. "In fact," he continued, "the audience makes a sportsman out of an actor."

5. By combining any of the above methods, while being careful to avoid using too many words in the lead.

EXAMPLES:

> After an introduction in which Burton Samson was described as a Renaissance Man and hailed as a "one-man cartel of the arts," the famous actor-producer-playwright attempted to describe the problems of the playwright in the modern American theater.

> Burton Samson came to Wheeling High School last Thursday to lecture on "The Modern Playwright in the American Theater," but the noted actor, playwright, and producer related instead his opinions and knowledge of many aspects of the theater, both in the U.S. and abroad.

Body of the Speech Story

In the body of the speech story the reporter will condense the speech by summarizing and by quoting the speaker directly and indirectly. In doing so he should take care to retain the spirit of the speech, be faithful to the speaker's original meaning, and be concerned with correct and accurate attribution. The length of the story will depend on the news value of the speech —the importance of the occasion or of the statements made, or the prominence of the speaker.

To begin the speech story, the reporter may want to expand on the element chosen for the lead. The sentences that make up the reporter's story should be well organized and relate to the main theme of the speech, even if the speaker himself rambled. As in other news stories, ideas should be arranged in order of decreasing importance (inverted pyramid style), even though this may not be the same order in which the speaker made his statements. The body of the speech story, like that of the interview story, will be made up of short paragraphs of direct and indirect quotations and summarizing statements. Quotations should not be selected at random but should serve to develop and illustrate the main theme.

In addition to the theme of the speech and supporting arguments, the reporter can also include in his story anecdotes, humor, and specific examples the speaker used to illustrate his ideas. The inclusion of this material will add life to the story.

EXAMPLE:

> Samson described his new three-act play, "The Generation Beat," as "unfashionable because people don't want to drink lemonade twice." This comment was one of many anecdotes that he used to brighten his talk. . . .

The Speech Story Conclusion

A speech story, like an interview story, should conclude with an air of finality. Often a speaker will conclude his talk with a summarizing statement. The writer may wish to use this quotation to conclude his story.

EXAMPLE:

> In conclusion, Samson said, "The theater is an instrument with which the playwright can do anything he likes, provided he can hold his audience. The playwrights are among the very few who can say what they think—with no fear."

If the speech is part of a lecture series, the writer could conclude his story by informing the reader of the time and place of the next event.

EXAMPLE:

The next speaker in the Drama Club Series will be Arthur Morton, a scenic designer, who will speak February 23 on the topic, "What High School Students Should Know About Scenic Design."

CHECKLIST FOR WRITING A SPEECH STORY

1. Have you done thorough research on the speaker and his topic prior to attending the speech?

2. While covering the speech, did you take accurate and complete notes, including significant direct quotations as well as summarizing statements?

3. Have you written a concise and effective lead which includes an important element of the story as well as identifies the speaker, the subject of the speech, and the occasion?

4. Does the body of your story present the speaker's remarks in an interesting, coherent, and well-organized manner?

5. Does your story have a conclusion?

6. Are all direct quotations in the speaker's exact words?

7. Have you retained the original tone and intended meaning of the speech in your story?

8. Does your story show that you thoroughly understood the speaker's main theme and his supporting arguments?

Sidebars to the Speech Story

As in a straight news story, a sidebar to a speech story often accompanies the main story about the speech. On occasion, developments prior to, during, or as a result of a speech will make good material for the writing of sidebars. If, for example, a speaker made certain charges against the school system in his speech, the reporter might wish to ask a school authority to answer the accusations. If protesters had stormed the stage and forced the speaker to delay his talk, a sidebar could be written about this disturbance. If certain groups had been barred from the speech, the reporter could write a sidebar based on interviews with leaders of these groups. The speech would be covered in the main story, while less important, though related, elements would be included in the sidebar. The following EXAMPLES, written by a journalism student now with the *Providence Journal*, show the difference between speech stories and sidebars to speech stories.

EXAMPLES:

Speech Story

Since we have the most technically advanced society in the world, we have no models. In fact, we are an experimenting station for other countries.

"Consequently, we should put more planning into our 'Choice of Communities for Tomorrow,' " Dr. Margaret Mead told 500 students in Hendricks Chapel Wednesday night. . . .

Carol Young

Sidebar to a Speech Story

Time—7:30. The lecture was scheduled for 8 p.m. Hendricks Chapel was gradually being filled, until stragglers were forced to use window sills and balcony steps for seats.

I sat fidgeting, but glad I had arrived early enough to grab a good seat. A crumpled copy of the school paper lay on the floor before me. The boldface headline read: "Margaret Mead on Campus Today." I wanted to pass the time, so I began to read the article. World famous anthropologist. Author of 11 books. Researcher of cultural patterns in South Sea islands and primitive areas of New Guinea, Bali, and Samoa.

Suddenly, I came to a conclusion. There I sat—a sophomore in college— a sophomore with hopes of being both a newspaper and sociology major—a sophomore who had said so many times "education means a lot to me." And

why was I there? Because of a course requirement.

A woman with a master's and Ph.D. degrees from Columbia University has been asked to share her knowledge and experience with today's students, and I began to wonder how many were awaiting the talk under their own initiative and desire to learn.

The girl next to me looked at her companion and said, "I'm not taking notes. I'm just here to meet a boy." I gazed about noting several frosh acquaintances, who were, no doubt, attending because of class obligations.

How many students are sincere? After all, I always envisioned myself as eager to learn, enthusiastic, and grateful for the opportunity to do so, but what had I done about it? Studied conscientiously? Most of the time. But what about *extra* reading, *extra* writing,

201

and taking advantage of *other* guest speakers? Rarely.

The murmuring drifted away. A woman in a green suit came up to the rostrum. She smiled at her audience and began. The audience was appreciative and attentive.

The lecture, "The Choice of Communities for Tomorrow," ended and the bid was made for questions. A seemingly long pause filled the room. "Come on, college students," I thought. "Are your minds *that* blank?" Finally, several hands shot up.

Time—9:10. It was over. I wandered toward the exit purposely listening to comments:

"She was great, but I disagree with her point on . . ."

"The topic was too generalized . . ."

"Her ideas were edging toward Communism . . ."

"I'm glad I *had* to come. She really was worth the time . . ."

"Gosh," I thought, "those students were *thinking*. Her lecture really stimulated minds."

Maybe this is what education is all about.

Carol Young

MEETINGS

Speeches, ranging from informal talks to formal addresses, may be given at meetings of any group or organization. At an hour-long PTA meeting, these speeches might consist of comments from the floor. At a five-day meeting of student editors, a great many speeches would be given. The school newspaper may want to cover the speeches at both these meetings— the PTA may be discussing a topic of significance to the school and community, and any large gathering of people, such as a student editor's meeting,

UPI

The Rev. Jesse Jackson, a dynamic speaker and the originator of "Operation Breadbasket," answers questions for mass media reporters and interviewers during an informal talk in Chicago.

is a newsworthy event. The reporter might want to summarize all significant speeches given at a meeting or, as in the following example, he may choose to write about one speech which effectively summarizes the most important developments which took place at the meeting.

EXAMPLE:

> As a result of the School Board meeting last week, Black student clubs will be allowed if these clubs follow the rules that govern all other school clubs.
>
> Speaking at the meeting, Superintendent Martin said that the name of the club "is of secondary importance."
>
> "Organizations, good and bad, go by the same name," he continued. "What really matters is not the name—but the goal. In setting goals, students have an opportunity for genuine educational experience," he said. . . .
>
> Martha Ojard
The Grantonian
Ulysses S. Grant High School, Portland, Oregon

PANEL DISCUSSIONS

The reporter will find that writing a story about a panel discussion will often present more problems than writing a story about a speech. However, many of the suggestions that were given for speech reporting will also apply to the panel discussion assignment. For example, the reporter would do research on the topic and on the panelists' backgrounds before attending.

If the panelists are in general agreement about the topic of discussion, the reporter could, as in the examples given below, write a lead in a variety of ways. The remainder of the story might then consist of significant comments made by the panelists.

EXAMPLES:

> With a prevailing note of pessimism, four high school teachers discussed "The United Nations in a World of Crisis" last week at the Warwood High School Auditorium. Participating in the panel discussion commemorating U.N. Day were Kevin O'Toole, William J. Pearson, Ishwer C. Kobe and Robert J. Thompson.
>
> Mankind is not yet psychologically ready to achieve international peace and harmony through an organization such

as the U.N., concluded four Warwood High School teachers appearing at the U.N. Day panel discussion last week.

An international panel of Warwood High School teachers expressed some grave doubts about the future of the United Nations last week at the auditorium.

If the participants are in disagreement, the story would consist of a presentation of the various opposing points of view on the subject of discussion. The fact that they are in disagreement could be used in the lead, as follows:

EXAMPLE:

A panel of experts last week differed sharply on whether the United States should provide military aid to Israel. Participating in a discussion on "The Mideast in Crisis," three authorities often became embroiled in heated and emotional outbursts during the program at the Washington High School auditorium.

The story might then continue:

EXAMPLE:

Senator Robert J. Lukas, who recently returned from a fact-finding mission to the area, charged that, "U.S. military aid to Israel could spell disaster to our goodwill in Arab countries." In answer to this, James B. Mason, U.S. Information Agency representative to Israel, said, "But we have no goodwill in Arab countries today. . . ."

PUBLISHED REPORTS

Published reports such as government documents, public relations releases, and magazine articles can be of great aid to the reporter as a source for background information for a news story or as a basis for writing an entire story. If a reporter writes a news story based on information contained in a published report, he will follow a procedure similar to that used in writing a speech story; that is, he will condense the material into a coherent story by choosing some passages to quote directly and indirectly and by summarizing other passages.

Government Documents—The U.S. Government Printing Office makes available a great many reports that often are of value to reporters. For example, a reporter writing a story about teenage car thefts could secure a copy of the FBI Crime Report. A reporter studying teenage marriage could write to the U.S. Bureau of Vital Statistics for information on the subject. For material on problems of education, the reporter would write to the U.S. Department of Health, Education, and Welfare, and the information obtained from the department could be used in a news story as follows:

EXAMPLE:

Two professors have just finished a major study of adolescents in three area high schools and have concluded—broadly speaking—that public high schools tend to inhibit rather than encourage independent thinking.

The recently published report, commissioned three years ago by the U.S. Department of Health, Education, and Welfare, suggests that high schools are failing miserably to stimulate original thought and are, in effect, crippling the very students they are supposed to serve. . . .

Public Relations Releases—Public relations offices may supply newspapers, magazines, and the other media with articles which are newsworthy. If newswriters use this material for news stories, they should check the accuracy of the releases and, in most cases, rewrite them. Following is an EXAMPLE of a lead from such a release.

EXAMPLE:

Baynor University has announced the completion of a major study by leading youth authorities Mario Delio and Rena Wilson. The study, conducted at local high schools, proves . . .

Magazine Articles—Magazine articles can be used by reporters as a source for background information for many assignments and for factual details needed to write a story. If the reporter uses any quotations, he should indicate the name and date of the magazine and, in some cases, obtain permission from the magazine to reprint the material.

Washington High School pitcher Warren Newton is the subject of an article in the April issue of *Sports Consolidated.* Author Tim Rice points out that Newton has signed a $75,000 contract to play professional baseball for the Los Angeles Angels this spring.

Because of the contract, Newton will be ineligible to pitch in any further Washington High games. Coach Robert Lawson made the following comment concerning the situation: "I'm only sorry that the Angels couldn't have waited until Warren graduated," he said. . . .

YOUR OPPORTUNITY TO THINK

Learning how to present the content of speeches, meetings, panel discussions, and published reports to readers is a valuable experience for the journalism student. While the reader benefits from reading these reports, the student writer may possibly benefit even more. From organizing his material into a coherent, newsworthy story and from his actual writing of the story, he has the opportunity to think and to evaluate the relative importance of ideas contained in the material about which he is reporting. And most importantly, by attending speaking events and reading published reports on important subjects, the student journalist will become a more mature, aware student of his society.

ACTIVITIES

1. List several preparatory steps that the speech story writer should follow before attending a speaking event.

2. Practice using research materials by doing advance research on a speaker scheduled to appear at your school. Sources can include newspapers and magazines as well as library materials.

3. Elements surrounding a speech, such as the speaker's appearance or mannerisms, interest-groups or prominent persons in the audience, audience reaction to the speech, and the setting of the event, can help to bring a speech story alive. During a school assembly or student council meeting, sharpen your powers of observation by taking notes on audience reaction and other aspects of the occasion. Compare your observations with the observations made by your classmates.

4. During a class lecture, practice your note-taking techniques. Try to determine your teacher's main theme or themes and supporting statements. Include in your notes both summarizing statements and direct quotations. Write a brief speech story based on the notes taken during the lecture. Be sure that your story has a lead, body, and conclusion.

5. Attend a court hearing, school committee session, town meeting, or similar event, and write a sidebar about a related development which took place prior to, during, or following the meeting.

6. Obtain an advance copy of a scheduled speech. Plan to attend the speech.
    a. During the speech compare the printed version with the speaker's presentation. If the speaker omitted or changed any parts determine why he did so.
    b. Write your own brief speech story about the event. Base the lead to your story on any new or important information introduced during the speech.

7. Write a news story based on the content of a government document. Your school library may have government documents and pamphlets on various subjects. If none are available, you may have to obtain material from the U.S. Government Printing Office or the appropriate government department.

8. Find a speech story in a daily newspaper and practice your editing techniques by eliminating any material you consider to be unessential to the meaning of the story. You may also want to summarize and paraphrase ideas expressed in long quotations which you think can be stated more concisely in your own words. Do not remove any important facts from the story. Discuss with your classmates your reasons for editing various paragraphs.

READING

ADLER, RUTH (Ed.), *The Working Press: Special to "The New York Times."* Putnam, New York, 1966.

ALY, BOWER AND F. LUCILLE (Ed.), *American Short Speeches.* Macmillan, New York, 1968. (PB)

BROCKWAY, THOMAS P. (Ed.), *Language and Politics.* Heath, Boston, 1965. (PB)

COPELAND, LEWIS (Ed.), *World's Great Speeches.* Dover Publications, New York, 1957. (PB)

HURD, CHARLES, *A Treasury of Great American Speeches.* Hawthorn Books, New York, 1959.

THONSSEN, LESTER (Ed.), *Representative American Speeches* (Annual). H. W. Wilson Co., Bronx, N.Y.

Feature Writing

THE OPPORTUNITY FOR CREATIVITY

Students often ask if there are opportunities for "creative writing" in journalism. Since all writing should, in a sense, be creative, the answer to this question hinges on what is meant by "creative writing." If what is meant by this phrase is the possibility of applying to journalistic writing the literary techniques used in fiction writing, the answer is "yes"; feature writers often use such literary techniques as establishment of tone and mood, development of character and plot, dialog, narration, and description. Because most feature writing is a creative process involving the writer's imagination, feature writers are often identified in print with by-lines. Feature writers must keep in mind, however, that although they use creativity and imagination in their writing, they are *not* writing fiction: they are, through the use of literary techniques, adding a new dimension to facts and ideas in order to most effectively present their material. Although feature articles are created from facts—but written with freedom of style and structure—there is

209

no set pattern for feature writing, thus allowing for creativity on the part of the writer. Skilled feature writers do, however, apply all the principles of effective writing to achieve unity, coherence, and emphasis—essential elements in all good feature writing.

WHAT IS A FEATURE?

Material written for the mass media that cannot be categorized as straight news or advertising is called feature material. Almost any topic that would entertain and interest consumers is an appropriate subject for a feature article. Feature articles lend variety to the newspaper's straight news presentations by adding color and extra dimensions to the news content.

Most news features are based, in some way, on news events: news features present entertaining news, explain and interpret facts, or present the human-interest side of the news. Other types of feature articles, also related to news, include most columns, editorials, editorial cartoons, detailed speech reports, personality interviews, fashion news, and radio, stage, motion picture, and television reviews. Non-news features are comics, crossword puzzles, book reviews, and humorous cartoons.

Purposes of Feature Articles

The primary purpose of the straight news story is to inform, and the primary purpose of the editorial is to persuade. While the feature story might inform and persuade to a degree, usually its primary purpose is to entertain. Above all, the feature story must be *interesting* to the reader. While straight news stories and editorials generally appeal to the reader's intellect, features usually appeal to the reader's emotions by arousing feelings such as joy, sympathy, and suspense.

The Definite Difference

Jack Cort, City Editor of Cocoa, Florida's *Today*, tells about a beginning reporter's first account of a man's operation to restore his sight. The reporter's first story was a simple presentation of facts in straight news story form. Cort suggested that the reporter rewrite his material as a feature article to show the readers what the blind man had been missing before his sight was restored. Following is the lead from the reporter's article, revised and resubmitted as a feature presentation.

EXAMPLE:

A blind man stood by his window after a summer rain. A cool mist touched his empty eyes.

Across the street, unnoticed, a little girl stirred a puddle with her toe to muss the rainbows and watch them form again.

Sights like the little girl have been missing from the world of Sam Cooper for 16 years. Now he will see again. . . .

THE IMPORTANCE OF STYLE IN FEATURE WRITING

In the straight news story the newswriter follows a definite style in presenting his material: the inverted pyramid. In the inverted pyramid style the newswriter reveals the most important elements in the lead and enumerates the remaining facts of the story, usually in order of decreasing importance, in an impersonal, straight-forward manner. By contrast, feature writing is less rigid in structure and allows the writer to inject his own personality and creativity into a story, and thus present a more *human* side of the news. Because the style of feature writing is informal, and because the writer is permitted to express his ideas in an imaginative and creative way, feature writing often requires more skill on the part of the writer than does straight news story writing.

In feature writing the newswriter's personal style (the way he puts his thoughts into words) is more important than in straight newswriting. Successful feature writers have an original, personal style to their writing—an individualism. To develop an individual writing style, students planning to become professional writers should first become familiar with, and study carefully, the elements of style used by skilled feature writers. They should also practice writing feature articles at every opportunity.

STRUCTURE OF THE FEATURE STORY

Though the writer is permitted greater freedom in writing a feature story than in writing a straight news story, he should keep in mind the basic elements of structure so that his feature story will have unity. In feature writing, the lead can be thought of as an introduction. Generally, the introduction should comprise about one-fifth of the length of the entire story. The body should comprise a little over three-fifths of the entire length, and the conclusion should comprise slightly less than one-fifth of the entire length. In contrast to the inverted pyramid structure of a straight news story, the structure of the feature story can be said to resemble a spool.

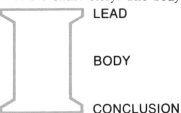

LEAD

BODY

CONCLUSION

211

Feature Article Leads

The purpose of the lead (introduction) in a feature article is to arouse the reader's interest and acquaint him with the general content of the article. By using an intriguing idea, a lively vocabulary, and an imaginative approach in his lead, the feature writer can successfully capture the reader's attention. The following examples, written by a journalism student, indicate a number of ways to begin a feature article.

The Serious and Thoughtful Lead—In a sense, this type of lead says to the reader, "This material should be important to you—no matter who you are." The tone of this lead is serious and thoughtful. The writer can create a sense of urgency by using short sentences.

EXAMPLES:

> Wisdom spoke to Tommie last night. She walked right into his dream. Tommie told me so.

> "Mommie, why is he so quiet?" asked little Susan.

The Problem Lead—This type of lead points to a significant problem and says, "Something's amiss here." The problem lead is informative and often presents conflict—one of the makers of news.

EXAMPLE:

> Six out of every ten students entering an institution of higher learning will never graduate.

The Shock Lead—Throwing the reader off guard and then shocking him is an effective way of capturing reader attention; however, the feature writer, in using this type of lead, should be careful not to resort to sensationalism. The reader should not be "let down" in the body of the story. The following feature is based on a report of the American Cancer Society. The humorous approach and the lightness of the tone in the first few sentences of the lead succeed in throwing the reader off guard.

EXAMPLE:

> Tobacco is a dirty weed. I like it.
> It satisfies no normal need. I like it.

It makes you thin, it makes you lean,
It takes the hair right off your bean,
It's the worst darn thing I've every seen, I like it.

Oh cigarette, cigar, and pipe smokers, join the crowd.
Chant the mighty ballad. Enjoy your simple pleasure. Relieve
your nervous and bored natures. Divulge your need to relax
with tobacco. Puff yourself from good health to ill. Curtail
your body's usefulness. Join the fun.

Die, oh die. Die of cancer. Die of heart disease. Die of
emphysema. Death comes to all—so, what does it matter how
we die? When it comes, it comes. Qué sera, sera.

Now abide foolish cigarette, cigar, and pipe smokers—
these three; but the most ill-omened is the cigarette smoker,
according to the latest report on smoking and lung cancer
released by the American Cancer Society.

The Mood Lead—Figures of speech are often used to set the mood in this
type of lead. Ideally, the mood lead gives the reader a feeling of expectation,
a feeling that there will be more to this story than might first appear.

EXAMPLE:

The winter sunset hinted at snow. The scene was grey,
like the inside of an oyster, and the sun appeared as white
and as precious as a well-kept pearl.

The First-person Lead—The first-person lead indicates that the writer will
inject himself into the story and take the reader into his confidence.

EXAMPLE:

Snow fell on Minneapolis the day I flew home to Washington, D.C., for Thanksgiving vacation. I looked out the
window when we took off, and as we rose in altitude . . .

The Alliterative Lead—Alliteration, the repetition of initial consonant sounds
in two or more neighboring words or syllables in a phrase, can be used effectively in a lead. Alliteration was used by Edgar Allan Poe in his poem
"The Bells."

What a tale of terror now their turbulency tells.

Feature writers might use alliteration in a lead to establish a light, easygoing mood. Writers who use alliteration in their leads can be said to be saying to the reader, "Take it easy. You don't have to be serious all the time."

EXAMPLE:

> Ah, Hollycrest, hilly haven for crazy college kids, over-worked snow shovels and perpetual precipitation—snow and hail love you, Hollycrest. They must—they come to us first and leave us last. . . .

The Historical Lead—Since the subject matter of an historical feature article may at first seem like "old news" to the reader, the writer should try to make his lead as interesting and lively as possible. In the following EXAMPLE the words "hugged" and "clawed" create vivid images for the reader, and conflict is placed early in the story.

EXAMPLE:

> The year was 1961. Intercollegiate wrestling champion "King" Larry Martin had hugged and clawed the challenger for his domain, and had reigned supreme for 10 years. Now, "King" Martin is facing the battle of his life for control of his kingdom, . . .

Body of the Feature Article

In writing the body of the feature article, the writer should keep in mind the three important elements contained in all good feature writing: unity, coherence, and emphasis.

Unity—To ensure unity in their feature presentations, many writers summarize the main idea or topic of their material into one brief sentence that is similar to a précis or thesis statement. The writer then uses the summary statement as the basis for expanding his topic in the body of the feature article. All of the material contained in the body of the feature article should be related to this summarizing statement. To further help achieve unity, many feature writers prepare, in outline form, a listing of all materials related to the summary statement that are to be included in the article. Each sentence in the feature article should relate to the summary statement, should expand on the main idea contained in the summary statement, and should serve either of the following functions:

1. Each sentence should add specific facts, or
2. Each sentence should entertain the reader.

Failure to achieve either of these functions can result in lack of unity and loss of reader interest.

Coherence—Because feature story sentences and paragraphs are usually much shorter than those contained in regular English compositions, coherence is often more difficult to achieve in feature writing than it is in English composition assignments. To guard against the possibility of reader misunderstanding, feature writers must be well organized in their presentation of materials and must carefully follow a well-prepared outline. Most feature writers try to use, in each sentence, transitional devices (words or phrases) that refer to the thoughts contained in the preceding sentences.

Emphasis—Feature writers, in order to highlight the main idea of their articles, often place all of their emphasis on the thesis statement. To ensure emphasis on their main idea many feature writers use repetition by stating the thesis statement in the lead, expanding on it in the body of the story, and again restating it in the conclusion. To avoid redundancy, they often state the thesis statement in a slightly different way each time.

Conclusion of the Feature Article

In his preparatory outline the skilled feature writer will have included all of the specific facts he wishes to present in the summary, or conclusion of his article. While some types of feature stories, when handled in chronological order, lead to a natural climax, others will not readily lend themselves to a "built-in" conclusion and the writer will need to plan a culminating paragraph. This paragraph should give an air of finality to the article, and should tie up all of the loose ends of the story. The conclusion may also utilize the "picture-frame" device by referring back to the lead.

TYPES OF FEATURE STORIES

While the types of feature stories are as numerous as the writer's imagination will permit, those most commonly used can be classified under the general categories listed in the following paragraphs. Beginning feature writers will find it helpful to become familiar with these most commonly used types of features.

Human Interest Features—The human interest feature, the most often-used type of feature article, appeals to the reader's emotions by offering the reader a glimpse of the successes and predicaments of ordinary human beings. Animals also make good subject matter for human interest feature stories. In the following feature, a journalism student describes a day in the life of a Head Start volunteer in Harlem. Though the feature is based on straight news material, the writer has added a new dimension to the story by using fiction-writing techniques. The tone and mood of the story are established in the lead. The writer has achieved unity by focusing on one day in the life of one teacher and one pupil. The writer appeals to the reader's senses and emotions by describing sights, sounds, and the human element.

EXAMPLE:

"Whatcha Doin' In Harlem?"

The bus halted on Lenox Avenue with the sigh of exhausted air brakes. The sudden force slammed me against the exit door, which then snapped open in reply. I was once again thrown into the screaming streets of Harlem—those streets that resounded with the wailing complaints of unwanted babies, and the ripping harshness of souped-up, relief-check Cadillacs.

Music descended from the windows that had been opened to the crackling heat of a New York summer. The beat was pounded out on the sidewalks by the click of heels on the slick new shoes that had been bought up on 125th Street.

I walked at a slower pace than the rest of Harlem. My rhythm was that of a sadder, less sure musician. I was unfamiliar with the melody of the neighborhood, and was hoping that maybe this day would bring me closer to the understanding of it.

Perhaps the classroom would provide refuge from the vibrating tensions of the streets. The contrast appalled me. Children were laughing here. Two or three plunked away at the piano, trying out original compositions for the first time. The various keys were hit mostly at random. Yet, when an appealing note was sounded, the respective pianist would repeat it a few times, and go on. To a five-year-old Head Start child, a piano is a new and thrilling toy— more fantastic, even, than the new dolls the children were given to play with, or the cement turtle to climb on out in the yard.

A crash interrupted the musical recitation. But this was no crash of a collapsing slum, no explosion of a policeman's pistol, no impact of chrome on flesh. Jimmy's creation, a skyscraper of blocks, had tumbled to the floor. Jimmy was a kid who was used to defeat. Yet now he was given the chance to rebuild something that had failed.

At lunch-time, silence prevailed as the children stuffed themselves on their sacred peanut butter on raisin-bread sandwiches. The only noise came as a response to my question. "How's the lunch, Jeff?" I asked. A moon-like smile shot up at me, followed by *Deelicious!* Delicious. I had taught him that word!

The work day left me tied a little closer to these children, who had seen and heard so much less than I (or was it more?). In any event, we were learning more about each others' lives as the summer wore on.

I slipped back out onto the streets, which were once more filled with the sloppy humming of transistor radios and screeching autos. A group of men in flashy clothes eyed me from the corner.

"Hey, Whitey!" one screamed. "How do ya like Harlem?"

"Just fine," I thought. "Just fine."

"Hey, Whitey! Whatcha doin' in Harlem? Huh, Whitey?"

Tired and angry, I wanted to tell them why I was in Harlem. I kept my mouth shut, however, trying to overcome my desire to run.

"Hey, Whitey, get out of Harlem!" he shrilled. "Get out!" I got out of Harlem. But I came back the next day. I had to.

Alice Silverstein
Syracuse University

Human interest features are enhanced when accompanied by human interest photos that help draw reader attention to the article.

Bruce Davidson, Magnum Photo

Autobiographical Features—Features that deal with the life or personal experiences of the writer can be classified as autobiographical features. Ordinarily, autobiographical features are written by well-known persons. However, anyone may have an interesting story to tell. In the following autobiographical feature, a journalism student explains how she became interested in writing. The form of the example is similar to that of the essay. The sentences flow smoothly because the ideas are well expressed and are presented in chronological order. Use of the "picture-frame" device (the conclusion refers back to the introduction) gives the article unity.

EXAMPLE:

JOURNALISM: A STEPPING-STONE

When I was ten years old, I fell in love with a library, neither very large nor ornate. It had at the most a few thousand volumes at hand. Just the same, I decided then and there that I would spend the rest of my life in a room whose very walls burst with knowledge and adventure. Perhaps it was the smell so peculiar to libraries, the odor of old pages and new bindings. It might have been the books themselves. Their titles fascinated me, the covers pleaded in various hues to be taken down and read. And of course, being ten years old, and not of a very steadfast nature, I was captured and bound.

Bound did I say? No, the very opposite. They showed to me lands and people I had never dreamed of. They loosed the bonds of the here and now and the chains of time and space. I created a world of my own, retreating further and further into my sanctuary of books. They became a haven of volumes, thatched with a roof of pages. There was only one difficulty. I had neglected to provide for the windows. Somehow, I had lost contact with the reality of a child's existence. I was completely alone.

As I grew older, I realized that everyone had dreams, but they had to be kept in their place. I had a responsibility to myself to live in a real world, populated with real people. I was learning to live.

It must have been then that I decided the only vocation possible for me was one in which I could write. To think, in this pen lie a million words. With it, I can draw a picture in your mind of ideas, beauty, moods, emotions, love, glory, eternity, and dreams. What world is not within the ken of my mind, and what can stop me from giving it to you in all its beauty and magnitude?

Here is a snowfall I saw in Vermont, here a glorious sunrise, here a tree, a cloud, a leaf, a storm. Here! Take it! I give it to you, as great men and women of the world gave to me the beauty beheld by their eyes.

I realized at once that I was not yet qualified to cast my thoughts before the world, nor did I think they would be accepted. There was and is much to learn. If one wants to write he must have a broad background of many dif-

218

ferent subjects. He must travel and know the world and its many peoples, their customs, ideas, and beliefs. He must know of the great philosophers of the past and the present; he must read and keep up with the knowledge of the present world. So each fact that I learn is another drop of ink in my pen. Each new door I open broadens the skies for me. Every talented and capable professor or lecturer helps to bring me nearer my goal. Each new experience broadens my senses and perceptions so that someday I will be able to return it one-hundred fold. That is the purpose of a liberal arts education.

The courses I will take .in journalism will aid me in another way; not so much in content, but in manner. I must learn clarity, unity, construction, and organization. What I write must be palatable to the reader or it serves no purpose. Very frankly, I want to use journalism as a stepping-stone to a final goal.

How will it help my fellow man? I will create a magic carpet, a space ship, a golden chariot to help him reach for the stars. I will make him laugh and cry at life and death. I will show him good and evil, right and wrong. I will stimulate his rage and his despair, his sympathy and love, for heaven knows, people do not feel strongly enough about things today. My words may light a fire, whether in a man's mind, or in· his wastebasket, I cannot know.

But this I do know. That, someday, my books will sit quietly on a crowded shelf, in covers of red and gold, and wait for a very little girl, lost in a very big world.

Sandra Altner
Syracuse University

Personality Features—Feature stories concerning the life, interests, and accomplishments of well-known or interesting persons can be categorized as personality features. Often a personality feature is based on material obtained from an interview. Whether the interview will result in a straight interview story or in a personality feature depends on how much creativity and imagination the writer chooses to put into the story. Often a personality feature will show how an average person gained fame or distinction, as in the following EXAMPLE:

EXAMPLE:

SUDSENLY, SHE'S A CELEBRATION —

And her entire life's churned potsy curvy

Schoolgirl Tessa Tracy's mangled maxims have made her a sudden celebrity.

Tessa, 17, is an attractive blonde long famous among family and friends for cunning puns and fractured phrases like:

"Where there's a ways, there's a means." "He's nothing but a liar and prefabricator." "It's so rheumatic to eat by candlelight."

Through the years her mother took notes and recently the Santa Barbara News-Press printed "The Collected

Sayings of Miss Tessa Tracy . . . a Born Malapropist."

The Associated Press carried them, and now Tessa's getting letters from appreciative readers from all over the country. . . .

Gene Handsaker
The Associated Press

How-to-Do-It Features—Many newspapers and magazines print feature articles which explain to the reader the practical steps to follow in order to do something. Examples of features in this category are "do-it-yourself" articles on crafts and home repairs, articles explaining how to improve your bridge or golf game, articles on diet and exercise, and homemaking articles on sewing and cooking. In the following "tongue-in-cheek" feature story a writer, irritated by the fact that many persons in public life avoid giving straight answers to interviewers, describes how to engage in the art of "non-speak."

EXAMPLE:

'Non-Speak' as Spoken By Two Who Are Fluent

One of the trade tricks every diplomat must learn is how to talk in "non-speak," how to say absolutely nothing when asked publicly to say something, perhaps about a talk he just had with a foreign official.

There are various ways of doing this, and a really professional diplomat can employ one, or several, or combinations or parts of each.

Yesterday, Secretary of State Dean Rusk and British Foreign Secretary Patrick Gordon Walker proved themselves masters of "non-speak" as they summed up a meeting they had just had at the White House with President Johnson. Their words were hearty, cheery, affirmative—and meant nothing.

In the process of skillfully saying nothing, the two men avoided the dangers of less refined techniques. One of the easier "non-speak" maneuvers, for instance, is to say, "No comment." But this involves certain hazards.

If said with a smile, "No comment" might indicate the just concluded talk had gone badly and lead to erroneous speculation. . . .

Another way is to say nothing when asked, lower the head and plunge past the persons, usually reporters, who are asking how the talk went. Some enraged diplomats follow this procedure. But, again, the plunge-silence response can indicate the just concluded talk was a real bust, an impression the diplomat might not want to create for distribution in a troubled world.

Possibly the best way for a diplomat to handle questions about a talk with a foreign official is to fall back on glowing words which, when weighed and studied, add up to zero. Mr. Gordon Walker and Mr. Rusk, in a brief session with reporters after the White House meeting yesterday, set an example of the empty-word technique which diplomats everywhere will applaud and envy. This is how they did it:

Mr. Gordon Walker said his talks with President Johnson had gone off remarkably well.

220

Mr. Rusk, beaming, said the talks were "extraordinarily valuable," adding, "We are off to a fine start."

"I can echo everything the Secretary has said," echoed Mr. Gordon Walker. "The talks were very valuable indeed."

On the subjects he had discussed with the President, Mr. Gordon Walker had this to say:

"We covered a very large field and have started with a broad identity of interests."

Expanding, he reported he and the President had talked about defense issues. But he would not elaborate.

"Will Britain's Labor government institute any policies which might affect Anglo-American relations?" someone asked, just as a matter of form.

"There might be changes of emphasis in certain policy questions, but they will not affect Anglo-American relations between us in any adverse way," Mr. Gordon Walker answered.

That query should be addressed to Mr. Johnson, Mr. Gordon Walker replied, employing still another variation of "non-speak," which might be called "bouncing the question back to the questioner."

However, Foreign Secretary Walker went on, "I certainly hope the meeting will take place soon." Some connoisseurs half-frowned, sensing a near-violation of "non-speak" in that reply.

But Mr. Rusk was quick to come to his colleague's side.

"A Presidential-Prime Ministerial meeting," he announced smoothly, "will be very welcome."

Tom Lambert
The New York Herald Tribune

Historical Features—Historical features, informative news features about past events, are usually written to observe national holidays, birthdates of historical personages, and anniversaries of important news events. For example, timely historical feature stories could be written for publication on Independence Day, on Thanksgiving, on the anniversary of a city founder's birth, or to recall such significant events as the ending of World War II. Source material for historical features can be found in your school or community library. The following is an EXAMPLE of an appropriate historical feature written during the Christmas season.

EXAMPLE:

'SILENT NIGHT' TO WARM 150th YULETIDE

VIENNA—"Silent night. Holy night."

The world famous song, which is sung the world over at Christmas, is 150 years old this year.

On December 24, 1818, Joseph Mohr, assistant vicar in the small Salzburg village of Oberndorf in Austria, hurried along the snow-covered lane to see his friend, Franz Xavier Gruber, the schoolmaster and organist at the nearby village of Arnsdorf.

He had, he told Gruber, a poem with six verses which he wanted set to music for two solo voices, with choir and guitar accompaniment.

Gruber was happy to oblige his friend. Within a matter of hours, the melody had been composed and copied out. That night, on Christmas Eve, the song was sung for the first time. . . .

Ritchie W. McEwen
Copley News Service

Explanatory Features—Because of the complexity of many news events, details of some news developments may need to be clarified for the reader in explanatory (or informative) features. The writing of explanatory features often requires that the writer do research or have a specialized knowledge of a particular subject. During the administration of Franklin D. Roosevelt, the press secretary called reporters together and announced: "We've gone off the gold standard." Probably the average newspaper reader would not understand the significance of such a statement without the help of a clearly written explanatory feature story. During the Roosevelt administration many newswriters were called "general assignment" reporters, meaning that they were considered to be capable of writing news stories about any type of news event. However, a good explanatory feature about the significance of the country going off the gold standard could probably not be written by a "general assignment" reporter: such a story would require a specialized knowledge of the workings of finance.

The writer for the school newspaper may want to write explanatory feature stories on such school-related issues as new course programs, how tax laws affect students, or what is meant by a proposed bond issue.

In the following example which explains the work of a presidential photographer, the reporter injects life into the story by using a humorous lead, by presenting part of the story in the form of a motion picture script, by giving the story an historical perspective, and by comparing the total of photos in the Lyndon Baines Johnson Library to the number of words in the *Old Testament*.

EXAMPLE:

LBJ Photo Job Far From 'Snap'

Maybe the Lyndon Baines Johnson Library in Dallas won't have enough room for books after all—just photographs by the ton of you know who.

It has been one of those extraordinary Washington secrets.

Alfred Hitchcock never dreamed up a more bizarre script.

For Act 1, Scene 1, enter Yoichi Robert Okamoto, born in—not Tokyo, Kyushu or Shikoku—but Yonkers, New York, who became "reputable" photographer for the U.S. Information Agency.

222

One assignment involved taking candids of then Vice President Lyndon Johnson. LBJ approved of the pics and Okie was okay.

Shortly after the tragedy in Dallas, President Johnson had Okamoto transferred to the White House as his personal photographer.

And what never had happened before at 1400 Pennsylvania Avenue had begun.

James Polk, the 11th President of the U.S., was the first ever to have his picture taken in the White House. The date was February 14, 1849, and Polk, his long hair, "gray and straggly," his face etched in deep lines from a terminal disease, sat in a straight-back dining room chair as photographer Matthew Brady held him erect with a head clamp for his daguerreotype. He died 18 days later.

Five administrations passed before President Lincoln went to Brady's studio "without any special regard to his dress . . . his long hair brushed with little care."

Robert Lincoln explained the feeling of the President on that day when he later wrote, "When any attempt was made to photograph my father he relapsed into his mood of melancholy."

Twenty administrations have come and gone since then and the attitude in the White House has come full circle.

You have heard the expression "I'd like to be a fly on the wall." Well, Okie was (and is) constantly clicking LBJ looking sad, glad, alone or with friends, family, and world leaders.

Said a colleague of Okie, "He has been in on everything taking pictures—even top secret meetings."

To give an idea of the scope of the assignment, Okie took 11,000 pictures of President Johnson in the first seven weeks after Dallas.

Today, five years and three weeks later, there are 250,000 (not counting those rejected) snapshots in LBJ's personal collection. If you can't picture how much that is, think of the King James version of the Bible. The number of words in all 27 books of the New Testament is 250,000.

Another comparison, the number of photos in LBJ's scrapbooks matches the number of words defined in Webster's unabridged Twentieth Century Dictionary published in 1964.

For processing and filing this colossus of candids, what used to be simply a house of Georgetown has been turned into a hush-hush "unmarked photo laboratory" at sssh—3248 M Street.

Nobody gets in; nobody, that is, but Okie's two assistants, a researcher, and about 20 lab staff members.

When the cost of the project was estimated at "around $250,000," one insider called the figure "on the low side."

Mary Cremmen
The Boston Globe

Color Features—Color features are sidebar stories concerning the trappings that add glamor to major events. For example, a main story might be written about the outcome of the Homecoming Game, whereas a color feature might concern the crowning of the Homecoming Queen. Other color stories might deal with what happens backstage during a Drama Club presentation, or in the football team's locker room during half-time. The following color story describes events occurring during half-time at a football game.

EXAMPLE:

SO WHO NEEDS HORSES?

The Greeks showed the Romans a trick or two at Syracuse University Saturday.

Romans put horses out in front of their chariots. Yesterday the Greeks (SU fraternity brothers) used each other.

This twang on an old saw came at the second "Greek Games" run off in Archbold Stadium as part of the last act of a campus "Greek Week" sponsored by the Interfraternity Council. The touch of Marx Brothers followed a week of social events, entertainment, speeches, scholastic competition, and alumni programs. The finale occurred during half-time of the Syracuse-Oregon State game.

The chariots—all hammered together in the fraternity houses with wood, bed sheets, flags, and bicycle wheels—carried two riders (a coed and a flyweight brother), hauled 100 yards by alternating teams of four students.

"I can't believe my eyes," a football fan said. "Are they really doing that?"

The stadium cinder track was wet, the midfield was wet, and riders and donors of horsepower were freckled with mud. . . .

Richard Case
Syracuse Herald-Journal

Interview and Speech Story Features—In most cases, the reporter writing an account of an interview or speech will emphasize what the interviewee had to say. Occasionally, the reporter may want to emphasize the circumstances surrounding a speech or interview, rather than the words spoken by the interviewee. This is especially true when the situation is out-of-the-ordinary, colorful, or glamorous. Assigned to cover a speech by presidential candidate Richard M. Nixon, a student journalist decided that, in addition to covering the speech, she should do a story on reporters caught up in the hectic pace of the campaign.

EXAMPLE:

"I'm a (yawn) UPI (yawn) Reporter"

A state of euphoria for just being on the ground and near food again prevailed. Reporters had gathered in gaggles, and flapping their wings like geese, honked away at each other, crowing at a colleague's typing style (like a charging two-fingered rhinoc-eros), or cackling at a fake Nixon press release (which had Mr. Nixon finally taking a stand on Motherhood and Apple Pie. In favor).

Suddenly, the dread double-headed phantom of Deadline-Pressure crept in, and the only clacking was from the 35 typewriters; the only human sound an occasional "For Heaven's sake, will *some*body get me a scotch-and-water . . . pleee-ease . . .?"

Next to one Smith-Corona a stack of once-white paper stubbornly resisted the efforts of a bleary-eyed young journalist to hypnotize it into a feature. Finally, he buried his campaign-weary head in his arms with a "why-didn't-I-go-to-medical-school" sigh. He was a correspondent for the Washington UPI Bureau, and this was the press room for Nixon's Boston visit.

Don Fulson has been traveling with Nixon since two weeks after the Miami nomination. While the pace is growing ever more frenetic with the approaching election (the step-up is due chiefly to the nearness of Nov. 5, rather than Humphrey's poll gains, Fulson feels), he finds that traveling with the candidate is "sometimes interesting and exciting, but always educational."

Always exhausting, certainly. That evening the corps had flown in with Nixon from Pennsylvania, and would spend Friday in Boston and Chicago, with Saturday in Chicago, Mount Pleasant, Ill., N.J., and New York City. Since Sunday was a "day off" the journalist would fly to Washington to prepare a feature for release Monday. Meanwhile, UPI expected to hear from him on Nixon's activities, so he filed stories in his "spare" time.

With such a schedule, and an increased push slated for the next fortnight's tour of the "key states" in the north, one wonders what ever prompts anyone to follow around a man who this November may be only a partner in the law firm of Nixon, Mudge, Rose, Guthrie, Alexander, and Mitchell. Certainly not a fondness for relaxation and creature comforts such as warm beer, cold coffee, strange hotels in strange cities, and ever so much plane riding.

Don Fulson started out as a "Top 40" disc jockey while at Syracuse University and "just sort of drifted into newswriting." He then found himself two years ago writing for the UPI Washington bureau. (No, it was not all that simple, but the campaign tends to dull one's senses at midnight and make biographical data sketchy at best.)

Four years ago, Fulson was assigned to cover Goldwater's bid for the presidency, and he notes a strong similarity between the crowds and their reactions to the two Republican candidates. But he feels there is a major difference in the handling of the campaign itself. "This will set a precedent for future campaigns. You leave your baggage outside the door in some hotels, and find it inside the room at the next stop. It is little incidents, such as these, that result in a well-managed tour, and good press relations," he said.

As far as future plans, at this stage disc jockey Don Fulson was not expressing any worries or hopes beyond the speech at Mount Pleasant, Ill.

And then the speech at Eatontown, N.J. And then. . . .

Carolyn Garrett
Boston University
School of Public Communications

Weather Features—Weather reporters for metropolitan dailies telephone the U.S. Weather Bureau each day to secure the information for their stories. To gain reader interest, weather reporters try to present interesting facts in their leads. A routine weather story lead might be as follows:

EXAMPLE:

> The first major snowstorm of the season is expected to move into the Midwest today with Chicago escaping most of the six inches of snow predicted for western and northern regions. . . .

Unusual weather conditions often make good material for imaginative feature stories. During one extended hot spell in the San Francisco area, a reporter wrote this award-winning weather feature:

EXAMPLE:

The Quietest Night Ever

"This," said one veteran moon-watcher in the San Francisco police department, "was the quietest night since the blizzard of '88."

In as much as San Francisco had no blizzard in '88, that makes it the quietest night ever.

Hall of Justice observers were puzzled.

Collectively, they constitute an "indisputable authority" on which things are learned. ("it was learned today, on indisputable authority . . .")

And when Hall of Justice observers can't agree on anything else they'll agree on this:

On a balmy summer evening, when the moon hangs in the sky like a lamp without a post, peccadillos are the rule.

Some people start shooting—and not necessarily at the moon.

Others take moonshine internally, with bizarre side effects.

Out at the zoo, the armadillos have eyes for the giraffes.

Real crazy.

But not last night.

Nobody leaped nude into the Palace of Fine Arts lagoon.

Nobody drove a sports convertible through Twin Peaks tunnel.

Usually busy Mission Police Station received no complaints except from householders who said neighbors' radios—what with everyone's windows open—were too loud.

No added starters joined the Alcatraz exodus.

The emergency ambulance service never got a call between sundown and sunup. . . .

There might have been an awful lot of conspiracy going on for all anyone knows, but the only overt felony all night was the $231 stickup of night clerk Richard Dye at the Roosevelt Hotel, 240 Jones St.

In Martin County, the bad guys were similarly becalmed.

The sheriff's office had only one call —to investigate a dog which was barking at the moon.

Open-air cafes and taverns did a booming business.

The Collins—Tom and John—were the heroes of the hour.

But nobody fell off a dock or stole a boat.

In San Mateo County, things were quiet—although it was not the kind of horse latitude quiet that so often prevails here.

"I can't figure it out at all," one old-time cop said.

"It must be because the Weather Man turned the heat on."

Andrew Curtin
San Francisco News Call Bulletin

Humorous Features—Writing humor is an art requiring an understanding of basic human nature. Associated Press reporter Hal Boyle, one of the best feature writers in the country, wrote the following humorous feature for publication in newspapers throughout the country.

EXAMPLE:

Those Gal Smokers Can Be Big Ordeal

One of life's little ordeals for the American male is the problem of taking care of the lady smoker.

It isn't enough today, in a woman's world, that a man open doors for the ladies, doff his bonnet in an elevator to them, give up his seat in a bus to them, and bring his paycheck home in his mouth to the fairest of them all.

No, indeed. One of the fringe benefits of manhood—and the sternest test of gallantry—is the privilege of helping the girls through the ceremonial rites of the nicotine habit.

Here are some types of lady smokers familiar to most men:

"Perky Pam"—This little doll thinks it is cute to droop a cigarette from the corner of her mouth, stand on tiptoe, look you square in the Adam's apple, and then demand in a sexy drawl, "light me, Big Boy!"

"Sandra Showoff"—This female powerhouse likes ostentation as well as attention. She waits until she's at the far corner of the room before pulling out her cigarette, thus forcing you to gallop over before everybody to ignite it.

"Golddigger Gertie"—No matter where you meet her, whether at a cocktail party or atop the Statue of Liberty, the cigarette she always pulls out is her last one. Somehow, somewhere, you have to manage to get her another pack immediately—if you're any kind of a man at all.

"Thelma Twitchy"—The gabby type. Keeps talking as you try to light her up, and the cigarette bobs around in all directions like a weathervane. When the match finally burns your fingers and you cry "Ouch," she asks loudly, "What's the matter? Got the shakes again? Maybe you'd better lay off the stuff for a while."

"Exotic Erica"—Can't stand anything except highly perfumed Oriental cigarettes which she puffs from the near end of a two-foot black and silver holder. After half an hour by her, you reel away smelling like an old Chinese temple.

"Bertha Beatnik"—She's the Bohemian type. Thinks cigarettes are strictly for the cowbirds at the party. Prefers an imitation corncob pipe encrusted with rhinestones. Gets ashes on the rug by knocking pipe against her shoe heel.

227

One nice thing about Bertha: your wife never invites her back again.

"Smudge-pot Nell" — This human chimney is a chain-smoker who feels socially insecure unless she has at least three cigarettes going for her at all times. A man really needs a blow torch to keep her lit up.

"Independent Inez"—Ruggedly self-reliant. Waits until a man gets his lighter out, then chills chivalry with the cold remark, "Oh, I'm a big girl now. I'm quite able to light my own cigarette." The man, crestfallen, withdraws his lighter, silently wishing he could cram it down her proud throat.

"Critical Kitty"—She blows smoke rings in your face for an hour. But when you light up a cigar yourself in self-defense, she wails, "Please put it out, won't you? I simply can't stand the smell of those awful things."

Dames like these are enough to give any fellow nicotine narcosis. They help explain why women may be smoking more—but men are enjoying it less.

Hal Boyle
The Associated Press

Satirical Features—In satirical features newswriters, through the use of wit, irony, and sarcasm, expose the folly or wrong-doing of persons in authority, of public institutions, or in political situations. Satire is one of the most difficult forms of writing and may present both the writer and reader with difficulties: the writer may not have the sophisticated vocabulary necessary to make his point, or the reader may not have enough knowledge of the situation to understand that the writer is using satire. Art Buchwald, one of the best writers of satire in the country, once wrote a satirical feature in which he stated that there was no such person as FBI Chief J. Edgar Hoover. Most readers would recognize Buchwald's statement as fictional; however, one newspaper received calls from a number of readers saying such things as, "Yes there is a J. Edgar Hoover! I met him in his Washington office last month!" When Congressmen were investigating reports that some agencies of the government were instigating trouble throughout the world, Buchwald wrote the following satirical feature.

EXAMPLE:

What? No trouble?

I just received a very heartbreaking letter from a friend of mine who happens to be the American ambassador to an African country which, to protect him, I will call Zemululu. He writes that he is in serious trouble with the State Department and doesn't know what to do about it. His problem first began when a year went by without any anti-American demonstrations in the country. Washington became suspicious and thought he was keeping something from them.

He received a cable which said, "CAN'T UNDERSTAND LACK OF ANTI-AMERICAN DEMONSTRATIONS YOUR

AREA. PLEASE CLARIFY WHY NATIVES ARE FRIENDLY."

My friend wired back he had no explanation for it unless the country's climate did not lend itself to demonstrating. He thought he would hear no more from Washington, but a week later he received a follow-up cable: "HOW COME YOU HAVE SENT IN NO REPORTS ON COUPS OR ATTEMPTED COUPS IN YOUR COUNTRY? YOU ONLY AMBASSADOR IN AFRICA NOT EXPECTING A REVOLUTION. WHAT HAVE YOU BEEN DOING?"

He replied, "ZEMULULU NOT COUP-CONSCIOUS. MILITARY GETTING ALONG FINE WITH PREMIER."

There was an ominous silence for a few weeks but then he had a bit of good luck and was able to wire, "PEACE CORPS SCANDAL MAY BE BREWING UP-COUNTRY. COULD CAUSE TREMENDOUS DAMAGE TO OUR RELATIONS HERE."

They immediately cabled back, "GOOD BOY. THIS MAY BE THE FIRST BREAK WE'VE HAD. SEND US FULL DETAILS."

After a thorough investigation he replied, "PEACE CORPS SCANDAL TURNED OUT TO BE FALSE ALARM."

A month went by and suddenly the code machines started clicking again. "CONGRESSIONAL JUNKET JUST RETURNED FROM ZEMULULU REPORTS THEY PLEASED WITH STABILITY AND PROGRESS MADE THERE AND VERY IMPRESSED WITH LACK OF SUBVERSION. SO YOU REALIZE THIS COULD HURT OVERALL BUDGET FOR UPCOMING YEAR? ALSO UNDERSTAND TIME AND NEWSWEEK CORRESPONDENTS HAVE MADE OFFICIAL COMPLAINTS TO THEIR EDITORS THAT ZEMULULU IS DEAD AS RUNNING STORY. EVERYONE HERE VERY DEPRESSED."

To save his job the ambassador wired back. "TWO CHINESE CULTURAL ATTACHES HAVE JUST ARRIVED FROM PEKING, AND HAVE OPENED CHINESE RESTAURANT."

An immediate reply from Washington said, "CONGRATULATIONS ALL OF US HERE DELIGHTED WITH NEWS. HOW MANY C.I.A. MEN CAN WE SEND YOU?"

Art Buchwald

Featured Brights—Newspaper editors often need short two- or three-sentence stories to fill out a column of type. If these stories are written in straight news story style, they are known as fillers or boilerplate. If the facts contained in such short stories are presented in feature story form, they then become featured brights. Featured brights are usually short, humorous features, often ending with a punch line or surprise climax. Some types of featured brights can be thought of as feature sidebars. For example, if at the scene of a fire, a dog were seen tugging at a fireman's coat in order to prevent the fireman from entering a burning building, such information could be presented as a feature sidebar to the main fire story. Following is an example of a featured bright.

EXAMPLE:

Two Israeli policewomen on a good-will tour of the United States were not over-awed by New York City traffic after directing cars for 10 minutes in Times Square. Roberta

Cohen, 19, conceded only that New York traffic snarls are "worse than Israeli traffic." But Janice Freedman, 20, said, "Traffic is more hectic during the rush hour in Tel Aviv."

Feature Photographs—Human interest photographs often make good feature material for newspapers. Feature photos can provide the reader with a welcome relief from pages filled with straight news copy. The following classified advertisement provided one photographer with a subject for an interesting feature photograph.

> **For Sale:** One old hound dog that is lazy and has fleas. Price: $500. Call 353-3484.

Intrigued, the photographer telephoned the man who had placed the advertisement. He learned that the dog's owner had given in to his wife's demands that he sell the dog, and had placed a classified advertisement in the newspaper—but he hadn't told her how the advertisement would read. The photographer asked if the advertisement had brought results: "Yes," replied the man. "One caller had offered to trade two $250 cats." Faced with the possibility of having two cats rather than one dog, the man's wife consented to keeping the dog. The man was happy to let the photographer take a feature picture of his son showing the dog licking the boy's face.

Jacqueline Karch

Animals and children lend human interest to feature photographs.

News Features—News feature stories often employ any of the devices of form and style that are common to the human interest story. News feature stories have, as a basis, a timely news happening with a human interest angle, and are generally more timely than straight human interest or long feature stories. News feature stories are usually about events that have already taken place or that everyone already knows about. Following is the lead from a news feature story.

Chute Fails to Open on First Jump

Editor's Note: The following story is true. This exciting incident relates a harrowing experience a young sophomore at MHS went through as he made a practice jump from an airplane over Orange, Massachusetts, in his desire to learn skydiving.

"It was my first time jumping from a Cessna 185. I had always wanted to learn how to jump and now my big moment had come. I was to be the first one out. Since I was a beginner, I was to jump at an altitude of 2,500 feet. . . ."

Betty Matta
Mustang News,
Medford High School,
Medford, Mass.

News Summary Features—News summary features summarize a series of news events, often by day, week, by month, and sometimes by year or years. Many newspapers feature news summary features in "capsule" form on their front pages, expanding them on the inside pages. School newspapers often use the news summary feature to summarize such events as all school dances for a particular year, all athletic competitions for a given season, or all of the fund drives. Following is the lead from a news summary feature story.

CLUB ROUNDUP — SPRING SALUTE PLANNED

Boom! Everything but fireworks is aiding Jackson High's salute to spring this year. Style shows, field trips, elections, and special presentations are only a few of the multitude of events scheduled. . . .

Feature Obituaries—School newspapers must, at times, publish obituaries that are presented as features. Such obituaries should be respectful and sympathetic without being over-sentimental, should be in good taste, and should be short, factual reports that state what happened, what accomplishments the person achieved, and the funeral details. When editorial comment is necessary, such comment should be placed in the editorial column.

EXAMPLE:

JOHN J. PAGET DIES AT 93; GAVE SWAN BOATS A 'HAVEN'

Thousands upon thousands they came —the children came. And they were of all ages and from all parts of the country.

They came to the Public Gardens to ride the Swan Boats while touring historic Boston.

And they became the life of John J. Paget who inherited the Swan Boat fleet from his father. Known as Commodore Paget, he began helping his father in 1889—at the age of 13—and devoted the rest of his life to what he said was "making children happy."

But the Swan Boats are not running today. Commodore Paget died this morning at the age of 93. Services will be held on Tuesday at 11 A.M. at St. Mark's Church.

Stories concerning the Commodore abound. For example, in 1900, six years before he graduated from Harvard College, he gave a Swan Boat ride to an Indian Rajah who, in payment, gave the Commodore a large lump of gold.

The passing of the Commodore will be noted by his thousands of friends, and the Swan Boats will not "die." The Commodore's life-long endeavor will be continued by his son Paul, age 32.

Society and Women's Features

Most newspapers contain columns and feature articles (on society and women's pages) on subjects primarily of interest to women. Society features include news of engagements, weddings, social events, and personalities. Also included in this general category are columns and feature articles offering practical information in the areas of health, child-rearing, family living, appearance and fashion, and "how-to-do-it" features on cooking and other homemaking skills.

Most school newspapers contain feature articles oriented to the interests of girls. These feature articles can be generally categorized as personality, occupation, social event, and appearance features or columns.

Personalities—One of the favorite pastimes of both men and women is "people-watching." Many women, interested in news of celebrities, enjoy reading

232

CHINESE CONTRASTS—The crispness of shredded iceberg lettuce, slivered scallions, carrots and green peppers contrasts with morsels of chicken just as the lemon flavoring points up the sweet sauce.

LEE LUM'S LEMON CHICKEN

4 whole chicken breasts, boned and skinned
2 tablespoons light soy sauce
¼ teaspoon sesame oil
1 teaspoon salt
1 tablespoon gin or vodka
3 egg whites, beaten until frothy
1 cup water chestnut flour or powder (available at Chinese grocery stores, including the Yuet Hing Market, 23 Pell Street)
Peanut or salad oil
¾ cup sugar
½ cup white vinegar
1 cup chicken broth
1 tablespoon cornstarch
2 tablespoons water
1 teaspoon monosodium glutamate
1 lemon, juice and thin yellow rind finely chopped
¼ head iceberg lettuce, finely shredded
3 small carrots, cut in julienne strips
½ large green pepper, cut in julienne strips
3 scallions, cut into julienne strips
½ cup shredded canned pineapple
1 one-ounce bottle lemon extract (see note).

1. Place the chicken in a shallow earthenware dish or bowl. Combine the soy sauce, sesame oil, salt and gin or vodka and pour over the chicken. Toss to coat and let sit 30 minutes.

2. Drain the chicken and discard the marinade. Add chicken pieces to the beaten egg whites and toss to coat. Place the water chestnut flour on a plate and coat the chicken pieces with the flour.

3. Add peanut oil to a skillet to a depth of one-half inch and heat to about 350 degrees. Add the chicken pieces, a few at a time if necessary. Brown one side, turn and brown the other. Drain

4. Meanwhile, place the sugar, vinegar, broth, cornstarch mixed with the water, monosodium glutamate and lemon juice and rind in a small pan. Bring to a boil, stirring until the mixture thickens.

5. Cut the drained chicken into one-inch crosswise slices and place it on top of the shredded lettuce on a serving platter. If necessary, keep it warm in a 200-degree oven.

6. Add the vegetables and pineapple to the sauce. Remove from the heat and stir in the extract. Pour over the chicken.

Yield: Four servings.

Note: This amount of lemon extract is accurate. It should be added at the very last moment.

Oriental tang

By CRAIG CLAIBORNE

One of the most interesting of the Chinese dishes available in Manhattan is a creation of Lee Lum, the highly skilled chef of Pearl's Chinese Restaurant at 149 West 48th Street. It is called simply Lemon Chicken and consists of boneless chicken breast, coated with water chestnut powder, crisply fried and served over crisp vegetables in a sweet and pungent lemon sauce, whose extraordinary flavor comes from the ounce of lemon extract that is added at the last moment. The recipe is given here for home cooks who would like to duplicate Lee Lum's triumph.

Features on cooking, like the recipe shown above, and features on homemaking skills are among the most popular types of features found on the newspaper's women's feature pages.

about other women with whom they share similar interests. In this category are feature stories about professional women and about wives of prominent men in such areas as sports, business, and government. The following is an example of the type of personality feature often found in school newspapers that is of particular interest to female students.

EXAMPLE:

> Typical of senior Susan Asche is the warm, friendly smile with which she greeted the members of the evaluating committee recently.
>
> Sue's quiet but effective type of service in many situations may go unnoticed by some, yet students and faculty members often turn to her for help, knowing that she will serve when and where needed.
>
> This Southwest senior's activities do not end with a few big publicized efforts. She quietly volunteers when there is work to be done and keeps on until it is finished.
>
> *The Southwest Lancer*
> Southwest Miami High School
> Miami, Florida

Occupations—Many feature articles of interest to feminine readers are based on employment and career opportunities.

EXAMPLE:

> Ten senior girls are enrolled in a new course with a salary of $1,200 or more in addition to their academic credit.
>
> The cooperative business education course offers participating students two credits and includes a four-hour work day with pay. Pupils attend their required classes in the morning, and then work in an office applying varied secretarial skills in the afternoon.
>
> *The Lancer*
> Arlington High School
> Indianapolis, Indiana

Information about the lives of professional women also makes appropriate material for women's page features, as shown in the lead of the following feature article about author Jean Kerr.

EXAMPLE:

Larchmont, N.Y. (AP)—When Jean Kerr was turning out $300 magazine articles in the back seat of the nine-year-old family Chevy, parked a few blocks from her houseful of boisterous boys, she never considered herself a serious writer. "I consider a writer serious when he makes more than $20,000-a-year," was the way she put it.

That was five years ago.

Today, two books, two movie sales, and a hit play later, Jean Kerr has had to revise her standard upward. Her royalties from the five companies of "Mary, Mary" average $20,000 a week. And she approaches her work with the same uncomplicated candor as when she heard MGM had paid $75,000 for the screen rights to her best-seller "Please Don't Eat the Daisies."

The venerable Chevy still holds down a place of honor in the Kerr garage, alongside a newer, more expensive vehicle, but its back-seat recluse has moved on to larger, more comfortable quarters. Jean Kerr now works in a corner of the bedroom amid a colossal chaos of Coke bottles, cigarette butts, and disorderly mounds of manuscript that, as the children know from past experience, constitute the rubbled construction site of a new play.

The Associated Press

Social Events—Throughout the school year, school newspapers include many feature articles on student social events. Including details (such as a description of the decorations at a school dance) will add life to a feature story and will help recreate the atmosphere of the occasion.

EXAMPLE:

Members of the Junior Class will sponsor a tea as a special Valentine's Day greeting for their mothers in the cafeteria this afternoon.

A Valentine motif of hearts and cupids will transform the cafeteria. In charge is a committee of 24 junior girls directed by Miss Martha White, junior counselor who will spend the seventh period decorating.

The tea table centerpiece and the refreshments of. . . .

The Lancer
Arlington High School
Indianapolis, Indiana

Appearance—Most women are interested in reading about ways to improve their appearance and the appearance of their homes. Feature articles based on beauty care, fashion, and interior decoration have high feminine interest. The following is a fashion feature oriented to the interests of female students.

EXAMPLE:

"Teens today are the best dressed in history," Chuck Mills, co-owner of the University Men's Shop told students in Journalism I and II classes last week.

He speaks often to women's as well as men's groups because, he says, "Seventy percent of men's and boys' clothing is bought under the influence of women and girls."

He finds that in schools where there is an ideal or program on proper dress the morale is higher and the influence on grades is enormous.

The Southwest Lancer
Southwest Miami High School
Miami, Florida

Feature Columns

School newspapers contain many types of feature columns. One of the most popular types is the social column which presents news about students and their activities. Information contained in the social column is usually presented in the form of brief news items. Most social columns are informal in style, often use humor and figures of speech, and are friendly and conversational in tone.

EXAMPLE:

Yorkshire Pudding a Real Enigma

In mid-April, forty-two Arlington Catholic girls set forth on a very enlightening journey to Canada. During their four-day expedition they learned such things as the true value of a dollar, how to load a camera, and just what Yorkshire pudding is. The last bit of information was my personal contribution to the treasury of knowledge gained from the trip.

I, being the hamburger-and-French-fries type, for a change of pace decided, on the last night of our sojourn, to dine elegantly. The only possible locale for such an event was "la grande salle à manger" of the Chateau Frontenac. The setting was in keeping, from the red and gold menu to the confusing array of tableware.

The ordering of the meal was a rather simple process since the only thing I recognized on the menu was roast prime ribs. . . .

A C Current
Arlington Catholic High School
Arlington, Massachusetts

School feature column writers should never resort to gossip about students. Unfounded gossip can be considered libelous. Many school newspapers, however, do carry feature columns which, while generally categorized as advice columns, can be considered as gossip columns. To avoid the possibility of libel, such columns usually use the signed question-and-answer approach. While some advice columns attempt to give serious advice, others depend on satire and humor to interest and entertain readers.

EXAMPLE:

Dear Sara:

Some of my teachers have criticized the length of my hair. I think that as long as it doesn't fall in my face and interfere with my studying my hair length is my own business. What do you think?

George

Dear George:

I think that as long as your hair is clean and well-groomed, its length is your own business. However, if it gets long enough to fall in your face I think you should consider braids.

Sara

SOURCES OF MATERIAL FOR FEATURE STORIES

Feature story material is easily found in any community. Any information having interest and entertainment value for readers makes ideal material for feature articles. Schools contain an abundance of feature material and writers often get feature story ideas from student activities, student organizations, individual students and teachers, or from offices that are set up to aid students. If a student were preparing an historical feature that compared the size of the school's first graduating class to the size of the present class, his research sources could be the yearbook, the student newspaper published by the school's first class, a teacher who taught the school's first class, and local citizen who was in the class. After researching these sources, the student would have the basic research materials for a good feature.

USE OF FEATURE STORIES BY OTHER MEDIA

Newspapers and magazines are not the sole media to use feature articles. Many public relations and advertising agencies prepare and distribute a variety of public service feature materials as well as feature materials concerning clients and advertisers, and radio and television news programs present many types of features.

Public Relations Agencies—Since newspaper editors prefer to use the best available feature stories, many public relations agencies hire writers who specialize in preparing features. Feature articles prepared by public relations writers usually concern the agency's clients. The following feature article was prepared by a public relations agency and distributed to thousands of newspapers and magazines.

EXAMPLE:

From:
Carl Byoir & Associates, Inc.
800 Second Avenue
New York, N.Y. 10017

For:
SCOVILL MANUFACTURING COMPANY

AMATEUR SOLVES PRESSING PROBLEM

A Wisconsin housewife had a pressing problem.

Literally.

But by solving it she became a successful businesswoman.

This is the success story of Mrs. June Tailor of Hartland, Wis.—whose invention now is being sold coast-to-coast by Dritz and Sons, a division of Scovill Manufacturing Company.

Like every other good home sewer, Mrs. Tailor knew that proper pressing is the secret of custom-made, rather than home-made clothes.

But what does a woman do when her ironing board remains uncooperatively flat when she's trying to iron a curved seam?

Mrs. Tailor invented her own ironing board.

The Tailor Board.

It has eight different surfaces—a straight edge, an inside curve, small, medium, and large outside curves, an angle for points and corners, a long curved edge, and a flat working area for small details. All in all, just about any shape that a home sewer would need.

And it's compact enough (14 inches)

to fit on any shelf and light enough so that any woman, even the tiniest, could easily set it up.

Ever since the Dritz people bought her invention, Mrs. Tailor has been busy with other home sewing ideas.

They are—?

She isn't talking until each one has been successfully tested in her own sewing room.

Advertising Agencies—The body copy for many advertisements is often presented in feature style. The advertising copywriter may peg his story on something that is in the news. For example, if city drivers were concerned about traffic congestion, a copywriter for a headache remedy might begin his copy with a reference to drivers. One major oil company has built an effective advertising campaign based on problems encountered by teenage drivers, and a recent advertisement for a car manufacturer was centered on winter driving problems.

Radio Stations—Feature articles presented on radio are prepared similarly to those written for newspapers and magazines. They must have a lead, a body, and a conclusion. However, the radio feature will be more similar to the "bright" because of the time limitations imposed by the tight scheduling necessary on radio stations. In many cases, the feature stories used by radio stations are only a few sentences in length. Following is an example of a radio station's public service type of feature presentation.

EXAMPLE:

CONSTRUCTIVE BOUNCE

Delivered by
Perry B. Bascomb—General Manager—WBZ

Young people today are full of both bounce and brainpower. One of the background papers for the upcoming Tufts Assembly shows how important it is to put that physical and mental energy to constructive use.

The author is Tufts education Professor William Kvaraceus. As he puts it, youth can be mined as a rich community resource. But in most communities today, young people appear as a surplus commodity on a glutted market.

They are kept powerless and often useless in adult society. The immediate concern about youth almost always revolves around delinquency. He feels that only when young people began to serve themselves and the community will the rising delinquency rate be cut.

The need for constructive involvement by young people goes far beyond the problems of those in or headed for trouble. Every young person needs to feel he has a place in society, that he can use his talents to help solve problems of real concern in the world around him. Many young people working for Senator Eugene McCarthy have shown they can be highly effective in the political arena. Other youths have worked with police and social workers in a number of cities to cool tensions in the ghettoes.

Dr. Kvaraceus feels that youth should be organized to take a regular part in the work of schools and colleges, police, health and welfare agencies, churches and the like.

That's easier said than done, of course. But to date there hasn't even been much recognition of the problem.

The Tufts Assembly next month can do a real service by getting the discussion rolling.

Broadcast on Radio
3/14/68—11:05 PM
3/15/68—1:05 PM; 6:28 PM
3/16/68—8:35 AM

WBZ Radio 103, Group W—
Westinghouse Broadcasting Company, Inc.
Boston, Massachusetts

Television—Television newscasters like to use at least one feature story on every news show in order to achieve variety and present "the lighter side of the news." Ordinarily, the newscaster or correspondent reads the feature story simultaneously with a filmed version of the story. Following is an example of a television script for a public service feature, while the illustration on page 242 shows a television public service "Job Bank" feature slide.

EXAMPLE:

SMOKERS ANONYMOUS/1–20V

MCU hand of cards, backs facing camera, held out for choice by second party. Lighted cigarette in ashtray on table.	ANNCR: IT SEEMS THAT SMOKING IS A POOR GAMBLE.
Hand selects card, places it face up next to ashtray . . . it's the Queen of Hearts. Camera tightens.	IF YOU SMOKE A PACK A DAY OR MORE . . . YOU RISK SHORTENING YOUR LIFE.
Second card selected; camera tightens. Card #2 is Ace of Spades.	MEDICAL RESEARCH HAS DEFINITELY LINKED CIGARETTE SMOKING WITH:
Third card—Cancer	CANCER . . .
Fourth—Emphysema	EMPHYSEMA . . .

240

Last—Heart Disease

AND HEART DISEASE.

Pick up all five cards, fan
toward camera, toss face down
next to ashtray and . . . put out
cigarette.

IF YOU'D LIKE TO QUIT . . .
SMOKERS ANONYMOUS
WOULD BE GLAD
TO HELP.

Key studio card:
Smokers Anonymous
w/phone number

SMOKERS ANONYMOUS. . . .

267–7733.

WBZ-TV 4
VTR PUBLIC SERVICE SPOT FOR SMOKERS ANONYMOUS
WBZ-TV 4, Boston, Massachusetts

CHECKLIST FOR PREPARING FEATURE ARTICLES

1. Is the lead designed to entice the reader, and is it different from a straight news story lead?

2. Does the story have unity, coherence, and emphasis?

3. Have transitions been used between sentences and paragraphs?

4. Is the story interesting and entertaining?

5. Does each sentence either interest the reader or add pertinent facts to what has already been said?

6. Have all of the trite, redundant words been edited out?

7. Has variety been achieved through the use of punctuation, vocabulary, and sentence structure?

8. Does the story have one main idea?

9. Does the story answer any questions the reader might have?

10. Does it have a lead, a body, and a conclusion?

11. Has the article ended once the story has been completed?

12. Are sentences, paragraphs, and the entire story short?

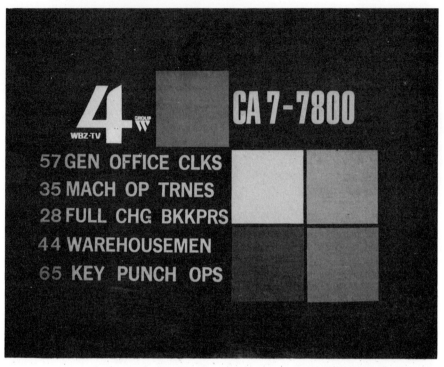

A television public service "Job Bank" feature slide.

TRIUMPH AND TRAGEDY

The student reading *Canterbury Tales, Romeo and Juliet,* or *Othello* can often see the qualities of the people he knows in the characters portrayed. The student may know persons as selfless as the clerk, as innocent as Juliet or Desdemona, or as ugly as Iago. While times may have changed since these masterpieces were written, human emotions haven't. In summary, the feature writer must be concerned with the triumphs and tragedies of the common man, and must have the ability to write about them with feeling in warm, human terms.

ACTIVITIES

1. Select five straight news stories from your daily newspaper. Rewrite each lead paragraph into a feature article lead, but maintain the basic facts. Use suspense, quotes, and shock leads to change the impact.

2. Each year many of the department stores select students for part-time employment. Plan an interview with one of these students and find out how they got their jobs, their hours, and what they think are the good and bad features of their work. Also find out any other interesting sidelights to their work. Then, prepare an outline form for a feature article based on the results of the information you obtained. Be sure to start the outline with one brief, summary statement.

3. All feature articles are based primarily on news information. Create a human interest feature story from one of the news items listed under *a* to *f* by making up your own facts. Remember to include the elements of unity, coherence, and emphasis.

    a. Mary Smith's dog was killed by a car.

    b. Petty thieves stole money from the church rectory.

    c. The goalie broke his leg during practice before the big game.

    d. Three false alarms have been rung this month at school.

    e. Cheerleader Mary Jones is very sick with pneumonia. It is believed she came down with it during the rainy football game.

    f. The Tower Ballroom, scene of last week's prom, burned down today.

4. Write a fictional featured bright elaborating on the following sentence:

The car stopped.

5. The Home Economics Department in your school often has available information on fashion news. Members of this department often work directly with local and national organizations that specialize in grooming and teen problems. Obtain any available information you can as the basis for a brief fashion news feature. Prepare your feature so that it is of interest to a feminine reading audience.

6. Many social and fashion newspapers can be made available, free of charge, for class use. For example, publications like *Sewing News* and *Women's Wear Daily* will be sent to your school's newspaper upon request. Compile an exchange list of similar newspapers so that your fashion research department can operate on a professional basis when reporting on fashion news events. Present the exchange listing to your school newspaper's circulation manager.

7. Personalities make up your student body. Select two students who have different opinions on the same issue (the dress code might be a start) and prepare a personality feature that stresses the students' attitudes towards this problem. Keep in mind that in writing a personality feature, home conditions, religious beliefs, and even the students' friends all work directly and indirectly to influence opinion. Dig into the students' backgrounds for clues to help you develop a feature angle for your story.

8. Contact a clothing manufacturing company that prints its own trade publication. Determine how this company fills page after page with interesting stories and features concerning their basic product. Prepare an interesting and entertaining feature article concerning the company's product and, after checking with your adviser, submit your article to the publication.

9. Prepare a feature story on how student fashions have changed since your grandfather's student days. Seek out old magazines and newspapers, and consult your parents for helpful suggestions.

10. Radio feature writers sometimes prepare featured brights that are included at the end of straight news broadcasts. Prepare three-line featured brights for a radio news broadcast for each of the following subjects:
  a. An apple.
  b. A pencil.
  c. A window.
  d. A clock.

READING

BAKER, RUSSELL, *All Things Considered.* Lippincott, New York, 1965.

BORLAND, HAL G., *How to Write and Sell Non-Fiction.* Ronald, New York, 1956.

BRESLIN, JIMMY, *The World of Jimmy Breslin,* edited by J. G. Bellows. Viking, New York, 1967.

BUCHWALD, ART, *And Then I Told the President.* Putnam, New York, 1965. (PB)

BUCKLEY, WILLIAM F., JR., *The Jeweler's Eye.* Putnam, New York, 1968. (PB)

ENGLE, PAUL (Ed.), *On Creative Writing.* Dutton, New York, 1964. (PB)

HARRAL, STEWART, *Feature Writer's Handbook.* University of Oklahoma Press, Norman, Okla., 1957.

HOGREFE, PEARL, *Process of Creative Writing.* Harper & Row, New York, 1963.

HOHENBERG, JOHN (Ed.), *Pulitzer Prize Story.* Columbia University Press, New York, 1959.

JACOBS, HAYES B., *Writing and Selling Non-Fiction.* Funk & Wagnalls, New York, 1969.

KAEL, PAULINE, *Kiss Kiss Bang Bang.* Bantam Books, New York, 1969. (PB)

KROCK, ARTHUR, *Memoirs: Sixty Years on the Firing Line.* Funk & Wagnalls, New York, 1968.

LEWIS, JERRY D. (Ed.), *Great Columnists.* Collier, New York, 1965. (PB)

MAILER, NORMAN, *Armies of the Night.* New American Library, New York, 1968. (PB)

———, *Miami and the Siege of Chicago.* New American Library, New York, 1968. (PB)

MEREDITH, SCOTT, *Writing to Sell.* Harper & Row, New York, 1960.

MURPHEY, R. W., *How and Where to Look It Up.* McGraw-Hill, New York, 1958.

PATTERSON, HELEN M., *Writing and Selling Feature Articles.* Prentice-Hall, Englewood Cliffs, N.J., 1956.

PEARSON, DREW, AND JACK ANDERSON, *Case Against Congress.* Simon and Schuster, New York, 1968.

RESTON, JAMES, *Sketches in the Sand.* Knopf, New York, 1967.

ROSS, LILLIAN, *Reporting.* Simon and Schuster, New York, 1964. (PB)

——, *Talk Stories.* Simon and Schuster, New York, 1966.

SCHOENFELD, CLARENCE A., *Effective Feature Writing.* Harper & Row, New York, 1960.

SNYDER, LOUIS, AND RICHARD MORRIS (Ed.), *A Treasury of Great Reporting.* Simon and Schuster, New York, 1962.

WARD, WILLIAM G., *The Student Journalist and Creative Writing.* Richards Rosen Press, New York, 1967.

WOLSELEY, ROLAND E., *Critical Writing for the Journalist.* Chilton Book Co., Philadelphia, Pa., 1959.

Chapter **12**

Sports Writing

Ron MacNeil

DREAMS OF A "WALTER MITTY" WORLD

Almost every man, at one time or another, will let his imagination drift off into a "Walter Mitty" type of dream world. In this "Walter Mitty" world of fantasy the average man often envisions himself as a celebrated sports hero: a sports hero who sinks a tie-breaking basket just as the buzzer sounds; a sports hero who runs at breathtaking speed to score a winning touchdown; or an Olympic diving champion, poised and ready to plunge, acknowledging the cheers and applause of delighted spectators. Such heroics, unfortunately, take place only in the average man's dreams—for we are a nation of "spectator" sports enthusiasts. Relatively few of us actively participate in sports: Most of us watch (at the actual event or on television), listen (on the radio), or read (in newspapers and magazines) about athletic activities.

Our newspapers contain accounts of athletic events and reports on the exploits of athletes, written by sports writers skilled in their craft. Most of today's

247

sports accounts, as read by both male and female readers, contain all the conflict, color, drama, and emotion found on the athletic field.

In recent years the sports world has become more complex, and the number of sports events of interest to spectators has greatly increased: there are fifty percent more major league baseball and hockey teams than there were in 1960, and professional football teams now play in thirty-eight cities. The city of Oakland, California, for example, had no professional sports representation until 1967, but by 1970 it had professional teams in football, basketball, hockey, and baseball. Athletic programs in high schools and colleges have expanded rapidly, and many of the schools that formerly featured only baseball and football now enjoy wrestling, basketball, tennis, swimming, bowling, boxing, hockey, and soccer. Recently, in some areas of the country, wrestling has outdrawn basketball as a spectator sport.

As more sports facilities are set up, attendance at sports events increases as does the number of persons actually participating in athletic events. The country's major participant sports are golf (there are approximately 8,525,000 golfers in America today), auto racing (not only in Indianapolis and Daytona Beach), skiing (snow-making machines have created ski-runs as far south as the Carolinas and Tennessee), bowling (which has recently greatly increased its following), and tennis (previously thought of as a sport for only the well-to-do).

Trends in Sports Reporting

To meet the demands of today's sports reading audience, a more discerning reading audience than ever before, newspaper sports sections and pages have changed radically during the last decade, the major changes being in the following areas:

1. *Amount of Space Devoted to Sports*—The number of newspaper pages devoted to sports coverage is constantly being expanded. For example, on an average Sunday, *The New York Times* features more than twelve pages of sports news. Metropolitan dailies devote, on an average, approximately seven pages to sports news in their Sunday editions, and at least two pages in each daily edition. Most school newspapers devote at least one page to sports stories, pictures, and columns.

2. *Elimination of the Trivia*—General sports articles are being condensed and trivial sports stories omitted in order to make room for expanded coverage of more sports events. For example, ten years ago many high school sports pages carried one or two long stories on intramural sports, whereas today similar stories are held to one or two paragraphs to allow space for more stories on the many different sports events.

3. *Specialization of Writers*—Sports editors now give assignments to the sports writers who are the most familiar with the particular sport to be covered. Pre-

viously, any general writer or reporter was thought to be competent enough to cover any sport. Today, most sports writers know almost as much as the actual players about a given sport. A writer who does not know the rules of hockey, for example, could probably not write a convincing, informative sports story about a hockey game.

Categories of Sports Page Readers

Sports reporters, including those writing for high school publications, must understand the reading audience for whom they are writing. Many professional sports writers categorize their reading audiences as follows:

1. *Readers Who Have Witnessed the Event*—Readers who have been to the game or who have seen it on television, who want to read a "behind-the-scenes" story.

2. *Readers Who Know the Outcome of the Event*—Readers who have not attended the game but in most cases, have heard the final outcome from radio, television, or from a friend. These readers will want to read accounts of the highlights of the action.

3. *Readers Who Do Not Know the Outcome of the Event*—Readers who want to know the final result of the game, as well as the highlights and "behind-the-scenes" story.

TYPES OF SPORTS STORIES

Every major sports event presents possibilities for a great variety of sports writing including such assignments as sports features, sports "spot news" stories, personality stories, sports interviews, sports sidebars, sports columns, sports speeches, personality stories, editorials, testimonials, and sports statistical reports. The three basic types of sports stories are usually categorized as *advance stories, game stories,* and *follow-up stories.*

The Advance Story

In the advance story, the reader is told *who* the participants and stars will be, *when* and *where* the event will take place, *what* the result can mean, and *why* the event is important. (Reporting *how* the event took place is usually reserved for game and follow-up stories.) As in most news stories the more background given, the more interesting the story. The major purpose of the advance story is to inform the readers about the event in the most interesting way possible. The second of the following two examples of types of advance story leads for sports stories includes the background information and is, therefore, the more interesting of the two.

The Wildcats will meet the Eagles on Friday at the Municipal Auditorium.

Frank Wolf and Ray Denfield, the best the Wildcats and Eagles have to offer, will be out of action Friday night at 8 p.m. when the teams meet for their annual clash at the Municipal Auditorium.

The remaining sentences in the advance story, presented in logical sequence, usually include the other facts needed to tell the complete story. The preceding example would be continued as follows:

EXAMPLE:

. . . Wolf, the leading scorer for Gibson, is hobbled by a badly sprained ankle, and Denfield, Wilson's Center, is suffering from the flu.

In place of Wolf, Coach Rudy Flowers will star Larry Haskins, the number six man on the team. Eagle coach Murray Berman has indicated that he will move sophomore Ray Santamaria into the lineup.

The Wildcats will be defending their 13-6 record for the Blue Division title.

The Eagles, who have the same record, won a tryout game played between the two teams earlier this season by a 63-60 score.

Coach Flowers has stressed the importance of the team's winning this game: "We still have a crack at the title, but a loss could hurt the excellent mental attitude our team now has."

Half-time entertainment at the game will be provided by pep bands from both schools.

The Game Story

From the timeliness point of view, the most important sports story is the one published immediately following the end of the game. To write as complete a game story as possible, the sports writer must secure as many of the specific facts as possible while attending the event. If such facts are outstanding, they may provide material for the lead. Among the specific facts secured at the scene of the event will be answers to the following questions:

What Were the Weather Conditions?—The wind, or lack of it, may affect a quarterback's passing. Cold weather may be the cause of fumbles. The sun may blind the outfielder and cause him to misjudge the fly ball. The All-State runner may lose because of a muddy track.

Despite a cross-wind that buffeted passes, quarterback Jack Wiseman rifled three touchdown aerials to lead Watkins High to a 21–0 triumph over previously unbeaten Brookside yesterday.

How Large Was the Crowd?—If the stands were packed, approximately how many fans were turned away? What was the approximate number of spectators? Did the cheering of the home crowd have any affect on the players? How did the fans behave? Did they celebrate the victory by tearing down the goal posts?

EXAMPLE:

More than 15,000 fans—the most ever to witness a high school basketball game in Centerville—saw the Lions down Lakeland 71–53 yesterday at the War Memorial.

What Was the Outcome of the Event?—Readers, of course, want to know who won. How was the event won? Did the victor "come from behind" to win? Any statistics about prior events that might possibly highlight the outcome of the event should be included.

EXAMPLE:

In the highest-scoring game in Baylor's history, the Generals downed undefeated Auburn 101–83 Thursday night.

Were There Any Spectacular Plays?—Accounts of spectacular plays may be included in the lead, especially if they affected the final outcome of the game. "The basket from mid-court as the buzzer sounded," "the punt-return for a touchdown," or "the bases-loaded home run" should be included.

EXAMPLE:

Harry Ashmore speared a line drive deep behind second in the ninth inning to prevent the tying run from scoring and preserve a 3–2 win for the pennant-bound Braves at Hanley Field yesterday.

Who Were the Individual Stars?—How did the stars perform? And, by the same token, if the star halfback didn't score, you have material for an interesting story.

EXAMPLE:

> Scoring two touchdowns and setting up two others, John Martin led the Hampton Beavers to a 27–14 victory over the Wykoff Tigers Wednesday. Star halfback for the Tigers, Steve Gordon, wasn't up to form when he fumbled . . .

Was There Any Significance to the Outcome?—This is another area that should be researched before covering an event. Was one team's undefeated string broken? Did the defeat cost a team the championship? Did the victor move up in the standings?

EXAMPLE:

> Handing Triadelphia the worst beating in the history of the school, Warwood continued its baseball supremacy Monday with an 18–0 shutout.

How Did the Teams Compare?—If the winners excelled in certain areas, this could well be mentioned early in the story. Did one team outweigh the other? Was the pass-rush effective? Did the full-court press hamper the loser?

EXAMPLE:

> Capitalizing on their height advantage, Moundsville's Trojans trounced the New Martinsville Blue Devils 71–34 last night on the loser's court.

The Follow-up Story

Because many school newspapers are published several days after a sports event has taken place, the written accounts of such events are presented as follow-up stories. Since follow-up stories lack timeliness, the writer must give such stories a different treatment than that given to advance or game stories. Follow-up sports stories may be generally categorized as follows:

The Wrap-up Story—If several games have been played prior to the publication of a school newspaper and space limitations prevent detailed accounts of the individual games, all of the information about the games is combined into one sports presentation that is called a wrap-up story. The wrap-up story should emphasize the most recent game and should briefly summarize the high spots of the individual games.

The Second-day Story—If a school's team performed spectacularly several weeks prior to the publication of a school newspaper, the paper will need to include a separate story on the game. However, since this information is "old news," the writer usually gives the story a second-day story treatment by answering any possible questions the average fan might still have. For example, such unanswered questions might be: Why did the coach alternate his forwards? Why did he use the man-to-man defense so early in the game? Why didn't the team use the fast-break more often? Often, as a basis for his story, the writer will interview the coach and players to find answers to such questions. Usually, the most significant of these answers is used as the lead for the second-day story.

The Evaluation Story—The evaluation story attempts to put the results of the game into an understandable perspective. To do this, many writers evaluate an entire sports season and present prospects for the rest of the season by answering questions such as: What does the outcome of the last game mean to the team? Can the team still hope to win the championship? Can the team rebound from their mediocre showing in the big game next week? Often, the reactions of players, coaches, and fans help make the evaluation story more interesting. Many sports writers and editors feel that the best evaluation stories about sports events can be obtained from the losing players' reactions, usually revealed in the locker room. There, the writer finds such elements as pathos, drama, and human interest. He talks to the coach, the stars, and the player who pulled the boner that resulted in the loss. The first of the following examples shows how a writer might present an evaluation sports lead if he hadn't done thorough background research. The second example shows a preferable handling of the same story.

EXAMPLES:

In a driving rainstorm Glenville's Hawks came from behind to edge the Wesleyan Eagles 8–7 two weeks ago, when guard Tom Hinkle tackled Eagle fullback Russ Wilson in the end zone scoring a safety. . . .

Russ Wilson sat alone in a dark corner of the Eagles' locker room. Other players were silently changing clothes, but Wilson, his head bowed and his eyes fixed on the floor, was trying to figure out what had gone wrong.

Without shifting his eyes, he muttered, "The rain-storm caused it. The field was just too muddy . . . I just couldn't get up any momentum. Before I knew it, Hinkle came through our line like a Mack truck and was on top of me. . . ."

WRITING THE SPORTS STORY

Because the sports story conforms in general to the principles that govern the straight news story, the sports story writer should handle his assignments the same way the news reporter handles a straight news story. The sports story writer must make the necessary advance preparation by researching for background material, must organize his story material, and must write the story (usually using the inverted pyramid style) in as interesting and informative a manner as possible.

Preparation—The sports reporter, if not an expert, should at least be well-informed or knowledgeable concerning the event he is assigned to cover. He should not only be familiar with the rules, but should also be familiar with the backgrounds and past performances of the individual players—especially the stars. He usually has read about the stars, is familiar with their records, and knows the background of the visiting team. He should also be able to reasonably predict the outcome of the event.

Organizing the Story—Since good sports writing is also good news writing, the sports writer should organize most of his stories in the inverted pyramid structure. Ordinarily, he will include the "five W's and the H" in his first few paragraphs and will include as many other news elements as possible (See Chapter 8, "Newswriting").

Writing the Lead—The lead for every sports story should include the names of the teams (or players), the score (if it is a game or follow-up story), and the place of the event.

SPORTS JARGON

In the past, many sports writers used a type of slang in their stories that, when overused, often became trite and hackneyed. Today, professional sports

Background information and highlights of the game are often included in the captions for photographs that accompany sports stories. Shown here is Lew Alcindor, chosen most valuable player in the 1968 ECAC Festival.

writers avoid using similar types of jargon in their stories. Many amateur writers continue to use such meaningless expressions as "split the ozone," "scorched the cinders," and "booted the pigskin." Because sports writers are permitted more freedom of style in their writing than are straight news story writers, the most-read sports writers use to an advantage such freedom of style to express themselves in a colorful, creative way. In sports writing the specific style of writing to be used is usually dictated, at least to a degree, by the type of story being written. The specific style of writing sports materials is also often predetermined by the media the material is to be presented in.

255

SPORTS FEATURES

Due to high reader interest in sports features, sports editors often request sports writers to prepare feature stories about the many different aspects of sports. When writing a sports feature, writers follow a procedure similar to the one suggested in Chapter 11, "Feature Writing." The major categories of sports features are as follows.

Celebrity Sports Features—The more famous the sports personality, the more articles printed about him. Sports feature writers preparing a celebrity sports feature usually prepare their material by interviewing a player after having read sufficient background material, or after having talked to the player's coach and to the player's friends and associates. The sports celebrity feature often takes the form of a biography, an interview, or a personality sketch.

EXAMPLE:

> When it comes to track, Steve Stageberg is a man possessed—possessed by an obsession to prove that he is the best.
>
> Ever since he was, in his own words, "humiliated" in the 880 in the state meet last year (if you can call a seventh-place finish because of a pulled muscle being humiliated), Steve has trained like a Spartan to prove that this year he is the best.
>
> "I see guys like Crunican (Mike, last year's state champ and state record holder from Roseburg) and I want to be like him," says Steve. "I want to be number one once in a while. . . ."
>
> Roland Cunningham
The Axe
South Eugene High School
Eugene, Oregon

Scene-of-Event Sports Features—Scene-of-event sports features focus on the specific area or arena in which a major event is to be held. For example, a number of scene-of-event feature articles have been written describing Houston's Astrodome. Other stories of this type detail the facilities and dimensions of the ball parks in which a World Series or Super Bowl game will be played. School sports writers may draw a comparison between the home court and the court on which the championship game is to be played.

JAPANESE HERE — FOR OLYMPICS

The island of Hokkaido, Japan, juts out northeast of the mainland. Except for its mountainous terrain, it is similar to Massachusetts in historical background, climate, and cultural interests. Here in Hokkaido, settled by the Japanese just a century ago, the next winter Olympics will be held in 1972.

With an influx of English-speaking tourists anticipated for the Olympics, the Japanese government, in cooperation with the U.S. State Department, sent a team of English teachers in Japanese high schools to this country to improve their English language ability so that they can return and teach English in Hokkaido. The teachers are living with families in Lynn, Wellesley, Framingham, Milton, Braintree, Salem, Worcester, Cambridge, and Weymouth. . . .

Evelyn Keene
The Boston Globe

Interpretative Sports Features—Readers are interested in the *Why* behind any sports event. An interpretative sports feature supplies the background information concerning sports issues and policies. Such an article might concern *Why* a team won the state championship, *How* the condition or abilities of the players might affect player performance.

EXAMPLE:

The year of the Panther is here . . . again. Thanks to the coaching of Byron Weaver and his hard-working assistants, North Central is out to top last year's fantastic season. Even greater finesse and more speed are the keys to this goal. With players returning in better condition, the coaches were able to start working toward greater dexterity and speed than ever before.

Chuck Tate
The Northern Lights
North Central High School
Indianapolis, Ind.

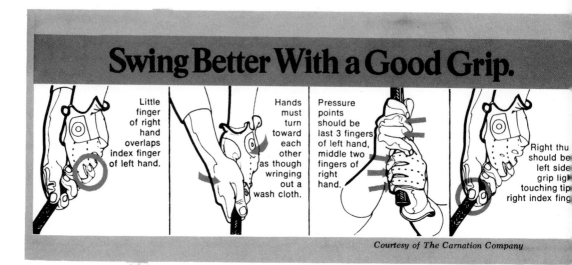

Swing Better With a Good Grip.

Little finger of right hand overlaps index finger of left hand.

Hands must turn toward each other as though wringing out a wash cloth.

Pressure points should be last 3 fingers of left hand, middle two fingers of right hand.

Right thu should be left side grip lig touching tip right index fing

How-to-Do-It Sports Features—As more people become interested in participant sports, the demand for how-to-do-it sports feature articles (sports features of an instructional nature) increases. Sports writers often prepare features on such subjects as how to play tennis, golf, soccer, or hockey. Many high school newspaper sports editors assign fledgling sports writers to prepare series of how-to-do-it features for use as fillers or for publication in each issue of their school newspapers. The following example lends a twist to the usual how-to-do-it sports feature. In a light, humorous way, the writer tells how to write a sports story.

EXAMPLE:

Pitching, Sox Achilles Heel

In the good old days, they tell me, writers didn't traipse around baseball locker rooms the way they do now.

Afternoon papers carried pretty much the same game material as the morning, with some sort of fresh angle in the opening paragraph. An afternoon baseball story might go something like this:

Walter Weakarm, veteran curveballer of the Red Sox, will go against Ed- die Erratic of the St. Louis Browns as the Hose attempt to square the series this afternoon at 3 at Fenway Park. Yesterday afternoon in the Jersey St. ballyard, the Brownies smashed 12 hits good for seven runs, etc., etc., etc. . . ."

Nowadays, that sort of thing doesn't go. An afternoon writer is required to probe the psyche of the athletes, supposed to get down there amid the adhesive tape and sweat socks, and ask penetrating questions.

So it was that a writer sat in the stands late Sunday afternoon and watched the Red Sox almost turn another pumpkin into a royal coach.

He saw the Sox score four runs with two out in the ninth and make a game out of a 7–1 runaway. He saw the Twins, who should have had an easy victory, panic over a pop fly that went 12 feet into the infield and about a thousand feet high.

He saw Twins' first baseman Rich Reese collide with third baseman Cesar Tovar and drop the pop fly but somehow reach out a big paw and catch it before it hit the ground, the way a football player would do in the end zone.

But most of all the writer saw the customers—standing, yelling, screaming for their cardiac kids, who so often battled from behind in the seven games of the present home stand.

Forgotten were the early inadequacies of the Sox' pitchers, and the supremacy of Twins' lefthander Jim Merritt. The rally was the thing, and the people got their money's worth.

"Money's worth," however, is not synonymous with pennant, and pennant is the word a man keeps hearing around Fenway Park these days. A sign in centerfield Sunday read: "Red Sox To Win Penant."

That's not the way you spell the word, and you don't spell it with bad pitching, either. Rallies are fun, rallies are exciting, rallies fill ball parks, but pitching wins pennants and lately the Red Sox aren't getting any.

In the seven games since the Red Sox came home to a welcome worthy of the Rolling Stones, not a pitcher has turned in a complete game.

Six innings is the longest a starter has gone. The Twins, who came in here with bats suffering from Dutch Elm disease, are hitting everything tossed their way. Holding Harmon Killebrew to a single is cause for burning incense in the dugout. Rod Carew stepped off a plane from Minneapolis after a weekend of Marine Reserve duty and hit four line drives.

The schedule is supposed to favor the Red Sox, with a pile of games in Fenway and not too many more on the road. "There is no way we can lose many games in Fenway Park," Carl Yastrzemski has said in assessing the team's chances.

The fact is, however, that Fenway has hurt the Sox against the Twins. "Our pitchers have been throwing the ball high," said Dick Williams, "and you can't do that in this park against that team."

"If we are a couple of runs down," said Mike Andrews, "I always feel we'll win it. But seven or eight is a tough proposition."

Williams knows pitching is the Achilles Heel of the club. Dave Morehead has been recalled and will pitch Tuesday. Morehead won 11 games at Toronto, which is fine, but there are few Killebrews in the International League.

The Red Sox are also trying to get Jim Grant from the Twins. Grant, having a bad year, is in the bullpen, and waivers have been put out on him.

So Morehead will be here and Jim Lonborg's flying up from Atlanta and maybe Jim Grant will join the club. The team is not standing pat, which is good news.

And here's something even better. The Twins are leaving town.

Ray Fitzgerald
The Boston Globe

Sports Features Based on the Writer's Involvement—Sports feature writers often become directly involved as sports participants in order to present readers with interesting feature materials. One such writer talked the coach of an undefeated football powerhouse into letting him participate in a practice session. The writer's lead read: "I felt like an ant among elephants." Author George Plimpton once masqueraded as a football player and went through training sessions with the Detroit Lions. Plimpton's book, *Paper Lion,* was based on these experiences.

To obtain background material for his book, George Plimpton masqueraded as a player and went through training sessions with the Detroit Lions.

Adding Interest to Sports Features

A leading newspaper sports editor prepared a listing of common football terms and then asked a group of girls for their definitions. Following are excerpts, based on the girls' definitions of the terms, from the sports feature story he prepared.

EXAMPLES:

BLOCK

"Trying to keep the ball from going over the goal."

"That is when someone is trying to stop someone from doing something sometime."

SPOT PASS

"A pass which is something like a spot."

"Pass spotted by the spotter."

"A pass is spotted by a player and he unexpectedly catches it."

FAIR CATCH

"Maybe it looked like the player dropped the ball, but he really didn't and so it is fair."

"Not a very good catch, but he caught it and that's all that matters, isn't it?"

THE CHAINS

"Some disease."

"The backfield."

"A group of players with connected hands going out to block."

HEAD LINESMAN

"Head person in football squad."

"The players on the front lines."

"Is the player that throws the ball to start the play into action."

STATUE OF LIBERTY

"A complicated play used in college more than high school."

"The symbol of American freedom located off the shore of New York City."

SNEAK

"The ball is passed secretly from one player to another."

"To move silently from one place to another without being seen."

6-2-2-1

"Count down before a play."

"Number of a play that has a special significance for different teams."

"A play in football only the particular team knows what it means."

"6 hits, 2 runs, 2 outs, 1 error."

The *News Register*
Wheeling, West Virginia

WRITING THE SPORTS COLUMN

On most school newspapers the sports editor writes a column for publication in each issue of the paper. In their columns, sports editors comment on sports events directly related to the school, often comment on sports events of concern to the school community, and, when space permits, also comment on the national sports scene. The following items may be used as a general guide for writing a school newspaper sports column.

Keep the Column Light—The sports columnist can make his column entertaining by using anecdotes and as much descriptive detail as possible. This writing style may be used even on those occasions when the sports columnist's basic purpose is to inform. Because readers do not appreciate lectures and sermons, the writer should avoid being preachy.

Keep the Column Accurate and Honest—The sports columnist should never stretch the truth. If a statement isn't exact, he should not use it. He should present only proven facts. To avoid the possibility of libel he should use constructive criticism rather than maligning or insulting statements. Being accurate and honest justifies the reader's faith in the writer.

Use a Number of Items—A sports column should rarely concern itself with only one topic or one sports event. The more items or events included, the more readers attracted to the column. Generally, sufficient comment on most sports events can be made in a few short paragraphs in a sports column.

Consider Including Pictures—The inclusion of pictures related to items mentioned in the sports column will attract readers to the column. For example, when presenting the coach's reactions to a game, a one-column headshot of the coach and a game-action picture may help attract the reader's attention.

Use the Personal Approach—Sports columnists, free to editorialize and inject their own personalities into sports stories, often do so by using the personal approach. Many sports columnists analyze the typical sports fan and present feature material based on the fan's likes and dislikes. In developing this type of sports feature, the average sports fan should be kept in mind and the material should be written especially for him. Sports columnists, because of high reader interest in their columns, must constantly be aware that they are in a position to create good will for their newspaper.

Always Be on the Alert for Possible Material—When *New York Times* Sports columnist Arthur Daley finished his first sports column on December 24, 1942, he collapsed over his typewriter, exhausted, and said, "Thank heavens, that's done." Then he sat bolt upright. "But what about tomorrow's?" This story exemplifies a major problem that most sports columnists have: the problem of where to obtain the material for their next column. To help ensure a fresh supply of ideas, many sports columnists jot down facts, figures, and any other available spur-of-the-moment material that might make interesting copy for inclusion in future sports columns.

Discipline Your Writing Habits—The sports columnist should set aside a specific time to write, and should not permit anything or anybody to disrupt this schedule. He should try to prepare the same-length column each time, proofreading and rewriting his material as needed. Above all, the sports columnist should never miss a deadline.

PITFALLS TO BE AVOIDED BY SPORTS WRITERS

The following list of eight pitfalls to be avoided by sports writers preparing material for newspaper sports pages was compiled by former sports writer and columnist Bill Ward. The list has been included in his book, *Newspapering*, published by the National Scholastic Press Association.

PITFALLS—"SPORTS STAFFS BEWARE"

1. *Writing in sports jargon*—Outlaw all sports language; write in clearcut language understood by the nonfan. Avoid such tangled construction as "The hurler unlimbered a blazer which the sticker cracked into the outer pasture for a one-bagger. The left gardener gloved it on the hop and sizzled it to the keystone sacker." One bit of sports slang is one bit too many.

2. *Organizing a game summary in chronological order*—Unless the kickoff is your most newsworthy element, organize the story with the most interesting details at the start. It is easy to tell a story chronologically; it usually is also dull.

3. *Narrating play-by-play*—This is dull, flat, routine, unimaginative, hard for the reader to follow, and stimulates few mental images. "Jones smacked the middle for six yards to the 18. Then Smith fired a pass to Smyth who took it on the 15 and ran to the 12. After two incompleted passes, Jones snaked to the 9. Funkle was thrown for a two-yard loss." Ad infinitum. Who cares? If you must include a play-by-play sequence, clip it short. Be sure it's important.

4. *Becoming a critic*—Your job is to report a game, not to coach a team. Frustrated athletes who become sports writers are a bane of coaches. Sports writers know very little about the techniques of the game; they know even less about the subtle problems that coaches and athletes encounter behind the scenes. I recall a metropolitan sports writer who criticized a collegiate halfback for loafing and losing. In truth, the halfback was badly crippled, a fact which had been hidden from the press and from the opposition before, during, and after the game.

5. *Failing to get specific, detailed facts*—Lazy, indifferent, unknowing? Whatever the reason, it's inexcusable. A sports writer must systematically dig, day by day, for any facts he may need for a story.

6. *Writing with too many adjectives and adverbs*—I have never visualized a "low flyball," so why a high one? There are also too many "vicious tackles, smoking slides, diving catches, smashing drives, blistering linedrives." Save your modifiers for moments of true impact.

7. *Including too many statistics*—Not many fans can tell what Biff McNasty hit in 1906; most don't care. Statistics are not sports, but merely a side-product. Thus, you must write about the action and the human interest. Don't turn a sports event into a bookkeeper's nightmare. "Tonight the Beaneaters (8 wins, 5 loses), averaging 6-2 in height and 195 pounds, meet for the second time the Yellow Sox (10 wins, 3 losses), averaging 6-1 and 184. The Beaneaters with a .321 shooting average came into the game with a 3-game winning streak (the longest in the conference this year thus far) after snapping a 5-game losing streak. . . ."

8. *Posing pictures*—Shoot on-the-spot action. There is little reason for posing athletes before and after games and then relaxing during the action.

ACTIVITIES

1. From newspaper sports stories, compile examples of both acceptable and unacceptable sports terminology. Use the examples to start your own sports jargon notebook. Keep in mind that because the average reader finds sports jargon difficult to understand, experienced sports writers avoid using it and, in order to keep their language colorful and interesting, use appropriate synonyms instead. Make a list of all the synonyms you can think of to replace the word *belted* in the following sentence:

> Jones *belted* off right tackle and scampered 25 yards down Medford's sidelines for the winning touchdown.

2. The standard "5 W's and the H" news lead is often used in sports writing. Using the results of the last sports event you attended, write six sports story leads. Use *Who* as the main "W" in the first lead, then the *What* in the second lead, etc., until you have completed six different leads, each based on the same basic facts. To gain practice in writing under pressure, establish a deadline time for completion of these leads.

3. Most daily newspapers will allow student journalists to use the newspaper's microfilm files or newspaper library if the request is properly made. Request permission to visit your local newspaper library to look up stories written about a major Thanksgiving Day football game from a previous year. Then, to test your recall of facts, write a second-day story about the game. Include any interesting sidelights you found during your research.

4. Quotations liven up any story, and good sports writers are constantly on the alert for usable ones. Your teacher will divide the class into four teams and, to obtain usable quotations, each team will plan to consult with cheerleaders, coaches, players, or fans. As a class activity have each of the four teams prepare and write its own sports broadcast based on the quotations it was able to obtain.

5. Most schools have an "eager-beaver" athlete, usually a sports enthusiast who comes early and stays late for practice. Often, he cleans the cleats, picks up the dirty towels, and brings water to his fellow athletes. He is, in many ways, as important as the star player. Seek out such a person and prepare a sports feature that uses the personal approach. Your teacher will evaluate your article for possible submission to the school newspaper. Such articles lend interest and variety to sports pages.

READING

ALLEN, MEL, AND FRANK GRAHAM, JR., *It Takes Heart*. Harper & Row, New York, 1959.

HARRISS, JULIAN, AND STANLEY JOHNSON, *The Complete Reporter*. Macmillan, New York, 1965.

HEATH, HARRY, JR., AND LOU GELFAND, *How to Cover, Write and Edit Sports*. Iowa State University Press, Ames, Iowa, 1968.

MARSH, IRVING T., AND EDWARD EHRE (Ed.), *Best Sports Stories*. (Annual). Dutton, New York.

MURRAY, JIM, *The Sporting World of Jim Murray*. Doubleday, New York, 1968.

RICE, GRANTLAND, *The Tumult and the Shouting; My Life in Sports*. A. S. Barnes, Cranbury, N.J., 1962.

SPORTS ILLUSTRATED, *Sports: The American Scene*, edited by Robert Smith. McGraw-Hill, New York, 1963.

STAPLER, HARRY, *The Student Journalist and Sports Editing*. Richards Rosen Press, New York, 1964.

WARD, WILLIAM G., *Reporting and Writing Sports*. Columbia Scholastic Press Association, Columbia University, New York.

WOODWARD, STANLEY, AND FRANK GRAHAM, JR., *Sportswriter*. Doubleday, New York, 1967.

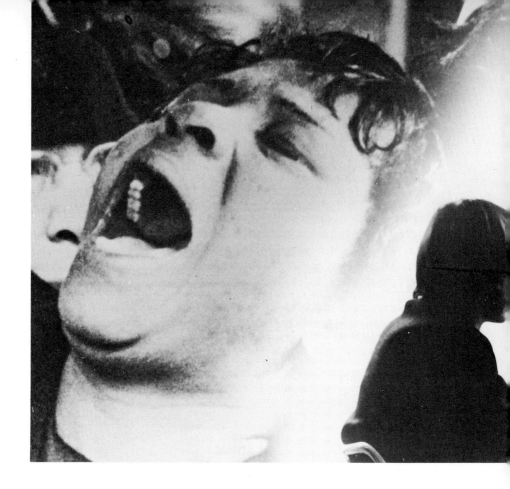

Chapter 13

Editorial Writing

EDITORIAL WRITING AND THE MASS MEDIA

Any listing of famous names taken from the history of American journalism would reveal that most of these persons, in addition to being newswriters, were also skilled editorial writers—writers who wielded great influence through their editorials during their particular eras. The names of Horace Greeley, Henry Grady, Henry Watterson, E.L. Godkin, Charles Dana, William Lloyd Garrison, William Allen White, Elijah Lovejoy, Walter Lippmann, and editor-poets William Cullen Bryant and Walt Whitman would be included in such a listing. Through effective, convincing editorials these men helped bring to light and resolve many of the major issues peculiar to their times. William Cullen Bryant, perhaps best-remembered as the poet who wrote *Thanatopsis*, was also the editor of the *New York Post* for fifty years. Thirty years before the tragic Civil War engulfed the country, Bryant conducted a well-planned editorial campaign against slavery. William Allen White, although living in and writing from a small town in Kansas, was read and respected by newspaper readers throughout the country.

Just as editorials expressing the opinions of these journalists exposed and helped find solutions for many of the problems peculiar to their times, editorials expressing the opinion of today's journalists expose and help find solutions for the problems peculiar to our times.

While the role of today's editorialist is, perhaps, not as dramatic as was a similar role during the days when Horace Greeley's writings were eagerly read throughout the country, today's editorialist is still an influential and respected member of our society. The editorial writer in today's society, while being concerned with many of the unsolved problems inherited from previous generations, is also confronted with the challenge of writing about newer problems—problems like nuclear armament, urban crises, over-population, race relations, and world peace. Today's editorial writer represents the conscience of his community.

Despite the fact that more people on any given day read their newspaper's comic section than read the editorial section (very few newspaper readers can actually identify one editorial writer by name), the thoughtful, concerned decision-makers of most communities invariably read the editorials. Among the first items the President of the United States reads each morning is a summary of editorials from the country's leading newspapers.

Editorial writing has become increasingly important in the electronic media. Radio and television stations frequently devote time to airing matters of public concern through editorials "in the public interest" prepared by station writers. Following is an example of a public service editorial prepared for radio and television.

EXAMPLE:

On the Outside

Delivered by
James R. Lightfoot—General Manager—WBZ Radio
Winthrop P. Baker—General Manager—WBZ-TV

Americans go to the polls today in the payoff of the American political system. Yet, in most of our states the law bars access to voting to some of our most interested and active citizens—youth between the ages of 18 and 21.

We think the time has come to lower the voting age across the country. Young people have shown their political ability in campaigns this year. They have won the right to full participation in our democratic process. This can be one part of a general drive to have our youth play a more useful and meaningful role in the world around them.

Some people have been soured on the lower voting age due to the excesses of protest groups here and elsewhere. But we see no excuse for penalizing the majority for the wild antics of a few. In fact, we think the voting privilege would serve as an antidote to some of the negativism that runs through the youthful protest movement.

Four states have already dropped the voting age below 21. Here in Massachusetts the Legislature has taken the first step toward making the voting age 19. But we think this is an issue that should be tackled on a national basis by an amendment to the United States Constitution. And the age should be set at 18—the age at which young men can be drafted, the age at which young people finish high school and go to work or on to higher education.

With prompt action in Washington and state capitols, this change can be effective by the nation's next big political payoff date in 1972.

Broadcast on Radio:
11/5/68—9:05 AM; 1:05 PM
11/5/68—4:05 PM; 6:28 PM

Broadcast on TV:
11/5/68—12:00 N
11/5/68—6 PM

WBZ TV 4—WBZ RADIO 103, Group W—
Westinghouse Broadcasting Company, Inc.

PURPOSE OF EDITORIALS

The editorials contained on any publication's editorial pages usually concern themselves with the same general issues found on the publication's news pages. The editorial page, regardless of who writes the editorials, is still a page of news although it is written and presented from a different viewpoint than that of other stories. While the news reports prepared by a reporter must be impartial presentations of factual information, the editorials written by editorial writers can reflect the writer's or publication's own appraisal and interpretation of events. The editorial is often called the "mouthpiece" of the publication it appears in. In no other part of the publication is that publication's character, personality, and policy so clearly shown. For this reason, crusades are often conducted through newspaper editorials.

The primary purpose of an editorial is to *convince*. The mark of a truly successful editorial is its ability to arouse readers to take action on the issue dealt with in the editorial. The writer of an editorial can be said to be saying, "Here is the evidence. The verdict should be as I have indicated."

What Makes a Good Editorial?

The most important element of an editorial is *effectiveness*. If an editorial is not effective, it will not fulfill its purpose. Because readers want news, effective editorials should be *timely* as well as *interesting*. For example, what students were discussing last month may well prove boring to them today. Editorials that preach and editorials containing uninteresting, poorly presented statements and assumptions often lose the reader's interest. "Preachy" editorials are usually ineffective because they fail to arouse a response in readers. With students, "preachy" editorials often arouse resentment; like all humans, students dislike being reminded constantly that they should or should not do something. But because a major purpose of all editorials is to suggest to readers what they should not do and encourage them to do what they should do, many editorial writers feel obligated to reveal only faults in their editorial writing and tend to preach about such faults. To avoid "preachiness," the editorial writer should consider the following points:

1. Rather than demand that readers must do something specific, editorialists can disclose a situation and challenge the reader to work out his own solution. In an editorial it is often more effective to suggest than it is to dictate.

2. Presenting a meaningful example can often eliminate the necessity for further lengthy comments that might sound "preachy." Meaningful examples can successfully arouse and influence the reader.

3. Being specific and using definite examples is usually more effective than using general statements and vague assumptions.

The successful editorial writer must be well acquainted with the elements of news discussed in Chapter 8, "Newswriting" (human interest, immediacy, proximity, conflict, emotions, and consequence), and should apply as many of them as possible to his editorial writing. The following are important qualities that contribute to making an editorial effective:

Conviction—Editorials, in order to be effective, must be convincing. To be convincing, the writer must understand thoroughly the situation or problem about which he is writing. The editorial must reflect the writer's belief in his point of view.

Force—An editorial must have an obvious purpose, clearly stated, that is the result of careful thinking. It must be presented forcefully enough to drive the idea home to the reader, thus evoking a responsive note while he reads. Forcefully written editorials inspire the reader to take action; the more readers who take action as a result of reading the editorial, the more successful the editorial.

Brevity—Well-planned, straight-to-the-point, short editorials are preferable to poorly planned, long-winded, lengthy editorials. Readers, when confronted with a solid body of unrelieved type, are predisposed to not want to read it. Short editorials (from two to three hundred words in length and less) more easily retain reader interest than do longer ones. Most editorial writers, in order to keep their material brief, choose only one aspect of a newsworthy situation or problem to comment on.

Consequence—Consequence is one of the most important elements to be considered by the editorial writer in his choice of topic. Minor news factors are seldom used as the basis for good editorials. In writing editorials for your school newspaper it is well to write about what you determine is significant about your school, and what concerns the student body.

Relevance—Among the most important factors contributing to a good editorial is relevance. The editorial must be relevant to the concerns, problems, and needs of the reader.

Each year one of the Pulitzer journalism prizes is awarded for the country's most outstanding editorial. The points on which the editorials are evaluated comprise a basis for preparing a good editorial. These points can be considered sound criteria for judging both school and mass media editorial writing. The points are as follows:

1. Clearness of style.
2. Moral purpose.
3. Soundness of reasoning.
4. Power to influence public opinion.

Editorial Research

One of the most important prerequisites for writing sound editorials is research. The writer must be in possession of all of the facts connected with the issue before he begins to compose his editorial. The actual writing usually takes but a fraction of the time spent talking to authorities, taking notes, reading about the subject, and compiling background material. Library reference materials such as the *Reader's Guide to Periodical Literature* and the *New York Times Index* are basic research tools for editorial writers. Before putting his neck on the chopping block, the editorial writer must be sure of all of the related facts and must be able to substantiate them.

TYPES OF EDITORIALS

Editorials written for publication in the print media or for presentation on radio or television are either formal or informal in their approach. Most of the editorials used by the mass media are of the formal type, while school newspapers usually feature informal editorials. The difference between the two is the writer's point of view: the formal type uses only the third person approach, while the informal type uses the second person form of verbs and pronouns, or the imperative form of verbs having an implied "you." Editorials don't usually make use of first person singular pronouns. Most editorials come under any one of the following classifications:

Editorials of Argument and Persuasion—Also called editorials of refutation, or editorials of criticism and reform, these editorials offer criticisms of existing conditions and try to persuade opinion by suggesting specific changes. Argumentative in nature, such editorials take a definite, convincing stand and, even though the editorial's object of criticism might not accept the writer's viewpoint, the editorial is effective if the object of criticism ceases the activities being criticized.

EXAMPLE:

The Y Affair

Iowa seems to grow tall corn and re-actionaries. Iowa State helps grow tall corn and inflames reactionaries. The continuing and serious YMCA controversy is a good example.

The Y has been changing its image from "that building with the columns" to a campus force for active discussion and inquiry. This change has transformed the Y from an insignificant "religious society" to a dynamic campus organization. Just when the Y was beginning to come into its own as a dialogue-producing catalyst the Ames community objected. The very roots of their objections pry into the freedoms and rights of expression and discussion. But the worst part of this reaction is its threat to knock the awakening sense of intellectual curiosity and inquiry in the head. If the reactionaries win, the Y will be demoted to the rank of hike leader for 10-year-olds and a meeting place for mental midgets.

Fortunately, members of the University community, who realize what the purpose of a university is, have come to

the defense of the Y. Unfortunately, these enlightened persons do not hold the life-or-death purse strings. We were glad to see that the dean of students chose to support the Y with a letter urging it to "continue to stimulate all segments of the University community." They desperately need this type of encouragement and we'd like to add our hope that the Y will continue its programs of rational discussion on controversial topics.

After all, if a university isn't the place for such inquiry, what is? Certainly, the churches won't take up the yoke or the high schools or the Federated Women's Club or the plant or the office. The university is the only social unity that can handle such inquiry into contemporary concerns.

The State Board of Regents realized this when it said, "We encourage students and staff to hear and discuss diverse points of view from speakers and programs sponsored by recognized student, faculty and employee organizations. This policy is entirely consistent with the aims of higher education. It is designed to emphasize that in a democratic society all citizens have not only the right but the obligation to inform themselves on issues of contemporary concern including politics, religion, ethics and morals."

A democracy must necessarily depend on an informed public—a public that isn't afraid to probe, pry and ask questions. If a university student can't inform himself now, it is doubtful if the habit will be formed for use in later life. E. N. Griswold of the Harvard Law School has said, "Great ideas can rarely be developed in an atmosphere of constraint and oppression. The university has a unique function not merely in systematizing the orthodox, but also in providing the soil in which may be nourished the speculative, the unfashionable and the unorthodox." How can University instructors exhort their students to be open-minded and searching inside the classroom and deny the same right outside the classroom?

The whole controversy boils down to the purpose and autonomy of the university. Maybe the Y should consider breaking away from the stifling Ames community.

Charles S. Bullard
Iowa State University
3rd Place, December 1967 Editorials
*William Randolph Hearst Foundation
Journalism Awards Program*

Editorials of Information—In order to prevent possible misunderstanding, editorials of information offer informative comments. Their success depends upon the influence of the information presented. These editorials do not attempt to present obvious conclusions, and they limit themselves to a review of the facts related to a given situation.

EXAMPLE:

LAWYER POOL COULD RESULT IN SAVING FOR STATE

Governor Licht has a good idea that might save the taxpayers some money and at the same time increase the efficiency of government. He is considering setting up a lawyers' pool in government instead of assigning lawyers to different departments. In this way he might be able to cut back on the number of lawyers needed. A plus in the proposal is that the lawyers will have a better idea of what's going on and maybe the gears of government will mesh better when all of the departments find it no longer necessary to have a private corps of lawyers to protect "private" interests.

The Citizen
Providence, R.I.

Editorials of Interpretation—These editorials present the facts or an explanation of the facts about timely situations of reader interest, including the writer's or media's opinion about such situations. Such explanations of facts may be presented as a penetrating discussion and are often of the personal essay type, using "I" and "me" (which are not often used in editorials) in their presentation to make them more forceful.

EXAMPLE:

UNIVERSITY ADMISSIONS CUT

Thousands of New York City high school seniors were hit hard by this year's 20% cut in admissions to the City University of New York.

What is surprising about this is that many of these students are good students—with averages in the neighborhood of 82% or 83%—who applied only to city colleges and, ordinarily, would have been admitted. Because of the drastic cut in admissions this year, however, they have been rejected by all of their choices, including the community colleges.

The reasons attributed to the overwhelming increase in the number of rejections this year are the financial and spacial limitations of the City University. Yet there were indications of the university's problems as far back as last fall—indications that went largely unnoticed by New York State and City legislators.

Back in November, City U. officials warned of the very crisis which forced the recent decline in admissions. Chancellor Albert Bowker, along with others, proposed the institution of a $400 tuition charge at the city colleges in order to raise sorely needed funds.

In the resulting clamor, however, the officials were made to back down, and the subject of how to obtain more money for the City U. was all but forgotten. The slight tremors which were

felt earlier in the school year were allowed to go unremedied until they developed into a full-scale earthquake, bringing with it a landslide of city college rejection slips.

Quite obviously, something must be done *now* regarding the City University's problems to avoid having to reject many qualified and deserving students in the future. The university officials, with their hands tied financially, can do little. It is the elected representatives of the people of New York who must act.

The city politicians must seek more state and federal educational aid, and they must explore new ways of raising money in order to enable the city colleges both to continue and to expand their current vital role in providing a college education for a significant percentage of N.Y.C. high school graduates.

And the state legislators must give New York City a fair slice of the state's educational aid pie. They must come to their senses and realize that the problems of the City University are far more important than the political power plays to give the state control of the university.

Howard Lemberg
The Chat
Far Rockaway High School
Far Rockaway, N.Y.

274

Editorials of Commemoration and Special Occasions—Editorials of commemoration and special occasions are usually about special events and occasions, holidays, campaign drives, and fund drives such as the Heart Fund, March of Dimes, and the United Fund Campaign. These editorials are often interpretive and narrative in nature.

EXAMPLE:

THE BLACK IRISH AND ST. PATRICK

March 17 has a mystical meaning for all who are Irish and it is that race's boast that on every March 17 "everybody is Irish."

We could begin with the late Dr. Martin Luther King, Jr. His grandfather was part Irish and a sharecropper in Stockbridge, Ga. The first Black Catholic bishop in America was the Rev. James A. Healy of Boston and Portland, Me.

Marcus Garvey Stokely Carmichael and the family of Malcolm X all hailed from the British West Indies . . . along with Harry Belafonte. In an earlier day it was home for Prince Hall . . . South Carolina Congressman Robert B. Elliott

. . . and a host of other prominent American Negroes.

British West Indians have much Irish blood. After the Battle of the Boyne in 1690 when Oliver Cromwell defeated an Irish rebellion, 10,000 Irish aristocrats were shipped to the West Indies to be slaves.

So, on the next March 17th St. Patrick's Day parade when McNamara's band passes by playing "It's a Great Day for the Irish," you can give a tug to your shamrock for on this day everybody really is Irish.

The Leader
Boston, Mass.

Editorials of Commendation—Written in praise of something or somebody, as expressions of appreciation, as a tribute to the deceased, or to commend a worthy cause or action, editorials of commendation are nearly always written seriously and are formal in approach.

EXAMPLE:

EDITORIAL

The Sands Point Academy has a self-assured, easy-to-get-along-with leader. His name is Mr. John Heller, our new principal.

Mr. Heller has brought a new firm, but quiet policy of leadership to our

school. Students who have met with him have found him to be definite in his ideas, but always open-minded and willing to listen.

This is the kind of leadership that a progressive school like Sands Point should have. Our principal's past experience gives him a unique and qualified basis for taking over at our school. In his years as principal at Jericho High School, he obviously learned the value of treating students, both younger and older, as responsible adults.

Though basically a member of the "old school, our new principal is willing," as administrative leaders too often are not, to give the student the benefit of the doubt. He realizes the value, in terms of mutual respect, that such a policy profers.

Mr. Heller's honesty is also appreciated. He is a very straight forward man, hardly a typical administrator. The students of our school have such trust and faith in him, that they have even found him ready to listen to, discuss, and offer advice about their personal problems. This is a rare thing in other, less personal schools.

We are very glad to see Mr. John Heller join our school's administrative staff, and we hope that his appointment will help to deepen the relationship of student and administration.

The Sandpaper
Sands Point Academy-
Country Day School
Sands Point, N.Y.

Editorial Brights, Fillers, and Liners—These editorials are usually short (often one-sentence) statements on a general or specific subject, and can be either serious or humorous depending on their topic of concern. Purposely brief, they are often placed at the end of editorial columns and are usually related to, or concerned with, the theme of the preceding editorial material.

EXAMPLES:

An Editorial Bright

REMEDY OF NATURE PERFECT MEDICINE

Mother Nature has managed to save the day again. Just as students and teachers were beginning to fall into a dreary, listless pit, spring entered the scene to shock all of us into awareness.

It's surprising what a little bit of sunshine and blue sky can do to revitalize an entire student body.

Spring's burst of energy may be just the shot in the arm we need to finish the last three months of school.

The Lancer
Arlington High School
Indianapolis, Indiana

An Editorial Filler

GENERALITIES

Attention students and faculty. Anyone ranging in age from 18–60 and in good health, your help is needed now for the treatment of hundreds of hospital patients who need someone else's blood to survive. You can help by donating only one pint of blood. Wednesday from 2:30–7:30 p.m. in the Alameda cafetorium, 2732 N.E. Fremont.

Unmarried persons under 21 years of age who wish to donate must bring signed parental consent.

FARRELL'S ICE CREAM PARLOR IS GIVING A FREE SUNDAE TO EACH DONOR.

The Grantonian
Ulysses S. Grant High School
Portland, Oregon

An Editorial Liner

> For finding out things one never knew about, there's nothing like opening the encyclopedia and reading away.
>
> *The Boston Globe*

Editorials of Humor and Entertainment—As their name implies, the purpose of these editorials is to entertain. Usually presented as humorous essays, many of them make use of analogy by drawing a parallel between a familiar situation or person and one that is fictitious or not familiar in order to show that what is true in one situation is also true in another. Editorials of humor and entertainment are often presented in order to get across subtly the writer's point of view.

EXAMPLE:

Editorially Speaking . . .

Turnabout Tale, Spring Cleaning . . .

Girl Shows Date 'How Not To Act'

The car horn blared, interrupting the early evening silence.

"Well, how do you like that?" John said to himself. "It's Turnabout night and she doesn't even come to the door for me."

He finally went out to the car and waited for Mary to get out and open the car door for him. "Hey, this is Turnabout, remember?"

"Yeah, yeah, I know. Just get in," she answered.

"Did you make me a corsage?" John asked after riding in silence for several minutes.

"Oh, I guess I forgot. I was kind of rushed all day. Sorry."

John started to complain. "Why start an argument so early in the evening?" he thought to himself. "Surely she'll be better at the dance."

They continued in silence . . .

. . . "Well, we came to dance didn't we? You're supposed to ask me tonight, you know."

"All right, all right," Mary said without enthusiasm.

"Dancing sure makes you thirsty,

277

doesn't it," John hinted.
    Mary grinned.
    John dropped another hint.
    Mary grinned wider . . .
    . . . They rode home in angry silence.
    "This has been a terrible evening,"

John thought indignantly. "She just treats me like . . . why . . . uh . . . like I treat her."

The Lancer
Arlington High School
Indianapolis, Indiana

Editorial Cartoons—Editorial cartoons are used by the print media on editorial pages to emphasize the point of view presented in the editorials. Often, these cartoons catch the reader's eye and generate enough interest to make the reader want to read the related editorial. Many editorial cartoons are political in nature. With their visual appeal, editorial cartoons add variety to the publication's editorial pages. Following is an example of an editorial cartoon dealing with a problem concerning many students.

EXAMPLE:

'Take care, son, eat proper food, don't protest in the rain'

Le Pelley in The Christian Science Monitor © TCSPS

Editorial Polls—An "Inquiring Reporter" column on editorial topics can lure a great many readers to the editorial page. Many editors base their editorials on the results of such polls.

EXAMPLE:

Students Poll on LSD

Students Favor Stronger Laws for LSD Control

Recent discoveries concerning harmful effects of LSD have sent students into discussions of laws governing the use of the halucinatory drug. A poll taken of Northwest students revealed that most favor laws which restrict users to those under a medical researcher's supervision.

Patsy Taylor, junior: There should be laws forbidding LSD because it destroys the user mentally and could cause deformation in their children.

Ellen Roberts, freshman: I'm in favor of laws concerning it because if LSD is dangerous to a person's health, it shouldn't be legal for one to destroy his health knowingly. . . .

The Shield
Northwest Classen High School
Oklahoma City, Oklahoma

EDITORIAL WRITING FOR SCHOOL NEWSPAPERS

School newspaper editorials regularly concern themselves with the betterment of the school and the student body. A reading of other school publications (through your school's publication exchange program) will show that there are many students in our schools today who are capable of meeting the challenges presented in editorial writing. While the larger daily newspapers usually employ from eight to ten full-time editorial writers, the average school newspaper may have but one—usually, the editor himself. Because of their many other publishing considerations most editors of school publications just do not have the time needed to write effective, hard-hitting editorials issue after issue. To alleviate this problem, the editor might well consider asking other student leaders to write guest editorials on topics of concern to the school community. The valedictorian, student body president, National Honor Society president, and leaders of other student organizations may be able to make contributions.

Value of School Newspaper Editorials

Through his editorials, the school newspaper editor has the opportunity to engage in a distinct kind of creative writing experience: in his editorials he can speak for the paper as well as present his own attitudes and beliefs. The editorial writer not only gains the personally satisfying experience of expressing himself creatively, but has the additional gratification of having contributed something useful to his reading audience and community. After carefully analyzing any given situation, the editorial writer is able to make his opinion known to the student body. He can gain considerable influence in his community if his editorials suggest positive courses of action. When editorials are written in an intelligent, mature manner, the student body comes to rely on the presentations contained therein for interpretations of and a better understanding of complex, often thorny, situations.

Most successful school and mass media editorial writers have the following characteristics in common: the ability to think clearly, a keen interest in and knowledge of society-at-large, and the ability to put opinions into effectively written, convincing editorial presentations. A skilled editorial writer's work requires knowledge of many fields and an aptitude for doing careful, thorough research. And, because he often writes about topics that are unpopular with many segments of our society, today's editorial writer must be able to withstand almost constant pressure and criticism.

Structure of School Editorials

Although creativity and originality are encouraged in preparing both mass media and school newspaper editorials, most school newspaper editorial writers follow a standard form that contains the following three divisions: the lead (beginning), the body (middle), and the conclusion (end).

1. The editorial's lead, or beginning, should acquaint the reader with the main idea of the editorial. The lead should also present the facts that support the main idea and should be interesting, clear, and should not contain superfluous words.

2. The body, or middle of the editorial, should build a logical case and should explain the causes or results of the situation in question. The logic presented in the editorial must be sound, and every point must progress to a reasonable conclusion.

3. The conclusion, or end of the editorial, should summarize the situation or the points made in the body of the editorial. The conclusion may suggest a solution, present the reader with a challenge, or drive home the purpose of the editorial.

Subject Matter for School Newspaper Editorials

Matters of concern to the school community are always appropriate subjects for school newspaper editorials. Events such as dramatic productions and art exhibits, programs sponsored by the various school clubs, athletic events, policy decisions affecting the student body, exhibitions by the school glee club, band, and orchestra are always good material for editorials of interest to the school community. School newspaper editorial pages also often deal with topics that touch upon the lives of students beyond the school itself. For example, good editorials can and have been written on such topics as the lowering of the voting age, the draft, the true significance of current events, consideration of changes in the political makeup of the community, the use of narcotics by teenagers, and the "drop-out" problem. Although many beginning editorial writers feel that they must be constantly critical, it should be remembered that constructive "criticism" often consists of praising worthwhile individuals and organizations.

Following is an example of a school newspaper editorial that comments on school government, a matter of direct concern to the student community.

EXAMPLE:

Head {

ELECT STUDENT OFFICIALS FOR STUDENT OFFICES

Lead {

It is unfortunate that the Executive Committee of the Student Council chose the election process that it did for this year's officer elections.

Body {

This method—having all the candidates run together and choosing the ones with the five largest numbers of votes as officers—turns these elections into popularity contests that might place some people in jobs for which they have no desire or qualifications.

This type of election process was chosen so that no qualified person's talents would be lost if he should lose one office. In other words, if a candidate came in second for president, he would be vice president rather than defeated.

However, it seems that this plan does not live up to its ideals; but rather, it may place some in office who do not feel they are fit for the job.   (*Continued*)

Body { -Since the purpose of an election is to choose the best man for each job, this method does not fulfill its objective.

If this is the case, then a better process should be found. This "better process" is the one used in all other campus elections—from classroom to student body.

Each candidate is required to file for a particular office, and then the voters choose who they want to serve them in each capacity. In this way the aspect of a popularity contest will be lessened by the fact that the students will be choosing between only a few qualified persons for each office. Also, only a person who really wants a certain job can be elected to that position.

Conclusion { It would seem advisable, then, that this method be adopted for all Loyola elections.

Paul Soukup
The Loyalist
Loyola High School
Los Angeles, California

Problems, common to all schools, that make grist for the editorial writer's mill also include over-crowded conditions in the school, traffic problems in and about the school, current clothes styles, and the quality of food and services in the school cafeteria. The following article is an example of an editorial dealing with overcrowded conditions in the school.

EXAMPLE:

Overcrowding Isn't Quite 'Licked' Yet

In October we were somewhat uneasy over which of several steps might be taken to correct overcrowding, Glenbrook's number-one problem.

A month later, the administration announced "Pafroc," an ingenious plan to both thin out a close-packed cafeteria and throw out the confusing "administrative period."

The administration rightly didn't try to tell anyone that "Pafroc" would be a permanent solution to overcrowding.

It plainly isn't, and never can be.

Not only the cafeteria was feeling the choking effect of over-crowding. On page 4 of this issue, we have shown how the history department library seemingly won't last much longer in its present closely-packed state.

In fact, we think that the history library is already too small and crowded to provide the service it should. And we think the programs of most history students are just a little below Glenbrook's high standards as a result.

Some overcrowding victims can't be saved by emergency measures like "Pafroc," so we were glad to hear that a more permanent answer is slated for the near future: a building addition in the fall of 1969.

We needed this added space a long while ago. So it should be kept in mind by those planning the addition that old deficiencies like the history library must not be forgotten just because we have put up with them this long.

At the same time, there must be some projected planning for the years after the addition is built.

We predict a rather large addition.

The Torch
Glenbrook High School
Northbrook, Illinois

An example of a school newspaper editorial concerning a situation beyond the scope of immediate school problems is as follows. This fine piece won the "Best Editorial Award" for 1967 in the ANPA *Quill and Scroll* competition, a competition for school newspapers.

EXAMPLE:

SHOW VOTING MATURITY

In the states of Georgia and Kentucky, an individual has the right to vote at the age of eighteen. In Alaska, one may vote in state elections past his or her nineteenth birthday. The cutoff point for Hawaiian residents is twenty years of age.

Are the youth in these states more mature than we in Utah? Of course not! But it appears that they have been able to prove or disprove the myriad of myths concerning teenage maturity by a more understanding adult public!

What has been the outcome? In 1964, while 62% of all "qualified" Americans were going to the polls, 88% of the eighteen to twenty-one group were voting in Georgia and Kentucky. Governor Sanders of Georgia has continually repeated his assertion that since 1941, when those under twenty-one in his state were first given the right to vote, the youthful electorate has demonstrated sound judgment and a knowledgeable attitude.

Utah can be the same! It is the monstrous challenge, however, facing all of us, to open the eyes of skeptics to the realities of our era.

An eighteen-year-old has the responsibility of operating an automobile, the obligation of paying taxes, the task of fighting for his country, and is considered adult in a court of law. The eighteen-year-old is still, in many instances, in the process of learning through formal education and this stimulates the desire to be properly informed. The

283

eighteen-year-old, because of the eagerness displayed in the above-mentioned states, can provide the impetus necessary to bolster a sagging adult voting populace, as well as acquire a background for future elections.

The time has come for Utah citizens, for Americans, to recognize this segment of society who accepts responsibility without the corresponding privilege; who is taxed and sent to war without so much as an audible voice in the formation of such practices. It is time for adults to turn their vision from the minority of publicized delinquents and vandals to the overwhelming majority of informed, capable, but silent teens.

How may an individual help to promote this cause? By (1) signing petitions supporting the Governor's proposal to lower the voting age requirement when they appear in the school or community; (2) writing letters to the *Tribune and News* and *Horizon* stating your convictions; (3) writing a letter to your district representative urging him to support the proposed amendment; and (4) displaying a responsible attitude and mature behavior becoming to a group deserving of the voting privilege.

Mike Kennamon
Horizon
Skyline High School
Salt Lake City, Utah

Organizing and Writing the Editorial

After thoroughly researching the background of his chosen topic, the editorial writer must organize his material. Successful editorials result from well-organized thinking. Preparing an outline from his background notes can be of great help to the editorial writer.

While organizing his material prior to writing, the editorialist should consider the following points:

1. He should understand thoroughly the problem or situation about which he is to write.

2. He should decide what is the basic purpose of his editorial.

3. He should analyze the causes of the problem or situation and determine his proposed course of action.

4. He should plan an interesting, striking method for getting his point across to the reader.

Choosing the Lead—Having determined these points, the editorialist should next decide on an interesting lead for his article. Effective editorials may begin in any of the following ways:
1. By presenting an interest-arousing statement that quickly gains the reader's attention and interest.

EXAMPLE:

Dan Mahoney is a student's student. . . .

2. By exhorting the reader to take a definite course of action, thus presenting him with an effective challenge.

EXAMPLE:

For the betterment of Northcentral, students should elect Dan Mahoney president of the Student Council. . . .

3. By giving, in a simple statement, an interpretation of the situation or problem which the editorial is to present.

EXAMPLE:

The best-qualified presidential candidate in the Student Council election is Dan Mahoney. . . .

4. By leading with a narrative statement. (While narrative leads can gain reader interest, they can often run so long as to be out of proportion with the body and conclusion of the editorial.)

EXAMPLE:

Last fall, when our Student Council was hampered by internal strife, a young delegate took the floor and made an eloquent plea for unity. . . .

5. By using a thought-provoking question which will gain the reader's attention and interest.

EXAMPLE:

Do you want the best possible leader for the student body next year? . . .

6. By using an interest-arousing quotation which is a vital part of the editorial's subject matter.

EXAMPLE:

"I will give the students a stronger voice in the operation of their school," Dan Mahoney has promised.

The Body of the Editorial—The body of the editorial should expand the lead statement by building a logical case in support of the lead. The body should explain the causes or results of the situation or problem in question. Each point of the supporting logic presented in the body should progress to a reasonable conclusion.

The Conclusion—The conclusion should sum up the points or situation covered in the body of the editorial. The conclusion can also suggest a logical solution or present the reader with a challenge, thus driving home the purpose of the editorial.

CHECKLIST FOR SCHOOL NEWSPAPER EDITORIAL WRITERS

1. Is the editorial's main idea of concern to your fellow students and to the school community in general, and does it have a moral purpose?
2. Did you thoroughly research and organize your material?
3. Have all the facts been checked and logically presented in a clear, interesting style?
4. Does your lead statement interestingly present the main idea of the editorial?
5. Is the stand you take definite and convincing, and is your reasoning sound?
6. Does your editorial have three parts: a lead, a body, and a conclusion?
7. Have you avoided being "preachy" and "over-sentimental"?
8. Is the entire editorial brief, interesting, and forceful?
9. Does the conclusion sum up, or suggest a solution to, the problem dealt with in the editorial?
10. Will your editorial effectively influence public opinion?

LIBEL CONSIDERATIONS IN EDITORIAL WRITING

In the 1830's an editorial in the *Louisville Focus* began, "President General Andrew Jackson is a lying, thieving scoundrel." Today, such an editorial would be discredited as libelous. Libelous matter is any material appearing in print that contains false information injurious to a person's reputation or business, whether that person is alive or deceased. Libel laws apply as much to editorial comment as to anything else in the publication. In America, in order for printed material to be considered libelous, the law usually requires that the material be proven to be malicious in its intent. The common defense against libel is to prove the truth of the matter published, to prove that the publication did no appreciable damage, or to prove that there was no malice aforethought. The school newspaper editorial writer must avoid any material that might recklessly endanger the reputation of anyone, and he must be careful to always be accurate in his presentation. All school publications support an editorial policy of truth and honesty in their presentation of published materials. There is no place in the school press for loose accusations of any kind.

IMPROVING EDITORIAL PAGE READERSHIP

In addition to placing "Letters-to-the-Editor" on the editorial page, the school newspaper editor can help improve readership by using attractive layouts that include good photos, cartoons, and special features. Editorial pages are visually more appealing when all stories used on the page are short and the editorials are set in a larger type size and at a wider column width than are the regular news stories appearing elsewhere in the publication. Interest-arousing headlines and leads for each editorial also help gain reader attention. Often, when especially significant issues present themselves, editors run them as featured editorials on page one.

School publications often expand their editorial pages into special editorial supplements when a major issue or situation presents itself. An excellent example of several pages from an editorial supplement of this type is shown on pages 288–289. The pages shown were taken from a sixteen-page supplement prepared by the staff of the *Mustang News*, Medford High School, Medford, Massachusetts. The supplement was published ten days after a fire had destroyed the school.

Most school publications keep their editorial pages free from advertising, thus allowing space for visually attractive groupings of editorial and feature material. Page two is usually set aside as the editorial page, and many schools

THE
FIRE
(Part One)

Leo McCabe
Medford Fire Chief

Heroic deeds of firemen are captured as they shoot hoses into the heart of fire, high on ladders, into the Distributive Education rooms on third floor crossover area.

Part of the thousands of spectators that watched the school burn look on as flames race out of control.

Ladders extend directly into blazing flames in firefighters' attempt to check fire's spread.

Mustang News Staff

The MUSTANG NEWS, student publication of Medford High School, is edited and published by the journalism classes at Medford High School, Forest Street, Medford, Massachusetts 02155.

Vol. IV   Nov. 1965   No. 1

Headmaster
Mr. William A. McCormack
Newspaper Advisor
Mr. Henry R. Selvitella
SPECIAL STAFF THIS EDITION:
Editor: Edmund R. Pignone. Reporters: Joanne Cecchini, Roberta Crafin, Patricia Dentamaro, Frances Salipante. Editorial: Linda Picilo. Lay-Out: Jeanne Lascone. Circulation: Diane, Gulino, Carol Ferrone, Louise Freni, Lucille Langone, Marjorie Lovering, Jutta Nahrgang, Nancy Philips, David Smith, Kathy Sweeney, Nancy Tankard, Rosemary Salvo, Patricia Moskos, JoAnn Aloisi, Stephen Umbro. Exchange: Charlene Jenkins, Judy Jeselonis. Art: Kathy Crehan.

Ex 'News' Photographer Really Hot On Fire Story

Robert Stanley was one of the early "pioneers" when the NEWS was born in 1962.

Bob was our top photographer when we were named ALL-AMERICAN last year, and his photos sure helped us earn that honor.

Now an apprentice photographer with Associated Press, we are proud to present some of the work of one of our first graduates whose major photo contributions dominate this issue.

We are sure that you will agree that Bob was really "hot" on this assignment.

While They Last

Copies of this special edition can be purchased in the Mustang News office now located in the Teachers Lunchroom, Room 023, directly beneath the School Committee Room or from the main office adjacent to the Headmasters office.

All proceeds will be applied to the Carol Baxter Journalism Scholarship Assistance Fund.

Tongues of flame shoot out of window in Dwight Davis' rear-view photo of Building C, which was completely destroyed.

Firefighters pour millions of gallons of water into girls' gym in a hard but vain attempt to save what remained of Building C. The effort of these typifies that displayed by all concerned with disaster.   (Boston Globe photo)

The Salvation Army and the Red Cross were on the job quickly and efficiently supplying coffee to the weary firefighters. (Photo by NEWS photographer Robert Crockford.)

Aerial hoses shower Building B at climax of multi-million dollar disaster.
(Boston Globe photo)

Girls' gym takes in torrents of water from ground hoses while Building C rages out of control.
(Boston Globe photo)

289

place their masthead (the publication's name, address, names of staff members, publication's affiliations, and advertising rates) on it.

"Letters-to-the-Editor"

In order to better judge reader response, editors encourage and evaluate letters from readers. "Letters-to-the-Editor," an essential part of a good editorial page, makes an interesting editorial feature and provides a platform for reader dissent. Such a platform is especially important for school publications—it shows that students are thinking about what they read. A school newspaper editor would do well to make it a rule that all letters to appear in print be signed, and he should always check that the signatures are authentic. Because libel laws also govern what can and cannot be published in the "Letters-to-the-Editor" section, the burden of proving that what is stated in the letters is the truth falls upon the publication's editor—despite the fact that the printed letters are genuine.

"WHY AREN'T YOU HERE?"

After Henry David Thoreau had been imprisoned for protesting taxation, he was visited by poet Ralph Waldo Emerson. Shocked by his disciple's plight, Emerson demanded, "Why are *you* here?" Thoreau, who had merely been following the advice of his friend, responded, "Why aren't *you* here?" Thoreau had taken a stand and was suffering the consequences.

Despite the advice of an old-time Chicago editor who said, "A newspaper's job is to print the news and raise hell," the scholastic editorial writer must remember that his duty is to attempt to help the student body to think *constructively*. An editorial writer—*any* editorial writer—must never tear down merely for the sake of tearing down: he must emphasize the positive approach. If an editorial writer cannot advance solutions to problems, he should not condemn those persons who do advance constructive, positive, well-intended solutions.

In summary, any editorial writer, before writing an editorial, must know all sides of the issue, must be qualified to offer opinions on the subject, must be fair and impartial to all sides and, lastly, must be positive enough in his suggestions to withstand any consequences for what he has written.

ACTIVITIES

1. Examine the editorial content of one back issue of your school's newspaper from the year 1964, 1959, or 1954. What were the issues that prompted

the editorials? Are the editorials contained in your school paper today concerned with similar issues? Are they presented in a similar way?

2. Invite a former editor of your school paper for a "briefing" from the current newspaper staff. Ask him if he would like to write a guest editorial on the changes or lack of changes he sees in his school.

3. Call the editor of the editorial page of your local newspaper and invite him to a staff meeting of your publication. Find out from him how he researches, organizes, and writes his editorials.

4. List five topics you would like to have considered for editorials in your school newspaper. Present them to your school's newspaper editor as suggestions for editorials.

5. Select an editorial from a recent issue of your favorite newspaper. Bring it to class and comment on such elements as lead, writing style, organization, effectiveness, and purpose.

6. List five suggestions for increasing your school newspaper's editorial page readership. Present your suggestions to the paper's editor.

READING

BLOCK, HERBERT, *Straight Herblock*. Simon and Schuster, New York, 1964.

DANIELS, JONATHAN, *They Will Be Heard: America's Crusading Newspaper Editors*. McGraw-Hill, New York, 1965.

KRIEGHBAUM, HILLIER, *Facts in Perspective: The Editorial Page and News Interpretation*. Prentice-Hall, Englewood Cliffs, N.J., 1956.

MAURY, REUBEN, AND KARL G. PFEIFFER, *Effective Editorial Writing*. Wm. C. Brown, Dubuque, Iowa, 1959.

RIVERS, WILLIAM L., *Opinionmakers*. Beacon Press, Boston, 1965. (PB)

SWADOS, HARVEY (Ed.), *Years of Conscience: The Muckrakers*. World Publishing, Cleveland, Ohio, 1962. (PB)

SWANBERG, W. A., *Pulitzer*. Scribner, New York, 1967.

VAN DEUSEN, GLYNDON G., *Horace Greeley: Nineteenth Century Crusader*. University of Pennsylvania Press, Philadelphia, Pa., 1953.

WALDROP, A. GAYLE, *Editor and Editorial Writing*. Wm. C. Brown, Dubuque, Iowa, 1967.

WARD, WILLIAM G., *The Student Journalist and Designing the Opinion Pages*. Richards Rosen Press, New York, 1968.

——, *The Student Journalist and Editorial Leadership*. Richards Rosen Press, New York, 1968.

WHITE, WILLIAM ALLEN, *The Autobiography of William Allen White*. Macmillan, New York, 1951.

Chapter 14

Social Responsibility
of Journalists

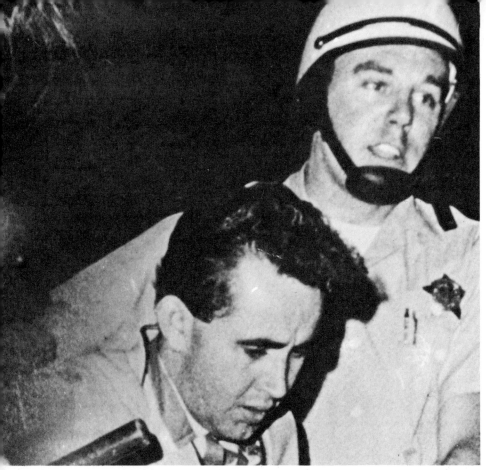

JOURNALISTS AS "OMBUDSMEN"

In Sweden when a citizen feels that he has not received true justice from the courts he goes to see his ombudsman, an official appointed by the government to guarantee the rights of the average citizen. The Swedish citizen knows that the ombudsman will fully investigate his grievance and quickly and impartially correct any injustices. To the ombudsman everyone—regardless of social position or wealth—is equal. He knows that his job is to serve the public and guard its rights. In many ways the mass media journalist in the United States is the ombudsman for the public. Though each mass communications medium has developed its own methods for serving the public, each subscribes to journalism's first real code of ethics—and its best-known creed—which in part reads:

> I believe that the public journal is a public trust; that all connected with it are, to the full measure of their responsi-

293

bility, trustees for the public; that acceptance of lesser service than the public service is betrayal of this trust.

Walter Williams
Grassroots

THE PRINT MEDIA

Newspapers have sometimes been called the "fourth branch of government" because, like the executive, legislative, and judicial branches in a democracy, they represent the will of the people. By providing the public with news and information, presenting and explaining the actions of the government, and exposing unjust and illegal activities, both newspapers and magazines have played and will continue to play a vital role in the lives of the citizens in a republic. To responsibly and effectively perform this role, the print media involve themselves in the problems and issues which face their readers in several ways.

"Ombudsman" Columns

Many newspapers and magazines now receive and investigate readers' questions and complaints about everything from the cracks in sidewalks to the malpractice of political officeholders. After researching and investigating authentic gripes, newspapers and magazines publish their responses in editorial, daily action-line, and ombudsman columns. For example, if a citizen has complained to his city administration about poor lighting on his street and has received no response, he might make his complaint known to the editor of his local newspaper. The editor, after determining the validity of the complaint by checking the proper city authorities and perhaps assigning a reporter to make a further investigation, would then answer the citizen's complaint in the newspaper's editorial, action-line, or ombudsman column.

Many readers make their grievances known through "Letters-to-the-Editor" columns. When these grievances are pertinent to the public-at-large, the editor may decide to base an editorial on a particularly forceful and informative letter from a reader. While an editor tries to publish every letter he receives, he realizes that some of the letters will be inaccurate—sometimes malicious—and therefore unprintable. On one occasion a newspaper editor discovered that a letter he had received was really a form letter prepared and distributed by an extremist group: the group, attempting to spread propaganda for its doctrine, had requested that each of its members sign a form letter and send it to his local "Letters-to-the-Editor" column. The editor, upon discovering the real intent of the letter, refused to print it.

294

Campaigns and Crusades

Famed author and reporter H. L. Mencken has said:

> It is the duty of the newspaper to comfort the afflicted and afflict the comfortable.

Many concerned editors attempt to follow Mencken's words by becoming aware of those people in their communities who are "afflicted," and then campaigning for an improvement in their conditions. These conscientious editors feel that if a newspaper or magazine is to become an indispensible part of its community, it cannot afford to become "comfortable": instead, it must fulfill its social promise through vigorous, independent, and courageous journalism.

In the past, newspapers that have served the public well have been awarded the journalism profession's most respected award, the Pulitzer Prize. For example, a Pulitzer Citation was awarded to newspapers in the Gannett Group for their excellence in community-service reporting. The president of the Gannett Group, Paul Miller of Rochester, New York, first became involved in public-service journalism when he became concerned about how his newspapers could constructively deal with the racial crisis in Rochester and other American cities. He sent the following memo to each newspaper editor in the group:

> Every city has the same problem. If it has not, it soon will have. Every city is trying to find answers. Have any cities found answers that might be useful in Rochester and elsewhere? If so, what are they?

Miller then assigned the group's executive editor, Vincent S. Jones, to organize and direct a series, titled "The Road to Integration," on the racial problem. Jones spelled out the objectives for the group's editors as follows:

> We would look for accomplishment, and for constructive, workable projects in the fields of jobs, housing, education, rights. We would use all of the techniques of newspapering —straight news reports, feature stories, interpretive pieces, interviews, pictures, and editorials. Our associated radio and television stations agreed to cooperate. We would *not* print just another series, however good, but set up coverage to be continued indefinitely.

To announce the series, a front-page editorial titled "Here's What We Can Do About Integration" was published in each of the Gannett newspapers. The editorial made the following suggestions:

> *Jobs:* Negroes should be welcomed to the ranks of the employed. Quotas were opposed as discrimination in reverse.

> *Housing:* The editorial urged support of sensible public housing; encouraged the conservation of existing buildings to preserve a normal neighborhood; asked enforcement of sanitary and building codes and a crackdown on delinquency and crime.

> *Education:* The editorial endorsed the best possible teaching, even special courses, for Negro pupils; opposed "crash programs" of school integration.

> *Representation:* The editorial urged the appointment of responsible Negro citizens to public boards and to the governing bodies of semi-public institutions and agencies.

Following the announcement of "The Road to Integration" series, Gannett reporters wrote and had published relevant articles, and many cities benefitted from the results.

Paul Miller was presented the "Brotherhood Award of the Council of Christians and Jews" and the Pulitzer Prize Committee, in praising Miller's civic responsibility, called "The Road to Integration" series "A fresh and constructive journalistic approach to a major social problem" and a "distinguished example of the use of a newspaper group's resources to complement the work of its individual newspapers."

THE ELECTRONIC MEDIA

The Columbia Broadcasting System, on the day after Thanksgiving, 1960, presented a one-hour documentary about migrant farm workers titled "The Harvest of Shame." The narrator, Edward R. Murrow (an early pioneer in electronic journalism broadcasting), ended the program by saying:

> The people you have seen have the strength to harvest your fruit and vegetables. They do not have the strength to influence legislation. Maybe we do. Good night and good luck.

In the days following the program Murrow received both praise and criticism. Some persons praised him for having dramatically and effectively exposed the terrible conditions of the migrant worker, while others condemned him for editorializing on a news program. Those who condemned Murrow claimed that by editorializing on a news program he had destroyed the impartiality. When Murrow was questioned about his lack of objectivity, he replied: "Would you give equal time to Judas Iscariot or Simon Legree?"

As illustrated by this incident, in matters of public interest the radio and television media act differently from newspapers: both radio and television appeal more directly to the emotions. Because radio and television announcers seem to be speaking directly to listeners and viewers, they can more easily arouse emotions and stimulate listeners and viewers to take action. This powerful quality of the electronic media provides great potential for the socially responsible electronic journalist.

Radio

A number of radio stations regularly schedule discussion programs that ask listeners to call and discuss current issues. Other stations broadcast public-service announcements that supply the public with the names of the city agencies that can be of help in problem situations. The broadcast editorial has also become a major part of the radio station's public-service responsibility, and many stations take a public stand on the problems of their communities. Broadcast editorials help to stimulate public participation in community affairs.

Television

Though often criticized for the violence and trivia presented in their programs, television networks have contributed much time and programming to the public interest. By focusing attention on Senate crime hearings, political party conventions, and the plight of the cities, television documentaries and news programs have helped to educate the American people about many of the problems and issues that directly affect them. For example, the Columbia Broadcasting System has won several awards for documentary films such as "Biography of a Bookie Joint" (a program that exposed the relationship between gambling and politics in a large city), and "Case Study of a Rumor" (a television program which showed how a malicious rumor can quickly spread across the country).

Local television stations also carry public-interest editorials and discussion programs. One television station began an "Air Your Gripe" show that encouraged its viewers to write to the station if they had complaints about conditions in the city. Upon receipt of complaints, camera crews were assigned to photograph the problems. On-camera interviews were held with public officials to discuss plans for solutions to the complaints. Some of the civic problems resolved through this method were littered playgrounds, damaged sidewalks, traffic congestion, and poor roads.

THE MEDIA OF PERSUASION

Because members of the mass media are basically profit-making business ventures, there is always the threat that enough pressure from the media of persuasion—advertising and public relations—could influence mass media standards. Mass media journalists are constantly aware that advertising, which pays most of the production costs in the mass media, might be withdrawn if journalistic content does not please advertisers. In general, however, most media editors present that news which they think is factual and which will appeal to the largest number of consumers. Advertisers, also concerned with reaching the largest possible number of consumers, rarely interfere with news content.

Advertising

The medium of advertising, well aware of its power to influence the public to buy certain products, has also become aware of its power to influence the public in other matters. With this increasing awareness, advertising has become more sensitive about its social responsibility. To demonstrate to the public how advertising can play an important role in bettering society in general, the medium banded together with business groups and formed the Advertising Council, an agency solely concerned with public service advertising. The Council, founded in 1942, operates under the following policies:

1. Accept no subsidy from the government and remain independent of it.
2. Conduct campaigns of service to the nation at large, avoiding regional, sectarian, and special-interest drives.
3. Remain non-partisan, and non-political; conduct the Council on a voluntary basis; and accept no project with a commercial interest unless the public interest is overriding.

from *The Advertising Council Annual Report—1967–1968*

Broadcast, print, transit, and outdoor advertising contribute millions of dollars each year in time and space publicizing such organizations as the Peace Corps, the National Safety Council, and the U.S. Department of Justice. The illustrations on page 299 show the types of public-service advertisements prepared by the Advertising Council.

NO CAMPING
NO SWIMMING
NO HIKING
NO RELAXING
NO FISHING
NO HUNTING
NO RIDING
NO SIGHTSEEING

Only you can prevent forest fires.

FOREST FIRE PREVENTION CAMPAIGN

Space contributed as a public service by this magazine.

One gift works many wonders

GIVE THE UNITED WAY

Photo contributed by Harold Halma

Help work wonders for the poor, the sick, the aged, the young. Give them
the hope, the health and the happiness they might never have without you.

Your fair share gift works many wonders ✓ THE UNITED WAY

27.5 million families benefit from child care, family service, youth guidance, health programs, disaster relief and services for the Armed Forces through 31,300 United Way agencies.

PUBLIC SERVICE ADVERTISEMENTS PREPARED BY
THE ADVERTISING COUNCIL

The Advertising Council

DON'T FENCE ME OUT.

If you don't help your school officials
open recreation areas nights, weekends
and during the summer, nobody else will.

DON'T
FENCE ME
OUT

For a free button and information to help you, write: Fitness, Washington, D.C. 20001
PRESIDENT'S COUNCIL ON PHYSICAL FITNESS

Published as a public service in cooperation with The Advertising Council

She can't come to you for the truth,
but you can reach her.

The truth can become a very precious
thing to a young mind in a closed country.
"Dear Friends,
I began listening to your broadcasts
when I was a small child.
Today I am 22.
And for most of what I know about the
world, I have to thank Radio Free Europe.
The young woman who wrote that letter
lives in Communist ruled Czechoslovakia.
Each year, one also, through the world
reeled with that only barbed wire fence.

Today she knows different. And what's
more important, she knows who built it.
There are 82 million people like her
living within the Iron Curtain countries
of Czechoslovakia, Rumania, Bulgaria,
Poland and Hungary. And more of them
listen to Radio Free Europe then ever
before.
The news, not only of their own country, but of the outside world, is broadcast
without bias or distortion and in their own
language.
Radio Free Europe is on the air up to

19 hours every day.
The one-time Communist monopoly of
information in Eastern Europe has been
broken.
The truth is getting through, helping
millions work toward their freedom.
And with that as a goal, a great many
people have a great many more reasons
to go on living.

Give to Radio Free Europe
Box 1966, Mt. Vernon, N.Y.

Public Relations

A public relations man, acting as the "ears" of his client, hears what the public thinks and feels about the company's products and services. Knowing this information, he can influence the operations of the company by presenting to management the complaints and advice he has heard from consumers. For example, if an automobile manufacturer's public relations representative receives many calls and letters complaining about the safety of the company's cars, it is the representative's job to transmit such complaints to the executives of the company, advising them that safer cars would restore public trust and increase sales. By identifying to management those company actions and policies which can help or harm the public, the public relations representative performs a crucial social function.

Some public relations firms have further contributed to the public good by offering, at no charge, their services to such groups as colleges, churches, and government agencies. Each year, one public relations agency volunteers a representative who visits school yearbook staffs with advice on promotion, layout, and writing.

THE PRESSURES AND PROBLEMS OF SOCIAL RESPONSIBILITY

An often-repeated story tells of an accused man brought before a judge for swinging his arms and hitting another man in the nose. The defendant, pleading innocent, asked, "Haven't I the right to swing my arms in a free country?" The Judge, answering the accused, said, "Your right to swing your arm ends where another man's nose begins. Ten dollars!" Though the defendant knew that the First Amendment to the Constitution guaranteed his right to freedom of expression, what he didn't know—and what the past has so often shown—is that freedom of expression has limits, and that freedom also implies responsibility.

The Meaning of the First Amendment

For the press the problem of what to print and what to omit is constant. A commission organized by Time, Inc., attempting to define how the press can act both freely and responsibly, divided the freedom of the press into two parts: "freedom from," and "freedom for." The Commission defined "freedom from" as:

A free press is free from compulsions from whatever source, governmental or social, external or internal. From compulsions, not from pressures; for no press can be free from pressures except in a moribund society empty of contending forces and beliefs. These pressures, however, if they are persistent and distorting—as financial, clerical, popular, institutional pressures may become—approach compulsion; and then something is lost from effective freedom which the press and the public must unite to restore.

To the Commission "freedom for" meant:

A free press is free for the expression of opinion in all its phases. It is free for the achievement of those goals of press service on which its own ideals and the requirements of the community combine and which existing techniques make possible. For these ends it must have full command of technical resources, financial strength, reasonable access to sources of information both at home and abroad, as well as the necessary facilities for bringing information to the national market.

A Free and Responsible Press
Copyright 1947 by the University of Chicago

As the Commission pointed out, maintaining a free and responsible press is not easy because of the many legal, political, financial, and criminal pressures which journalists face.

Legal Restraints

Any journalist working in the mass media understands the adage, "The pen is mightier than the sword." However, if a journalist does not recognize that his statements—spoken or in print—must be truthful, impartial, fair, and non-malicious, he would be wise to choose another field of endeavor. While the mass media are looking for courageous men and women to be their reporters and editors, they don't need reporters and editors with more nerve than discretion.

Though the First Amendment guaranteeing the freedom of the press is sacred to the journalist, the Fifth Amendment stating that no person shall be deprived of life, liberty, or property without due process of law, and the Sixth Amendment guaranteeing a speedy and public trial by an impartial jury, are equally important to him. Journalists know that because words and pictures can create or destroy a man's reputation, they must be exceedingly careful about what they say and how they say it. If they are not careful, the medium they represent may have a lawsuit to contend with. The two types of lawsuits of major concern to media journalists are libel and slander.

Libel—The majority of legal cases concerning the print media are in the area of libel. A libelous statement is any false or malicious representation, written or printed, which hurts the reputation of a person; exposes him to hatred, ridicule, or contempt; injures him in his occupation; or which damages his firm financially.

The two types of libel are criminal libel and civil libel. Criminal libel covers the publication of obsence, blasphemous, or seditious material and since this offense is considered a felony in most states, conviction carries a jail sentence. Civil libel consists of publication of material that unjustly defames a person's character or hurts the operation of his business. In most cases, this crime is considered a misdemeanor and conviction can result in a fine or a jail sentence.

Slander—While libel laws govern false and maliciously written statements, slander laws pertain to spoken defamatory remarks. In the early days of radio and television, a person who had been slandered by a radio or television commentator had little recourse in the courts. If he sued and won the case, the settlement was often so small that it was hardly worth the plaintiff's time. Because of the large audiences of the radio and television media, such suits are now handled under the more harsh libel provisions. Usually, the more persons that hear the slander, the more severe the penalty.

Defenses Against Libel and Slander Suits

Legal arguments in libel and slander cases are usually very complicated, but, in general, three defenses have been developed for protecting the members of the mass media: truth of report; privilege of reporting; fair comment and criticism.

Truth of Report—Truth is the major defense in any libel suit. The editor or publisher accused of publishing a libelous statement must be able to prove the truth of the statements he made. When a national magazine published a report saying that two well-known football coaches had conspired to "fix" a game between their two teams, the magazine publisher was sued by the two coaches. For the libel suit to be dismissed, the law required that the magazine prove that the coaches had been involved in a conspiracy. The magazine's publisher, however, was unable to substantiate his report of a "fix," and the coaches were awarded over a million dollars for damage to their reputations.

A person's name does not necessarily need to be used in a defamatory story for a libel action to take place. If the person in the story can be identified, he can sue the publication for damages. To avoid libel suits, reporters avoid expressions that give the impression that a person accused of a crime has been adjudged guilty of that crime. On one occasion, a newspaper carried a story that quoted the police as saying that a woman was charged with shoplifting. The newspaper's headline read:

Shoplifter Nabbed in $100 Theft

The police had not told the reporter that the woman was a shoplifter—only that she had been *charged* with shoplifting: only a judge and jury (not the newspaper) could, on the basis of evidence, find the woman *guilty* of shoplifting. The headline should have read:

Woman Accused of $100 Theft

A week after the first headline was published, the judge, on the basis of insufficient evidence, acquitted the woman. She then sued the newspaper and collected a large sum for damages. Media journalists must always keep in mind that a person is innocent until *proven* guilty.

Privilege of Reporting—This defense grants the press immunity from libel damages for fair and true reports of government or other official proceedings. For example, if a mayor fires a police commissioner, the mayor's reasons, whether given at a news conference or in writing, can be published without fear of a libel suit being filed by the dismissed police commissioner. Similarly, any comments or accusations made by government officials during public hearings can be published.

Fair Comment and Criticism—Without this defense, many editorials, movie, stage, television, and book reviews, feature stories, and letters-to-the-editor could not be printed. This defense permits editors, feature writers, and columnists the freedom to express their opinions as long as they are not malicious. If *fair comment and criticism* were not a defense against libel, no reporter would be able to include in his news stories any quotations which criticize a person or business.

Political Pressure

Since it is the right of people in a democracy to know how government officials function, and the duty of the mass media to transmit information concerning government operations, journalists and government officials are often at odds: journalists try to uncover facts while government officials sometimes try to keep such facts secret. For example, during the Viet Nam War the government became concerned about the unfavorable reports coming from the battle zone and tried to pressure *The New York Times* into transferring its reporter, David Halberstam, from South Viet Nam to Poland. The *Times* refused to transfer Halberstam who later received a Pulitzer Prize for his coverage of the war. No journalist, however, believes that the press must know everything—he realizes that some confidentiality is necessary in order for the government to successfully conduct its foreign, defense, and domestic policies.

The conflict between the people's right to know and the government's need of secrecy was summarized by John Hohenberg, a former foreign correspondent for *The New York Times* when he said:

> The responsible news media . . . are torn between a desire to respect the processes of government that clearly demand a certain amount of confidentiality and to check the growth of such objectionable official practices as holding unnecessary executive sessions and maintaining unnecessary secrecy over public records.
>
> *The News Media: A Journalist Looks at His Profession*

Political pressure on the media is always present regardless of which political party is in power. For example, a newspaper that published a critical story about its city administration had the streets leading to its pressroom closed by the city, and a magazine that criticized the federal government had its income tax statements repeatedly investigated. The confrontation between the journalist and the politician reached a new peak during the 1968 Democratic National Convention. A presidential commission, called to investigate violence in American life, issued a report on the convention entitled *Rights in Conflict*. In its section on "The Police and the Press," the report stated:

> A total of 49 newsmen were hit, maced, or arrested, apparently without reason, by the police. . . . The Chicago Fire Department inspected television equipment vans just prior to the convention and ordered them re-wired, saying that

they didn't conform to the Chicago code. Police imposed a parking ban on television camera vans. The police ordered television cameras off sidewalk locations near the convention hotels and threatened, according to one television technician on the scene, to take the cameras apart piece by piece if they weren't removed.

This and other attempts at indirect censorship led Columbia Broadcasting System's News President Richard S. Salant to say that the restrictions on the press formed "a pattern well beyond simple labor disputes, logistics, and security problems." The morning after CBS newsman Dan Rather was knocked down by an employee of the convention's sergeant-at-arms (while on-camera before millions of viewers), National Broadcasting Company newscaster Chet Huntley said, on an NBC newscast:

> We in the calling of journalism have hesitated to talk about our problems in Chicago . . . but the hostility toward any kind of criticism, and the fear of telling how it is, has become too much and it becomes our duty to speak out. . . . The significant part of all this is the undeniable manner in which Chicago police are going out of their way to injure newsmen and prevent them from filming or gathering information on what is going on. The news profession is now under assault by the Chicago Police.
>
> "The Police and the Press"
> *Rights in Conflict*

Chicago journalists were in a particularly sensitive position during the violence. Knowing they would have to work with local police and politicians following the convention, they did not wish to antagonize city officials by being too critical and perhaps cut off important sources of future news stories. Following the convention some Chicago journalists concerned about the conflict between their newspaper's interest in retaining good relations with city government and the public's right to unmanipulated and unmanaged news founded a magazine called *Chicago Journalism Review*. The magazine was established to discuss the problem of political pressure on the mass media.

Financial Problems

In order to be socially responsible, a newspaper must be financially sound. The publishers of financially unsound newspapers usually cannot afford the independence necessary for courageous journalism. Newspapers having economic troubles often have to compromise themselves to business interests that limit their freedom to criticize business, while others are often forced to become members of newspaper chains, thus sacrificing some of their former independence for financial soundness.

Commercial pressure also comes from unscrupulous advertising and public relations agencies. For example, a national magazine once ran an article entitled "Beware of Hearing-aid Gyps." The story did not say that hearing-aid manufacturers were unethical or that the manufacturers were defrauding, or misleading, the public. The article—with a number of specific examples—merely said "Beware. . . ." But, as a result of the story, $60,000 in hearing-aid advertising was taken away from the magazine.

Advertising and public relations agencies are also subject to commercial pressures. Following the assassinations of Dr. Martin Luther King and Senator Robert F. Kennedy, a Chicago advertising agency prepared a series of public service advertisements proposing strict gun-control legislation. Opponents of this legislation pressured the agency by contacting agency clients with threats to boycott their products unless they fired the agency. Many of the agency's clients, bowing to the pressure, withdrew their accounts, and the agency suffered a serious financial loss.

Criminal Pressure

Criminal pressure on the mass media does occasionally occur. Organized crime, wishing to keep their operations secret, has sometimes threatened harm to journalists in order to frighten them into silence. Two newspapers in Utica, New York, experienced intimidation when they crusaded against the influence of organized crime in their city. Their articles resulted in the arrest and conviction of a number of criminals and politicians, and the two newspapers shared a Pulitzer Prize for their courageous journalism.

REGULATION IN THE MASS MEDIA

The mass media try to ensure accuracy, fairness, and good taste in their news presentations, and avoid government pressure, libel suits, and public disapproval by conforming to a number of written and unwritten restrictions. A major responsibility of mass media editors is the protection of consumers from journalists who overemphasize the sensational, ridicule religion, report rumors, and spread malicious gossip in their news presentations. Media editors further regulate news presentations by rejecting all writing

Former President Harry S. Truman is shown shortly after his election holding a copy of "The Chicago Daily Tribune" with its banner headline proclaiming "Dewey Defeats Truman." The paper's lead story predicted a nationwide G.O.P. sweep with Republican candidate Thomas Dewey leading the presidential elections by a wide margin.

that doesn't measure up to the ideals of the journalism profession. Skilled journalists, however, seldom need to have their material "censored" by editors. Columnist Jimmy Breslin, for example, has said that he cannot remember ever having had his copy changed by an editor.

Guidelines for Journalists

To further ensure against violation of the written and unwritten codes of the journalism profession, the mass media have created some specific guidelines for journalists.

Guidelines for Covering Public Disorders—After a number of peace demonstrations and race riots in which several persons were injured, leading

307

editors met to set up guidelines to prevent the mass media from contributing to a disturbance. Among the provisions set forth were:

> Because inexpert use of cameras, bright lights, or microphones may stir exhibitionism in some people, great care should be exercised by crews at scenes of public disorders. Their presence should be as unobtrusive as possible.
>
> All news media should make every effort to assure that only seasoned reporters are sent to the scene of a disaster.
>
> Every reporter and technician should be governed by the rules of good taste and common sense. The potential for inciting public disorders demands that competition be secondary to the cause of public safety.

"The Police and the Press"
Rights in Conflict

Photograph by Bruce Davidson,
Magnum Photos

Government pressure and public disapproval often have an effect on members of the mass media who, in their efforts to ensure accuracy and fairness, have tried to "tell it like it is" in matters such as police brutality.

Guidelines for Covering the Arts—Another example of self-imposed restriction concerns the arts. If a reviewer too harshly criticizes every movie, play, art show, or musical event offered in a community, people will either stop attending events or will soon completely ignore the criticisms. Therefore, reviewers try to temper their statements. For example, in reviewing a presentation of *Romeo and Juliet* by a local dramatic group, the reviewer should keep in mind that the actors are amateurs. Instead of saying that the housewife who portrayed Juliet didn't begin to compare with the actress who played Juliet on Broadway, the reviewer might emphasize the difficulty an amateur actress encounters when performing in one of Shakespeare's works for the first time.

Guidelines for Covering the Courts—To ensure an accused defendant a fair trial, mass media journalists must keep in mind the fact that an accused person is innocent until found guilty by a judge or jury. The American Bar Association (ABA), an association of lawyers, has frequently charged that some stories carried by the mass media prevent the accused from receiving a fair trial as guaranteed by the Sixth Amendment. Though the ABA cannot place restrictions on the mass media which would violate the First Amendment pledge of a free press, the ABA can recommend that police and court officials withhold certain information from reporters. An ABA committee on "Free Press, Fair Trial," headed by Judge Francis Reardon, recommended that the following facts be withheld in criminal cases:

1. The suspect's prior criminal record.
2. Existence or contents of a confession.
3. Lie detector test results or whether the suspect takes the test.
4. Identity of prospective witnesses.
5. The possibility of a guilty plea.
6. General comments about the suspect's guilt or innocence.

Though many newsmen have protested that these recommendations constitute censorship of the public's right to know what the police and courts are doing, court officials in most states are following the Reardon Report. Continuing studies are being conducted by mass media organizations, the ABA, and universities in an attempt to see if newspaper publicity—"trial by newspaper," as it is called—has any effect on the decisions of juries. Two University of Chicago Law School professors, investigating the effect of pre-trial publicity on jury trials, studied 3,000 criminal trials and made note of the "impressive" fact that not a single case indicated that a judge believed the jury to be swayed by pre-trial publicity. Another researcher, James B. Lemert of Southern Illinois University, came to these conclusions:

People are less likely to jump to news-based conclusions about guilt or innocence when they are actually in a jury situation.

Despite this, the possibility remains that news about the existence of a confession could bias a jury when the confession is not admitted as evidence.

Editor and Publisher

Professional Codes of Ethics—Most of the mass media have written codes to which their members subscribe. The Appendix of this book contains the American Society of Newspaper Editors' *Canons of Journalism*, the *Production Code of the Motion Picture Association of America*, and the *TV Code of the National Association of Broadcasters*.

Plagiarism—The word "plagiarism" is defined as the presenting as one's own the ideas or words of another. While news facts are not copyrightable, the style of writing them is. A newswriter, however, is permitted to rewrite material presented in another story provided that he gives credit to his original source. It is not only unethical to use passages of another writer's story, it is also illegal. The original writer may have invested a great deal of time and energy in a sentence (it is said that Ernest Hemingway rewrote one particular sentence one hundred times), and as the originator, he is entitled to compensation if another writer uses his work.

IS OBJECTIVITY POSSIBLE?

Journalists are told by their editors to be objective in their news presentations—to report all facts without distortion, prejudice, or personal feelings. They are also advised by their editors to gather and present news which will stimulate and involve readers. Sometimes these two demands seem to conflict. If news stories are presented without personal involvement and interest readers may become bored; if news presentations express personal feelings readers might think they are biased and unreliable. And if news presentations are written as though by a robot, the words used would convey some feeling to the readers—if the readers were robots.

Choice of Words

Though newswriters are reasonably sure of the distinction between fact and opinion when writing a news story, they are often not quite so confident

310

in their choice of words for their story. Editors and reporters, being very sensitive to the power of language, realize that certain words in news copy can create positive or negative feelings. For example, does a student group "demand" or "request" a change in the school dress code? If the writer presenting a story on this subject uses "demand" he must be sure that the student group proposing the change is really "demanding" and not just "requesting" a change, because some readers might react negatively to student "protest" but positively to student "participation." To avoid taking sides in any dispute and spreading propaganda for any cause through their use of language, journalists take great pains in writing a story, deleting any words or sentences which will misrepresent a person or event.

Taking Sides

A newspaper's job is to clarify issues and events, not to confuse them. To do this, journalists must decide *how* to report an event. Newspaper coverage of the foreign and domestic policies of the government differ in part from one newspaper to another because different publishers have different viewpoints about government activities. For example, a newspaper in favor of capital punishment might feature a series on "The Death Sentence—A Crime Deterrent" while a newspaper favoring abolition of the death sentence might provide front-page space for an article titled "Reforming the Penal System." Individual newspapers usually cannot avoid taking a position on the issues facing the public (during election campaigns newspapers openly support their candidates in their editorials), though the best newspapers try to prevent prejudice in their news reporting.

To avoid the tedium of facts without feeling, and the preaching of feeling without facts, the news media continuously and earnestly attempt to be fair to all sides at all times. But some pictures and stories are so powerful—like the highly publicized picture of a Buddhist monk burning himself in the streets of Saigon—that editors decide to use them even though they may be criticized for sensational and unethical journalism.

RESPONSIBILITY OF THE SCHOOL JOURNALIST

School publications report to students, faculty members, alumni, members of the community, and parents about what a school has done, and what it plans to do. In addition to being a "bulletin board" of student activity, school newspapers often attempt to clarify problems and issues which confront the student body and the administration. By accurately presenting all sides of an issue in its news, and by thoughtfully stating a position in its editorials, a school newspaper indicates its social responsibility to its school and community. To ensure meeting this responsibility, editors and reporters work closely with faculty advisers on any complex issue. If a school newspaper should decide to cover a serious and controversial issue like the use of drugs, it must carefully prepare its presentation, making sure that all sides of the problem are revealed. One school newspaper, by failing to present an open discussion on the use of drugs, advocated the use of certain narcotics. Some students believed the one-sided reports of the paper and began taking drugs. Most editors and reporters, however, recognize the power of the press and the need for impartial and accurate news stories.

Relevant Reporting

Many school newspapers, in trying to describe and relate student activities both in and out of school, have added many new features to their newspapers. Realizing that their readers have opinions and feelings about many subjects including drugs, sex, politics, music, television, and dress, the editors of these newspapers believe that the student newspaper must be relevant in order to attract student readers. *The Midway,* the newspaper of University High School in Chicago, Illinois, in order to compete with a popular underground newspaper and to increase its own meaningfulness to students, reported on and became involved in the following relevant issues:
1. "A New Look at Teens and Marijuana."
2. Reported on the "new" image of the Blackstone Rangers, a neighborhood street gang.
3. Investigated high school fraternities and sororities.
4. Found that "Distillery Execs Oppose Teenage Drinking."
5. Found that at "adult" films, teens get in.
6. Conducted a survey on the dating game as played by U-Highers.
7. Followed the protest scene and U-Highers involved.
8. Found that "What U-Highers See on TV Affects Their Stand on War."
9. Had our reviewer review *Playboy* magazine.
10. Conducted several all-school surveys on presidential preferences.

Dick Dworkin
Scholastic Editor/Graphics/Communications

Increased relevance of news and comment included in the newspaper increased concern with school problems. The same newspaper also:
1. Related recent items on classroom freedom.
2. Asked faculty members about parental pressure.
3. Took a look at U-High's dress code.

312

4. Surveyed student reaction to plans for the school's sex education program.
5. Conducted dozens of interviews with student government leaders and prospective leaders about their plans.
6. Devoted a page to the curious business of college admissions and one to college counseling, U-High style.
7. Investigated a rise in cafeteria prices.
8. Followed development of a new plan for student government.

Dick Dworkin
Scholastic Editor/Graphics/Communications

The Goals of School Journalism

Working on a school publication trains students for a productive role in the community as it trains them to become journalists. In addition to providing students with the opportunity to explore journalism as a possible career, other goals of journalism training for students are:

To Provide a Laboratory in Writing—Staff members on school publications will not only be writing for themselves, but will be writing for an audience that includes other students, faculty members, alumni, members of the community, and parents. Student journalists learn the necessity for accuracy in all their writing.

To Teach a Sense of Responsibility—Student journalists learn of the power of freedom of the press and learn that freedom of the press cannot exist apart from responsibility of the press.

To Develop an Understanding of Journalism—By becoming aware of journalistic techniques used in the mass media, student journalists will better understand what constitutes news, what makes a news story permanent and significant, what makes propaganda, how to distinguish fact from opinion, and how to analyze stories in the mass media.

To Make the School a Part of the Community—Student publications help to educate the community about the school's programs, express student opinion, and increase school spirit.

To Teach Important Social Skills—Student journalists develop a sense of awareness, group cooperation, and pride in their work.

To Furnish a Valuable Supplement to the Language Arts Program—Student journalists learn to "listen" and become involved in numerous oral and speech activities outside of their English class.

THE FUTURE OF A FREE PRESS

Today, the President of the United States and the Premier of Russia can communicate with each other immediately on a "hot-line," a telephone link constructed to lessen the danger of accidental nuclear war. The general principle behind the phone is that when two people communicate their thoughts and feelings to each other they are less likely to settle differences through battle. Similarly, by keeping the public informed, the mass communications media can contribute to a more ethical and peaceful world. In *A Free and Responsible Press*, the Commission on Freedom of the Press pointed the way for journalism in the future when it said:

> With the means of self-destruction that are now at their disposal, men must live, if they are to live at all, by self-restraint, moderation and mutual understanding. They get their picture of one another through the press. The press can be inflamatory, sensational, and irresponsible. If it is, it and its freedom will go down in the universal catastrophe. On the other hand, the press can do its duty by the new world that is struggling to be born. It can help create a world community by giving men everywhere knowledge of the world and one another, by promoting comprehension and appreciation of the goals of a free society that shall embrace all men.
>
> *A Free and Responsible Press*
> Copyright 1947 by the University of Chicago

ACTIVITIES

1. What problems in your school and in your community most anger and upset you? Is anything being done about it? Have your local newspaper and radio station taken a stand on these problems? Is the community apathetic about them? What can the local mass media do to change the situation? If you were a Pulitzer Prize-winning journalist, how would you attack these problems? List the ways you would go about stimulating community actions.

2. Bring to class two different newspapers or magazines covering the same news event. Compare the headlines, pictures, amount of coverage, depth of coverage, placement of the story, and style of reporting in the two different publications. Which publication seems to provide the most accurate, de-

tailed, and impartial information? Which one is more responsible? What reporting changes would you make in the less responsible publication?

3. Compare press freedom in the United States with that in other countries. Do other countries have guarantees of a free press similar to America's? Are their newspaper presentations and television programs independent of government control? How do their governments regulate the mass media?

4. Do you feel a newspaper can "hang" a suspected murderer before he goes on trial? Why are reporters and photographers banned from court rooms in major criminal cases while artists are not? What are the problems for newspapers covering such capital crimes as the murder of Senator Robert Kennedy or Martin Luther King? Do you think the legal restrictions on trial coverage violate the public's right to know, or that they guarantee an accused criminal a fair trial? Explain your position.

5. Divide the class into two groups, one acting as jurors, the other as reporters. The reporters will cover the arrest of a man accused of a crime, including in their report all information and interviews pertinent to the crime. The jury, after reading the reporters' stories, will decide whether the defendant can be judged guilty or innocent from the accounts given by the reporters. How can a jury be influenced by reports they have read in the newspapers or seen on television?

6. Select an evening when all members of your class can watch the same two or three "prime-time" television programs. In class the next day discuss the following questions:

   a. Did any program give a distorted picture of events, people, and facts? How?

   b. Did you find any program annoying or offensive to your taste?

   c. Would you censor any of the programs? Why? How?

   d. Would you remove any of the programs from the air? Why? What would you show in their place?

   e. Which program(s) showed the greatest social responsibility? How do you think this was accomplished?

7. Select either a particularly good or an especially bad editorial from a magazine or newspaper. Investigate the subject of the editorial, gathering facts to affirm or deny the position taken by the editor. Then, write a letter-to-the-editor. If you disapprove of the editorial, you might express anger, surprise, irony, or humor. If you approve of the editorial, you might express your vigorous support or hearty congratulations. Mail your letter to the editor of the publication.

8. After losing a presidential election, a defeated candidate said good-bye to the press with these words: "Well, boys, you won't have me to kick around any more." What do you think the losing candidate meant? Can the press "kick around" a candidate for public office? What is meant by "slanted" reporting? Can the press create favorable and unfavorable opinion for a candidate? How?

9. Select a controversial public figure to write a news story about, making up what happened to that person. Read your story to the class and see if they can guess what your feelings are about the individual. How did your feelings come through? Which sentences, phrases, and words gave you away? Did those who agree with you about the individual like your story? Can opinion ever be completely concealed? Rewrite your story trying to keep as much of your personal feelings out of the story as possible.

10. How can book, play, and movie reviews be "unfair"? Can a critic be sued for insulting an artist in his review? What is the difference between a critic writing for a professional newspaper and a critic writing for his school newspaper? Do student critics have the same freedom as their mass media counterparts? Attend a movie and write a review pretending that you are the reviewer for a very influential publication, and that your review can make or break a film. Read your review to the class and see if they think you were accurate and fair.

11. A reporter for an underground news service, *The High School Independent Press Service* (*HIPS*), when questioned about the impartiality of his news bureau, said,

> I suppose we're just as bad as the *Times* in being biased.
> But underground papers are more interesting to read than
> the *Times*. They don't start with the usual 'who, where,
> when, what, why.' *HIPS* gets people to think.
> *Scholastic Editor/Graphics/Communications*

Do you agree or disagree with the preceding statement? Why? Can a newspaper be interesting and impartial at the same time? Is there a conflict between exciting and accurate reporting? Does a traditional news story get people to think? Can any newspaper completely avoid bias in its reporting? Obtain a copy of an underground newspaper and discuss its strong and weak points. How could the publication be improved? What aspects of the paper do you think might be incorporated into your school's publication? Why might they be appropriate?

12. If you were the publisher of a "crusading" newspaper that was having financial troubles, what would you do to save the paper without compromising your ideals? What are some of the other pressures you might be faced with as a "crusading" newspaper publisher? How can such pressures be controlled or ended? Prepare a report on the effects of outside pressures on the mass media, selecting a particular publication, or radio or television station as an example. Explain how the publication or station responded to the pressures brought to bear on it. Would you have acted similarly under the circumstances?

13. Prepare a report explaining the conflict which has developed between the government and the press in any one of the following areas:

    a. Censorship
    b. News management
    c. The "credibility gap"
    d. News "leaks"
    e. Covering demonstrations
    f. War correspondents
    g. National security

Do you feel conflicts improve or impair news reporting? How?

READING

ASHLEY, PAUL, *Say It Safely*, Fourth Revised Edition. University of Washington Press, Seattle, Wash., 1969.

BARTH, ALAN, *The Loyalty of Free Men*. Shoe String Press, Hamden, Conn., 1951.

BECKER, CARL L., *Freedom and Responsibility in the American Way of Life*. Vintage Books, New York, 1945. (PB)

BLEUM, WILLIAM A., ET AL, *Television in the Public Interest*. Hastings House, New York, 1961.

BRUCKER, HERBERT L., *Freedom of Information*. Macmillan, New York, 1949.

CARR, EDWARD HALLETT, *The New Society*. Beacon Press, Boston, 1957. (PB)

COHEN, BERNARD C., *The Press and Foreign Policy*. Princeton University Press, Princeton, N.J., 1963.

COMMISSION ON FREEDOM OF THE PRESS, *A Free and Responsible Press*, edited by R. D. Leigh. University of Chicago Press, Chicago, Ill., 1948.

CROSS, HAROLD L., *The People's Right to Know*. AMS Press, New York, 1953.

EMERY, WALTER B., *Broadcasting and Government: Responsibilities and Regulations*. Michigan State University Press, Lansing, Mich., 1961.

FRIENDLY, ALFRED, AND RONALD L. GOLDFARB, *Crime and Publicity*. Vintage Books, New York, 1967. (PB)

FRIENDLY, FRED W., *Due to Circumstances Beyond Our Control*. Vintage Books, New York, 1967.

GERALD, JAMES EDWARD, *The Social Responsibility of the Press*. University of Minnesota Press, Minneapolis, Minn., 1963.

Gross, Gerald (Ed.), *Responsibility of the Press*. Fleet Publishing, New York, 1966.

Gordon, George N., and Irving A. Falk, *Television Covers the Action*. Messner, New York, 1968.

———, *Your Career in Television and Radio*. Messner, New York, 1966.

Hale, Oron J., *The Captive Press in the Third Reich*. Princeton University Press, Princeton, N.J., 1964.

Head, Sydney, *Broadcasting in America: A Survey of Television and Radio*. Houghton Mifflin, Boston, 1956.

Lang, Kurt, and Gladys Engel Lang, *Politics and Television*. Quadrangle Books, Chicago, Ill., 1968.

Lerch, John H. (Ed.), *Careers in Broadcasting*. Appleton-Century-Crofts, New York, 1962.

Levy, Leonard, *Legacy of Suppression*. Harvard University Press, Cambridge, 1960.

Lloyd, Herbert, *The Legal Limits of Journalism*. Pergamon Press, Long Island City, N.Y., 1968.

Miller, John C., *Crisis in Freedom*. Little, Brown, Boston, 1964. (PB)

Minow, Newton N., *Equal Time: The Private Broadcaster and the Public Interest*, edited by L. Laurent. Atheneum, New York, 1964.

Neal, Harry Edward, *Communication*. Messner, New York, 1960.

Phelps, Robert, and E. Douglas Hamilton, *Libel: Rights, Risks, Responsibilities*. Macmillan, New York, 1966.

Quill and Scroll Society, *The Principal's Guide to High School Journalism* (Laurence R. Campbell). State University of Iowa, Iowa City, Iowa, 1966.

Randall, John H., *The Making of the Modern Mind*. Houghton Mifflin, Boston, 1940.

Schramm, Wilbur, *Responsibility in Mass Communication*. Harper & Row, New York, 1969.

Siebert, Frederick S., *Freedom of the Press in England, 1472–1776*. University of Illinois Press, Urbana, Ill., 1965.

———, *The Rights and Privileges of the Press*. Appleton-Century-Crofts, New York, 1934. (PB)

———, Theodore Peterson and Wilbur Schramm. *Four Theories of the Press*. University of Illinois Press, Urbana, Ill., 1956. (PB)

Skornia, Harry J., *Television and the News: A Critical Appraisal*. Pacific Books, Palo Alto, Cal., 1968.

———, *Television and Society*. McGraw-Hill, New York, 1965. (PB)

Stein, M. L., *Freedom of the Press: A Continuing Struggle*. Messner, New York, 1966.

Talbot, Daniel (Ed.), *Film: An Anthology*. Simon and Schuster, New York, 1959.

Walker, Daniel, *The Walker Report: Rights in Conflict*. Bantam Books, New York, 1968.

Wiggins, James Russell, *Freedom or Secrecy*. Oxford University Press, New York, 1964.

PART THREE

The School Media

Chapter **15**

Photography in the School Media

SHUTTERBUG OR PHOTOGRAPHER?

If, as a professional media photographer, you were assigned to make a feature picture of trumpeter Louis Armstrong and had available every resource you might want—what would you take? Noted magazine photographer Art Kane was assigned to make such a picture. After putting much thought into the assignment, the imaginative Kane decided to photograph Louis playing his horn while sitting in a rocking chair in the Mojave Desert with the setting sun as a background. This, Kane felt, would visually tell a story—the picture would symbolize that the trumpeter was nearing the end of his career. To make the picture, Kane chartered a small plane to fly from New York to California. As the plane soared above the clouds, Armstrong picked up his trumpet and began to play. "It was just like going to heaven with Gabriel at your side," recalls Kane. While few high school photographers have the money or the facilities needed to make this type of picture, the story shows what can be done by a photographer with imagination.

In today's age of automatic cameras almost anyone can take a satisfactory picture; the difference between the pictures taken by a successful "photographer" and those taken by the amateurish "shutterbug" is that the photographer's work shows imagination. The successful photographer, in order to visually tell a story, must have imagination and the ability to implement his imaginative ideas in the taking of a picture. For example, if the school's football team captain plays center, the shutterbug assigned to take the captain's picture might submit a face-on, head-and-shoulders shot. An imaginative photographer, however, might decide that the best camera-angle would be from underneath the player. He might try to persuade a local glass dealer to lend him a large plate of very thick glass and, after placing it on heavy supports, ask the player to take his position on the glass and center the ball. Then, the picture could actually be taken from under the player. An assignment of this type would, of course, take imagination and time—but the end-product would be well worth it. Such a picture would attract reader interest for any school publication. And, because all pictures can be considered as visual storytelling, such a shot would illustrate the expression, "A picture is worth a thousand words."

Ron MacNeil

Creative techniques help attract reader interest for any school publication, as shown in this example of multiple printing from three negatives combined with a solarization exposure during development.

IS IT WORTH A THOUSAND WORDS?

Any beginning school newspaper photographer might ask of his work, "Are the thousand words pictured here worth reading?" "Reading" some pictures can be compared to reading the dictionary: interesting, but no plot. Before submitting his work to his editor, the school photographer would do well to make sure his "thousand words" have a plot. He can best gain interest in his photographs by keeping in mind the following factors, each of which contributes to making successful school publication pictures:

People—Because the human-interest touch enhances the effectiveness of most photos, people usually make the most successful subjects. Imagine a picture of a chemistry lab that doesn't show the students? Often, you will need to take some students with you on photographic assignments for inclusion in your pictures.

Action—Whether or not your subject is at work or play is unimportant. It is important, however, that your subject be doing something (and in the opinion of most publication judges, merely shaking hands does not constitute doing something). There is no deadlier type of picture than the one that shows a rigid lineup of people looking directly into the camera.

Telling a Story—Never be in a hurry to snap your picture and run. Try to arrive early enough to talk to the subject(s) and solicit advice and ideas about what type of picture will best tell the story. Keep in mind that your subject—like you—wants the best possible picture taken. Photography subjects are usually more than happy to offer suggestions. Also consider using pennants, flags, posters, signs, costumes, and any other available props to better help you to visually tell the story.

Closeups—Try to avoid having more than three or four people in your picture. Suggest that your subjects stand close together to eliminate the possibility of large gaps of wasted space between them. You may want to take your picture from either side in order to eliminate other possible wasted space. When you print the negative, remember to enlarge it enough to allow for deletion of unwanted areas around the edges. Don't leave the cropping for your editor; he may forget to do it.

School Tie-in—Try to find ways to show that the persons in your pictures are from your school. Uniforms and banners help to accomplish this. Rather than taking a picture of the Student Council Officers with a plain background, for example, photograph them outdoors with a part of the school in the background.

Technical Quality—A good photographic print consists of areas made up of shades of gray ranging from solid white to solid black. Prints with no solid black areas should be reprinted before being submitted for publication. A print that "sparkles" is one that has an entire range of gray tones. One of the easiest ways to make your prints sparkle is to expose the negative a normal length of time. Film is relatively inexpensive so don't hesitate to take a number of shots, varying your exposure for each.

Angles—Beginning photographers often use only one angle in their pictures: head-on. Variety and impact can often be achieved by the use of high or low angles. A football rally, for example, might best be taken from a third-story window. And a basketball star can often be made to look taller if he is photographed from a very low angle.

Lighting—Most basic photography books suggest that beginners take their pictures with the light source coming from over their shoulder. More advanced photographers often have the illumination (flashbulb, sun, floodlight, etc.) coming from the side or from behind the subject.

Posing—In photography an area in which you can fully exercise your imagination is "posing" your subject. First, think of what a "head-on" picture of the subject would look like. Next, imagine how the subject would appear in a photo if his head were turned and he were looking over his left shoulder. To get a posed picture to look candid (unposed) is an art. Handshaking and presentation shots, because they often look the same, should be avoided. If assigned to photograph a dramatic club production, you might want to wait until after a dress rehearsal to pose the actors in order to be sure to capture the exact expressions and action you want.

USING A CAMERA

While many school photographers prefer to use Polaroid cameras, most journalism courses advocate use of one of three other types of cameras: the Speed Graphic, the 35mm, or the 120mm. The current trend in many schools is toward the use of the smallest of the three (the 35mm) because it is less obtrusive, has a faster lens, and does not need flashbulbs. The mechanical operation of each of these cameras is similar: once the use of one of them is mastered, it is easy to learn to use either of the others. The following steps are suggested to help you to better understand how to use a camera:

Setting Speeds—First, set the shutter speed indicator. Set it at a fast speed (around 1/100th to 1/200th of a second) to prevent blurring in your picture. Camera and shutter movement are two factors than can ruin any picture. If you are photographing a sports event, shoot at the fastest speed possible: 1/400th or 1/500th of a second. For indoor pictures using natural light you may have to set the indicator at a slower speed. Should you take a picture at a very slow speed, like 1/30th of a second, be sure to steady the camera by bracing it against your shoulder or by using a tripod.

Exposures—When possible, estimate the light exposure by using a light meter. If a light meter is unavailable, use the chart included with the film. Typical exposure settings for fast film (Plus-X or Tri-X) at a speed of around 1/100th of a second are: bright sunshine, f/22; open shade, f/11; dull day, f/5.6; indoors f/3.5.

The brighter the light on the subject, the larger the number on the lens needed to give the proper exposure. This procedure can be compared to the way the iris in your eye operates. For example, if you entered a darkened theater you would have difficulty distinguishing objects. After a few minutes, your eyes would become accustomed to the dark and you would be able to see. Your brain would have "instructed" your iris to open wide (even more than f/35 on a camera). When you left the darkened theater and

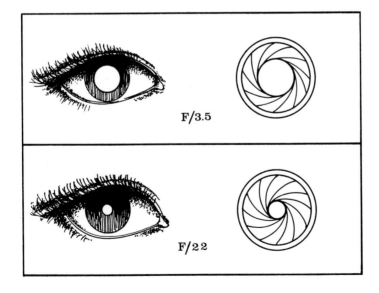

F/3.5

F/22

emerged into the bright daylight your eyes would probably hurt for a few seconds and you would want to shield them from the sun. Once your eyes have "stopped down" (to a possible f/22 on a camera), they would no longer hurt. The brain performs this function for humans. In photography the photographer must act as the brain for his camera and must adjust the exposure on his camera to accommodate the amount of light available.

The Shutter—Locking the shutter, or readying the shooting lever, is a simple operation. The cocking lever is located on the top portion of the lens on a Speed Graphic, but is located under the lens on some 120mm cameras. Most 35mm cameras, however, are cocked automatically.

The Viewfinder—Look through the viewfinder to be sure that the picture you see is exactly the picture you want. If it isn't, rearrange the subjects or try different camera angles until you are satisfied that what you see through the viewfinder is what you want to have appear in your picture.

Focusing—There are three ways to focus the Speed Graphic: with the range-finder, with the venier scale, or with the ground-glass. Focusing with the range-finder is usually the quickest, most ideal way to focus. Looking through the two windows on the top of the camera (not through the viewfinder) and tilting the camera slightly will enable you to see two images—one clear, the other fuzzy. The camera is in focus when, by turning the wheel at the front of the camera bed, these two images come together. The focus can be double-checked by the vernier scale (located near the focusing wheel on the bed). This scale indicates, in feet, how far away you are from the subject. For example, should the arrow on the scale indicate fifty feet after you have used the range-finder to focus on a subject seven feet away from the camera, you know that you have not focused properly (or that the range-finder is broken).

Reflex cameras (35mm and 120mm) may be focused through the viewfinder by using the ground-glass at the top of the camera, or with the vernier scale which is usually used for taking action photos. Most sports photographers avoid using the ground-glass to focus because it takes too much time and trouble. Because it is difficult to focus on a moving object, sports photographers often estimate where the action will be and, using the vernier scale, focus on that spot. For football action shots, photographers usually set the distance at about 25 feet, and for basketball action shots they set the distance at about 15 feet. For baseball coverage, photographers often focus on the base where they expect the most action. Many 35mm miniature cameras are not reflex cameras and must be focused using the range-finder or the vernier scale.

326

Loading the Film

Speed Graphic cameras are loaded by inserting the film holder into the back of the camera and then pulling out the side of the holder having a silver-edged slide. The silver-edged side of the holder indicates an unexposed sheet of film. When loading most 120mm cameras, the roll of film is placed into the back of the camera and wound until the arrow on the back of the paper covering the film can be seen. This arrow should align with the arrow on the inside of the camera. With 35mm cameras, the roll of film is inserted into the back of the camera and fed (or wound) onto the sprocket. The film should be secured within the camera before the back is closed. At least three exposures should be clicked off to make sure that only unexposed film is behind the camera lens.

Exposing the Film

The film is exposed and the picture is taken when the shutter lever is pushed down. The camera is made ready for the next picture by advancing the film to the next number. On Speed Graphic cameras the slide holder must be turned over or replaced (see instructions for loading film in Speed Graphic cameras in previous paragraph) to ready the camera for the next picture.

DEVELOPING THE FILM

Many school photographers have their film developed by commercial firms, usually a time-consuming procedure. Other high school photographers who have available facilities prefer to save time by doing their own developing. All film developing is, of course, done in a darkroom. Speed Graphic film negatives are developed by placing them on hangers and immersing them for approximately five minutes in a $68°F$ film-developing solution called DK60A. The negative is then removed from the developing solution and immersed for another five minutes in an acid fixative (or hypo) bath that stops the developer's action. The negative should be constantly agitated while in the developing and fixing solutions. Finally, the negative should be washed in cold running water for about ten minutes (to remove all chemicals) before being hung up to dry.

A similar procedure is followed for developing roll film for 35mm and 120mm cameras, the exception being the necessity for using a light-proof tank and a plastic film-apron (the apron must be the same size as the roll of film—35mm or 120mm). The film is placed in the covered, light-proof tank which is filled (through a small opening) with a developing solution. Microdol is a suitable developing solution for roll films. The film should be left in the tank for usually about fourteen minutes, depending on the type of film. Next, the developing solution is poured out of the tank and replaced by an acid fixer, or hypo, for approximately five minutes. Lastly, the tank cover is removed. The roll of film should be washed in cold running water before being hung up to dry.

PRINTING AND ENLARGING

Once the film is developed, the resulting negatives are ready to be printed. If an enlarger is not available, contact prints (prints that are the same size as the negative) can be made using the following procedure. In a darkened room that is lighted only by a dim yellow or red darkroom light bulb, place the negative on a sheet of sensitized photographic paper covered by a plate of clear glass. Expose the paper directly under a white, high-watt light bulb for approximately two seconds. Then, immerse the exposed paper in a Dektol developing solution, slightly agitating the solution, until a satisfactory image appears on the paper. Should an image appear instantly (which would make it so dark as to be indiscernible) repeat the procedure, decreasing the exposure time. When you are satisfied that you have a good print, immerse the photographic paper in an acid fixer solution for approximately five minutes before finally washing and drying the print. The print can be dried on blotters, on ferrotype plates, or in a print dryer.

Too dark *Too light* *Out of focus* *Correct exposure*

Ron MacNeil

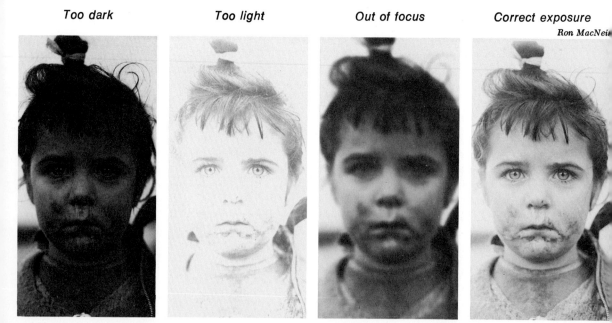

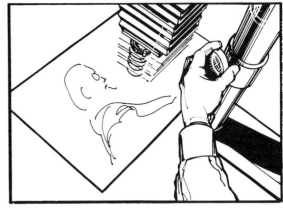

Step 1: Insert negative into the negative carrier.

Step 2: Turn on the enlarger light.

Step 3: Focus until the image is sharp.

Step 4: Expose the paper.

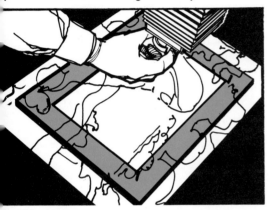

Enlarging the Negative—To make an enlarged print from a negative place the negative emulsion-side down (dull-side down), in the enlarger's negative holder. Turn the enlarger light on and slowly raise or lower the top portion of the enlarger until an image appears on the enlarger's easel exactly as you want it to appear on your print. Carefully focus the enlarger to get the clearest possible image, deleting unnecessary outer portions from the image. The enlarger is equipped with a lens similar to the one on your camera. Then reduce the amount of light falling on the easel by stopping down the enlarger lens a few clicks. Turn off the enlarger light. In the dark, insert sensitized photographic paper under the frame on the easel and turn on the enlarger's light for about ten seconds. Next, develop the print by using the previously explained procedure for developing contact prints. Should the print lack contrast (no clear distinction between blacks and whites), repeat the procedure using a harder (higher number) printing paper or filter. Or, if the print has too much contrast, use a softer (lower number) paper. Some photographers prefer to use polycontrast enlarging paper. With this type paper, contrast can be controlled by the use of filters used under the enlarger lens.

329

THE THREE C'S OF PHOTOGRAPHY

Creativity, communication, and craftsmanship are considered by many school photographers to be the "three C's" of photography. The school photographer has the opportunity to *create* a work of art with any picture he takes by using his imagination. For example, if three imaginative photographers covered the same assignment, each one would take a picture that was entirely different from those taken by the others. The imaginative photographer has the ability to *communicate* an idea in a photograph—to visually tell a pertinent story. *Craftsmanship* is important in photography because, without a knowledge of and the ability to use the techniques of lighting, composing, focusing, exposing, developing, and printing, the elements of creativity and communication would be lost. The student interested in a career as a photographer can develop a knowledge of what constitutes art in photography by taking courses to become more conscious of texture, color, line, and composition. He can further improve his photographic technique by reading books on the theory of photography. His school photography experience will prove helpful as background for a career as a photographer in the mass media.

WRITING CAPTIONS

After taking the picture, it is important that the photographer secure as many facts as necessary to properly identify the picture. When taking a picture of a group, the photographer should be careful to take down all names of all persons included in the group, listing the names from left to right. Since it is important that names be spelled properly, the photographer should consider printing the names rather than writing them. When photographing a sports event, the photographer should take down the numbers of the players shown, the quarter or period during which the picture was taken, and a brief description of the action portrayed. As soon as possible, he should type up his information, supplying any further information needed for identifying purposes. For example, if a right halfback is shown beginning a run for a 43-yard winning touchdown, the photographer should so indicate this information.

When a photographer is expected to write an entire caption exactly as it is to appear in print, he should be sure to include the five *W*'s and the *H*. If the picture is to be published without an accompanying story, the caption should contain even more detail. In such a case the photographer should briefly tell the entire story in his caption. If the picture is to be published with a story, the photographer should then keep his caption material as brief as possible, describing only what is going on in the picture.

USING MOTION-PICTURE CAMERAS

Film-making has become increasingly popular in American schools and, with recent improvements in motion-picture camera manufacture, this once complex and expensive procedure has become less complicated and less expensive. Courses that formerly only taught journalism students how to use the motion-picture camera have developed into detailed courses in film-making. Many students, to better prepare themselves for careers in the mass media, take and produce their own documentary, educational, and news-films for use in journalism laboratory courses.

The basic operational procedure for motion-picture cameras is, in many ways, similar to that used for still cameras. The lens aperture must be set according to the amount of available light and, should the camera not have a built-in light meter to automatically set the lens opening, a separate light meter must be used. The light meter should be set in relation to the "speed" of the film. Instead of setting the shutter speed (as on a still camera), the motion-picture camera operator must set the "frames-per-second" speed indicator. For normal motion the indicator should be set at 16 frames-per-second, and for sound cameras it should be set at 24 frames-per-second. For a slow-motion effect the indicator is usually set at about 48 frames-per-second. A motion-picture camera must be held firmly, or placed on a tripod to prevent unnecessary camera movement and blur. Film is loaded into most of the latest-model motion-picture cameras by simply snapping into place a cartridge containing the film. The film-developing process for motion-picture cameras is the same as that used for developing still-camera roll film. For expedience, many students prefer having their motion-picture film developed commercially.

Making Motion Pictures

The motion-picture and television media are closely related. Both of these media use sight and sound to put across their messages, and both media are powerful, "made to order" forces when used to influence people's thinking. Each one can be a dangerous device when used *only* to shape people's minds for propaganda purposes. Movies and television shows produced in our country and viewed by people in other countries are often the basis for the opinions these people form about life in the United States. While most American viewers know that filmed shows, on television or in motion pictures, are often illusions of reality rather than factual portrayals of life as it is actually lived in this country, many viewers still accept (as they often do with the printed word) anything seen on film as the truth; people usually tend to accept, and believe, that the camera doesn't lie.

A knowledge of the techniques used by cameramen in making films for movies and television will help develop viewer appreciation for camera art, and will also help television and motion-picture viewers become more discriminating, informed consumers. An important element that contributes to the success of any filmed presentation is its continuity and, like any news story prepared for the print media, its scenes should proceed in a logical sequence from a beginning, to a middle, and then to an end (or conclusion). Because communication is the basic aim of all filmed events, many of the skills you have studied and developed in writing for the print media can be applied to making films.

Ordinarily, the basic method used for filming any event is similar to that used by still photographers when photographing a picture story. Like the still photographer, the motion-picture cameraman can achieve variety in his

| *Long shot* | *Medium shot* | *Close-up* |
| | | **Ron MacNeil** |

filming by using various lighting, camera angles, and distances from the subject. A cameraman on a typical assignment, rather than moving the camera when filming an event, usually selects the spot where he anticipates the action will take place and lets his subject(s) come into view before starting to film. When the cameraman does pan (or follow) the action with the camera, he does so very slowly in order to establish his position in relation to the subject and setting. When panning, he first takes what is called an "establishing shot" (or long shot) at a short distance away from the subject. He then moves in closer to the subject for a medium shot which still shows the entire subject but only a part of the setting. Next, he moves in for a close-up which shows in detail the most important part of the subject (or action). Most of the action is filmed as closely to the subject as possible, and close-up shots often show only the face and head of the subject, leaving room for nothing else in the picture. Lastly, the end of the filming is usually done as the cameraman slowly moves back to the medium-shot position, and then further back to the long-shot (or "establishing shot") position, concluding the filmed event with a distant overall view of the subject and setting. The technique for operating a television camera is similar to that used to operate a motion-picture camera.

As in still photography, the cameraman must act as the "brain" for the motion-picture camera. All of the necessary techniques and theory that help the cameraman to visually convey a message on film would be wasted if the cameraman lacked imagination and creativity. Because the basic purpose of all filmed material is communication, motion-picture and television cameramen, in order to successfully communicate, must have imagination and creativity and be able to best apply photographic techniques and theories to film-making.

ACTIVITIES

1. List five feature-photo ideas for suggested use in your school newspaper. For each idea on the list present details for effective camera angles, lighting, and setting. Include suggestions for possible ways the photographer could most effectively tell an imaginative picture story through each photograph.

2. Ask a friend to stand outdoors at noontime, facing in the following directions: toward the sun; back to the sun; side to the sun. Write a brief description of the subject's location in relation to the sunlight, including your observations on the seeming change in the shape of the subject's face.

3. Invite a student photographer from your school paper to show the class the various steps involved in taking, developing, and printing photographs.

4. Select a photograph from a current magazine or newspaper. Write a brief one-sentence explanation for each of the following points:

   a. What is the story told in the photograph?

   b. What are the techniques the photographer used to tell the story?

   c. What do you think were the photographer's reasons for choosing the angle, distance, action, lighting, and setting he used?

5. Select what you decide is the best photograph from a current issue of *Life* or *Look* magazine. Mount the photo on a sheet of paper that also has a brief explanation of why you like the picture. With other members of your class, prepare a bulletin-board display made up of similarly mounted pictures chosen by your classmates. Then, take an informal poll of your classmates to determine their choice of the three most popular pictures in the display. Discuss with your classmates their reasons for their choices. How many of their reasons were similar?

6. Many good photographs have been turned into posters. If available, bring one to class and analyze its technique and content.

   a. Why is it appealing?

   b. What was the photographer's intention?

   c. Does the size of a photograph affect viewers? In what ways?

   d. Write an appropriate caption for the poster.

7. Prepare a listing of constructive comments suggesting what points you think should be considered when choosing student-submitted photographs for the school yearbook. Include suggestions for writing interest-arousing, comprehensive picture captions. From the listing prepare, in outline form, a photograph-evaluation suggestion sheet for submission to your school's year-book committee.

8. Prepare a list of five future school events that you think would lend themselves to imaginative motion-picture coverage. Prepare brief, one-paragraph suggestions as to how you think each event could best be covered in order to gain student interest in the films.

READING

BRODBECK, EMILE, *Handbook of Basic Motion-Picture Techniques*. Chilton Book Co., Philadelphia, Pa., 1966.

BOUCHER, PAUL, *Fundamentals of Photography*. Van Nostrand, Princeton, N.J., 1963.

CARTIER-BRESSON, HENRI, *The World of Cartier-Bresson*. Viking Press, New York, 1968.

CAPA, CORNELL (Ed.), *The Concerned Photographer*. Grossman Publishers, New York, 1968. (PB)

COSTA, JOSEPH (Ed.), *Complete Book of Press Photography*. National Press Photographers Association, New York, 1950.

DESCHIN, JACOB, *Photography in Your Future*. Macmillan, New York, 1965.

DUNCAN, DAVID DOUGLAS, *Self-Portrait: U. S. A.* Harry N. Abrams, New York, 1969.

EASTMAN KODAK COMPANY, *How to Make Good Pictures*. Random House, New York, 1957.

EISENSTAEDT, ALFRED, *Witness to Our Time*. Viking, New York, 1966.

FEININGER, ANDREAS, *The Complete Photographer*. Prentice-Hall, Englewood Cliffs, N.J., 1966.

——, *Creative Photographer*. Prentice-Hall, Englewood Cliffs, N.J., 1955.

——, *Successful Photographer*. Prentice-Hall, Englewood Cliffs, N.J., 1954.

FOX, RODNEY, AND ROBERT KERNS, *Creative News Photographer*. Iowa State University Press, Ames, Iowa, 1961. (PB)

GERMAR, HERB, *The Student Journalist and Photojournalism*. Richards Rosen Press, New York, 1967.

GERNSHEIM, HELLMUT AND ALLISTON, *The History of Photography*. McGraw-Hill, New York, 1969.

LEABO, C. J., AND FRED BAURIES, *Photography: An Introduction to Photo-Journalism for Student Publications*. National Scholastic Press Association, Minneapolis, Minn., 1967.

LLOYD, IRVING, *Creative School Photography*. American Yearbook Co., Topeka, Kan., 1962.

LOOK MAGAZINE, *School Photojournalism*. Cowles's Magazine and Broadcasting Co., New York.

LYONS, NATHAN, *Photographers on Photography*. Prentice-Hall, Englewood Cliffs, N.J., 1966.

McCALL, FLOYD, AND ROBERT B. RHODE, *Press Photography*. Macmillan, New York, 1961.

MANOOGIAL, HAIG P., *Film-Makers Art*. Basic Books, New York, 1966.

NATIONAL EDUCATION ASSOCIATION, *Telling Your School Story in Pictures*. National Education Association, Washington, D.C., 1958.

PAYNE, LEE, *Getting Started in Photojournalism*. Chilton Book Co., Philadelphia, Pa., 1963.

ROTHSTEIN, ARTHUR, *Photojournalism*. Chilton Book Co., Philadelphia, Pa., 1965.

SIDEY, HUGH, AND RODNEY FOX, *One Thousand Ideas for Better News Pictures*. Iowa State University Press, Ames, Iowa, 1956. (PB)

SPINA, TONY, *Press Photography*. A. S. Barnes, Cranbury, N.J., 1967.

Chapter 16

Organizing and Writing
School Newspapers

SCHOLASTIC JOURNALISM

The production of school publications has mushroomed into a big business operation in the United States. Each year thousands of school newspapers, literary magazines, and yearbooks are written, edited, and published by hundreds of thousands of student journalists. This number of student journalists is currently more than the total number of persons employed by the country's approximately 1,750 daily newspapers. Budgets for student publications now amount to an annual $75,000,000 — a figure predicted to increase yearly.

Today's students, increasingly more aware of and concerned with the world they live in, have become more interested in working on school publications. Recent studies show that school publications have not only increased in student appeal, but that staff members working on them are among the top students in their classes.* As well as helping to fulfill the

---

* *The Saturday Review*, September 14, 1968.

TYPICAL STAFF ORGANIZATION FOR A SCHOOL NEWSPAPER

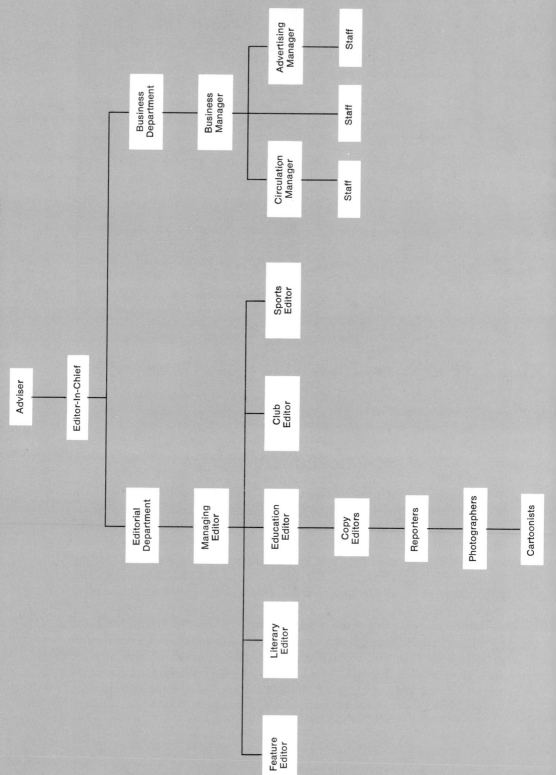

training needs for aspiring young media executives, editors, and writers, working on school publications offers valuable business and writing experience for students planning to enter other fields of endeavor.

SCHOOL NEWSPAPER ORGANIZATION

Because the variances in local conditions necessitate adjustments in any school newspaper staff organization, there are considerable staff organization differences from school to school. The following outline of a school newspaper staff organization is, therefore, intended as a suggestion only. All staff members on school newspapers, of course, are responsible directly to the newspaper adviser and indirectly to the head of the school. Like their mass media counterparts, the staffs of most school newspapers are organized to include an editor-in-chief, a managing editor (sometimes called news editor), editors of the various departments (feature, literary, education, club, and sports), a business manager, an advertising manager, a circulation manager, copy editors, reporters, and photographers. The following paragraphs outline the general duties of the key members of the school newspaper staff, and the chart on page 338 shows the organization of a typical school newspaper.

Duties of the Editor-in-chief

School newspaper editors-in-chief, as well as having to be competent administrators, should have the ability to write (and rewrite) news stories, make attractive page layouts, write effective editorials and eye-catching headlines, and should be able to use their imaginations in order to suggest stimulating ideas for articles, page makeup, and headlines. He serves as contact man with the newspaper's readers, receiving complaints for which, with the help of the adviser, he tries to work out solutions in the best way possible. Because the editor-in-chief fulfills many of the most important functions on the school newspaper, it is necessary that he be a responsible person. Some of his most important areas of responsibility are as follows:

Supervising the Staff—While journalism students often comprise the majority membership on many school publication staffs, the more competent editors-in-chief, in order that all members of the student body will be equally represented on their newspapers, attempt to recruit staff members from other departments and classes. Generally, editors-in-chief perform their supervisory duties as follows:

1. The editor-in-chief acquaints himself with the problems of all members of his staff — editors, advertising salesmen, circulation personnel, reporters, writers, and photographers. The editor-in-chief should be familiar with the functions performed by all of these staff members. Frequent personal contact with each staff member is usually the best way to maintain favorable relations with staff members.

2. The editor-in-chief is well acquainted with the writing abilities of each member of his staff. Often, he permits the use of by-lines as a reward to writers for outstanding work.

3. The editor-in-chief plans specific staff assignments, usually assigning articles to reporters according to the reporter's particular area of interest. Realizing that many new reporters aren't yet capable of handling more complex assignments, he assigns them to minor stories. The more a new reporter writes, the more competent and skilled he becomes — and the more he likes to write. New reporters can often be encouraged by being given assignments that are chosen to be well within their abilities.

4. The editor-in-chief can expect some staff members to lose their enthusiasm for working on the paper. To keep up the morale of other members of the staff, the editor-in-chief should make no concessions to disinterested staffers. Staff members who are deadwood often cause trouble with other more productive workers. It is usually good policy not to retain such people.

Attending Staff Meetings—Planning and conducting staff meetings, with the consent of the adviser, are important functions of the school newspaper editor-in-chief. The editor-in-chief acts as chairman at all such meetings.

1. During his term in office the editor-in-chief regularly schedules and conducts meetings with his staff and, to keep himself informed, often schedules informal get-togethers with individual staff members.

2. Prior to each issue of his newspaper, the editor-in-chief holds planning sessions and editorial meetings with staff members to discuss suggestions, assignments, content possibilities, problem areas, and various ways for improving each issue.

Keeping Informed—The editor-in-chief, after devoting much of his energies to his publication, does not have the time to participate in as many school organizations and activities as he might wish to. He should, however, keep himself informed of possibilities for newsworthy material involving all of the organizations and activities associated with the school.

1. In order to see that school-related organizations and activities are properly covered the editor-in-chief should prepare a *beat sheet,* a listing of all of the school's organizations and activities to be covered for news possibilities. The editor-in-chief usually prepares his beat sheet by obtaining from the

340

school's administrative office a listing of all of the organizations and activities connected with the school, plus the names of the presidents and the faculty advisers of each organization. From this information the editor-in-chief can have typed an alphabetical listing of the various groups, with several carbon copies being made for posting throughout the newsroom. At one of the first general staff meetings, reporter assignments should be made from the beat sheet. At this meeting student reporters should be impressed with the need to be thorough in their coverage of assigned beats.

2. Recognizing news that has importance and interest to readers takes experience and perception. The editor-in-chief must determine the importance and reader interest of each story and, based on his decision, must decide where to locate each story in the newspaper. He must also decide on what amount of space to assign to each story.

Writing Effective Editorials—One of the most important functions of the editor-in-chief is to stimulate student body thinking through effective, meaningful editorials. If his editorials are successful, the editor-in-chief will have performed a valuable service for his readers.

1. The editor-in-chief should constantly keep in mind that to be effective, his editorials should be timely, interesting, forceful, and relevant.

2. Most school newspaper editorials advocate those things which will benefit the school and the student body. The editor-in-chief, aware that the newspaper's chief concern is the school and the student body, usually bases his editorial writing on matters related to them.

3. Through his editorials, the editor-in-chief should be constantly aware that he is carrying the burden of speaking for the paper. Usually, his editorials are planned with the help of the adviser and are printed with the approval of the adviser.

4. The editor-in-chief knows that well-planned editorials can bring results. For example, one school newspaper's editor-in-chief received a letter from a graduate now serving in the Peace Corps. The letter requested that students donate used books for children in the Philippines. The editor published the letter along with an editorial urging student action and, in the next five issues of his newspaper, ran pictures, news stories, and follow-up editorials. As a result, some 7,000 books were collected by students, teachers, parents, and publishers. Officials at a nearby Air Force base heard about the campaign and volunteered to fly the books to their destination. A few months later the editor-in-chief received a letter from the President of the Philippines thanking him for his efforts.

Establishing and Meeting Deadlines—Because of the amount of time needed by printers to set stories and headlines into type, have engravings made, make up pages, and print school publications, it is necessary to carefully plan and schedule editorial preparation time well in advance of the newspaper's proposed publication date.

1. Ideally, the editor-in-chief should meet with the printer before the beginning of the school year in order to work out the scheduling details necessary for establishing realistic deadlines for submission to the printer of all copy from the edtiorial staff. When such a meeting isn't possible, it should be planned for as early in the school year as convenient.

2. Although printers usually want all photographs and most of the news copy as early as possible, it is often necessary to submit some last-minute stories, heads, and layouts at a later date so that the news can be kept timely.

3. Established deadline dates should be prominently posted in the journalism classroom, on bulletin boards throughout the school, and in the newsroom.

4. Preparatory work on the school paper should never be put off until the last minute, and it is always wise to schedule editorial work well enough ahead to avoid any chance that the paper might come out late.

5. Editors-in-chief often maintain files of general feature stories and pictures for emergency use in the event that a story or picture for which space has been saved is received too late to be included in a particular issue.

6. The editor-in-chief is responsible for seeing that staff members are constantly made aware of the importance of meeting deadlines.

Working with the Printer—Printers of school publications are usually conscientious men who cooperate with the editor-in-chief to help make each issue of the school newspaper the best news presentation possible.

1. The editor-in-chief should cooperate with the printer; the printer's time and advice are valuable.

2. The editor-in-chief should see to it that all stories are typed neatly and, when copy is difficult to read after having been heavily edited, he should plan to have it retyped.

3. Many editors-in-chief help the printer by writing *fillers* (one- and two-sentence stories). The printer sets the fillers into type and uses them to fill any extra space left at the bottom of columns, thus making unnecessary any last-minute rearranging of stories to fill columns.

4. When the editor-in-chief knows of a late-breaking story, he should call the printer and explain the situation. For example, if the school's basketball team was scheduled to play in the state finals on the day established as the deadline date for submission of copy to the printer, the printer should be requested to leave space on the front page layout in which to insert the last-minute copy for the game story.

5. The editor-in-chief is responsible for seeing that all copy and photographs to be submitted to the printer are checked to be sure that they meet the printer's specifications for submission of copy.

Working with the Adviser—The editor-in-chief must maintain close communication with his adviser on topics such as budget, policy, staff, deadlines, printing, and editorial campaigns. In many schools the editor-in-chief and most key members of the staff are appointed by the adviser, while at other schools they are elected by general student vote.

1. Because some stories may involve poor taste, inaccuracy, or potential libel, such close communication is necessary in order to obtain competent advice when needed.

2. School newspaper advisers are usually chosen on the basis of past experience as advisers. The professional advice obtainable from an interested, experienced adviser is an invaluable aid to the school newspaper editor-in-chief.

3. Staff members who are not working to the best of their abilities should be discussed with the adviser. Often, the adviser can suggest discreet solutions to personnel problems.

Duties of the Managing Editor

While the editor-in-chief is responsible for the administration of every operation on the school newspaper (including business, advertising, and circulation), the managing editor (on some papers called the news editor) limits his function to the newspaper's editorial operation, making sure that each departmental editor is doing a thorough job in covering and reporting his assigned news beat. The managing editor helps prepare the beat sheet and often supervises its preparation. On many school newspapers, the managing editor is also responsible for editorial production (editing and layout). Directly responsible to the editor-in-chief and the adviser, the managing editor must carry out their instructions whether or not he agrees with them. The managing editor assumes the role of editor-in-chief in the absence of the editor-in-chief.

Duties of Departmental Editors

Departmental editors, with the staff members assigned to them, cover and report the news obtained from their appointed beats. For example, the education editor assigns his staff reporters to cover stories affecting the education of students in the school, proposed courses, new faculty members, and school facilities. A member of the education editor's staff should periodically consult with the principal on matters concerning the overall educational environment. Departmental editors should periodically discuss with the editor-in-chief and the managing editor the major coverage of all beat areas. The departmental editor also should know approximately how many stories the managing editor expects his department to submit for each issue of the newspaper. Departmental editors are often in charge of makeup for the pages their material is to appear on and are responsible directly to the editor-in-chief and indirectly to the adviser.

Duties of the Business Manager

The school newspaper business manager's primary function is to keep the paper financially sound. To do this, the business manager must maintain thorough records. By working closely with the advertising and circulation managers he can keep a close check on his two main sources of revenue: advertising and circulation. The business manager must also prepare budgets for each issue of the paper, as well as for the entire school year, taking into account proposed income from advertising and circulation as well as expenses for printing, supplies, and operation. The business manager has the responsibility for recording all of the newspaper's financial affairs. He receives and deposits in the bank to the newspaper's account such funds received from advertising and circulation and, through the direction of the adviser, he allocates money for all necessary newspaper supplies and equipment.

Duties of the Advertising Manager

The advertising manager and his advertising space salesmen are responsible for the sale of all advertising space in the school newspaper. The advertising manager works closely with the editor-in-chief, the managing editor, the business manager, and the adviser. The advertising manager's role is essential to the financial security of the newspaper. To be profitable, at least sixty percent of the space in each issue of the newspaper should be devoted to advertising. Advertising managers usually prepare a listing of all business establishments in their communities, assigning advertising men to canvass each establishment for ads. Selling school newspaper advertising space is an important function: in spending some twelve billion dollars yearly, today's students are forming buying patterns that may last a lifetime. The advertising manager supervises and assists his salesmen in the preparation of advertising layouts as needed. With the aid of the adviser, he helps establish newspaper advertising rates. He must also maintain records for all advertising space sold or contracted for, and should supervise the collection of payments for all advertising.

344

Duties of the Circulation Manager

The major function of the circulation manager is the supervision of the distribution (dropping-off, delivering, and mailing) of the printed newspapers to all subscribers. He should keep careful records of all money collected, submitting such records to the business manager. Ideally, the circulation manager should have access to a car, enabling him to more easily pick up and deliver the printed newspapers. The circulation manager has a number of assistants to help him and, with the aid of the advisor, plans newspaper circulation campaigns when necessary. Because of his continual contact with the public, the circulation manager must be aware of his responsibility for promoting good will for the newspaper whenever possible.

Duties of Copy Editors

These young men and women, working with the managing editor, help to proofread, edit, write captions, and supply headlines for every story. They also help to lay out each page of the newspaper. Copy editors are responsible directly to the managing editor. Usually, because copy editors are stu-

Copy editors, usually responsible to the managing editor, help to proofread, edit, write captions, supply headlines, and sometimes lay out pages.

Ron MacNeil

dents who have previously worked as reporters, they are aware of the problems reporters have and are more experienced writers than are new reporters. The amount of editing necessary often depends on the proficiency of the writer of each story. In some cases a story might need complete rewriting, while in others only very minor copy editing is necessary. Good copy editors should have a good vocabulary and the ability to write interesting headlines. Copy editors having an interest in design and makeup often help in laying out the pages.

Duties of Reporters

One of the most exciting, interesting, and rewarding positions on the school newspaper staff is that of the reporter. He is "where the action is" and, in many cases, has a "front-row seat" for news events. Because of this, many school (and professional) reporters pass up promotion opportunities in order to continue covering news events. The reporter is responsible directly to the managing (or news) editor and, like his mass media counterpart, the school reporter is the backbone of his newspaper. His contribution can make the difference between an uninteresting or a lively newspaper.

Duties of Photographers

The motion-picture stereotype portraying a brash, unkempt, rude news photographer unthinkingly whizzing from tragedy to tragedy with press card in hat is often misleading and inaccurate. By contrast, the school photographer, as a representative of the student body, should be thorough, neat, courteous, professional, and serious, and should be constantly aware of his role as a good-will representative for his newspaper. A school newspaper photographer receives from the managing editor and departmental editors assignments to photograph newsworthy events of interest to school newspaper readers. He is responsible directly to the managing editor and indirectly to the adviser, and is usually responsible for developing and printing his own material, thus supplying photographs that are cropped and ready for the printer.

WRITING FOR THE SCHOOL NEWSPAPER

The abilities of the members of the school newspaper staff are best shown by the quality of the paper's written content. News stories, editorials, speech stories, interview stories, sports stories, and feature articles must be honest, objective, and accurate presentations that reflect the school to the best of the student writer's ability.

Copy Preparation—Stories should be typed on standard 8½ by 11 inch copy paper. When more than one of the school's publications use the same editorial room, or the same printer, it is advisable to color-code the copy paper. For example, the newspaper could use pink copy paper; the yearbook could use yellow; and the literary magazine, white. All news copy should be double-spaced, leaving generous margins on the top, bottom, and sides of all pages. More space is needed at the top of page one for use by the copy editor and, as an aid to the printer, it is preferable to end a page with the end of a paragraph. In general, the procedure for copy preparation outlined in Chapter 8, "Newswriting," should be followed when preparing copy for school newspapers. Student reporters often find that it's a good idea to keep on file carbon copies of all stories.

Writing News Stories—The more "makers of news" included in school news stories, the better. Many similar, but significant, stories must be covered each year. Writers, aware that readers become bored with the same story year after year, often capture reader interest by using "secondary" or "feature" leads. The following student example is a lead from a school newspaper story dealing with the opening of the school year, a significant story that is covered each year by most school newspapers.

EXAMPLE:

Student Power Finds New Leader

R-r-r-ring—The sound of the first bell on the opening day of school marked the beginning of a new era of Belmont High School life as Mr. Robert J. O'Donnell assumed the duties of principal. With his leadership have come his views that students should be involved fully in the business of their school. Under the fresh administration the once dormant Student Council shall have more power and make decisions concerning their "own" issues. . . .

Barbara Finigan
The Highpoint
Belmont High School
Belmont, Massachusetts

Writing Spot News Stories—Unexpected newsworthy events of general interest to the student body are written and presented as spot news stories. The following example of a school newspaper spot news story bases each paragraph on a specific fact.

EXAMPLE:

JUNIOR HURT IN CAVE ACCIDENT
LISTED SERIOUS AT COMMUNITY

Junior Chad Hall is currently in serious condition in Community hospital.

Saturday, December 28, Chad was with his Explorer Scout troop on a weekend outing of spelunking in Bloomington, Indiana.

As he was descending by rope further into a cave, his hands slipped and Chad fell from 40 to 65 feet into the cave. Chad remained there helpless until the Sputniks — Professional Rescuer team arrived some four hours later.

Chad is now suffering multiple bone fractures, including a broken back.

Chad's sister, senior Patty Hall, commented that although visitors are not encouraged, any cards would be appreciated. His room number at the hospital is 2517-A.

The Lancer,
Arlington High School
Indianapolis, Indiana

Writing Interview Stories—In the interview story, the writer presents the opinion of the student, teacher, or administrator being interviewed. Many school newspapers carry an "Inquiring Reporter" column in each issue. Such columns gain reader interest by dealing with significant topics. The following example was carried under a standard news headline.

EXAMPLE:

"What Are Teens Saying?"

With SDS gaining popularity throughout the nation, Knights are almost unanimously negative in their reaction to the organization.

Junior Linda Rosenquist: "They're revolting without a purpose; they're trying to destroy the capitalist system without replacing it with something, and without making constructive suggestions."

Senior Jan Behrman: "They have a Communist background."

Senior Jim Lane: "They just want something to gripe about."

Senior Tisha LeMaster: "SDS began as an organization without a purpose; however, the group has been directed into Communist channels."

Junior Amy Pheasant: "I don't like the way they go about reforming society."

The Lancer,
Arlington High School
Indianapolis, Indiana

On the editorial page of each issue of *The Grantonian,* the school newspaper of the Ulysses S. Grant High School in Portland, Oregon, an inquiring reporter column is combined with an interpretive interview article as shown in the following example.

348

The General's Comment . . .

Marriage: the union of a man and woman in holy wedlock. Do teenagers really realize the meaning of the word marriage, and the responsibilities, advantages, and sacrifices that lay between the lines of its definitions? Do teenagers jump into marriage with their eyes closed, or are they actually awake to the joys and problems marriage may present?

"I'm against teenage marriage," commented senior Pat Neupert, when asked about the situation. "I don't think most teenagers are grown up enough to realize that in marriage you must give as well as take, and many times you must give a little more than you take.

"Also, a lot of kids don't realize they will continue to change and mature after getting married early," continued Pat. "These further mental developments could cause problems in a marriage," Pat asserted.

"No," stated Matt Hewitson, a junior, firmly. "I don't think a teenager can support a family. I think one reason many marriages break up is because the couple can't afford to live comfortably, and is constantly struggling with money problems.

"A lot of marriages also break up because the couple thought they were in love before they were married, but after they were married they realized they didn't know the real meaning of love," concluded Matt. . . .

Marlene Feves
The Grantonian
Ulysses S. Grant High School
Portland, Oregon

The preceding article served as a sidebar for the following in-depth story on teen-age marriages. The story includes source material obtained from the Census Bureau, Family Service Association, and from an interview with a school administrator.

Successful Marriages for Teenagers?
Census Bureau Statistics Offer Answers

Can teenage marriage really be a success? According to the Census Bureau it depends upon four things: age, education, income, and where you are living after you get married.

Statistics prove that 21 per cent of the men who marry before the age of 18 are divorced or separated within three to five years. Women that marry before the age of 18 are twice as likely to be divorced or separated as women who marry after the age of 22.

Sixty-four per cent of the women that get married after the age of 22 are usually married to the same man when they are 60. By 1985 this per cent is expected to rise to 72 per cent.

It has been proven that couples that marry as teenagers and do not finish high school are most likely to end up in a divorce court or separation. Those who wait until they have finished their educational training and marry when they are older usually have a much longer, more stable marriage.

"It is all lovey-dovey the first year or so," commented Mrs. Melva Andersen, girls' vice-principal. "When the bills start to pile up, and the pressure gets so bad that the husband can stand no more, he can just take off, leaving the wife to support herself."

Shotgun weddings (matrimony by force) are becoming more and more popular these days because of the rise of the "new morality." Teenagers now seem to have their morals set too loosely according to society's standards. This is now becoming a major reason for "forced" marriages. Over one-half of these "forced" marriages never really last for more than one week to one month. The husband-to-be starts thinking about all of the pressures and responsibilities he must face, and realizes that he cannot cope with them, so he does not show up for the wedding. This creates a very big problem, increasing the enrollment in hospitals and homes for unwed mothers.

According to the Family Service Association of America, marriage falls into five categories: 1) The Fun Marriage, 2) High-Companionship Marriage, 3) Minimal-Interaction Marriage, 4) Peripheral-Husband Marriage, 5) Nestling Marriage.

Teenage Marriages are considered to fall into the first category: "The Fun Marriage." They are just another fun experience that the teenagers want to try. When the fun stops, marriages end, either in divorce or separation.

If a man and a woman want to engage in matrimony, they should take into consideration three things: Can they support a family now? Are they ready to face the future? Are they really in love? If they feel they can answer these questions honestly and meaningfully then they actually are ready to be married.

Kathi Robinson
The Grantonian
Ulysses S. Grant High School
Portland, Oregon

Writing Speech and Meeting Stories—Speeches and meetings of interest to school newspaper readers should be considered by writers as possible material for news stories. The managing editor or departmental editor assigns reporters to attend and write articles based on speeches and meetings of concern to students. Meetings and speeches can vary from reports on the status of a student council committee to reports on meetings at which several speakers present material of student concern. The following story, based on a speech, won first place in a *Journalism Awards Program* sponsored in cooperation with the Columbia Scholastic Press Association and Quill and Scroll.

EXAMPLE:

Mr. Farrell Discusses Bethpage Drug Problems; Blames Parents, Claims School's Hands Are Tied

Assistant Principal Harry G. Farrell directly confronted the narcotics issue Thursday by admitting that a drug problem exists in Bethpage. He made his views known in a joint program with Leonard Victor, the author of a recent series of articles in the Long Island Press, before two hundred students and teachers.

Mr. Farrell placed the responsibility for the narcotics problem on apathetic parents in the community. "The family is no longer the unit of civilization." He condemned parents who allow their children to wander the streets at night, and who never ask where they have been or whom they have been with.

He pointed out that since the establishment of a health program in Bethpage High School, a unit on drugs had been included (the health program started in 1959). The biology curriculum also contains a unit on drugs. He praised the Senior Patrol and the Receptionists for their roles in keeping strangers out of the building, and the Student Council and Student Court for their roles in teaching individual responsibility and self-government.

After showing how the school is endeavoring to educate the student body to the dangers of using drugs, Mr. Farrell explained that the "hands of the school are tied." The actions that a school may take are severely limited by the difficulty of catching people in the act of taking drugs. He then called upon the legislature to provide stiffer penalties for pushers of narcotics and more people to help enforce the laws.

Mr. Farrell cited the two assemblies scheduled for January 28 and February 4 as evidence of the administration's efforts to alert the student body to the problems of drugs.

It was also announced that on February 7, the film "The Decision" will be shown in conjunction with a lecture by the police narcotics squad for interested parents and students.

Mr. Leonard Victor came to address the Student Council, Student Receptionists, and Senior Patrol at the request of Dr. Charles Bryan, Superintendent of Schools. Mr. Victor is the author of a series of eight articles on the narcotics problem, which appeared in the Long Island Press.

Mr. Victor's primary purpose in coming to Bethpage was to seek the responses of students to the problems of drugs and to elicit suggestions on possible solutions.

Mr. Victor's concern for the narcotics "disease" is the result of conclusions he drew in two months of studying the problem on Long Island. He found that "an astounding amount" of addiction exists in the richer, as well as average and above average, areas of Long Island—Great Neck, Levittown, Bethpage, Massapequa Park.

Actually, few in high schools fool with heroin because it is much harder to get than pills. Unfortunately, even this causes addiction. Mr. Victor pointed out that everyone who was hooked sincerely believed that he could break his habit. But in reality only "one in a million can do it."

Twenty percent of the high school addicts are girls.

Suggestions from students included an intensive education program for students and parents, trips to see addicts in withdrawal, and inviting former addicts to speak.

Immediately following the discussion, Mr. Victor met with about twenty students to further explore teenage attitudes toward the problems that face all of us from drugs.

He claimed that narcotics is definitely a problem in the Bethpage area. He refused to state that the sale and use of drugs takes place on high school grounds or during school sessions. But he stated emphatically that narcotics are being sold on the streets around the school. He commented that pills could be purchased in the area of "six for a buck" when they are cheap.

He pointed out how life loses all meaning to the addict. Everything—cars, sex, grades—is subordinate to the desire for a pill. Addicts, he said, can be easily recognized by their semi-con-scious state and constant weariness. He discussed withdrawal and told a grue-some tale of autopsies he had seen on addicts. Of course, there are many cases where the addicts lost control of them-selves and caused severe damage to themselves and others.

David Schlachter
The Eagle's Cry
Bethpage High School
Bethpage, New York

Writing Feature Stories—Writing feature stories for school newspaper pub-lication affords talented writers the opportunity to be creative. Feature sto-ries can appeal to the reader's emotions as well as supply information. Gifted feature writers have the ability to supply an interesting approach to almost any situation. The feature approach used as the basis for the following story was a program established by a school's drama coach.

EXAMPLE:

COACH STIRS DEBATERS TO PEAK OF SUCCESS

It may be as old as Socrates, but de-bating is as "in" and "now" at North-west as the Bugaloo.

This isn't just another happening. It is the labor of love of a dedicated coach, Mrs. Charline Burton, who in two short years has more than doubled enrollment in debate classes, filled sev-eral cases with trophies, and made a lasting name for herself in the state an-nals of forensics.

Why are pupils enrolling in a course they once bypassed? Students are at-tracted to debate for the same reasons they participate in sports; it is an outlet for their natural competitive drive.

All students are not physically en-dowed for participating in athletics or performing in musical organizations, but all can and do talk. With proper direction in research and logistics, they can channel this natural inclination into debate.

"Life itself is competition," Mrs. Bur-ton explained. "I feel we need more competition, and more tournaments are the only answers."

There are no "bench warmers" in Mrs. Burton's classes. Everyone, not just the varsity, is permitted to engage in tournament competition. Winning is not the prime consideration, even though they do a lot of that, too.

Matching wits with a serious oppo-nent is "game experience" that all en-rolled in debate get. This is the part of the excitement that is padding the en-rollment at Northwest.

"We go to tournaments for the same reason the football team plays games. Of course, this takes time outside of class, but no speech teacher worth her

352

salt refuses to work after hours," she laughed.

As a result of their active participation, her teams have chalked up an impressive record. They have in two years attended 28 different tournaments, compiling the enviable record of 49 debate trophies: 25 firsts, 17 seconds, and 7 thirds. Her teams have been ranked third in the national forensics, and school trophies include first, second, and third, in regionals; first in state in '66, second in state in '67, and first at NFL District, '67.

This year's question: Resolved: That Congress should establish uniform regulations to control Criminal Investigation Procedures, has sent scholars even into court rooms and judges' colleges. Legal libraries and newspaper morgues are gleaned for information to add to their bulging briefcases. They learn to interview public figures. Classwork also includes instruction and practice in extemp speaking, radio speaking and oratory.

Revitalizing the high school debate program really is worthwhile, and it can be done!

The Shield
Northwest Classen High School
Classen, Oklahoma

Writing Sports Stories—A great variety of sports events are covered in school newspapers. Every major athletic contest (including girls' sports) participated in by the school should be the subject for advance and follow-up stories. Because of space limitations, however, many sports activities must be presented as wrap-up stories. Sports writers can also write sports features, columns, and interview stories based on interviews with players or coaches. Following is an example of a follow-up sports story.

EXAMPLE:

SWIMMERS DISPLAY ABILITY IN FINAL MEETS OF SEASON

After three weeks with no meets, Loyola's swim team roared back to upset a heavily favored St. John Bosco team by five points and in the process set three school records. Three days before, the Cubs smashed an outclassed Hawthorne High by sweeping all divisions. Also the team did fine in the Inglewood Invitational and won the State-wide All-Catholic Divisional Diving Championships.

For the St. John Bosco meet the varsity squad of Pete Worden, George Kerker, Jerry Hankins, Tim Ryan, Jim Henneberry, Roger Burshe, Dan Terheggen, and Rick Hayes was beefed up by the addition of Dave Oyster, Alex Vdacin, and Chris Richard. Greg Spinner led the Bees and Mark and Kevin and Phil Doi led the Cees.

It was a cold, windswept, rainy day when Loyola challenged St. John Bosco in their own outdoor pool. After a slow start and a new 200 Medley record by Jim Henneberry, the Cubs came back with a 1–2 in Diving and Butterfly. George Kerker placed first in the 100 freestyle setting a school record. The team of Jerry Hankins, Pete Worden, Tim Ryan, and George Kerker won the 400 free relay setting a record and winning the meet. An elated Coach Gubser received an untraditional, fully clothed swim in the pool after the meet.

On a windy afternoon three days before, the Cubs smashed Hawthorne High by sweeping all of the firsts and most of the seconds and setting a record in the 200 Medley. The Bees also won by a good margin and there were no Cees.

At the Inglewood Invitational the team performed excellently against L.A.'s best swimmers. Pete Worden placed third in the 100 Butterfly and set a school record. He also placed first in diving and his younger brother Kevin placed sixth.

At the All-Catholic Diving Championship Loyola won when Pete Worden placed first. Kevin Worden placed fifth at this meet.

Jim Henneberry
The Loyalist
Loyola High School
Los Angeles, California

Because of the great variety of sports events covered by most school publications, writing sports stories affords student writers a challenge in that every major athletic contest participated in by the school can be the subject for advance, interview, on-the-scene, and follow-up sports stories.

UPI

The following is an example of a featurized wrap-up sports story.

EXAMPLE:

WITH A RUMBLE AND A SHAKE

Opposing teams cringe, the ground shakes, and Middlebury citizens quake. What is this phenomenon that casts fear into the hearts of all those associated with it? Could it be superman? No, it is only the extraordinary athletic ability of the girls at Westover.

Hockey at Westover has become the most popular fall sport, and is of an unusually high caliber. (How could we fail to be good with all that energy supplied by recess-lunch sparking through the student body?) The Varsity captain is Whitney Neville, while Claudia Orr heads the J.V. This year's squad has led an undefeated season so far with victories over Forman with a varsity score of 6–0 and J.V. score of 5–0, and St. Margaret's (played the first day of snow) with the Varsity winning 6–2 and the J.V. 7–0. The game with Kent was unfortunately called off because of bad weather, as was the Farmington game, which has been rescheduled for later in the season. Ethel Walker and, of course, The Marvelous Mothers of Middlebury will be the only other opponents Westover will face this season. Can we keep our undefeated record?

For those not on the squad, however, a playday may be scheduled where Westover can once again prove its phenomenal athletic prowess. And just so Trinity will not be the only boys school to challenge and confront Westover skill on the hockey field, a game with Hotchkiss may be arranged.

Hockey this year looks promising, and who knows what heights this fall's team will attain? Will it be the big league in '67?

Fall tennis this year has been given a new lift by the new tennis teacher Mrs. Shealy. She and her young son Eric are new faces at Westover this year, and we would like to extend to them a warm welcome. Our new pro, who is the wife of a Woodbury doctor, handles two periods of tennis daily; one made up of underclassmen, and one composed of Seniors. Though her pupils range from beginners to advanced, Mrs. Shealy has done a terrific job in coaching Westover's Wimbleton aspirants.

Toni Walker captains this year's expanded soccer squad. From a total of sixteen in 1966, the squad this fall has jumped to twenty-six girls. Although most of the girls are inexperienced, everybody seems to be full of spirit. The fact that everyone eventually ends up on the ground has not dampened their enthusiasm for a possible game with Ethel Walker. Whatever the soccer squad does this year, we'll all be behind our team of potential Pélés.

Obviously, then, athletics at Westover are something with which to be reckoned. So, the next time you hear of something fantastic happening in the Middlebury area, you can be fairly sure it is Westover marching on to another of their countless victories.

Gigi Bradford
The Wick
Westover School
Middlebury, Connecticut

355

Like the editorial writer, sports columnists often have the opportunity to express their own opinions in their writing. Many sports columnists base their writing on short interviews with athletes and coaches. Many sports columnists resort to the colorful use of language and sports jargon in their written presentations, sometimes to an extreme. Other than to keep in mind that his material should always have reader interest, the sports columnist need follow few rigid writing "rules." School newspaper sports columnists may comment on a variety of sports happenings taking place at their school, or they may choose to feature only one sports topic as was done in the sports column shown in the example on the following page.

Amateur sports events are often featured in school newspaper sports columns.

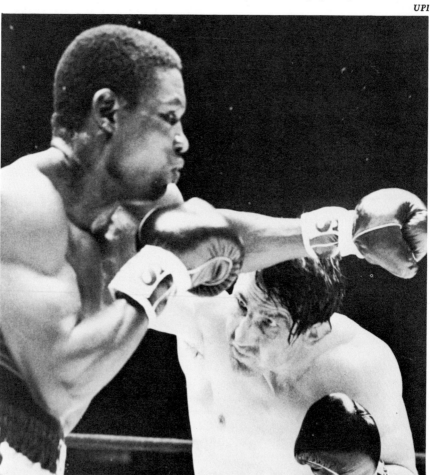

THE HIPPODROME

The Plight of Boxing

Can you name ten professional boxers? If you can, you're definitely in the minority. The sport of boxing has slipped from its position of eminence earlier in this century to the point where most people are completely indifferent towards it. There are several reasons why.

First, boxing has traditionally been a sport which has appealed to both the upper and lower classes. The rich have always maintained an interest in "the manly art of self-defense," while the poor see fighting as some sort of escape from their drab existences. This fact is proven by the crowd seen at a fight. At ringside you find businessmen, movie stars, etc., who have paid an exorbitant price to see two young men attempt to maim each other. Then there is the rest of the crowd, often members of some minority group, passionately supporting one of the two contestants.

If boxing's appeal lay only in these two groups, it would be obvious why the sport has lost popularity, for the middle class in America is constantly expanding, leaving fewer rich and fewer poor. However, the average, middle-income, man-in-the-street type can and does get interested in "the big fight," usually a title bout. But boxing has been unable to come up with enough of these major attractions in recent years to sustain any sort of steady interest.

With the departure of Muhammad Ali from the scene, boxing has lost its colorful personality and drawing card. The current heavyweight championship tournament, sanctioned by the inept World Boxing Association, cannot excite too many people with relatively unknown names like Thad Spencer and Jerry Quarry because no one knows a thing about them.

Paradoxically, the only two heavyweights whom the public knows or cares anything about, Joe Frazier and Floyd Patterson, are not in the tournament. Frazier wisely took the advice of his backers and avoided it. As a result, all he has to do is wait for the whole affair to end, then fight the winner. After being eliminated from the tournament by losing a controversial decision to Jerry Quarry two weeks ago, Floyd Patterson appears to have little in the way of a future.

Consequently, we are faced with the strange situation of having a tournament for what is supposedly the most glamorous title in sports filled with contestants who are about as glamorous as a frosh-soph soccer announcement. Boxing is indeed in sad shape. What it needs is more responsible administration than that afforded by the WBA, a sensible way to rank fighters, and most important, more exciting performers. If it does not get them, boxing may be moving towards quick extinction.

Bob Hibbert
The Deerfield Scroll
Deerfield Academy
Deerfield, Massachusetts

357

CHECKLIST FOR COVERAGE OF SCHOOL EVENTS

Elementary School

1–Special unit features
2–Field trips
3–Special day projects (Valentine's Day, Thanksgiving, etc.)
4–Students entertain parents
5–School plays, pageants, etc.
6–Building additions for kindergarten
7–Intra-school sports, contests
8–Music programs, operettas, etc.
9–Special education-speech correction, mentally handicapped, oral-deaf, etc.

Junior High School

1–Shop and homemaking features
2–The junior high guidance program
3–Clubs
4–Music, dramatics, and dance activities
5–Students study foreign languages (use of displays, foreign books)
6–Student publications
7–Honor societies, student council
8–Honor rolls
9–Students help in office, library
10–Special trips, projects

Senior High School

1–Business education feature
2–Clubs, publications, etc.
3–School productions-drama, music
4–Special projects (shop, physics, home, etc.)
5–Students prepare for jobs after graduation
6–Scholarships, guidance talks
7–Honor rolls
8–Contests, sports events
9–Print shop, auto shop
10–Student government

General School

1–School board
2–School elections, referendums
3–Teaching staff
4–School finances
5–Parent-teacher associations
6–Citizen's committees
7–Professional conferences
8–Maintenance and janitorial activities

From Let's Go To Press, Copyright 1956,
National School Public Relations Association

THE SCHOOL NEWSPAPER NEWS BUREAU

Many stories concerning scholastic events are often newsworthy enough to be of value to the editors of local newspapers. School newspaper editors-in-chief often appoint students—preferably ones who plan to enter public relations or newspaper work—to serve as the school newspaper's press representatives. The press representative is responsible for preparing and sending school news to the local newspaper editor. When in doubt as to whether or not the editor will be interested in a particular story, the press representative can check by telephone. Most school news bureaus prepare and maintain listings of all major school events worthy of news coverage.

On the preceding page is a checklist, prepared by the National School Public Relations Association, that may be used as a guide to determine coverage of specific school events. The guide may also be used by school press representatives to determine the types of school news usually of interest to local newspaper editors.

ACTIVITIES

1. Prepare a *beat sheet* for your school and assign yourself to cover one of the "beats." List all of the school activities which you would cover as the reporter for your "beat." Compare your coverage choices with those made by the school newspaper. How does your coverage differ from the school newspaper's? How is it similar?

2. If the last edition of your school newspaper had to be made smaller, what articles, features, and editorials would you leave out? Why? Which stories would you cut in length? Why? Select one story and rewrite it so that it occupies only half of the space it currently fills. If the last edition of your school newspaper had to be made larger, what would you add? Why? Are these stories that could be meaningfully expanded? How?

3. Select a photograph caption from an edition of your school newspaper and expand it into a detailed news story. Write a headline and a new picture caption for the story.

4. Prepare a list of questions that you would want to ask if you were assigned to interview a suspended student. Write an interview story based on your interview, either arranging an actual interview with such an individual or making up responses for your proposed questions.

5. During the next month what are the student, faculty, and community activities that should be covered by the school newspaper? Plan to attend one of them and write a news story about it. Perhaps you can get one of your classmates to act as photographer for the event. Present your story to the class and compare it with the one appearing in the school newspaper. How does its coverage differ from yours? Why?

6. Does your school newspaper contain fillers? What subjects do they cover? Are they topical or are they designed to fill up space? Write three brief, interesting fillers about your school that could be included in any edition of the school newspaper.

7. Draw up a staff organization table for a school newspaper, filling all of the positions on the chart with the names of those members of your class you think would most suitably fill the positions. Do your job assignments agree with those made by other students? Why is it sometimes difficult to assign people jobs? Is it sometimes necessary for the editor-in-chief to assign staff members jobs which they might not want? How can friction between staff members of a school newspaper be avoided? What procedures would you institute on a school newspaper to ensure a harmonious relationship among its staff members?

8. Using an agreed upon organizational chart containing the class job assignments decided upon in activity 7, plan a class newspaper, setting a deadline for its completion. Structure its content, size, and format by taking into consideration the time and facilities you have available. Prepare a list of business establishments that might want to advertise in your paper, and decide on the advertising rates. Do you think your class newspaper could succeed?

READING

ALLNUT, BENJAMIN W. (Ed.), *Springboard to Journalism*. Columbia Scholastic Press Association, Columbia University, New York, 1965.

ARNOLD, EDMUND C., AND HILLIER KRIEGHBAUM, *The Student Journalist: A Handbook for Staff and Advisor*. New York University Press, New York, 1963.

BASTIAN, GEORGE C., ET AL, *Editing the Day's News*. Macmillan, New York, 1956.

BARKER, BRYAN, *Humor Hints for School Publications*. Columbia Scholastic Press Association, Columbia University, New York, 1967.

CLAY, ROBERTA, *College Newspaper*. Pageant Press, New York, 1965.

GARVEN, CHARLES, *The Student Journalist and Editing*. Richards Rosen Press, New York, 1968.

GREENAWALT, LAMBERT (Ed.), *Newspaper Fundamentals for Student Publications*. Columbia Scholastic Press Association, Columbia University, New York, 1965.

JULIAN, JAMES L., *Practical News Assignments for Student Reporters*. Wm. C. Brown, Dubuque, Iowa, 1967.

McLure, Leslie W. and Paul C. Fulton, *Advertising in the Printed Media*, Mac-Millan, New York, 1964.

Presson, Hazel, *The Student Journalist and Interviewing*. Richards Rosen Press, New York, 1967.

Stapler, Harry, *The Student Journalist and Sports Reporting*. Richards Rosen Press, New York, 1964.

Ward, William G., *Newspapering: A Complete Guidebook for Better School Newspapers*. National Scholastic Press Association, Minneapolis, Minn., 1967. (PB)

——, *Reporting and Writing Sports*. Columbia Scholastic Press Association, Columbia University, New York, 1967.

——, *The Student Journalist and Creative Writing*. Richards Rosen Press, New York, 1967.

——, *The Student Journalist and Editorial Leadership*. Richards Rosen Press, New York, 1968.

——, *The Student Journalist and Editorial Writing*. Richards Rosen Press, New York, 1968.

——, *The Student Journalist and Thinking Editorials*. Richards Rosen Press, 1969.

Wood, James Playsted, *This Is Advertising*, Crown, New York, 1968.

Chapter 17

Producing and Financing
the School Newspaper

PRODUCING THE SCHOOL NEWSPAPER

The successful production of school newspapers, like the production of metropolitan newspapers, should be the result of careful thinking and planning. An efficient system for obtaining news, converting that news into a suitable newspaper presentation, and then preparing the presentation for publication in a newspaper doesn't "just happen" — such a system must be the result of careful planning.

Successful school newspaper production results from the careful planning and scheduling of all of the elements within a well-established system. To prepare an appropriate system, it must first be determined how often the the school's newspaper will be published. In deciding how often to publish (daily, weekly, biweekly, triweekly, monthly, or bimonthly), the following points should be considered:

1. How great a demand is there for the paper?

2. How is the paper to financed?
3. What are the advertising prospects?
4. How large and how competent is the staff?
5. How much editorial time can staff members devote to planning and producing the paper?

The major steps for producing letterpress, offset, and duplicated school newspapers are outlined in Chart *A*, page 365.

PRINTING THE SCHOOL NEWSPAPER

After deciding how often to print, you must next decide *how* to print. Most schools prefer commercially printed offset or letterpress newspapers because they are easy to read, look more professional than newspapers prepared on spirit duplicator or Mimeograph machines, afford more opportunities for effective layout and advertising display, are usually more rapidly and efficiently produced, and the newspaper's staff members—not concerned with the details and responsibilities of the actual printing—can more advantageously spend their time writing.

Printing Processes

The current trend with most school newspapers is toward offset printing (see Chapter 2, "Newspapers," for a detailed description of this process). The chief disadvantage of the printed newspaper is, of course, its cost. The approximate cost per issue for printing 500 copies of a four-page tabloid-size newspaper is usually from $150 to $250 (including composition and photoengraving), depending on the number of pictures. This cost, multiplied by the number of issues per year, is usually the basis on which the school newspaper's budget is established. Schools that do not have their own print shops or that do not have their newspapers printed by letterpress usually produce printed materials, including newspapers and news sheets, by using any one of the nine low-cost printing processes shown on Chart *B*, page 367.

The information contained in the chart is useful to staff members of school newspapers who are often consulted about other types of printing jobs (literary publications, yearbooks, announcements, posters, programs, etc.). "Changing Times," *The Kiplinger Magazine,* lists the possibilities and limitations to consider with each process as follows*:

---

* Excerpted by permission from *Changing Times,* The Kiplinger Magazine, (November 1968 issue). Copyright 1968 by The Kiplinger Washington Editors, Inc., 1729 H. Street, N.W., Washington, D.C. 20006.

MAJOR STEPS FOR PRODUCING LETTERPRESS, OFFSET, AND DUPLICATED SCHOOL NEWSPAPERS

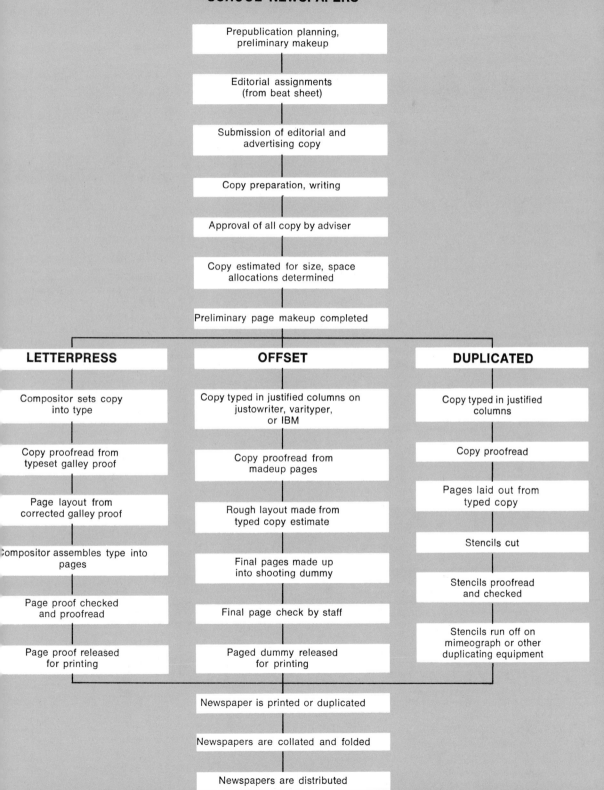

Prepublication planning, preliminary makeup

Editorial assignments (from beat sheet)

Submission of editorial and advertising copy

Copy preparation, writing

Approval of all copy by adviser

Copy estimated for size, space allocations determined

Preliminary page makeup completed

LETTERPRESS

Compositor sets copy into type

Copy proofread from typeset galley proof

Page layout from corrected galley proof

Compositor assembles type into pages

Page proof checked and proofread

Page proof released for printing

OFFSET

Copy typed in justified columns on justowriter, varityper, or IBM

Copy proofread from madeup pages

Rough layout made from typed copy estimate

Final pages made up into shooting dummy

Final page check by staff

Paged dummy released for printing

DUPLICATED

Copy typed in justified columns

Copy proofread

Pages laid out from typed copy

Stencils cut

Stencils proofread and checked

Stencils run off on mimeograph or other duplicating equipment

Newspaper is printed or duplicated

Newspapers are collated and folded

Newspapers are distributed

Photocopy—Xerox, the comparatively recent development that revolutionized the field of "instant copying," is best known in this class. Some models can copy almost anything from books to birth certificates in seconds and on ordinary white paper. If you have access to a copier, each item can be reproduced for less than five cents a copy. Libraries charge about ten cents, while commercial houses charge up to twenty-five cents a copy. The smallest Xerox copiers can be rented for about $45 a month.

If you want a few high-quality copies of anything in a hurry, Xerox is a good bet. However, it will not ordinarily reproduce photographs and shaded drawings very well, nor provide enlarged or reduced copies. For these, you would have to use other photocopying devices, such as the Photostat, which will enlarge or reduce documents and reproduce photographs satisfactorily.

The Copymate, a small machine that can make black and white copies up to 8 by 10 inches on chemically treated dry paper, is the newest development in the field of inexpensive photocopying. The machine costs around $30 and makes same-size copies in a minute. Copies cost about ten cents apiece.

Spirit duplicator—If you have less than $10 to spend and need up to 300 copies of anything that can be written, typed, or drawn, a spirit or "fluid" or "liquid" duplicator may be the answer. Dye carbon on the master copy is moistened with a special solvent just before it contacts the paper to be printed. Spirit duplicators can handle up to five colors simultaneously—red, blue, green, black, and the most commonly seen, purple. A spirit duplicator can be bought for $80 and up.

Hectograph—For under 50 copies of a notice, memo, etc., you can use a hectograph, which is a smaller, cheaper version of a spirit duplicator. It works by transferring the image of the master copy onto gelatin and then onto blank paper. A hectograph can handle up to four colors simultaneously.

Mimeograph—Most small job shops and lettershops, as well as many offices and schools, have Mimeograph machines, ideal for newsletters, press releases, reports, résumés, and anything else that can be written, drawn, typed, or ruled.

Lettershops usually charge about $2.50 to cut each stencil sheet and $1.50 for the first 100 copies run off. Mimeograph is most economical for runs of from 50 to 3,000 copies.

Recent improvements allow a Mimeograph to use smoother, harder paper finishes than formerly. Modern machines can print with two or more colored inks simultaneously if the colors are well separated. A new electronic stenciling process, such as Mimeofax, permits duplication of solids, bold headlines, and even photographs.

366

NINE LOW-COST PRINTING PROCESSES

	HOW IT WORKS	ITS COMMON USES	QUANTITIES IT'S BEST FOR
PHOTOCOPY	Transfers images by light. Provides black on white or white on black copies.	Documents, letters, drawings, memos.	1–50
HECTOGRAPH	Transfers dyes from typed, written, or drawn master sheet. Can print colors simultaneously. Most copies are purple.	Memos, notices, diagrams, instructions.	10–50
SPIRIT DUPLICATOR	Same as hectograph.	Same as hectograph plus programs, price lists, tags, labels, business forms.	50–300
MIMEOGRAPH	Rotating drum forces ink through typed, written, or hand-drawn stencil. Colored inks may be used.	Newsletters, form letters, memos, reports, résumés, diagrams, instructions, labels.	50–3,000
SILK SCREEN	Ink is forced through screening onto paper, cardboard, glass, or other materials.	Signs, posters, billboards.	10–2,500
MULTIGRAPH	Raised type prints directly onto paper. Various colors may be used, but not simultaneously.	News and sales letters, reports, résumés, business forms, menus, tickets, postcards.	500–10,000
MULTILITH	Image from inked master is picked up by rubber roller, which then transfers or "offsets" image onto paper.	Same as Multigraph, except that photographs and wash drawings may be reproduced.	150–40,000
OFFSET	Same as Multilith. Can reproduce color artwork.	Magazines, booklets, brochures, pamphlets.	1,000 plus
THERMO-GRAPHY	Heat applied to a powder sprinkled on wet ink produces raised letters resembling engraving.	Business cards, letterhead stationery, announcements	any quantity

Changing Times, The Kiplinger Magazine, November 1968

Chart B

The very smallest Mimeographs, for post-card-size printing, are available for under $20. They are hand-operated and hand-inked. Larger, automatic models begin at about $150.

Silk screen—The silk-screen process is by far the best bet for up to 2,500 bright, bold, eye-catching posters, car cards, or window and display signs of simple design.

If you need less than ten posters, have them done by hand. If you need more than 2,500 or want to reproduce photographs and small lettering, an offset printing job should be considered. Silkscreen can be used to decorate felt, glass, metal, and other materials. A 14 by 22 inch poster in three colors costs about $35 to prepare and about 30 cents a copy to run.

Hand-operated equipment to handle 12 by 18 inch sheets costs under $10.

Multigraph—Like letterpress, which is used for big printing jobs, Multigraph prints directly onto paper from raised type mounted in slots on a revolving drum or on etched, curved plates.

Multigraph printing, though no longer widely used, is generally clearer than Mimeograph or spirit duplicating processes. It is most economically used for 500 to 10,000 copies.

In the silk-screen process (often used for posters and window signs), ink is forced through screening onto paper, cardboard, and other materials.

Ron MacNeil

Offset—This process is called "offset" because, rather than printing directly onto paper, the master copy prints onto a rubber roller, and the roller then prints onto the paper. Full-size offset presses can economically handle jobs ranging from national magazines to newsletters, circulars, and brochures when runs of at least 1,000 are involved. Price varies widely, depending on many factors, including the nature of the job and the quantity needed. Offset printers are also known as lithographers.

Multilith—The Multilith machine is really a small offset press. It can reproduce anything that can be written, lettered, typed, drawn, traced, stamped, ruled, or printed on the master copies. Multilith is economical for runs of 150 to 40,000. It can print several colors on slick as well as dull papers and can handle photographs as well as line drawings. However, quality can fluctuate widely and depends on the operator's skill. Photographic reproductions are generally not as good as those produced from more expensive processes.

Thermography—This process duplicates and is almost indistinguishable from the high-quality raised printing associated with engraved announcements and business or calling cards. It is also known as plateless engraving or raised printing and is considerably cheaper than the real thing. Announcements produced by thermography cost about $12 to $20 per 100; business cards are $4 or $5 per 100.

To get the most satisfaction from what little printing money you have to spend, try to see specimens of the work that have been produced by each of these processes. In most sizable cities you will find several pages of printing firms listed in the yellow pages of the telephone directory. Many advertise their specialities and indicate which processes they use. Often it is helpful to take your work to a shop that does specialize in what you have to be done. The people there can give you good advice on preparing copy or layout and selecting colors and papers.

If you have more than a few dollars' worth of printing to be done, get several estimates. Printing is a highly competitive trade. Its practitioners will be glad to bid for your business.

THE MIMEOGRAPHED NEWSPAPER

Faced with rapidly rising printing costs, many schools depend on mimeographed newspapers. A description of the mimeograph process is given in Chart *B*, page 367, and in the material following the Chart. Although cost often dictates the kind of newspaper a school has, it need not dictate the quality, and many mimeographed school newspapers reflect credit on their schools and newspaper staffs. To give a mimeographed newspaper a professional look, the lines of type in the columns must be the same width. To accomplish this copy must, after editing, be typed twice. Most mimeographed newspapers run three columns wide, and stories are typed on an elite typewriter at a 26 character width. On a pica typewriter the character width per column is 22 characters. Following is an example of the justified typing necessary to make the column widths of a mimeographed newspaper equal. The slashes shown in the first column of the example are replaced with spaces between the words in the second column.

EXAMPLE:

```
    Graduation exercises for/         Graduation exercises for
130 seniors will be held///       130  seniors  will  be  held
Friday in the school audi-/       Friday  in  the  school  audi-
torium at 7:30 p.m. Dr.////       torium  at  7:30  p.m.  Dr.
Allan Mendell of Northern//       Allan  Mendell  of  Northern
State will give the class//       State  will  give  the  class
address.                          address.
    Eleven seniors will grad-         Eleven seniors will grad-
uate with 3.4 or above/////       uate   with   3.4   or   above
grade averages.                   grade averages.
```

After the pages are pasted up, the typist cuts the stencil by following the copy on the dummy, and lastly, illustrations and heads are cut in, on the stencil, by hand, and the stencil is run off on a mimeograph machine. A mimeographed newspaper page is illustrated on page 480.

EDITORIAL PRODUCTION

To ensure a regulated and consistent flow of editorial materials, a carefully planned editorial production schedule should be made. The editorial production schedule should state specific deadlines and should clearly note the time allowed for each step to be taken in producing the school newspaper. Most school newspaper staffs program their newspapers by days (rather than by hours, as on mass media daily newspapers). Production schedules should be posted prominently on bulletin boards throughout the school. Chart C, page 371, illustrates a suggested production schedule for a monthly school

EDITORIAL PRODUCTION SCHEDULE
FOR A MONTHLY SCHOOL NEWSPAPER

October 10th Edition

August 20
Prepublication planning session with adviser and all staff members.

August 22
General news assignments made from beat sheet.
Feature assignments made.
Editorial page assignments made.
Sports assignments made.
Pictorial assignments made.

August 27
Editorial page assignments due.
First advertising copy due.

August 31
Advertising layouts made.
Editorial and news page layouts planned.
First third of picture assignments due.
First third of sports copy due.
First third of feature copy due.

September 5
News assignments made for scheduled events.
First third of general news copy due.

September 12
Second third of picture assignments due.
Second third of sports assignments due.
Second third of feature copy due.
Second third of general news copy due.

September 17
Copy starts to printer.
Advertising and editorial page layouts completed.

September 19
Second third of copy (pictures, sports, feature, and news) starts to printer.
Last third of picture assignments due.
Last third of sports copy due.
Last third of feature copy due.
Last third of news copy due.

September 23
All remaining copy to printer.

September 29
Galley proof checked and proofread.

September 30
Final layouts made for all pages.

October 3
All proof and layouts released to printer.

October 5
Page proof checked and proofread.

October 7
Newspapers are printed.

October 8
Newspapers collated and folded.

October 9
Newspapers are distributed.

Chart C

newspaper. Many school newspapers maintain, under the supervision of the adviser and through the advertising or business manager, separate advertising production schedules that are similar to the editorial production schedule shown in Chart C.

Copy Editing

School newspapers have an obligation for accuracy and reliability in their presentation of material to readers. Student editors must constantly be aware of this obligation and must, at all times, protect their readers from carelessness, inaccuracy, and bias. Newspaper copy editors (or copy readers) can help the editor-in-chief achieve the goals of accuracy, reliability, and good taste for their school newspaper.

From the many stories submitted for each issue of the school newspaper, relatively few are chosen for publication. All of the stories submitted must be approved by the adviser and the editor-in-chief, and then checked for grammar, spelling, organization, and factual correctness. The copy editor should be a more experienced writer than the reporter. Most school newspaper copy editors, rather than rewriting entire stories, mark all errors and then check the errors with their adviser before making corrections.

Following are a few of the specific points a copy editor checks for (usually referring to an editorial style sheet), when editing news copy:

Accuracy—Every fact should be double-checked. The copy editor usually checks facts in reference works such as encyclopedias, dictionaries, almanacs, and previous issues of his own and other newspapers. The copy editor checks with the writer of the material and with the adviser, when necessary.

Spelling—If no directory of students is available, a city telephone book is a good source for checking the spelling of names. Other words can be checked in a standard dictionary.

Grammar and Punctuation—A comprehensive handbook on grammar should be kept in the newsroom for general reference purposes. Because a major reason for having a school newspaper is to provide a laboratory in which good writing, grammar, and style may be learned, it is essential that only correct grammar appear in print.

Verbosity—Don't waste newspaper space (and the reader's time) by using unnecessary words. Keep in mind that conciseness is one of the major goals in the presentation of all news materials. The first sentence in the following

372

example is verbose and confusing. A competent copy editor might make it more concise by changing it to read like the second sentence.

EXAMPLE:

> Twenty years ago the greater of the number of people addicted to the taking of drugs in America were in the latter half of the entire life span.

> Twenty years ago the majority of American drug addicts were over thirty.

Sentence Structure—The portion of the *Gettysburg Address* that most of us remember is an example of parallel structure:

> . . . a government of the people, by the people, and for the people . . .

When dealing with a story that does not contain parallel construction, rewrite sentences as needed to obtain parallelism.

Libel—Keep in mind that truth is the only defense against libel charges. The burden of proof is not on the person who was allegedly libeled, but is on the publication. Avoid printing any material that might, however remotely, endanger a person's reputation.

Good Taste—In the early 1900's an editor was rebuked for calling a limb a leg. Although times have changed, it is still necessary to delete material that might be considered by any member of the student body as offensive.

Buried Leads—Seek out any possible buried material that might more appropriately be presented as a lead. For example, if the head of a school gave a talk titled "Good Citizenship," and following the talk mentioned that construction on a new science wing was about to begin, a reporter writing the story might present the material concerning the construction at the end of his story. An observant copy editor might decide that the material concerning the science wing could be the basis for an interesting lead, or he might further suggest to the reporter that more specific details be obtained to present, as a separate article, the information about the science wing construction.

The examples on the next two pages are the preparatory stages for an article submitted to a school newspaper for publication. The first is the story containing the copy editor's markings; the second is the same story, copy edited, retyped, and ready for the printer. (See Appendix X for the standard symbols used on newspaper copy desks in preparing copy for the printer.)

EXAMPLE:

Tridel's Senior class has topped the jr. class in the school spirit contest sponsored by the student council, edging the ~~Upperclassmen~~ *underclassmen* by 3%.

Having just twelve per cent, the sophomores are behind the elventh grades 16 percent and the senior average of 19 per cent. This contest will be continued ~~thruout~~ *throughout* the home basket ball season. Two council members take the tallie during the ~~hardwood contests~~ *basketball games*, and ~~a sign is~~ *(a sign)* posted on the second-floor bulltein board announcing the weakly class standings.

Supervised by Vice-President Judy Jefferson, the contest, which began on January twenty-first, nineteen hundred and seventy, is designed to increase ~~the~~ schools spirit. At the end of the year, the President of the winning class will be presented with a pewter cup.

EXAMPLE:

Tridel's Senior Class has topped the Junior Class in the School Spirit Contest sponsored by the Student

Council, edging the underclassmen by 3 percent.

Having just 12 percent, the Sophomores are behind

the Eleventh Grade's 16 percent and the Senior average

of 19 percent. This contest will be continued throughout

the home basketball season.

Two council members take the tally during the

basketball games and post a sign on the second-floor

bulletin board announcing the weekly class standings.

Supervised by Vice-president Judy Jefferson, the

contest, which began on Jan. 21, 1970, is designed to

increase school spirit. At the end of the year, the

President of the winning class will be presented with

a pewter cup.

WRITING HEADLINES

After the story has been copy edited, the copy editor must supply an appropriate headline. To write an appropriate headline, the copy editor must first determine, in terms of action or unusualness, the one essential element of the story to be used as a basis for the headline. Next, using short, vigorous words, he states this essential element in one brief sentence. From this summarizing sentence, he edits out unnecessary words in order to make the sentence fit into the space allowed. When preparing headlines, copy editors give particular attention to the use of verbs, usually using those that are short, active, forceful, and vivid. The tense must either be future (to speak, will speak) or historical present (speaks). The past tense of verbs is only used in headlines when the story deals with something that happened in the distant past. The word "is" is usually unnecessary in headlines, and a comma is often used in place of "and."

Headline writers avoid trying to be too clever: what is clever to one person is often not clever to someone else. Headline writers also avoid wooden, lifeless headlines. The Columbia Broadcasting System, concerned about the low viewer ratings of presidential nominating convention television coverage, attempted to attract viewers to the network by presenting Robert Trout as the news commentator. The following two heads, written by a copywriter assigned to write headlines for the story, were presented for publication:

EXAMPLE:

CBS to Dangle Trout for 'Bait'

(18 pt. Bodoni Bold)

CBS to Try to Increase Ratings

(18 pt. Franklin Gothic Extra Condensed)

The first headline, which was published, was preferred by some readers, while other readers claimed it was "too far out." Very few readers liked the second headline. A compromise might have been preferable.

One-line headlines are often easier to write than are two- or three-line headlines, and in all headlines, no matter how many lines therein, each line should be able to stand alone. It is preferable never to end the first line(s) of a more than one-line headline with a preposition, article, or adjective, and verbs should never be split, as in the following example:

EXAMPLE:

PRINCIPAL DEAD
SET AGAINST   *can be corrected to:*
NOISE IN HALLS

PRINCIPAL OPPOSES
NOISE IN HALLWAYS

(18 pt. Alternate Gothic No. 2)   (18 pt. Alternate Gothic No. 2)

Accepted spellings should be used in school publications. Even though some professional newspapers use shortened versions (such as "tho," "foto," "nite"), school publications should use the preferred dictionary spellings. Headlines containing slanted or double meanings should be avoided.

HEADLINE SCHEDULE

89 Senator Proxmire Speaks at Commencement   5/48
Goudy Bold
8 Count Per Column

0 **News Briefs from School of Journalism Alumni**   4/36   Bodoni Bold
7 Count Per Column

1½ Bartell Resigns As Athletic Director   3/36   Goudy Bold 11 Count Per Column

8 Memento Given Dean   18 – Bodoni Bold Flush Left

22 *Amusement That Purifies*   3/36 – Bodoni Bold Italic 7 Count Per Column

1
30 '5-footers' overcome size in gym   Mighty-mites   14 – Tempo
3/30 – Tempo in 3/4 Hood
11½ Count Per Column

22 Five New Staff Members   2/36 = Goudy Bold 11 Count Per Column
22 In Various Departments

21 Dr. Mills Enjoys Brazil: 2/36 = Goudy Light 10 Count Per Column
19 Discusses Past Visits

20 Pupils define patriotism   2/30 ≡ Tempo 11½ Count Per Column

26 Varsity squad 'haunts' Attucks   2/24 = Tempo 14 Count Per Column
25 win insures successful season

1 *Senior Coed*   36 ≡   9½ *Newhouse,*   24 ≡   11 **Guys 'n dolls**   18 –
10 *Has Varied*   Eusibius   11 *Wife Cited in*   Bodoni   Tempo
10 *Background*   11 Count Per   10 *Who's Who*   Bold Italic   Extra Bold
Column   11½ Count   12 Count Per Column
Per Column

11½ **Deans Clark,**   24 ≡   14 Music, Readings   24 ≡   18½ 2 Business Pupils Get   14 ≡
10½ **Spencer To**   Bodoni Bold   14 To Be Featured   Goudy   20 Lions Club Recognition   Tempo
11½ **Cite '41 Class**   11½ Count Per   Bold   20 Count
Column   14 Count Per   Per Column
Column

It is important to remember that type is made of metal—not rubber. Because the printer cannot squeeze in extra letters, it is better to allow the lines in a headline to run short rather than have them "bounce" (not fit).

Copyfitting Headlines

There are several adequate methods for counting the units of space in a headline. Many school newspaper copy editors find it easiest to count each letter and each space as one unit. A slightly more complicated way is to count narrow lower-case letters (*i, l, t, j, f*) as half units, and the wide lower-case letters (*m* and *w*) as 1½ units. All remaining lower-case letters are then counted as one unit, and capital letters are counted as 1½ units, except capitals *M* and *W* which are each counted as 2 units, and capitals *J* and *I* which are counted as one unit. The safest count for numbers is 1½ units. Most printers set spaces between words, leaving approximately one-half unit per space. The current trend has been to "open up" the headline (making it easier to read) by inserting one complete unit of space between words. Most newspapers maintain a "flush left" headline style for news stories.

EXAMPLE:

18 Units
{
EAGLES WIN,
22-14, AFTER
SURVIVING LATE
COUGAR RALLY
}

(18 pt. Spartan Black Condensed)

18½ Units
{
EAGLES WIN,
22-14, AFTER
SURVIVING LATE
COUGAR RALLY
}

(18 pt. Spartan Black Condensed)

The overall unit count for letters and spaces for column widths varies depending on the printer and on the type face used. Bold and expanded type faces take more space than do condensed type faces. Many printers supply headline schedules that show which type faces they have available. These schedules indicate exactly how many units the type face used allows per column width. Most school newspaper columns are two inches wide. Many school copy editors determine available headline widths by placing a ruler over each face shown in the printer's headline schedule, then drawing a vertical line every two inches (if this is the width of the column), and counting the number of units column. They then post the headline schedule (see illustration, page 377), indicating the unit counts, in the newsroom.

When determining type sizes for headlines, headline writers give the lead story the largest type size. They then observe diminishing graduation of type size by using the heaviest heads at the top of the page. The bottom anchor story, however, is usually given a 30- to 36-point size headline in order to make it stand out from other stories. The least important stories are usually given 18- to 24-point headlines, each line usually set "flush left."

"Don'ts" for Headline Writers

1. Avoid using unnecessary words. Avoid using part of the verb *"to be,"* articles *"a, an, the,"* and the conjunction *"and."*

EXAMPLE:

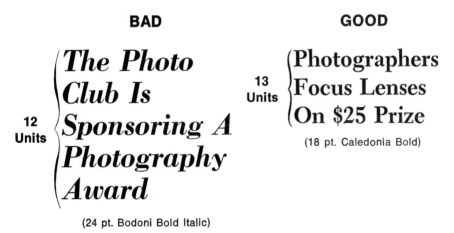

BAD

12 Units { *The Photo Club Is Sponsoring A Photography Award*

(24 pt. Bodoni Bold Italic)

GOOD

13 Units { Photographers Focus Lenses On $25 Prize

(18 pt. Caledonia Bold)

2. Avoid ending a line with a modifier or conjunction.

EXAMPLE:

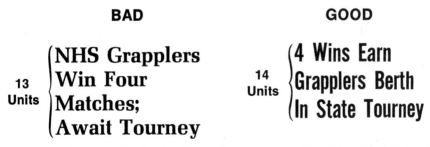

BAD

13 Units { NHS Grapplers Win Four Matches; Await Tourney

(18 pt. Melior Semi-Bold)

GOOD

14 Units { 4 Wins Earn Grapplers Berth In State Tourney

(18 pt. Alternate Gothic No. 2)

379

3. Avoid using the past tense.

EXAMPLE:

BAD	GOOD

BAD

13 Units { VHS Principal
Urged Change
In Curriculum

(18 pt. Caledonia Bold)

GOOD

13 Units { VHS Principal
Urges Change
In Curriculum

(18 pt. Spartan Heavy Italic)

4. Avoid lines that are more than three unit counts shorter than the other lines in the headline.

EXAMPLE:

BAD

14 Units { STUDENTS
FAVOR
LOWERING
OF AGE FOR
VOTING TO 18

(18 pt. Century Bold Condensed)

GOOD

19 Units { STUDENTS FAVOR
LOWERING OF AGE
FOR VOTING TO 18

(18 pt. Spartan Black Condensed)

5. Avoid using confusing terminology.

EXAMPLE:

BAD

17 Units { COUNCIL SETS
DATE—SO AVOID
THE RUSH

(14 pt. Times Roman Bold)

GOOD

15 Units { FIVE JUNIORS
JOIN RACE
FOR COUNCIL

(14 pt. News Gothic Bold)

380

TABLOID PAGE MAKEUP AND LAYOUT

Although some schools still publish standard-size newspapers with eight columns per page, the most common size for school newspapers is the tabloid size, approximately 11 inches wide by 17 inches long. Because the current trend is toward the increasing use of tabloids, the following material deals with page makeup and layout for this size newspaper. Tabloid newspapers usually contain five columns per page, each column being two inches (12 picas) wide. Recently, some schools have converted to four columns per page. Column lengths for both tabloid and standard-size newspapers vary according to press capacity and paper dimensions.

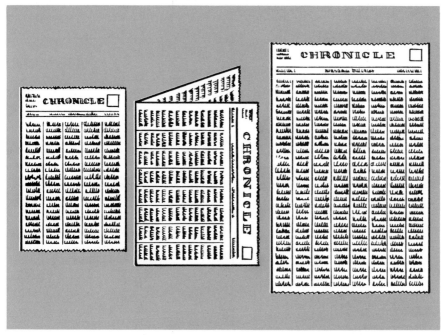

Comparison of tabloid with standard-size newspaper.

Basic Types of Tabloid Makeup

The basic types of tabloid page makeup are: formal, horizontal, focus-and-brace, and a combination of horizontal with focus-and-brace. Each of these four layout types is illustrated on the following pages 382 through 385. Often, in newspaper pages using horizontal page makeup, two or more stories are indicated to be set in one-and-one-half column measures in order to achieve the effect of more white space.

Formal Page Makeup—Formal page makeup attempts to balance each headline or picture with another element of equal weight. A two-column headline or picture in columns one and two would be balanced by a two-column headline or picture in columns four and five. An example of a formal layout is shown in Fig. 1, below, and an example of a school newspaper page made up from that formal layout is shown next to it in Fig. 2.

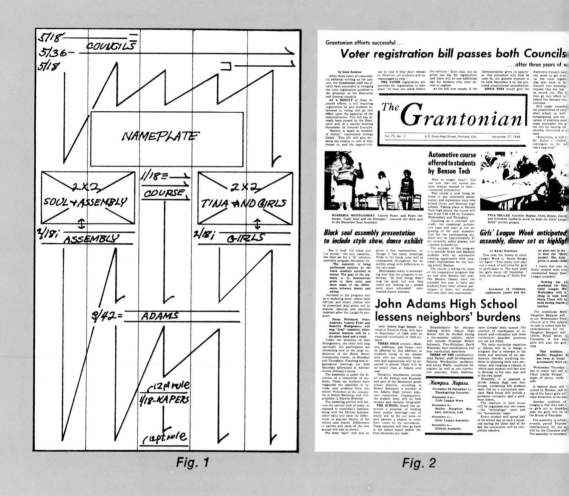

Fig. 1   Fig. 2

FORMAL LAYOUT

The Grantonian, Ulysses S. Grant
High School, Portland, Oregon

Horizontal Page Makeup—In horizontal page makeup, headlines, stories, and photographs are located so that they visually appear to form large horizontal blocks. Wide, shallow photographs are ideal for horizontal page makeup. Headlines are usually set in three-, four-, or five-column widths. An example of a horizontal layout is shown in Fig. 3, below, and an example of a school newspaper page made up from a horizontal layout is shown in Fig. 4.

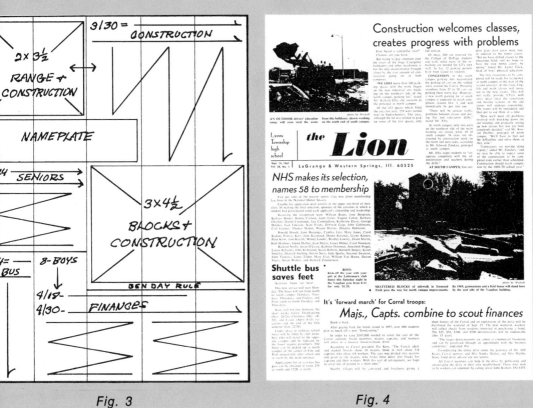

Fig. 3

Fig. 4

HORIZONTAL LAYOUT

The Lion, Lyons Township High School,
LaGrange & Western Springs, Illinois

Focus-and-brace Page Makeup—In focus-and-brace makeup, the main story is located in the top, right-hand corner of the page. Other stories are located, in order of lessening importance, following an imaginary diagonal line running from the main story (top right) diagonally across the page to the bottom, left-hand corner.

Many school newspaper editors feel that the focus-and-brace type of layout is the most suitable of the four basic types of tabloid layouts because it creates an impression of action. The focus-and-brace type layout is used by many professional newspapers, both dailies and weeklies, and by some magazines. An example of a focus-and-brace layout is shown in Fig. 5, below, and an example of a school newspaper made up from that focus-and-brace layout is shown next to it in Fig. 6.

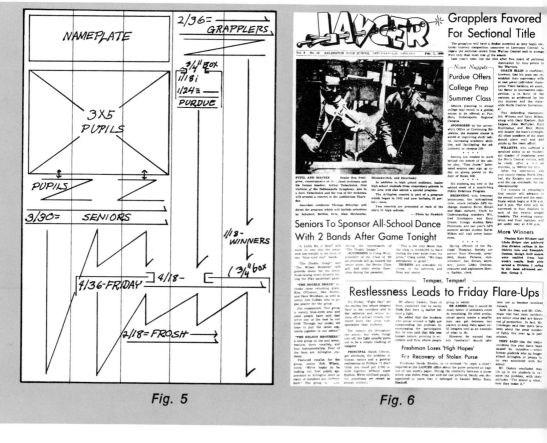

Fig. 5

Fig. 6

FOCUS-AND-BRACE LAYOUT

The Lancer, Arlington High School, Indianapolis, Indiana

Combination Horizontal with Focus-and-brace Page Makeup—This type of page makeup is a variation of the horizontal and the focus-and-brace types. This type of page makeup often utilizes a page-width photograph across the top of the page, with a four-(and sometimes five-) column headline serving as a visual anchor for the page. Masses of type in the center of the page are broken up with one-column headshots or bold-face stories referring to important articles appearing on inside pages. Bold face, capitalized lead-ins break up the stories, and white space is achieved by adding extra space (leading) between paragraphs. An example of a combination horizontal with focus-and-brace layout is shown in Fig. 7, below, and an example of a school newspaper made up from that combination horizontal with focus-and-brace layout is shown next to it in Fig. 8.

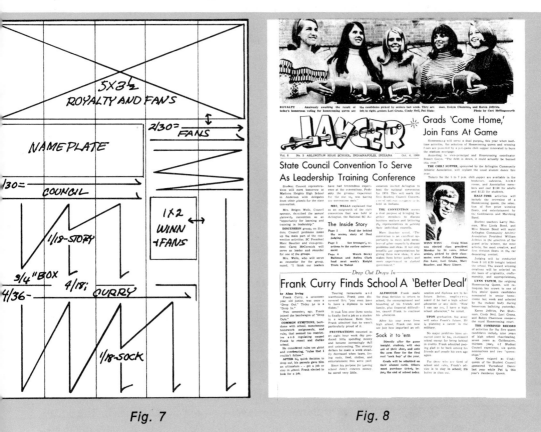

Fig. 7

Fig. 8

COMBINATION HORIZONTAL WITH FOCUS-AND-BRACE MAKEUP

The Lancer, Arlington High School, Indianapolis, Indiana

Planning Page Layouts

One of the prerequisites for success as a layout editor is having the ability to judge, by importance, what constitutes news. Using as criteria the makers of news (see Chapter 8, "Newswriting"), the layout editor must first decide the importance of each news item. Based on that order of importance, editors prepare a list of all materials, with proposed locations, to be printed.

The layout editor can begin planning preliminary page layouts as soon as editorial and news assignments are made, realizing that there will be some changes before final layouts can be prepared. Many school newspaper pages follow the same general layout (or format) in every issue, with most of the advertisements appearing on pages three and five. Because page one is considered the most important page, layout editors usually work on it first. Most page one stories should be hard news (non-feature news). However, layout editors sometimes place well-written feature stories at the bottom of page one. Once the photos have been selected for page one, there is usually only enough room left for five or six short news stories. In the average eight-page school newspaper, page two is usually the editorial page (the first two columns being devoted to editorials, and columns four and five being devoted to a cartoon, letters-to-the-editor, or other feature material). Page six often starts the sports section. The top of each page should carry an important story with a picture, and a large (three-to-five-column) headline.

Before starting their layouts, layout editors usually sketch, on scrap paper, a tentative layout plan for each page, often attempting to make slight variations from the layouts used in previous issues. The news value of the stories to be used can often contribute variety to the layout. For example, with a lead story that deals with a student council election that affects the entire student body, a five-column headline might be used, while with a lead story concerning the drama club's spring presentation a two-column headline with a three-column picture across the top of the page could be used.

Having decided which stories and pictures to use, the layout editor next writes the name of the newspaper (called the nameplate or flagge) in location on the *dummy* (a small diagram or template of the page). If a page dummy is not available, a sufficient supply can be mimeographed from a ruled-off master. On the layout dummy it is wise to indicate, in inches, the proportions to the full-sized sheet (see Figs. 1, 3, 5, and 7 on pages 382–385, for typical tabloid page dummies). Having written the name of the newspaper in location on the dummy, the layout editor next writes in the locations for the main story, pictures, and all other material to be contained on the page. The layout editor makes sure that every corner of the page is anchored with a short two- or three-paragraph story. Layout editors often consider using two- or three-column headlines in the middle of a page to prevent the page from looking too gray (because of a solid mass of body type). They also often use kickers (small headlines) above or below the headlines of long stories to help achieve a more open look. Currently, most schools delete the column rules (ruled lines between columns) to further achieve a more open look. The white space that results from using kickers usually makes a page look more open and inviting to the reader.

EXAMPLE:

Drastic Cuts Predicted

COUNCIL VOTES MAJOR CUTBACKS

Achieving Variety in Page Layouts

Layout editors can achieve visual variety on each page by breaking up solid masses of type with headlines, white space, and pictures. It is always best not to place pictures or headlines side by side (this is known as *tombstoning*). When the placing of headlines next to one another cannot be avoided, they are usually less offensive if one is set in an italic type face.

The continuation of a story from page one to an inside page should be avoided. It is preferable to print the entire story on page one. Because news stories are written in the inverted pyramid style it is possible to shorten a story by deleting the last few paragraphs, retaining an accurate news presentation with the remaining facts (the five W's and the H) contained in the beginning (usually the lead) of the story.

In school newspapers that have advertisements, the advertising manager should dummy in the ads for the inside pages (there is usually no advertising on page one). The layout editor must then fit the remaining pictures and stories around the advertisements, attempting to locate at least one picture on each page and using any of the remaining, less-important news stories to fill the pages. Advertisements are usually *pyramided*, the larger advertisements being located at the bottom of the page and the smaller ones placed above them.

Determining Lengths of Copy

The easiest way to determine how long a story will run when set in print is to count the numbers of typed lines in the article. When typed on an 8½ by 11 sheet of paper with one-inch margins on each side, four lines of copy will equal approximately one inch of standard newspaper print. For example, if the story consists of 24 typed lines, it will be approximately six inches long when set in type. The headline depth can be approximated by adding one more inch to allow for the average one-column, two-line headline.

A more complex system for keeping track of how much copy is needed is as follows: if a page runs 15 inches deep and is five columns wide, 75 inches of heads, stories, advertisements, and pictures will be needed to fill the page. Following is a suggested form for keeping track of the amount of copy needed to fill pages.

	Head Size	Length of Story and Head	Total No. of Inches	Slug
1.	2/48/2	12	12	Council
2.	3/36/1	10	22	Musical
3.	1/24/3	7	29	Library
4.	Picture (2x5)	10	39	with Library

Under Column 1, Head Size, the figures 2/48/2 are an abbreviated way of referring to the number of columns, the size of type, and the number of lines in the headline. To write out this information would take too much time and space: it would be necessary to write "two columns, 48 points, two lines." Layout editors usually maintain, for each page in their papers, similar charts that list each story and picture schedules to appear on a particular page. When the total number of inches comes to 75, they know that they have enough material to complete a page.

One way layout editors prepare copy (preferred by most printers) is by using the paste-up method. With the paste-up method a dummy page is laid out as previously described, and is retained by the editor while the printer sets all stories and headlines into type. The printer then has proofs made of all copy and pictures, which he returns to the layout editor. The layout editor next pastes these elements onto actual-size master dummies (or templates), which are then returned to the printer. Using the pasted-up master dummy as a guide, the printer locates the metal for the type and headlines and the engravings for the pictures in the exact positions indicated on the master dummy.

Selecting Effective Photographs

Scholastic newspaper editors, to ensure that they have selected effective pictures, should be able to answer the following four questions with a "yes."

1. Is the picture of good quality?
2. Does it tell a story?
3. Does it create a favorable impression of the student body?
4. Will using it help create an attractive layout?

Is the picture of good quality?—Although non-color photographs are referred to as black-and-whites, such prints actually consist of hundreds of shades of black, white, and gray. A photograph will make a good engraving only if it has many gradations of gray, ranging from solid black to pure white. If a photograph has too much contrast (mostly black and white with few grays), or is too flat (over-all gray) it should be reprinted.

Does it tell a story?—If the picture shows nothing more than a group of students in a row, the editor might suggest that the picture be retaken. Head-and-shoulder photographs are usually more effective if the person portrayed is doing something. Rather than using full-face headshots, many school newspaper editors prefer to show a ball player about to catch a pass, a stagehand moving scenery, or a club member cleaning up the club room.

Does the picture create a favorable impression of the student body?—Photographs can often create undesirable impressions. One consideration in choosing photographs for use in school newspapers is to be sure that the ones chosen for publication create a favorable impression of the school.

Will using the picture help create an attractive layout?—At least one photograph should appear on each page. Strong vertical and horizontal pictures add variety and lend a feeling of action to the pages of any newspaper.

Location of Photographs

Once the editor has chosen photographs that meet the preceding requirements, he must decide where to locate them. If a picture accompanies a story, both should appear on the same page. Layout editors often use pictures that are the same width as the headline of the accompanying story. For example, when using a two-column picture in the top left-hand corner of page one, standard usage is usually to precede the story by placing a two-column headline under the picture.

The layout editor needs to know, for layout purposes, the approximate final size of the engraving. The final size can be estimated by looking at the cropped photograph. If it is a vertical composition that is planned for a two-column width, chances are that it will run approximately five inches deep (length). A horizontal two-column picture will usually run approximately

389

three inches deep. Headshots usually run about one column wide by three inches deep. Since most high school editors have proofs submitted to them by the printer, the depths of photographs can be accurately measured from the printer's proof. The caption (cutline for the photograph) will, of course, add depth to the photograph, and captions should be planned for all photographs. A rule of thumb to follow when preparing captions is to keep them as short as possible. When a photograph is used without a story, the caption should tell the story as briefly as possible.

Cropping Photographs

Unless the photographer is experienced, the editor will need to crop the pictures to eliminate all of the dead space. Pictures that are not properly cropped often show more background or foreground than they show of the subject. If the layout editor places two L-shaped cardboard strips over the picture (see illustration) he can zero in on that portion he wishes to have

To visualize what a final reproduction of a photograph will look like, many editors and photographers place "cropper L's" over the photograph to form a rectangle. Moving the L's together or apart frames that part of the photograph to be reproduced, and final crop marks are made on the photograph.

Jon Halberstadt

printed. Next, to ensure that only the best part of the picture will appear in print, he draws heavy lines on the portion of the photograph that is to be eliminated by the photoengraver. By carefully cropping photographs, editors can also convert vertically shaped pictures into horizontally shaped pictures, and vice versa.

On publications using Scan-engravings, engravings are made exactly the same size as the print. Therefore, the photographer should be asked to reprint his picture to the desired column width and depth by following the editor's crop marks. For example, the final width of a print chosen to fit a three-column space should be the exact width of three columns plus the amount of space included between two of the columns.

Layout editors are often called the story's surgeon, the writer's conscience, and the reporter's best critic. Like the members of the stage crew of a dramatic production, the layout editor's skill puts into the presentation of material the quality that draws the applause. Excellent staffs without layout editors sometimes produce fair newspapers; mediocre staffs with competent layout editors often produce acceptable newspapers; but excellent staffs, backed by excellent, experienced layout editors, almost always produce excellent-quality newspapers.

FINANCING THE SCHOOL NEWSPAPER

As with mass media newspapers, the two main sources of revenue for school newspapers are advertising and circulation. The latter is most important: a newspaper without a guaranteed circulation (a specific number of readers who would see the advertisements) would be useless to advertisers. On school newspapers both the advertising manager and the circulation manager are usually responsible directly to the business manager and indirectly to the adviser.

School Newspaper Advertising

The financial success of school newspapers depends largely on the effectiveness of the advertising staff. In addition to contributing to the financial stability of the school newspaper, advertising contributes a genuine service to the school's business community by fostering good will and making the entire community aware of the total school program.

Advertising Sales—Members of the school newspaper advertising staff must be courteous, resourceful, honest, dependable, and well-organized. Most members of school newspaper advertising staffs work from an advertising beat sheet similar to the editorial assignment beat sheet described in Chapter 16, "Organizing and Writing School Newspapers." From the advertising beat sheet they usually organize advertising prospects by territories that include streets or sections of the community to be covered by specific salesmen, or by a listing of businesses categorized by types. Many salesmen prepare prospect cards that contain the name and address of a business concern, the advertising manager's name, and any other information that might be of assistance in selling newspaper advertising space. School newspaper advertising managers often maintain advertising production schedules similar to the editorial production schedule shown in Chart C, page 371.

Advertising Rates—Advertising salesmen must be familiar with their newspaper's advertising rates. Most school newspapers have an established policy on rates, as determined by the advertising manager, business manager, and adviser. Often, these rates may be presented to advertising prospects in the form of a printed advertising rate card. School newspaper advertising rates are usually determined by charging a flat rate per column inch for all advertising (regardless of size of advertisement, type of advertising, or number of insertions) or by a sliding scale of charges. With the sliding scale of charges, advertisers are given reductions for inserting larger advertisements, inserting advertisements in more than one issue, or for inserting more than one advertisement in an issue.

Advertising Layout—While many merchants specify definite copy and layouts for their advertisements, advertising salesmen must be prepared to suggest effective advertising layouts and copy for those who don't. Planning an advertising layout is beneficial to the advertising salesman because the layout will show how much copy (headlines, illustrations, and body copy) is needed to fit the available space. An effective advertising layout will also show the advertiser how his advertisement will appear, and will show the printer exactly how the advertisement is to be set up. Advertising managers on many school newspapers, responsible for helping layout editors locate advertisements on dummy layout pages, often use the salesman's advertising layouts in making up page layouts.

Advertising Contracts—Many school newspaper advertising managers formulate and have printed supplies of advertising contracts that contain space for such information as the advertiser's name, the size of the advertisement, the issue the advertisement is to appear in, the price of the advertisement, the copy to be contained in the advertisement, the salesman's name, and the date of the advertising insertion order. Then, from the advertising contracts submitted by salesmen, the advertising manager maintains a running record of all advertisements, usually alphabetically, by issue, that is made readily available to the editor-in-chief, the business manager, and the adviser.

Statements of Account and Billing—As soon as possible following the publication of each issue of the school newspaper, advertising managers and advertising department staff members must make out statements of account (to be delivered or mailed) for each advertiser. The statement of account contains the advertiser's address, the size of the advertisement, the price of the advertisment, and the advertisement's location in the paper. Most school newspaper advertisements appear as *R. O. P.* (run of paper) advertisements, meaning that no definite location has been specified. A tear sheet (a printed newspaper page showing the advertisement) should always be sent with the statement of account. Many schools prefer to send the entire newspaper with the statement of account. When this is done, the advertisement being billed is usually circled, making it easier for the advertiser to locate his advertisement. Tear sheets are usually sent with a statement of account for display advertisements only, and not for classified advertisements. Delivering the tear sheet (often called the billing copy when submitted with a statement of account) enables the advertising salesman to pursue possible future sales.

School Newspaper Circulation

The school newspaper circulation manager and his staff of circulation representatives are responsible for newspaper sales, deliveries, subscriptions, mailings, and sometimes for promotional and subscription campaigns that are planned to increase the newspaper's circulation. Many schools do not conduct subscription campaigns, and allot specified amounts of money to the newspaper from funds acquired through student activity fees. School newspaper circulation departments are often responsible for delivery of the printed newspapers from the printer to the school.

Circulation managers often name representatives to sell the paper, and also make sure that all students have access to newspaper stands throughout the school. Such stands are best located in areas where students congregate, such as student lounges, cafeterias, libraries, and locker rooms.

The sale of advertising, the main source of income for any newspaper, depends on the circulation. Advertisers have the right to expect the newspaper to reach all of the students. It is the circulation manager's primary duty to ensure that the printed newspapers are distributed to the best of his ability.

Selling the Newspaper—Most school newspapers sell for from five cents per copy to twenty-five cents per copy. Sales to the student body of from 75 to

80 percent are considered satisfactory. Many schools sell subscriptions either for one semester or for one year, and subscription rates often vary from year to year depending on the financial state of the newspaper, the number of issues printed, and the cost of producing the paper.

Mail subscriptions are usually sold at a student rate plus postage expense, or at alumni rates plus postage expense, and many schools sell subscriptions to residents of the community outside the student population. Such residents can be considered as potential buyers of advertising space, and can often be sold congratulatory advertisements.

Sales Campaigns—A sales campaign, designed to promote the sale of the newspaper and increase its circulation, must be intelligently planned and carefully carried out. Such campaigns usually have a theme around which slogans, contests, and activities can be built. Many circulation sales campaigns are based on salesmen increasing the number of subscriptions sold, while others depend on editorial contests and crusades to increase sales.

Keeping Records—School newspaper circulation managers must maintain an accurate record of all newspapers sold, delivered, mailed, or sent to advertisers. Many circulation managers keep records of subscription sales and deliveries by using simple receipt books, while others maintain more extensive records in ledger form. All records maintained by school newspaper circulation managers should, at all times, be available to the editor-in-chief, the business manager, and the adviser.

Exchange Newspapers—Most school newspapers maintain an exchange newspaper system with other school newspapers. On many school newspapers an exchange editor is assigned, usually as a member of the circulation department, to handle this function. Most exchange editors work directly with the circulation department to mail copies of their newspapers to all schools involved in the exchanging of newspapers. The exchange editor has the responsibility for maintaining records for all newspapers received. He also studies copies of the newspapers received from other schools in order to suggest to appropriate staff members of his own newspaper new ideas for layout, handling of copy, promotion campaigns, and production procedures.

School Newspaper Business Management

On most school newspapers the business management function is placed directly under the journalism department adviser or the school's commercial department. The school newspaper business manager's major function is to help keep the newspaper financially sound. Because even the smallest school newspapers incur expenses, handle money, purchase supplies, and pay for producing newspapers, the business manager's role is an important one. School newspaper business managers receive valuable training in business procedures, and the student selected to fulfill this function is usually chosen from commercial or business courses.

The business manager works closely with the advertising and circulation managers so that he can be constantly aware of any changes in the newspaper's two main sources of revenue: advertising and circulation. He must prepare budgets to show where all monies are to come from and how they are to be spent, listing each source of income as well as the amount of income expected. Budgets, as soon as they are approved and finalized by the adviser, become the basis for all of the newspaper's financial records. Preparation of the budget is usually followed by the preparation of contracts to suppliers (typesetters, printers, and engravers).

Usually, the business manager has the added responsibility of depositing in the newspaper's bank fund all money received from advertising and circulation. Through the direction of the adviser, he is also responsible for the expenditures involved in the purchasing of newspaper supplies and equipment. To meet these responsibilities, many business managers keep a cash record that shows the actual amount of money on hand, as well as a separate ledger that lists all expenses and all income. Most business managers use a system by which all payments are made by check, thus providing a thorough and accurate record of expenditures and simplifying the record-keeping details.

ACTIVITIES

1. From a recent issue of your school newspaper select several headlines that you think could be improved. Rewrite the headlines retaining their original unit counts. Rewrite them with five to ten fewer units.

2. Select a topic to write a short news story about, including in it a headline, kicker, and lead. Select a fellow student to be your copy editor and exchange news stories with him. Using the style sheet in the appendix edit his news story for content and expression, and confer with him about the reasons for your editing. Rewrite the story to your copy editor's specifications.

3. Using the page makeup examples on pages 382–385 as a guide, make up a page one dummy layout for the first fall issue of your school newspaper, maintaining its current size and number of columns. Specify the amount of space to be alloted for whatever stories and pictures you intend to include.

4. Using a printer's rule, measure the point sizes of the type used in the headlines of your school newspaper. What is the one-column unit count for each measured headline? Prepare a "headline schedule" for your school newspaper, listing the one-column counts for each size of headline type.

5. Analyze the layout of your school newspaper for the following:
   a. Readability.
   b. Variety and placement of headlines.
   c. Size and placement of photographs.
   d. Space between columns and paragraphs.
   e. Placement of advertising.
   f. Eye-catching devices like cartoons, illustrations, and type faces.
Select a particular page from the newspaper and describe how you would rearrange it, using the present pictures and stories.

6. What layout and copy suggestions would you make to an owner of a clothing, music, or food shop who wished to purchase space for an advertisement in your school newspaper? Make up a dummy advertisement for one of these stories, including any copy and illustrated material you think would appeal to its owner.

7. What changes would you like to see in the content of your school newspaper? Are there any areas of student life that your school newspaper doesn't cover well? Write a letter to the editor suggesting possible changes in coverage that might well benefit the paper's appeal.

8. Prepare a business campaign for your school newspaper, attempting to increase its circulation and advertising. How would you increase student readership and interest? How would you create a demand for the paper? How would you get local business to advertise more?

9. By what printing process is your school newspaper produced? How can you tell? What are the relative costs of the current printing procedure used by your school newspaper, as compared with other printing methods? Could the newspaper save money on its production? If the newspaper changed its method of printing, what changes might occur in content and format? How does the printing process influence what a newspaper prints? Why are colors seldom seem in newspapers?

READING

ARNOLD, EDMUND C., *Functional Newspaper Design.* Harper & Row, New York, 1969.

BAKER, STEPHEN, *Advertising Layout and Art Direction.* McGraw-Hill, New York, 1959.

CALLIHAN, E. L., *Grammar for Journalists*. Chilton Book Co., Philadelphia, Pa., 1969.

COLUMBIA SCHOLASTIC PRESS ASSOCIATION, *Style Book*. Columbia Scholastic Press Association, Columbia University, New York, 1965.

CURWEN, HAROLD, *Processes of Graphic Reproduction in Printing*, edited by Charles Mayo. Dover, New York, 1958.

ESTRIN, HERMAN A., AND ARTHUR M. SANDERSON (Ed.), *Freedom and Censorship of the College Press*. Wm. C. Brown, Dubuque, Iowa, 1966. (PB)

FELDMAN, SAMUEL M., *The Student Journalist and Legal and Ethical Issues*. Richards Rosen Press, New York, 1968.

HOHENBERG, JOHN, *The New Front Page*. Columbia University Press, New York, 1965.

HOLDER, ROBERT, *The Complete Guide to Successful School Publications*. Prentice-Hall, Englewood Cliffs, N.J., 1964.

HUTT, ALLEN, *Newspaper Design*. Oxford University Press, New York, 1960.

HVISTENDAHL, J. K., *Producing the Duplicated Newspaper*. Iowa State University Press, Ames, Iowa, 1966. (PB)

KARCH, ROBERT R., *Printing and the Allied Trades*. Pitman, New York, 1962.

McCARTHY, HELEN, *Advertising in School Publications*. Columbia Scholastic Press Association, Columbia University, New York, 1958.

POWERS, VERNA, *Mimeo*. National Scholastic Press Association, Minneapolis, Minn., 1964.

SCHLEMMER, RONALD M., *Handbook of Advertising Art Production*. Prentice-Hall, Englewood Cliffs, N.J., 1966. (PB)

SCHMID, CALVIN F., *Handbook of Graphic Presentation*. Ronald, New York, 1954.

SEEBER, EDWARD D., *A Style Manual for Students*. Indiana University Press, Bloomington, Ind., 1967.

TURNBULL, ARTHUR T., AND RUSSELL N. BAIRD, *Graphics of Communication: Typography, Layout, and Design*. Holt, Rinehart & Winston, New York, 1968. (PB)

WHITBECK, EARL C., (Ed.), *Duplicated Publication Fundamentals: For School Periodicals*. Columbia Scholastic Press Association, Columbia University, New York, 1965.

WIMER, ARTHUR AND DALE BRIX, *Workbook for Head Writing and News Editing*. Wm. C. Brown, Dubuque, Iowa, 1957. (PB)

WOODS, ALLEN, *Modern Newspaper Production*. Harper & Row, New York, 1963.

WRIGHT, GLEN, *The Student Journalist and Making Advertising Pay for the School Publication*. Richards Rosen Press, New York, 1968.

Chapter **18**

Organizing and Writing
the School Yearbook

PLANNING THE YEARBOOK

Few books in the average home are read and referred to as often as the school annual, or yearbook. Because the information, the pictures, and the layouts contained in the yearbook will be seen by the children and the grandchildren of the members of the graduating classes depicted therein, it is essential that the writers and editors chosen to work on school yearbooks be intelligent, responsible individuals. They must be capable of giving future readers an accurate view of what took place during a given year at the educational institution the yearbook represents.

Planning the yearbook should begin as early in the school year as possible. A full year is usually sufficient time in which to complete the average yearbook, provided that the staff is well organized and competent. The techniques used to produce successful yearbooks do not differ greatly from the techniques used to produce successful school newspapers: like work on the school newspaper, all work on school yearbooks must be well-organized and carefully scheduled. Organizing, copy editing, proofreading, writing, selecting and cropping photographs—all techniques similar to those used on school newspapers—are the techniques that members of the yearbook staff will need to utilize. Because you have learned many of these techniques in previous chapters in this book, this chapter will deal only with those techniques necessary to organize and write for school yearbooks.

Organizing the Yearbook Staff

Various schools select their yearbook staffs in different ways. Students chosen to fill the major staff positions on the yearbook may be selected by the yearbook adviser, by the previous year's yearbook staff, or by a board of publications. The chart on page 401 shows the staff organization for a typical yearbook, and the following paragraphs describe the functions of the key members of the yearbook editorial staff.

The Editor-in-chief—The yearbook editor-in-chief must be a competent organizer, capable of organizing and administrating the yearbook staff and scheduling the flow of materials to and from the printer. Directly responsible to the adviser, the editor-in-chief has the overall responsibility for meeting an established deadline. To do this, the editor-in-chief must select competent students to help him succeed in his efforts. Final decisions concerning the yearbook cover, theme, sections, budget, and policy rest with the editor-in-chief who must be capable of commanding respect from printers, suppliers, and fellow students, must be tactful but firm in dealing with staff members, and must be a conscientious, diligent worker. Intelligent direction and leadership must be given to staff members by the editor-in-chief.

The Business Manager—The yearbook business manager has an important function, equal in importance to the function of the yearbook editor-in-chief: the business manager must ensure that the yearbook is a financial success. After carefully estimating the amount of revenue to be secured from subscriptions, advertising, patrons, and any other areas, the business manager, working with the editor-in-chief, sets up a budget for the yearbook. From the budget he determines the approximate overall cost per page, and the total number of pages the budget will allow. Having established the proposed income for the yearbook, the business manager must know approximately how much money should be allocated for photography, covers, printing and engraving, office supplies, and miscellaneous expenses. For example, if new typewriters or file cabinets are needed, the business manager must take this into consideration when preparing a budget for the yearbook. He should set up an efficient bookkeeping system if one is not already

TYPICAL STAFF ORGANIZATION FOR A SCHOOL YEARBOOK

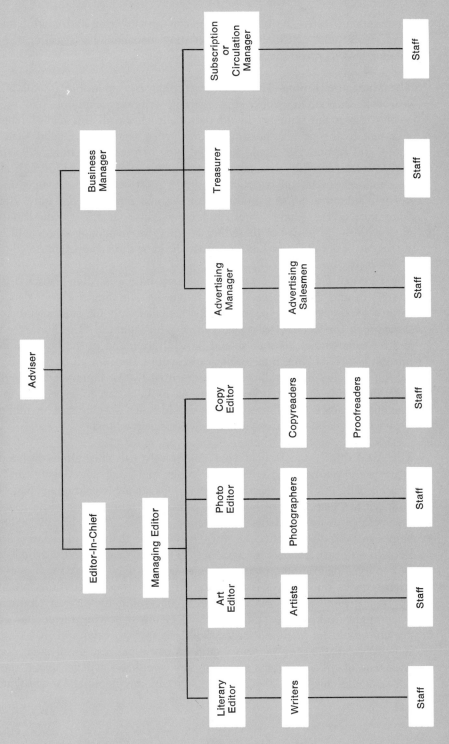

in operation. Lastly, the business manager must oversee and coordinate the work of his major assistants: the advertising manager, the treasurer, the circulation manager, and the subscription manager.

The Managing Editor—The managing editor is responsible for all of the yearbook editorial functions: copy editing, write-ups, captions, photos, and layouts. Since this student should personally check all this material before it is sent to the printer, he should know what comprises a good write-up, photo, and layout. He should have the type of personality that will enable him to work smoothly with not only the editor-in-chief, but also with all of his subordinates on the yearbook staff. In most schools the managing editor will submit a list of candidates for the major posts under him: literary editor, art editor, photo editor, and copy editor. If his recommendations meet with the approval of the editor-in-chief, the managing editor will have succeeded in obtaining key staff members he knows are competent.

The Literary Editor—The yearbook literary editor is often chosen for his interest in and love for the English language. He should know what constitutes good prose and poetry, and when choosing his staff members he should look for students who share these same qualities. The literary editor and the members of his staff should be well grounded in the basics of English grammar: spelling, punctuation, and syntax. Because all of the yearbook stories, captions, and headlines will be written by the literary editor and his staff, these people must be consistent slaves to accuracy—especially in the spelling of names. The literary editor should name specific staff members as copy writers, caption writers, headline writers, and editors.

The Art Editor—Since school yearbooks rarely use illustrations by student artists, most yearbook art editor jobs consist mainly of page layout—an "art" in itself. The art editor must be able to look at a blank dummy page and visualize the placement of headlines, print, illustrations, and white space in the most pleasing, readable presentation possible. If he has assistants to help him with the layouts, he must make sure that his ideas are carried through on every page. If he does not do this, the completed yearbook may lack unity. For example, pictures in one section may be too small, while in other sections the pictures may be too large. Yearbook art editors often set up, as a general guide, rules of thumb concerning the size of engravings. They might decide, for example, that all pictures showing fewer than three persons would be made no larger than four inches wide, and that pictures showing more than ten persons would be made at least seven inches wide. After one of the art editor's assistants has completed a page layout, the art editor should check the layout at once, offering any necessary suggestions on how it might be improved. The art editor also has the major responsibility of helping to choose the theme and planning the opening section. The person chosen as yearbook art editor must be responsible and reliant. If he is negligent about having page layouts finished on time, the yearbook may miss its publication deadline.

The Photo Editor—The photo editor chosen to work on the yearbook should have many of the qualities essential to the art editor. In addition to these qualities, he should be tactful in his choice of photographs. Knowing what constitutes an ideal yearbook picture, he will encourage his photographers to take pictures that tell a story, have action, are different, are closeups, and are technically of good quality. He should never accept prints that do not have solid blacks and whites plus a complete range of grays. The photo editor works closely with the managing editor to make certain that all requests for photo coverage are fulfilled. Should the managing editor desire a photograph that will be used in unusual dimensions, the photo editor will relay the specifications to the photographer. Lastly, the photo editor is responsible for the safe-keeping and distribution of school-owned photographic equipment and supplies.

The Copy Editor—Among the hardest workers on the school yearbook staff are the copy editor and the members of his department. Upon receipt of articles from the literary editor, the copy editor and his staff must double-check every word. Since it is difficult for a writer to do a proper job of editing his own writing, this must be done by the copy editor or a member of his staff. To ensure uniformity, copy editors often prepare their own style guide for use by the entire yearbook staff. A typical style guide prepared by a yearbook copy editor would include at least four main areas: spelling, punctuation, capitalization, and abbreviation.

1. *Spelling*—Although dictionaries often list more than one acceptable spelling for the same word, it is important to be consistent regardless of which spelling you choose. For example, here are three spellings for the same word: goodbye, good-by, and goodby. The copy editor's style book should list the spelling that has been decided on, and this spelling should be the only one used throughout the yearbook.

2. *Punctuation*—All articles in the yearbook should conform to rules for formal grammar and punctuation. The "when-in-doubt, leave-it-out" rule used by some newspapers is seldom permitted on yearbooks. A comma should follow the last word in a series preceding a conjunction, and hyphens must be placed between two or more words when used as one.

3. *Capitalization*—Most yearbooks follow an "up" style, meaning that the first

403

letters in titles, points of the compass, and proper names are capitalized. For example, while some school newspapers use a "down" style (as in *Wykoff high school*), the "up" style capitalizes the *h* and the *s* (*Wykoff High School*). Many newspapers use the "down" style with titles following names, as: *Roger Qualman, principal of Coos Bay high school*. Most yearbooks, however, would run this material as: *Roger Qualman, Principal of Coos Bay High School*.

4. *Abbreviations*—Most yearbook copy editors avoid abbreviations. However, when it is necessary to use them, they must be used the same way each time. For example, editors in states like California and Pennsylvania should decide whether to use Calif. or Cal., Pa. or Penn. Parochial schools should be careful when using abbreviations for the title of clergymen: if the Bishop's title is The Right Reverend Monsignor, the proper abbreviation is Rt. Rev. Msgr.

After a story has been edited the copy editor should have it retyped, making at least one carbon copy for the files. The carbon copy can be referred to when copy has been released, or can be used in the event that the original becomes misplaced or lost. Following completion of the retyping, the copy is again checked by the copy editor to make sure there are no further typographical errors.

The Advertising Manager—As with school newspapers, the two main sources of revenue for school yearbooks are circulation and advertising (including patrons). The yearbook advertising manager's main goal is to publish the best yearbook possible without incurring any debts. Without advertising, yearbooks often have financial difficulties. Recently, many yearbook editors, feeling that advertising is not appropriate in school yearbooks, have given up advertising space in favor of use of the space to depict school activities. And advertisers, feeling that yearbook advertisements are not as effective as newspaper advertisements, have been reluctant to advertise in yearbooks where their advertisements are often bulked at the end of the book, making them easy to skip over. While the advertising manager's chief duty is to see that advertisements are sold, his function doesn't stop there: he must also make sure that the advertisements that are sold are in good taste and that advertising copy is received on time and sent to the printer promptly. In addition to supervising the proofreading of all advertising copy, the advertising manager usually sees that advertisements are located on the proper pages. Many school yearbooks offer students as photographer's models for some advertisements. The school yearbook advertising manager's job is often more difficult than the school newspaper advertising manager's job. Advertising rates for yearbook space—sold by the page or fraction of the page rather than by the column inch—are often determined by a sliding scale, based on the size of the advertisement. Usually, about one third of the production cost of the yearbook is absorbed by student subscribers, the remainder being borne by advertisers. The per-page advertising rates are determined by dividing the remaining production costs (after student subscriptions) by the number of advertising pages desired. This rate should be checked against the per-page production costs and adjusted so that each advertising page not only pays for itself, but also pays for another page not containing advertisements.

The Treasurer—In many schools the actual billing and paying is done not by the business manager, but by a yearbook treasurer. The yearbook treasurer is responsible for supervising all financial matters and dealing with the bank. Much of the yearbook bookkeeping is supervised and carried out by this person. The yearbook treasurer's duties are similar to the duties of the school newspaper business manager's duties described in Chapter 16, "Organizing and Writing the School Newspaper."

The Subscription Manager—An important staff member on the yearbook is the subscription manager. Without sales, the best-written, edited, and produced yearbook would be a failure. Although potential buyers are often reluctant to spend the money charged for the yearbook, every student wants a copy and those who put off buying a subscription usually regret having done so later. The subscription manager must post notices in strategic places throughout the school so that each student knows where he can be contacted. While subscription managers often name other students as subscription representatives, the subscription manager himself must keep track of all sales and must be sure that all students are contacted. If some students cannot afford to buy a copy of the yearbook, the subscription manager should find ways for these students to get a free copy. For example, such students might be asked to make posters or take part in promotional projects in exchange for a free copy of the yearbook: ideally, a copy of the yearbook should be placed in the hands of each student. In addition to selling advance copies, the subscription manager also explores ways of promoting the book. He may write articles for the student newspaper, place a few promotional pictures in the literary magazine, supervise the making up of posters, and plan other similar activities designed to sell the book. When the completed yearbooks are delivered, the subscription manager may wish to sell any extra copies to businessmen, alumni, and teachers.

PLANNING THE FORMAT

Two items of major concern in planning any school yearbook are emphasis and unity. Usually, it is best not to overemphasize any particular aspect of the entire school year, but to give equal emphasis to all aspects. The yearbook should reflect an honest appraisal of the entire school year, so that years after its publication date a reader will be able to look at the yearbook and say, "That's the way it was." Unity is achieved by using one main theme, or central idea, throughout the yearbook.

The Theme

The central idea underlying the yearbook is called its theme. The entire format for the yearbook is planned around the theme. The yearbook theme must be pertinent to:
1. A specific school.
2. A specific senior class.
3. A specific school year.

It is better to have no theme at all than to have one that doesn't apply to all three of these categories. The advantages to having a theme are many: a theme can give unity to all of the sections of the yearbook; a theme can make the yearbook different from any other yearbook in the country; a theme can make the yearbook timely; a theme can make the yearbook more creative and unique; and lastly, a theme can give the yearbook real meaning to the graduate in the years to come.

An example of the successful use of a theme is the Museum of Modern Art's inspiring picture book *The Family of Man*, photographed by Edward Steichen. The cover picture, which shows a happy Peruvian youngster playing a flute, was used as the theme throughout the various sections of the book. Pertinent quotations were also used on the beginning pages for each section. Some school yearbooks use the school emblem on the beginning pages for each section, while others use the entire opening section to set the theme. An example of this would be: "Let's take a look at the year 19—— at _____ School through the pages of The _____." Pictures throughout the opening section could illustrate such phrases as: It's Friendly, It's Fun, It's Hot, It's Cold, It's Studious, It's Work, It's Play.

One High School used "time" as a theme. The cover and opening section used the quotation from Ecclesiastes III, 1–8.

EXAMPLE:

To everything there is a season, and a time to every purpose under heaven. A time to be born, and a time to die, a time to keep silence and a time to speak, a time to weep, and a time to laugh, a time to embrace and a time to be far from embraces. A time to get, and a time to lose, a time of war, and a time of peace.

406

Photos throughout the opening section illustrated phrases taken from this quotation. The division pages throughout the yearbook contained other quotations concerning time.

"Time, you old gypsy man, will you not stay, Put up your caravan just one day?'
— Ralph Hodgson

SENIORS

"to everything there is
a season,
and a time to every purpose
under heaven.

a time to be born,
and a time to die . . .

a time to keep silence, and a time to speak . . .

A leading yearbook publisher, Wm. J. Keller, Inc., offers the following guidelines for use when thinking of adopting a theme:

1. Is it right for your school? Does it show the school off at its best? Does it typify your school? Does the administration approve? Does it cater to one group or is it representative? Does it ridicule or poke fun at individuals?

2. Can it be effectively translated into visual or verbal expression? Can it easily be illustrated with the time and talent available? Is it too abstract for illustration? Will it work in all sections of the book? Is it too contrived or "worked" . . . is it far-fetched?

3. Is it hackneyed? Does it represent the talents of a "budding" artist or the whole staff? Is it childish, crude, or otherwise not up to the capabilities of the yearbook staff?

4. Would the yearbook be better without a theme? Will the theme cause so much trouble and effort that not enough time can be given to the rest of the book? Is it really an honest effort to say something or a way of filling up empty division pages?

When deciding on a theme, the editor-in-chief and his art editor should try to select one that meets the preceding four requirements. After screening several possibilities, they should submit their results to the entire editorial staff and the adviser, listening to constructive comments before choosing the one theme that will have much influence on the final makeup of the yearbook. In considering a theme possibility, the editor-in-chief should ask for picture suggestions that illustrate the theme, and should consult with photographers to discuss picture possibilities. Also, Bartlett's *Familiar Quotations* is often an invaluable aid when choosing a theme.

Ideally, the theme should be carried through on the cover, end pages, table of contents, page one, opening section, and division pages. If a talented student has written a poem about the year's activities, the editor-in-chief might consider it as the theme (but should never commit himself to any one idea until the entire staff discusses it). The yearbook staff should be prepared to abandon any theme they find too difficult or impossible to carry out. Lastly, all staff members concerned with choosing a theme should keep in mind that what may seem clever, witty, and humorous today may well seem trite and in poor taste years from now. They should avoid editorializing, "funny" pictures, and "clever" write-ups and captions.

Yearbook Sections

Before the yearbook staff members can begin their work on the yearbook, they need to know what sections will be included, approximately how many pages will be allocated to each section, and the page size. In making these decisions, the editor-in-chief and his top aides should look at the year-books from the preceding years. These yearbooks can give a general idea about the number of pages to allocate to each section. Once the business manager presents the yearbook budget, the number of pages in the book can be established. The overall number of pages will, of course, depend both on the budget and on the amount of material to be included. The overall number of pages desired can be determined by first estimating the number of pages that the pictures will occupy, and then estimating the amount of space to be devoted to all other sections based on their relative importance.

When choosing a page size, yearbook staff members should avoid non-standard sizes. Standard page sizes for most yearbooks are 9″ x 12″, 8½″ x 11″, and 7¾″ x 10½″. Irregular sizes should be avoided to prevent printing problems and paper wastage. Margins should be determined, with the help of the printer, based on the amounts of space necessary to achieve the most attractive-looking pages.

If it has been decided to use a theme, an opening section devoted to words and pictures depicting this theme might be suggested. Although the arrangement and names of sections can vary considerably from school to school, most yearbooks include the following sections: opening, faculty, graduates, classes, features, organizations, athletics, and advertisements. Larger schools having larger yearbooks often have several other feature sections. Material concerning yearbook covers is contained in Chapter 19, "Producing and Financing the School Yearbook."

Opening Section—First impressions mean a great deal. Therefore, the opening section should have a major impact on the reader since these pages will be the first ones he sees. This section usually presents the most opportunity for creativity. (Often, the other sections of many yearbooks retain about the same general format from year to year.) As with every section in the yearbook, the opening section should be broken down into workable units. Considerable thought must be given to the opening section's end pages, the title page, table of contents page, and to illustrations. Usually, each part of the opening section is assigned to a different person.

1. *End Pages*—Since most printers prefer (for binding purposes) to use heavier paper as stock for the end pages, it is best not to consider placing photographs on end pages. However, many school yearbooks place line drawings on the end pages. The end paper should match or complement the color of the cover, and it is usually best not to use solid black ink on them or on any other pages in the book. When a line drawing is used on the end pages in the front, the same illustration is usually repeated on the end pages in the back.

2. *Title Page*—The yearbook's title page presents an opportunity for a great deal of creativity in the use of type, art, and overall design. The title page should always include the name of the yearbook, the year, and the name and address of the school. Regardless of whether it precedes or follows the pictorial portion, the title page should be an odd-numbered (right-hand) page.

3. *The Table of Contents*—Included on this page will be the various section titles and their page numbers. In listing the contents the material contained within each major section may be broken down into comprehensive descriptions. Many yearbooks place a full-page picture on the page facing the table of contents, thus balancing such elements on the table of contents page (another odd-numbered page) as the school seal or large type faces. As on all other special pages, it is best not to crowd too many elements onto one page. Combined masses of typographical elements with white space usually produce an artistic effect. Some schools reproduce small pictures of the division page illustration on the contents page.

4. *Illustrations*—Ideally, the photos used in the opening section should set the theme for the yearbook. They should be top-quality pictures, and should be given enough space in order to have an impact. One picture (or at the most two pictures) should be used per page. Their sequence should have unity and coherence. If a poem is used as the theme, an attempt might be made to have each photograph illustrate a few lines of the poem. Editors should consider having a professional photographer take the pictures for the opening section as well as having him take any color and division-page pictures. Division-page photographs should continue the yearbook theme, and should also depict the subject of the section. While some yearbooks use one full page as the division page, other yearbooks use two full pages. Photographers, before taking pictures, should know how their pictures are to be used: if a picture is to be used on one page, the photographer should take a vertical picture; if the picture is to be used on two pages, he would need a horizontal composition.

Faculty Section—A formal arrangement of photos and layouts is often used for the faculty section. A few schools, having tried to use candid photos for this section, have been unsuccessful. For example, candid shots of a bishop and other diocese officials, deans, principals, and superintendents of schools are difficult to obtain. When a photographic montage division page (many photos cut apart and mounted as a composite) is used to introduce the faculty section, it should show as many faculty members as possible.

Often, school officials write congratulatory messages to the members of the graduating class. These messages should be placed on the same page as the picture of the official who wrote the message. When printing a handwritten message, the message must be reproduced large enough to be easily read and, because yearbook editors can usually complete this section early in the school year, such messages and their accompanying pictures should be secured as soon after school starts as possible. Many times faculty mem-

412

bers do not have portraits available, and yearbook staff members assigned to the faculty section will need to remind the faculty members to obtain them, often setting up appointments with the photographer. Some schools have descriptive material of faculty members set in type for emergency use when photos are unobtainable.

Many schools place faculty pictures in alphabetical order, while other schools segregate teachers by the departments they teach in. Still others place teachers in the faculty section according to their length of service at the school. Yearbooks often print each teacher's degrees and alma mater with the teacher's photograph.

Class Section—The class section can often be scheduled for early completion. Since most students enroll the first day of school, they should be available for pictures immediately. The class section is usually one of the most important and popular sections of the yearbook, provided that each student has his picture in it. The portrait photographer, often chosen during the summer, can usually schedule sittings immediately after the opening of school. A number of schools have found it convenient to also have the portrait photographer take the group pictures. One photographer told a high school adviser he could afford to take the group pictures free, and then take the portraits at a nominal charge. His reason? He found that once a resident of the community was satisfied with the work of one photographer, he usually went back to the same photographer, and that many of his wedding assignments came from girls for whom he had taken yearbook pictures.

The yearbook editors often place candid photos throughout the class section that show the activities of the various classes. Other editors frown on this practice because experience has shown that candid shots—usually taken by amateur shutterbugs—tend to reduce the quality of the entire section.

To help achieve uniformity, editors should advise students on what type of clothing to wear for their portraits. It is essential that the photographer be informed of these decisions so that he can make sure the students are properly attired before taking their pictures. The photographer should also be told what color background to use for every picture. A medium gray is usually recommended because it provides good contrast regardless of the student's hair color. Poses and headsizes must be uniform, and the photographer must submit identical picture sizes to the yearbook staff. The best size for class section portraits is two inches wide by three inches deep. Because they yield better-quality engravings, engravers prefer working with glossy prints. Some photographers volunteer to place adhesive backs on the prints (for layout purposes), a suggestion that is often discouraged because the pictures stick together and are ruined before release to the engraver.

After all of the yearbook pictures have been obtained, they should be filed in alphabetical order. Some yearbooks use only the student's name with his picture; however, most yearbooks use other descriptive information such as course of study, student organizations, and offices held. It is, of course, imperative that the student names be spelled correctly. Spelling—in this and in all other sections—should be triple-checked. No degree of artistic perfection in the other sections will be compensation to a student whose picture and write-up are not perfect.

Feature Section—The feature section of the yearbook usually singles out students who have made outstanding contributions to the school, and contains material about activities students will want to remember. Some schools place a dedication in this section, while others locate the dedication in the opening section. Regardless of placement, the dedication must be as well written as possible. The student assigned to write the dedication must research his subject thoroughly. The dedication should not be maudlin, nor should it sound like a sermon: it is usually more effective when kept light, informative, and interesting. A large, excellent-quality photograph usually accompanies the dedication.

Although the feature section is an ideal place to recognize the class valedictorian and salutatorian, close deadlines often prevent knowing who will win these honors in time for inclusion in the yearbook. As an alternative, editors often consider devoting the space to students who are named as members of the National Honor Society, thus helping to present a balanced perspective at an *educational* institution. For differing reasons yearbooks all too often emphasize only the extracurricular activities.

Other features often included in the feature section are: Homecoming activities, Thanksgiving and Christmas programs, Dramatics Club productions, Student Council election and events, and special assemblies.

Organizations Section—Yearbook editors usually plan to devote a great deal of time and effort to the organizations section of the yearbook. In addition to scheduling pictures and getting accurate identifications, yearbook staff members must produce interesting, well-researched write-ups about each of the organizations in their schools.

First, staff members for the organizations section usually plan to have the yearbook photographer come to the school to spend an entire day or two taking group pictures. Schedules for such pictures are approved through the school's administrative offices and usually allow for at least a half-hour to photograph each organization. Organizations should be informed a few weeks in advance of the scheduled dates. In addition to notifying the officers of each organization, posters and newspaper notices will serve as reminders to students to be photographed. If the students don't know how they're expected to dress, they should be told. Staff members should be available at all times during the shooting schedule, and it is advisable to secure membership lists from each club or organization president or adviser to be checked a few minutes prior to the time scheduled for the organization's photograph. Staff members often have mimeographed a form that facilitates the accurate recording of identifications. Staff members should be sure that proper photograph identifications are taken before allowing a group to disband. Identifications can be double-checked with the organization's president after the photographer submits proof of the prints.

After all organizations have been photographed, the photographer should be informed that glossy prints will be needed, at least five inches by seven inches in size. When prints are delivered to the yearbook staff, great care must be taken with them. Sloppy handling can result in the emulsion cracking and the print being ruined. Prints should be filed and the organizations' names written lightly on their backs. Write-ups for each organization should be completed by the time the photographer delivers the prints. Write-ups, captions, headlines, and photos should be shown to the club president and the faculty adviser. Corrections will be unnecessary if staff members have done a responsible job.

Sports Section—The amount of space allocated to the sports section is usually determined by the degree of student interest in the various sports. While football, basketball, baseball, and track are the major sports at most schools, other sports such as ice hockey, soccer, swimming, golf, and tennis may also be stressed. Once priorities and amounts of space have been assigned for each sport, coverage should get under way. Group pictures of each team (in uniform) will, of course, be needed. The sports department of the local newspaper can often provide glossy action photos, and extensive photo coverage should be planned early in the school year. Football action pictures should be assigned early in the school year because weather conditions may be bad later in the season. If the game is played in the rain (or in snow in some regions), the pictures will not be of good quality. In the case of night football games, the photographer—using a flash or strobe attachment—should watch for end runs because his light source will be ineffective for distance shots. He may, however, take an overall view of the stadium with the team on the field by shooting at a slow exposure (about 1/10th of a second). The photographer should also watch for "color" shots: the coach on the sidelines, cheerleaders in action, spectators cheering, the band playing during halftime, and the team coming onto the field.

Yearbook basketball coverage is similar to yearbook football coverage. However, since the yearbook sports deadline is close to the basketball season, basketball action shots should be taken during the first few games of the season. Spring sports present still another problem. Because they take place after the yearbook deadline is past, some yearbooks must use pictures taken during the previous season; other yearbooks limit their coverage to posed shots of the various teams. An ideal way to handle this problem is to talk to the coaches in the fall and, since the coaches have a good idea who will be on their teams, you may be able to take posed "candid" shots of the team members.

Advertising Section—While the actual work on the yearbook's advertising section is done by members of the advertising staff, the yearbook editorial staff members can help the next year's advertising salesmen by making the advertising section as attractive and attention-getting as possible. If the advertising section doesn't look good, advertisers will often be reluctant to renew their advertisements. The introductory division page for the yearbook's advertising section might well be a general view of the community's commercial area. To eliminate distractions when taking this type of photograph, such a picture could be taken at night.

The advertising section is usually a good place for those snapshots that don't fit into any other portion of the book. Advertisers are often pleased to have such photographs included in this section, as it ensures that students will look at every page, and thus see every advertisement.

For practical reasons, the advertising section is usually one of the last sections of the yearbook to be completed. It is always advisable to plan to have a number of photographs available for fillers in this section. When advertising space is sold the photos can be replaced with advertisements, and the photographs retained when advertising space isn't sold. Many schools carry the label "Autographs" at the top of each blank page at the end of the advertising section, but also replace such blank pages with last-minute advertisements when obtainable.

Imaginative handling of the advertising section is essential because the revenue derived from it is of the utmost importance to the financial success of the yearbook.

WRITING FOR THE YEARBOOK

Since the words published in the school yearbook will live for many years, they should be chosen with the utmost care. Skilled student writers who have done well in their composition classes are usually assigned to the yearbook section according to their special interest areas and abilities (such as feature writing or sports writing). Ordinarily, the yearbook editor-in-chief will write the dedication, the foreword, and the epilogue. Reporters should interview the presidents of the various school organizations to get the facts for the stories that accompany the pictures of each school activity. The reporter should find out the group's major accomplishments, and should try to find "the story behind the story."

There is an art to the ability to summarize the year's activities of an organization in a few sentences, and yearbook writers should concentrate on learning how to say a great deal in a few, well-chosen words. Yearbook writers must also concentrate on what the organization has done during the year, supplying specific facts rather than vague generalities. All write-ups must complement the photographs, not compete with them: they should be kept concise, to-the-point, and well-written.

Because most yearbook articles are written early in the school year, writers should include activities that have not as yet taken place. When the writer interviews an organization's president, he must be sure to ask what future events the group is planning. In his writing he should mention only those activities that are definitely scheduled. Yearbook writers must be constantly aware of grammar, spelling, punctuation, and above all, accuracy. Following is an example of a write-up for a yearbook's organization section.

EXAMPLE:

One of the outstanding honors a student of Gloucester High School may receive is election to the Sherman B. Ruth Chapter of the National Honor Society. To be considered for membership, a student must exhibit not only scholarship but also leadership and character.

Each year a scholarship is awarded by the Honor Society to one of its members who plans to further his education. The organization sponsors many fund raising activities, such as selling stamps and candy. Members also act as guides for all official ceremonies held at the school. Miss Claudia Perry is the Chapter's sponsor.

Flicker
Gloucester High School
Gloucester, Massachusetts

An opportunity for creative writing is offered by such yearbook features as the foreword, the epilogue, and the dedication. Although the writer is permitted to "pull out all the stops" and let himself go, he must, at the same time, be brief and make every word count. Under the headline "BLITHE SPIRIT," the Hanover (Mass.) High School *Hanoverian* published the following dedication.

EXAMPLE:

A bubbly personality . . . an exuberant spirit . . . a zest for life and her work—the essence of the teacher whose warm heart and understanding nature have helped us bear the "slings and arrows" of our year at HHS. She was not only a teacher, but a friend. Her classes and her homerooms were always exciting. We have been guided by her friendly co-operation, her enthusiasm—and we shall remember it always. In grateful appreciation we dedicate this yearbook to Mrs. Olga Garick.

Hanoverian
Hanover High School
Hanover, Massachusetts

In the foreword, the yearbook editor-in-chief may want to establish the yearbook's theme. This is often done either by choosing an appropriate poem or by presenting the editor's own words. Choice of an appropriate poem for the foreword is usually made by the editor-in-chief in consultation with the members of his staff. The following foreword was written on the theme of "friendship."

EXAMPLE:

The students with whom we share our days and experiences are truly our friends. The strong ties among them are obviously held as the Alma Mater is sung at the assemblies and games, and there is a friendly atmosphere throughout the halls and classrooms.

A friend is, as exactly defined, more than one whom you know; he is one who answers all your needs. He brings special happiness into your life.

As we gaze at the individual pictures of all the students, we remember the joy and fun each one brought Stonewall. The great bond of friendship is truly a General Quality.

Jacksonian
Stonewall Jackson High School
Charleston, West Virginia

Class write-ups should summarize, in a concise way, the *unique* aspects of the year. How did this year differ from all the others? The following is such an example.

EXAMPLE:

BWHS's Senior Class spent their last year of high school actively participating in the many school activities of the year. Senior girls and boys served their school faithfully through the many service clubs and organizations at West High. The members of the class discovered many rewards in being upperclassmen during an exciting year of games, pep assemblies, and dances. There were disappointments such as a wet, snowy Homecoming, and triumphs such as the third consecutive victory over Senior High on the gridiron, and then finally the Senior Banquet, Senior Week, Baccalaureate, and Commencement. The Senior Class ended the last year of high school with a profitable year behind them and the future they had been preparing for throughout their years at West waiting ahead of them.

Westward
Billings West High School
Billings, Montana

Some yearbooks publish a Class Ode written by one of the senior staff members. Ordinarily, this poem summarizes the writer's philosophy of life.

EXAMPLE:

Quickly we must climb aboard,
    The ship will wait no more.
We must leave now this snug harbor
    And embark for a strange, new shore.

We must leave that which is familiar
    And sail toward what is new.
So powerlessly we watch and wait
    As our harbor fades slowly from view.

Straining, we try to recapture
    The moments which are slipping away.
But the progress of the ship is steady.
    Only memories are left us today.

We should not linger at the stern,
    For we must hurry to the bow.

Only there, we may hope to catch a glimpse
Of the new life which beckons us now.

What will this new life mean for us?
What events does it secretly hold?
Only God knows the answers
Which He will in time unfold.

For God is the weathered pilot
Guiding always our ship of time.
And in His wise hands lies the destiny
Of the crew, which is mankind.

Christine Gattinella
Westerdays
West Senior High School
Pawtucket, Rhode Island

In the Epilogue, the writer, most often the editor-in-chief, is given the opportunity to present his own Commencement Address. He is also given the chance to present his advice to the Class and to give his philosophy on life. Mary Ellen Conlon, Editor-in-chief of the Salem High School *Witch*, wrote the following:

EXAMPLE:

How difficult it is to relinquish the carefree ways of youth, and assume the responsibilities of adulthood. As a child's first steps are often unsure, so are our first ventures into the adult world. We are eager for new experience, challenges, and achievements; yet, are we ready to tuck away our youthful irresponsibility?

The era in which we live has an atmosphere of constant change. As the growing child discards toys and games, so does youth reject the ideals of adults. Time proceeds, and no segment of the population can impede progress. What we reject today as absurd and ridiculous will probably be an accepted part of our life in later years.

So we are no longer children, we must now try to assume the responsibilities of society. As we seek success in our diverse fields we shall discover it also will come in varied guises. For some individuals wealth will measure success;

others will attain power or prestige. Perhaps, our success will be the personal satisfaction derived from knowing that we have found our identity and place in a complicated society. Hopefully, success will be the attainment of happiness. This quest is the challenge of youth. As part of a perceptive generation, the Class of '68 must now accept life's challenges.

Youth contains hope for the future; awareness is the hope for youth.

Mary Ellen Conlon
The Witch
Salem High School
Salem, Massachusetts

Captions—A glance at any yearbook will show that the majority of material set in type consists of the names that are included in the captions. Every picture (even the candid snapshots) used in the book should have some sort of identification. Such identification often consists merely of labels such as "Gary and the Gang." Often, picture identifications need not be complete sentences. Usually, the more names used, the better. Captions for pictures accompanying writeups should be short, but should always contain the names of all of the persons depicted. If no write-up is used with a picture, the story should be told in a caption. Organization pictures must always have complete name identifications. If two pictures of different organizations are placed on the same page, readers might be confused as to which picture went with which write-up. To guard against this, it is advisable to precede the list of names with the name of the organization. The style for captions, determined by the editor-in-chief, should be consistent throughout the yearbook.

EXAMPLE:

HOCKEY TEAM: First Row, l. to r.; John Flahive, Don Zeilski, David Burgoyne, Robert Waugh, Bruce Tierney, Richard Critch. Second Row, l. to r.; Coach Bradley Nelson, Tom Gordon, John Ansaldo, Robert Crowe, Lennie McCabe, Duane McCormick, Norman Erskine, Sam Hickman, and Paul Wilson.

Index—Yearbooks containing more than 100 pages usually contain an index carrying the names of all organizations, activities, and persons appearing in the book. Page numbers beside each index entry should indicate the page on which material about the index entry may be found. One general index, presented as an easy-to-read reference section in which everyone is listed, is preferable to several smaller, complicated indexes. The index should be prepared from the final dummy as each section is completed, usually with each entry typed on a separate 3 x 5-inch file card. The cards are then organized alphabetically and a master list, from which the printer sets the copy, is typed from them.

ACTIVITIES

1. Write five ideas for suggested themes for your school's next yearbook.

   a. Discuss these ideas in class, comparing your theme possibilities with those of your fellow students.

   b. Select, with your fellow students, the one idea for a theme that has the most appeal to your classmates.

   c. As a class endeavor, plan ways to utilize the chosen theme in the school's next yearbook.

   d. Present the theme and its suggested usages to your yearbook committee for consideration.

2. What yearbook position do you feel you are best qualified to fill? Briefly explain why you think you could fill this position, describing the contribution you could bring to it.

3. Study a copy of last year's yearbook and make a list of suggested improvements for this year's yearbook.

4. Discuss in class any faults found with last year's yearbook and make suggestions as to how similar mistakes might be avoided in this year's book. Add these suggestions to the suggested list of improvements you made in question 3. Submit your list of suggestions to the yearbook committee.

5. Write a short article about a school organization, suitable for publication in your school's yearbook, and submit the article to the yearbook editor-in-chief for his consideration.

6. List five ideas for picture stories suitable for the opening section of this year's yearbook. Expand the listing to include suggested ways for handling the photo assignments for these picture stories.

7. Present to your yearbook committee, in outline form, a unique possibility for handling the material in the feature section of your yearbook. Be specific about suggestions for a balanced representation of both academic and extracurricular activities.

8. Write a 200-word yearbook dedication about a faculty member of your choice. Interview the subject to obtain pertinent information for inclusion in the dedication. Be sure to obtain reactions from your fellow students concerning your subject. Consider these reactions for possible inclusion in the final draft of your dedication.

READING

ALLNUT, BENJAMIN W., *Practical Yearbook Procedure*. H. G. Roebuck and Son, Inc., Baltimore, Md., 1964.

ARNOLD, EDMUND C., *Ink on Paper*. Harper & Row, New York, 1963.

———, *The Student Journalist and the Yearbook*. Richards Rosen Press, New York, 1966.

BIGGS, JOHN R., *An Approach to Type*. Farrar, Strauss and Cudahy, New York, 1952.

JOHNSON, EVE BUNNELL (Ed.), *Yearbook Fundamentals for School Publications*. Columbia Scholastic Press Association, Columbia University, New York, 1966.

LEWIS, JOHN, *Typography: Basic Principles*. Reinhold, New York, 1964. (PB)

LLOYD, IRVING, *Creative School of Photography*. American Yearbook Co., Topeka, Kan., 1962.

———, *The Photo and Its Use in Yearbook Journalism*. American Yearbook Co., Topeka, Kan., 1969.

McGIFFIN, VIDA B., AND ORISSA A. KINGSBURY, *Creating the Yearbook*. Hastings House, New York, 1962.

———, *Creative Yearbook Journalism Workbook*. Hastings House, New York, 1964.

MAGMER, JAMES, *Yearbook Editor's Workbook*. Midwest Publications, Birmingham, Mich., 1965. (PB)

———, AND FRANKLIN RONAN, *"Look" and "Life" as Guides for the Successful Yearbook Editor*. Midwest Publications, Birmingham, Mich., 1964. (PB)

MEDLIN, CALVIN J., *Planning Your Yearbook*. Iowa State University Press, Ames, Iowa, 1968. (PB)

———, *Yearbook Editing, Layout and Management*. Iowa State University Press, Ames, Iowa, 1966.

ROOT, ROBERT, *Modern Magazine Editing*. Wm. C. Brown, Dubuque, Iowa, 1966.

SAGE, KATHLEEN, *Yearbooking*. National Scholastic Press Association, Minneapolis, Minn., 1966.

SKILLIN, MARJORIE E., et al., *Words into Type*. Appleton-Century-Crofts, New York, 1964.

SPENCER, O. C., *The Art and Techniques of Yearbook Photography*. Hennington Publishing Co., Wolfe City, Texas, 1966.

WHEELER, JOHN, *Yearbook Planning* (Filmstrip). National Scholastic Press Association, Minneapolis, Minn.

WISE, DEWITT D. (Ed.), *Yearbook Fundamentals for School Publications*. Columbia Scholastic Press Association, Columbia University, New York, 1966.

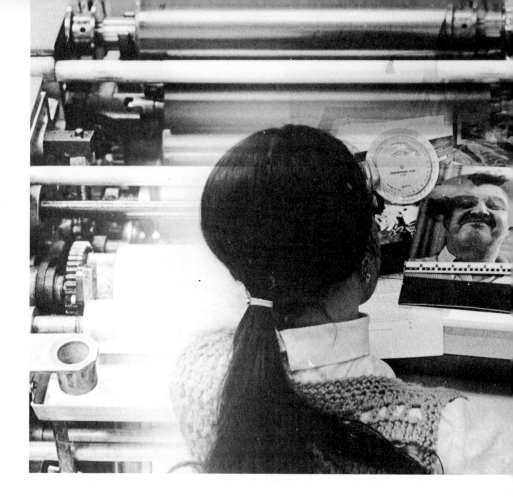

Chapter 19

Producing and Financing the School Yearbook

PRODUCING THE YEARBOOK

Once the yearbook budget has been established, the theme determined, the page size and overall number of pages decided on, and the raw materials (write-ups and photographs) for the various sections secured, the copy editor, the layout editor, and the art editor are given the opportunity to test their abilities. This phase (the actual production of the yearbook) is considered by many yearbook staff members to be the most interesting: it is also one of the most important. Carelessness and inept handling during this phase can often defeat the previous achievements of other staff members. The copy editor, concerned with polishing the raw materials, and the layout and art editors, concerned with effectively and artistically placing these raw materials in the yearbook, must, at all times, be aware of the importance of their contributions to the overall success of the book.

The first part of this chapter offers suggested procedures to be followed by the yearbook's copy, layout, and art editors in order to successfully fulfill their functions as staff members on school yearbooks, and deals primarily with the basic techniques of printing, engraving, and binding: the second part of the chapter discusses such aspects of yearbook financing as advertising, promotion, and subscription campaigns.

COPY EDITING THE YEARBOOK

The yearbook copy editors who handle write-ups, headlines, photographs, and layouts are usually the last staff members to see the material to be included in the yearbook before that material is released for printing and binding. Careless copy editing of write-ups and articles, trite headlines, improperly cropped photographs, sloppy layouts, and poor proofreading can ruin any yearbook.

Following Style

Feature articles, write-ups, captions, and headlines must be edited to conform to the established style set up for the yearbook as well as to the accepted standards of formal grammar. In addition to checking spelling, grammar, and sentence structure, copy editors should attempt to eliminate expressions that are trite, juvenile, or that contain clichés. Copy editors must know the amount of copy necessary to fill each page and, because write-ups about the various school organizations are best kept to consistent lengths, must often shorten articles that run too long: if an article is too short, the copy editor must turn writer-reporter and add more facts. Thorough copy editors, assets to any yearbook staff, follow the copy-editing procedures described in Chapter 17, "Producing and Financing the School Newspaper." Standard copy-editing symbols are contained in Appendix X at the end of this book.

Proofreading

Because the yearbook copy editors are usually the last staff members to see the final yearbook materials before the materials are released for printing and binding, yearbook copy editors have the additional responsibility of proofreading all final copy. In proofreading final copy, proofreaders and copy editors should be aware that changes made on final galley proof are costly and can often introduce further errors. It is always wise to keep in mind that it is better not to rewrite merely for the sake of rewriting: if a sentence is acceptable as it stands, it should be left as is. The work involved in unnecessary rewriting takes time and often demoralizes staff writers. The standard proofreading symbols used by most yearbook proofreaders are contained in Appendix IX at the end of this book.

Writing Headlines

Before making decisions on the type of headlines to be written for each group portrayed in the yearbook, copy editors must know the total number of pages planned for the book. When more than one organization is placed on each page because of space limitations, copy editors often use, with the pictures for each organization, a headline consisting of only the organization's name. When each group is allocated an entire page, more creative, lengthier headlines and kicker lines can be considered. Once the headline type sizes have been selected, the maximum count for each headline should be determined (the count refers to the total number of letters and spaces contained in a line of print). A simplified count of one unit for each letter and space is usually acceptable. For example, if a 36-point type face is selected for many of the yearbooks' headlines, the editor might decide that each headline should be between 20 to 25 units in length.

When writing headlines, copy editors should try to prepare interesting phrases that "swing" but that aren't juvenile, trite, or cliché. Headline writers often try to be unique in their presentations by using portions of well-known sayings, popular songs, or alliteration. Headline writers sometimes find they don't have enough room for necessary verbs: they then try to "peg" the headline to the accomplishments of the group being written about. Following an undefeated basketball season one school headlined its yearbook basketball squad's picture page with "Quite a Quintet!" Another school used "Miami's Math Marvels" above a picture of its math club, and "The 'Reel' McCoys" was used with the picture of an audio-visual club. Other examples of unique yearbook headlines are: "A Goalie's Nightmare," "The Groups Behind the Teams," "Thespians of the Future," "Latin Linguists," and "Neophyte Nurses."

Cropping Photos

Since the largest portion of space in yearbooks is devoted to photographs, establishing the correct proportions for photographs is of major importance in yearbook production. When the copy editor has decided on the layout for a given page, he should instruct the photographer to print photographs in dimensions that will enhance the page layout. If the editor has access only to a vertical photograph when he needs a horizontal shape to suit the format, the layout may suffer. A good practice is to encourage photographers to take several photographs, each one from a different angle, in order to present a choice of sizes suitable for use with differing formats.

Once the photograph to be used has been selected, the copy editor must indicate any of the unnecessary portions not to be printed. To do this, he usually makes grease-pencil crop marks (delete marks) to indicate the portions to be deleted. The pencilled crop marks enable the engraver to reduce or enlarge the remainder of the print to the specified size, giving emphasis

Photographs reduce proportionately in height and width. The measurements of the rectangle I-G-B-H will be the measurements for the reduced print.

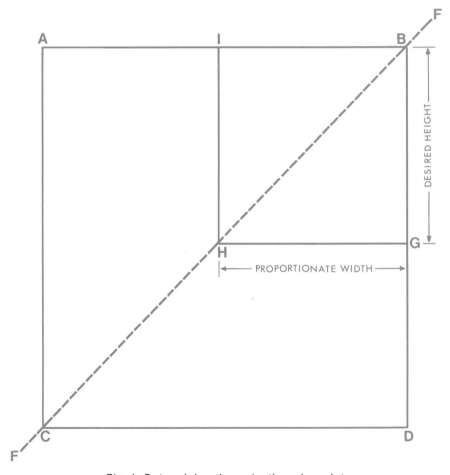

Fig. 1. Determining the reduction of a print.

428

to the most important, remaining area of the photograph. When too much of the photograph has been marked for cropping, it is often necessary to have the photographer reprint, reproducing only the area specified. If an engraver enlarges from a photograph that has been cropped too much, the quality of the remainder of the photograph may be endangered. After cropping, the copy editor must determine the amount of space the engraving will occupy on the page. When a photograph is reduced in height, it reduces proportionately in width. Fig. 1 on page 428 shows how the width and height of a photograph are affected when the original is proportionately reduced. In Fig. 1, A, B, C, and D represent the four corners of the photograph. The measurements for a reduction can be determined by drawing a ruled line diagonally across the back of the photograph (dotted line E-F) and marking off the desired height of the engraving (G-B), and drawing from the bottom of that point (G) a horizontal line (G-H) that intersects the ruled dotted line (E-F), then drawing a vertical line (H-I) to the top of the print. The measurements of the rectangle (I-B-G-H) will be the measurements for the reduced print.

Next, the exact size of the engraving is drawn in location on the page layout. The final size is marked lightly on the back of the print (or pasted so that the front of the print is not harmed). The picture should be checked against its caption to make sure that both are accurate and, for identification purposes, the picture, its caption, and the layout should each be coded with the same coding symbol, letter, or number. Once the page layouts are completed, the pictures can be sent to the engraver and the picture captions and page layouts to the printer. Photographic enlargements are seldom used in yearbooks because reproduced enlargements often lose their detail and are not as sharp as photographic reductions.

LAYING OUT THE YEARBOOK

Just as an architect works with wood, stone, and space to plan a building, a layout editor works with pictures, type, and space to plan his yearbook layout. Both the architect and the layout editor are artists: there is an art to handling yearbook layout elements, and yearbook layout editors, using artistic skills, have the opportunity to create an artistic achievement. In every school there are students who have a creative and artistic flair. These students have an instinctive knack for effectively placing the layout elements on a page, and an inherent sense of order and simplicity. They are aware that the three elements mentioned in writing for the yearbook—unity, coherence, and emphasis—should be stressed when laying out the yearbook.

Unity

A theme and a consistent style for layouts help a yearbook achieve unity. Usually, to further ensure unity, layout editors work on facing pages at the same time, using a uniform amount of copy, headlines, and pictures on each page, making the layouts for each section similar in general style. The editor-in-chief can be helpful by setting up a few rules of thumb: for example, he can establish that not more than three pictures, six sentences, or one headline may be used on any one page. He might also decide on the physical boundaries for photographic layouts suggesting that whenever possible the edges of pictures be aligned. He might further decide that a definite margin should be maintained with at least one photo touching this predetermined margin at least once on each two-page spread. In the style shown in Fig. 2, below, the pictures are squared off with the margins. If the editor-in-chief prefers to bleed pictures (extend the pictures beyond the margins to the edge of the page), he might decide that photos ought not to bleed more than once from each edge of a two-page spread (see Fig. 3, below). Fig. 4, below, shows the variety that can be achieved by using equal-sized layout elements three different ways.

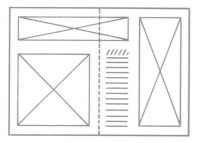

Fig. 2. Layout with photos.

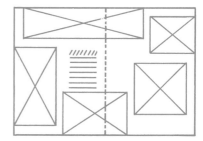

Fig. 3. Layout with bleed photos.

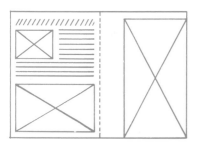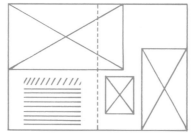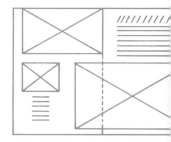

Fig. 4. Three layouts using equal-size elements.

430

Coherence

With yearbook page layouts, coherence can be said to be synonymous with balance. For example, a skilled layout editor would rarely face a full-page picture with a three-inch square picture: the pages would not be balanced. Some layout editors think of a two-page spread, imagining that a fulcrum has been placed at the bottom center of the pages: when a layout element is placed on one of the pages, that page will tip down. To equalize the pages, an element having approximately the same "weight" is placed on the opposite page. For example, layout editors consider that photos with predominantly dark tones have more weight than do lighter pictures having light backgrounds, and equalize (or anchor) pages by placing the darker pictures on the bottom. They can then locate the "lighter" elements on the page above a heavy, strong element.

Emphasis

Because the most important elements on a page should be the ones to attract immediate attention, layout editors accomplish emphasis by making the most important elements the largest elements on the page. Photographs can be emphasized by presenting them as strong horizontal and vertical shapes, avoiding square compositions (the least effective shape). Standard size photos (4 x 5, 5 x 7, or 8 x 10 inches) can usually be cropped to make the most important parts of their compositions more forceful.

In order to ensure that the principles of unity, coherence, and emphasis have been followed, yearbook editors-in-chief should go over all page layouts before the layouts are released for printing. Often, some layouts will have to be redone. When it becomes necessary to redo layouts, the person who did the original should be shown what was wrong and how it should have been done.

Formal and Informal Balance

The two basic layout patterns used in most yearbooks are called formal and informal. (See Figs. 5 and 6.) White both patterns use the same basic layout elements—type, pictures, and white space—each of these patterns is distinctly different from the other. With formal balance, a page can be said to be a reversed reflection of the page it faces. The advantage to using a formal layout pattern is that such a pattern assures that the yearbook will have unity in visual appearance. The disadvantages to using a formal layout pattern are that the layouts can often look static and lifeless and the use of photos is limited (layout editors may have difficulty finding a photo suited to the shape needed for a page).

With informal balance, the layout elements for each page (while often retaining similar weights) are not placed in an identical pattern. The chief advantage to using an informal layout pattern is flexibility. For example, on a two-page spread the layout editor, not having to conform to the standard photo sizes imposed by formal layout patterns, can better emphasize the most important picture on the spread by making it a completely different size than any other photo on the spread.

Many layout editors prefer allowing the photos to dictate, at least to a degree, the final outcome of the two-page spread, rather than having a preconceived pattern worked out before seeing the actual pictures. Studying the layouts in such publications as *The Family of Man, Life,* and *Look* can give layout editors helpful ideas for their yearbook layouts. Many mass media layout editors use more headlines and type on the left-hand pages than they do on the right-hand pages because the reader's eye is conditioned to read from left to right.

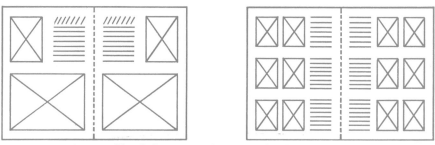

Fig. 5. Layouts using formal balance.

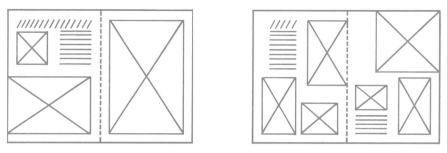

Fig. 6. Layouts using informal balance.

432

School yearbooks, the creations of student artists who create with words, cameras, and layouts, reflect the degree of student enthusiasm, talent, creativity, and intelligence available at the schools they represent. Each step taken to help produce the yearbook must be carefully weighed and considered: only when each member of the yearbook's staff conscientiously performs to the best of his ability can the yearbook be something the school can be proud of.

SUGGESTED DEADLINE SCHEDULE
FOR YEARBOOK EDITORS

Spring—The editor-in-chief, with the help of the adviser, should select a printer, a professional photographer, and key yearbook staff members. The editor-in-chief will need at least three key assistants: a business manager to oversee the advertising and subscription sales, a managing editor to supervise the writing and photographic assignments, and an art editor to supervise page layouts. Special concern is necessary when choosing photographers: a poorly written news story can be successfully edited, but a poorly taken photograph must be discarded.

Summer—The editor-in-chief should schedule meetings with the yearbook managing editor, art editor, and business manager. A proposed budget, based on the predicted number of advertisements and subscriptions, should be established. Some picture assignments can be made during the summer. Pictorial shots (of the school campus) and many color pictures can be made at this time. With the art editor, the editor-in-chief should study other school yearbooks to help get ideas for the theme, format, division pages, and opening section. The editor-in-chief may also want to prepare contracts for the printer, photographer, and cover manufacturer. The managing editor and the business editor should propose the names of their suggested staff members. The summer preceding the opening of school is the best time to get as much preliminary planning done as possible.

September—With such demands on their time as class routine and homework, yearbook staff members should carefully plan and schedule the time they will have available for work on the yearbook. Once all of the staff vacancies have been filled, the editor-in-chief should call a staff meeting to discuss the overall plan for the book, attempting to inspire enthusiasm on the part of the staff members. Each staffer must understand his job. After reviewing the yearbook's general format, the editor-in-chief should divide the staff into groups to allow the managing editor, art editor, and business manager to discuss assignments with their assistants.

CHECKLIST FOR YEARBOOK LAYOUT EDITORS

1. As soon as the yearbook editor-in-chief and adviser establish a stylesheet and the ground rules for layouts, begin working on rough, thumbnail sketches for each two-page spread in the section that has been assigned to you.
2. As soon as layout sketches have been completed for all pages in your assigned section, review them for consistency of picture sizes, headline sizes, and length to copy.
3. Discuss the layout sketches with the editor-in-chief, the yearbook adviser, or the designated staff member.
4. Redo the layout sketches as necessary, transferring approved layout sketches to final layout sheets.
5. Be exact. When a photograph is to be bled into the margin, the layout *must* so indicate.
6. Sketch in all headlines exactly as they are worded.
7. Mark every copy block and picture indicated on the layout. Work with each two-page spread until every element has been located in its desired position.
8. On the layout, mark the first picture on the left-hand page as "Picture *A*," the next one as Picture *B*, etc. Also mark (or attach) these same identifications on the backs of each picture. Each block of copy should be similarly marked with a code symbol, letter, or number, both on the page layout and on the copy itself.
9. Print the page numbers at the bottoms of all layout pages, keeping a record of all of the materials that have been placed on each of the pages.
10. Secure final approval for the layouts and send them, with their accompanying pictures, copy, and headlines, to the printer.

October—The exact number of pages in the book should be determined, based on the business manager's quotes for advertisements and subscriptions. Staff members who are not serious about their assignments should be weeded out. Preliminary sketches for the cover design should be selected and sent to the cover manufacturer. Photographs showing the opening of school, freshmen, football action, etc., should be submitted. The budget should be reviewed with the business manager and adviser to see if any item is out-of-line.

434

November—Subscriptions, advertisements, copy, and pictures should be pouring in by now. November is often the staff's busiest month. The managing editor should be concerned with expediting initial copy and photographs to the printer, keeping in mind that he cannot let yearbook material pile up. As soon as yearbook items have been approved, he must either deliver them personally or put them in the mail. This is the ideal month in which to take class and organizations section pictures. Seniors should begin having their portraits taken at this time. Candid photos of parties, assemblies, and Thanksgiving programs should be taken. The football section can be closed out now. The staff should also have some idea about how close they are to achieving the goals of the circulation drive.

December—Unless you planned for this short school month well in advance, December may throw the yearbook staff behind schedule. Several sections should be finished prior to the Christmas Holiday: the opening section, the faculty section, the class section, and the organizations section. Cover and end pages can be released. The fall sports portion of the sports section can be completed, and more than half of the yearbook should be at the printers. The editor-in-chief should plan a meeting with his art editor, managing editor, and business manager during the holidays in order to determine what remains to be completed. At this meeting the editor-in-chief should also determine exactly how many advertisements remain to be processed, as well as the exact number of subscriptions and advertisements the staff has sold to date. The results of this information should help to determine an approximate price for the yearbook.

January—Galley proof for copy, captions, photos, and advertisements should be returned to the printer in January. All material should be proofread carefully, and checked for typographical errors. If the proof for an engraving is bad, discuss possible solutions with the engraver. He may be able to replace the plate with another one of better quality. Winter events such as plays, musicals, and social functions can be photographed. The yearbook salesmen should make their last rounds of potential advertisers.

February—The advertising sales should be completed. Page numbers should be located at the bottom of each dummy page. Galley proof should be checked, with special consideration being given to the spelling of names. The sports section can be completed, with the exception of one page that can be put aside for inclusion of last-minute sports events (such as the winning of a tournament by the basketball team). Spring activity pictures should be sent to the printer. By the end of this month only the remaining few pages of the yearbook should be left to be closed out.

March—Early in March the remaining pages should be released to the printer who should be consulted to ensure that *everything* has been received. Final galley proof must be checked and final plans for distribution of the book can be made. If the printer suggests a paste-up printer's dummy as a guide, the dummy can be done in March. The dummy can also serve as a check on whether or not the printer has received all of the yearbook material. Spring sport and activity assignments can be made to the photographers of *next* year's book.

April—Final page proof should be checked to ensure that captions have been placed under the proper pictures and that no picture has been lost. Page proof must be checked for typographical errors and returned early in the month. Subscription sales should be carefully re-checked in order to determine the number of copies to be printed. It is always wise to plan to have about twenty extra copies printed to avoid the possibility of not having enough yearbooks to distribute.

May—First copies of the completed yearbook should be available, and the most efficient method of distribution should be decided on. Dependable staff members should be assigned to distribute the copies, making sure that everyone who has paid for a copy receives one. All bills should be checked and paid. A meeting with the staff members of next year's yearbook could be planned in order to discuss with them helpful suggestions and advice.

WORKING WITH THE PRINTER

The companies that print school yearbooks can usually be divided into two general groups: local and national. The major advantage to using a local printer is accessibility: yearbook materials can be dropped off at a local printing shop, thus saving mailing time and because the local printer usually knows everyone in the community he will hope to maintain his reputation by doing the best job possible. Local printers are better able to discuss immediate problems, and deadlines can usually be more easily extended because finished books don't have to be shipped long distances. Yearbook staffers have the opportunity to learn about printing from a local printer by observing his work on each section of the yearbook. Local printers, however, must often charge more than a specialized, national yearbook printing company does because local printers usually aren't set up to mass produce yearbooks. For example, because printing presses are expensive and better processes are constantly being developed, small print shops often cannot afford to keep up with the newest equipment and production techniques. The advantages for choosing a national printer are the lower production costs and the quality obtained by his use of the latest production techniques.

The yearbook editors-in-chief and advisers should plan to spend some time during the summer talking to both local printers and to representatives of the national yearbook printing companies. They should discuss the cost-per-page per 100 books, quality, and deadlines schedules, comparing yearbooks produced by both. It is advisable to talk to editors of other schools to discuss the advantages of choosing one type of printer over the other. When judging sample yearbooks presented by the printer's representative, consider such factors as the following: Are the pictures uniform? Does the ink seem to be darker on some pages than it seems on others? Are the engravings washed out? Were parts of pictures at the tops and bottoms of pages cut when the paper was trimmed? Are the captions and headlines set in typefaces that look attractive? The production cost per book may seem high and will, of course, vary considerably depending on the section of the country it is printed in, the printing process, the current cost of supplies, and whether it is produced by a union or non-union shop. The cost will also vary depending on the page size of the book. The most common yearbook size is 8½ x 11 inches: however, both smaller and larger formats are available. When determining the page size it is helpful to know the total number of pages to be included. Because a 250-page 7¾ x 10½-inch yearbook will be too bulky, it would be preferable to consider fewer pages in a 9 x 12-inch size. The printer can be of great help when deciding on the page size.

YEARBOOK PRINTING METHODS

Imagine producing a yearbook if you lived prior to the Fifteenth Century: for each book you would have to draw by hand each illustration as well as write in each headline, write-up, and caption. If you were to produce a yearbook using this painstaking process, you might come to resent every illustration and word that did not contribute to the total impact of the book. Today, while being spared from such a tedious chore because of technological advances in printing and production processes, it is still advisable to make every word and picture included in the yearbook contribute to the total impact of the book.

The two major printing processes used to produce school yearbooks are letterpress and photo offset. The trend is toward the latter: of the 1,253 entries submitted in a recent Columbia Scholastic Yearbook Competition, the vast majority were produced by the photo offset method.

Letterpress

As its name implies, in the letterpress process each "letter" to be reproduced is cast in metal and "pressed" against paper. Most newspapers and many magazines and books are published by this process. This process is also known as "hot type" because the metal—usually lead—is melted and forced into matrices (molds), thus casting the letter in relief (similar to the raised letters on a rubber stamp). Each photograph is engraved on a metal plate—zinc, but sometimes copper—by etching away with acid the non-printing areas so that only the printing image stands high enough to receive ink. All makeup elements—headlines, type, and photoengravings—are then assembled and placed into page forms. Following the yearbook page layouts, the printer places each of the makeup elements into metal page forms exactly as indicated on the layout. The page forms are then placed on a flat-bed printing press, inked, and pressed against large sheets of paper (see Fig. 7). These printed sheets are stored until all of the yearbook pages are printed. Then they are cut, collated, bound together, and placed within the yearbook cover.

Photo Offset

The "cold type" photo offset printing method reproduces type and pictures electronically. Special machines (similar to electric typewriters) reproduce, on enamel-coated white paper, all headlines, write-ups, and captions in the type faces, sizes, and lengths desired. These makeup elements are then pasted onto a master dummy-page as indicated on the layout, leaving blanks (or windows) for the photos and artwork. Negatives are made from the page dummy by photographing the page dummy on a reproduction camera. The glossy photographs and artwork are photographed separately through a halftone screen (as they are in the letterpress process) to convert the continuous tone image into a series of small dots. Although they cannot be seen without the help of a magnifying glass, these dots produce the light, dark, and medium tones of the printed picture. The completed halftone negatives (which may have been reduced or enlarged) are next stripped (or located) into the windowed areas on the negatives already made from the paste-up dummy of the yearbook pages. Then, in negative form, the pages are joined together to form what is called a flat.

Printing plates are made from the flats (combined negatives) by exposing the negatives onto aluminum plates in a vacuum frame. The aluminum plate, which is coated with a light-sensitive coating in order to pick up the image from the negative when exposed to light, is then coated with a chemical preservative before being placed on the printing press.

438

Offset printing is based on the adage that water and grease won't mix. While the plate receives the ink, the plate does not deposit the ink directly onto the paper. The plate prints its design onto a rubber blanket which, in turn, transfers the design onto the paper (see Fig. 8).

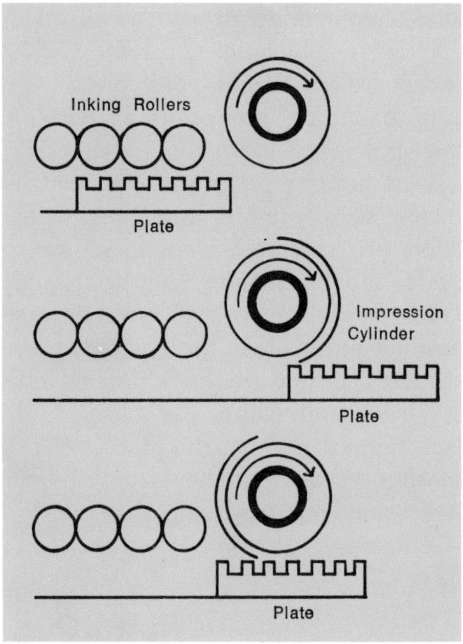

Fig. 7. Flat-bed cylinder press.

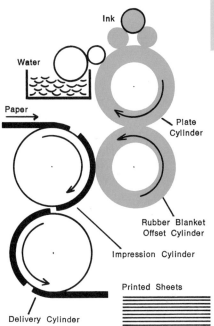

Fig. 8. Offset printing press.

Use of Color in Yearbooks

The printing process chosen (letterpress or offset) becomes more complicated when it is decided to use color in the yearbook: the printing flat must be run through the press an additional time for each color used. However, a total of four times through is all that is necessary to reproduce all colors: different combinations of red, yellow, and blue produce all of the secondary colors. A four-color picture (such as used in quality magazines) must go through the printing press four times to receive red, blue, yellow, and black inks.

Most printers prefer working with 4 x 5 or 2¼ x 2¼-inch color transparencies: some printers are able to use 35mm transparencies. The primary colors are separated from these transparencies in a complex process and made into black-and-white prints, one print for each color to be used. These "separation prints" are then made into engravings or negatives, depending on whether the printing process is letterpress or offset. Yearbook printers can help yearbook staff members decide on how to most effectively use black and white, tint blocked, duotoned, and one-color photographs (see Fig. 9). Because the process of printing in color is complex, it is an expensive process that should only be considered for yearbooks having financially sound budgets.

YEARBOOK COVERS

Although they may often be misleading, first impressions can also be lasting impressions. For this reason most yearbook staffers prefer covers that are modern, creative, or unique. The three basic types of yearbook covers are: hard, padded, and paper. Most yearbooks use hard covers because their stiff, fiberboard construction offers durability. The least-expensive type of yearbook cover, the paper cover, is used only for books having fewer than 100 pages. Paper covers are manufactured from heavy-weight paper stock.

Regardless of the type of material chosen for the cover, a cover layout, prepared by a yearbook staff member, must be submitted to the cover manufacturer. The layout is then readied for printing by an artist employed by the manufacturer. The yearbook cover design need not be elaborate: some of the best yearbook covers use only the name of the book and the school seal. Others try to work in an idea based on the theme of the book.

While local printers usually have covers produced by outside cover manufacturers, most national yearbook publishing organizations manufacture

BLACK and WHITE   TINT BLOCK

Fig. 9. Four reproductions of the same photograph.

DUOTONE   ONE COLOR

their own. These companies usually suggest the use of a standard type cover that is relatively inexpensive but similar in design to covers used by other schools throughout the country. Standard covers provide blank areas in which are printed the different school seals, titles, and dates.

Costs of covers can range from about fifty cents each to over one dollar each. If the yearbook budget permits, embossed, silk-screen, or four-color photographic covers might be considered. These types of covers are considerably more expensive than standard covers.

FINANCING THE YEARBOOK

Just as the costs for producing the yearbook can vary depending on price fluctuations, the income for producing the yearbook can also vary depending on the sources of income at different schools. At most schools, yearbooks are financed through subscriptions, advertising, clubs, activity fees, and picture sales. Some yearbooks, however, carry no advertising, do not charge clubs to have their pictures included, and do not sell the pictures at the end of the school year. For example, one school yearbook that didn't sell advertising space or have access to student activity fees showed a profit of $216 after selling for only $2.75 per copy. This particular school's yearbook budget was as follows:

INCOME		EXPENDITURES	
Subscription sales =	$3,876	Printing 1,360 136-page	
Club fees =	490	books =	$2,636
Picture sales =	702	Engraving =	1,300
Miscellaneous income =	214	Covers =	858
Total =	$5,282	Miscellaneous =	271
		Total =	$5,065

The Budget

The yearbook business manager must know how much money is needed to produce the yearbook and how that money is to be obtained. His budget must be set up and approved early in the school year. Staff members incurring expenses that affect the yearbook budget should clear such expenses through the business manager who should, at all times, know the exact amount of the expenditures contracted for to date, the balance available, and the possibility of situations that might cause expenditures in excess of budget allowances. He might well consider setting up a form similar to the

SUGGESTED YEARBOOK BUDGET FORM

Name of Book _____   Date _____

INCOME

    CIRCULATION _____

    ADVERTISING _____

    ACTIVITY FEE _____

    PATRONS _____

    CLUB FEES _____

    PICTURE SALES (PROJECTED) _____

    TOTAL INCOME _____

EXPENDITURES

    PRINTING _____

    COVERS _____

    ENGRAVINGS OR NEGATIVES _____

    PHOTOGRAPHY _____

    BINDING _____

    OFFICE COSTS _____

    MISCELLANEOUS EXPENSE _____

    TOTAL EXPENSES _____

_____
Business Manager

Suggested Yearbook Budget Form shown on page 443 for bi-monthly submission to the editor-in-chief and adviser.

The business manager should make sure that yearbook staff members are aware of ways to help save money. Among these are the following:

Meeting deadlines—Printers operate on tight schedules and must stagger their work loads in order to accommodate work that has been received off-schedule. When the printer's schedule is not met, the printer must double-up on his work, often having to charge extra for overtime. Such overtime increases the production costs of the yearbook.

Editing copy correctly the first time—If, after the copy has been set in type, it is noticed that there are several misspellings, such misspellings must be corrected. The printer, having to reset the copy, must charge extra for such alterations. Such alterations are called *author's alterations.*

Knowing how many photos are needed—Photographic equipment and supplies are expensive. If 300 photos are assigned when only 200 are needed, the overall costs for photography will, of course, be higher than necessary.

Being aware of production costs—When yearbook editors consider using student artwork, they should be aware that such material usually involves a much greater expense than does the use of photographs. Knowing what the yearbook production costs are, and keeping within these costs is an important part of each yearbook staff member's job.

YEARBOOK ADVERTISING

Yearbook advertising space salesmen are often faced with the fact that some potential advertisers will need to be convinced of the value of yearbook advertising. Other potential advertisers, aware that lifetime buying habits are often formed during school years, are more easily convinced. Yearbook advertising space salesmen, aware of these differences, must plan their sales campaigns to conform to the individual needs of the advertiser being contacted. Ideally, the yearbook advertising salesman will have prepared at least two advertising layouts before calling on a potential advertiser, asking that the customer suggest a preference. Only unimaginative advertising space salesmen ask clients to run congratulatory advertisements such as "Compliments of Ace Garage." Advertising salesmen, when drawing up proposed advertising layouts for clients, should keep in mind the following basic suggestions:

Attention—The advertisement should immediately capture the prospective buyer's attention. The copy and any illustrations should be planned to gain the attention of the intended consumer audience.

Interest—The headline, illustration, and body copy should capture and hold the consumer's interest.

Conviction—The advertisement should convince the consumer that what is being advertised is ideal for him.

Desire—The advertisement should inspire the desire to purchase the advertised product.

Action—The total effect of the advertisement should be to encourage the consumer to obtain the advertised product as soon as possible.

Yearbook advertising managers may want to train space salesmen in effective selling techniques. Because potential advertisers will be impressed —one way or the other—by student salesmen, the salesmen must always keep in mind that they are representing their schools and should conduct themselves in as professional and businesslike a way as possible. They might consider preplanning their sales talks, and should always arrive on time for appointments with potential advertisers.

Yearbook Advertising Rates

Yearbook advertising rates should be based on per-page production costs. It is financially unsound to sell a full-page advertisement for $50 if it costs $100 to add that page to the yearbook: it is equally unsound if the production cost per page is $50 and the advertising rate is the same—nothing is gained by advertising. A general rule is that a full page of advertising must not only pay for itself, but for another page (without advertising) as well. Determining the advertising rate, patron fees, and subscriptions are discussed in Chapter 18, "Organizing and Editing the School Yearbook."

YEARBOOK PROMOTION CAMPAIGNS

The yearbook promotion manager works with members of the staffs of both the advertising and subscription departments. Placing posters throughout the school to announce subscription drives, and planning yearbook promotional activities such as dances, bake sales, or contests are the types of activities of concern to yearbook promotion managers whose job is to publicize the yearbook and solicit funds to defray production expenses. Yearbook promotion managers also concern themselves with supplying information about how, when, and where members of the student body may obtain copies of the yearbook.

The school newspaper is often used by promotion managers to present news, feature stories, and pictures that publicize the yearbook.

YEARBOOK SUBSCRIPTION CAMPAIGNS

When subscription sales are planned to completely compensate for the yearbook, any income derived from advertising can then provide for extra, more expensive touches such as quality covers and color printing. Because subscription sales should provide the yearbook with its major source of revenue, they should receive the greatest emphasis.

A yearbook staff planning to conduct a subscription-sales drive should schedule the drive soon after the beginning of school with subscription salesmen being assigned to contact each student organization, teacher, and alumni group. Such a drive must be coordinated with the promotional campaign: poor organization and bad timing can result in the loss of sales. Usually the most effective selling for a subscription drive is last year's yearbook.

A second major subscription drive can be held early in the spring. The yearbook staff should make sure the drive doesn't conflict with other school events. Members of the student body should be made aware that this is the final deadline for ordering yearbook copies. All members of the student body can be contacted by obtaining from the administrative office a list of the names of the entire student body. Those students who ordered during the first drive can be eliminated from the list, and plans can be made to contact the others personally or by memo. While a successful subscription sales campaign can often result in an ideal 100 percent sale of yearbooks to the members of the student body, a sale of over 85 percent is usually considered satisfactory enough to meet the costs for producing the yearbook.

ACTIVITIES

1. Obtain the page size of your yearbook and cut out a piece of white paper with similar dimensions. Then, from colored construction paper, cut out several rectangles and blocks to represent yearbook makeup elements (copy and photographs). Arrange the makeup elements on the white paper in as

visually pleasing a manner as possible. When you are pleased with the results, paste them down. Compare your layouts with those made by your fellow students. Select the three best.

2. Try to improve on the layouts of two sections from last year's yearbook by drawing new layout sketches of a two-page spread for each of the sections.

3. Using the copyreading symbols given in Appendix X, edit a magazine feature story of your choice.

4. Cut five small headshots from a magazine. Using as a basis the magazine caption material that accompanied each of the photographs, prepare "yearbook type" captions for each.

5. Using the headshots and caption material you prepared in the preceding question, paste up a yearbook page layout with headlines, kicker lines, and page numbers.

6. Clip a vertical photograph (at least 5 x 7-inches in size) from a magazine. By proportionately reducing and cropping the picture, give the picture a horizontal format.

READING

BERRY, WILLIAM TURNER, A. F. JOHNSON, AND W. P. JASPERT, *The Encyclopedia of Type Faces*. Pitman, New York, 1962.

DAIR, CARL, *Design with Type*. University of Toronto Press, Toronto, Ontario, Canada, 1965.

HLASTA, STANLEY C., *Printing Types and How to Use Them*. Carnegie Press, Carnegie-Mellon University, Pittsburgh, Pa., 1950.

JACKSON, HARTLEY EVERETT, *Printing: A Practical Introduction to the Graphic Arts*. McGraw-Hill, New York, 1957.

KARCH, R. RANDOLPH, *Graphic Arts Procedures: Offset Processes, Strike-On and Film Composition*. American Technical Society, Chicago, Ill., 1965.

LATIMER, H. C., *Advertising Production Planning and Copy Preparation for Offset Printing*. Art Directions Book Co., New York, 1969.

LONGYEAR, WILLIAM, *Type and Lettering*. Watson-Guptil Publications, New York, 1966.

McCARTHY, HELEN M., *Advertising in School Publications*. Columbia Scholastic Press Association, Columbia University, New York.

TARDY, WILLIAM THOMAS, *Money-Making Ideas for School Yearbooks*. Banks Upshaw & Co., Skokie, Ill.

UNIVERSITY OF CHICAGO PRESS, *A Manual of Style*. University of Chicago Press, Chicago, Ill., 1969.

WRIGHT, GLEN, *The Student Journalist and Making Advertising Pay for the School Publication*. Richards Rosen Press, New York, 1968.

Chapter 20

Organizing and Writing the School Literary Publication

THE STUDENT VOICE

The rich and noble heritage of literary publications in this country's schools can be traced back to 1777—less than a year after the signing of the Declaration of Independence. Although there are no existing copies of the first issue of our country's earliest school journal, *The Students' Gazette* (dated June, 1777), other copies produced later in the same year have survived. *The Students' Gazette*, hand-written by students at the William Penn Charter School in Philadelphia, was not limited to school news alone: one of its first articles discussed "The many Disturbances which have arisen in this State," thus bringing about the start of our tradition for student comment on social, moral, and political issues. Fifty years after the founding of *The Students' Gazette*, the first printed school publication, *The Literary Journal*, was launched on May 9, 1829, at the Boston Latin School.

Today, thousands of literary publications are written and produced by students throughout the country. These student publications provide a voice

449

for students interested in literary expression, the opportunity to read works of literary value written by other students, and a practical application for the development of writing skills and language abilities in an informal atmosphere. The student writers and editors who work on school literary magazines also learn to accept and evaluate constructive criticism.

Purpose of School Literary Publications

In order to justify their existence, school literary publications should serve, in completely different ways than school newspapers and yearbooks, a definite purpose for both the members of the student body and the school itself. To accomplish this, school literary publications should:

1. Present a balanced offering of top-quality, tasteful material that will be of genuine literary value to the members of the student body, the faculty, and the community.

2. Aid in teaching literary publication staff members technical competency, discrimination, and good taste.

3. Make literary publication staff members aware of the positive effects of the printed word.

4. Achieve the widest possible distribution at the lowest possible price.

TYPES OF SCHOOL LITERARY PUBLICATIONS

While the scope of school literary publications varies considerably, most school literary publications can be categorized under any one of the following three general classifications:

Literary-art Oriented—Most school literary publications are literary-art oriented. Contents include (almost exclusively) poetry, plays, fictional short stories, artwork, and creative photography. Nonfiction articles are excluded.

Combination Literary Magazine-Newspaper—While many combination literary magazine-newspaper publications use high-quality illustrations on their covers, the contents often consist of interview features, sports features, and feature news stories of interest to members of the student body. The combination literary magazine-newspaper also features poetry, artwork, and fiction in special sections.

Miscellaneous—The school year's final issue for many literary publications appears as a yearbook supplement in the spring. The yearbook literary supplement usually contains coverage of the school activities and events that took place after the final yearbook deadline. Graduation events, spring sports, and student awards are the subjects most often written about and photographed for the yearbook literary supplement. Some school literary publications devote complete issues to artwork and photography, humor, or to creative class writing projects. Titled *53 Voices on Little Red Riding Hood*, a special issue of the literary magazine produced by Notre Dame High School, West Haven, Connecticut, contained fifty-three rewritten versions of the well-known children's story, each version imitating a famous writer or distinctive literary style.

ORGANIZATION OF SCHOOL LITERARY PUBLICATIONS

The staff of the school literary publication usually consists of an editor-in-chief, associate editor, layout editor, an editor for each of the sections in the publication (section editors), business manager, advertising manager, circulation manager, promotion manager, illustrators, proofreaders, and typists (see chart on page 454). The editor-in-chief, who delegates responsibility for each section to the section editors, is responsible to the literary publication's adviser.

Editor-in-chief—The editor-in-chief has the overall responsibility for every aspect connected with the production of his publication. Working with the adviser, associate editor, and business manager, he helps determine format, choice of printer, number of pages per issue, number of issues, and price per issue. In conference with section editors he helps make content decisions on theme, percentage of poetry and drama, percentage of fiction and nonfiction, artwork and photos to be used, and helps establish policy on any other general types of editorial materials to be used.

Associate Editor—The associate editor and the copy editors have the responsibility for editing all articles and captions, writing titles and headlines, and assigning the type and layout specifications for any poetry and articles to be illustrated.

Layout Editor—After all of the material to be printed has been selected and edited, and after the artwork has been submitted, the layout editor and his staff members make dummy page layouts by locating the material to be printed on layout sheets. The layout editors must indicate the area (width and depth) that each poem or article will occupy when set into type. The exact placement of the illustrations and titles for all material should be indicated on the page dummy. In order to know exactly how long an article will run when set into type, the layout editor must be acquainted with the basics of copyfitting (see Chapter 21, "Producing and Financing School Literary Publications"). Before cropping an artistic photograph and determining its final size, the layout editor should discuss with the photographer exactly what the photographer's intentions were when taking the picture, and what the photograph is intended to express. When picture stories are planned for inclusion in literary publications, layout editors often consider having the photographer help with the layout.

Section Editors—Ideally, the section editors are the best writers on the staff. Although section editors often assign articles to other members of their staffs, they are usually responsible for supplying the bulk of the written material for each issue. Section editors attend all pre-planning and staff meetings, and participate in all editorial discussions concerning content.

Business Manager—The literary publication business manager's job is similar to, yet less complex than, the yearbook business manager's job. The business manager must formulate the publication's budget for the year as well as for each issue. His primary responsibility is to see that the publication is a financial success. On many school literary publications the business manager and advertising manager functions are combined.

School literary publication copy editors usually edit all articles and captions, write titles and heads, and assign type specifications.

Ron MacNeil

Advertising Manager—Because of the expense involved in producing literary publications, literary publication advertising managers play an important role in helping to maintain their publication's financial stability. Ideally, the advertising manager and his staff should contract for enough advertising to fill about fifty percent of the total number of pages in the publication. When advertising revenue doesn't compensate for a substantial portion of the production costs, the price of the publication often becomes prohibitive for many students. Advertising salesmen for literary magazines sometimes canvass alumni to solicit contributions. Additional revenue is often gained by including the names of donors on pages titled "Patrons."

Circulation Manager—The circulation manager and his staff members must make sure that all students have the opportunity to purchase copies of the publication. Circulation representatives are often assigned to specific areas such as student lounges, cafeterias, etc. Tables displaying copies for sale are sometimes set up throughout the school on the day the publication is issued. Many publications send circulation representatives throughout the community to solicit sales from such places as doctors' and dentists' offices. Since many literary publications do not sell advance subscriptions, the circulation manager must determine with the business manager and the editor-in-chief exactly how many copies are to be printed.

Promotion Manager—While most school literary publications do not have promotion managers, the establishing of such a post might well be encouraged. There are often persons in journalism classes who are interested in entering the field of public relations, and the responsibility for being a literary publication's promotion manager offers these students ideal training as well as an opportunity to fulfill an important function for the publication. The duties of the promotion manager include various ways of making the student body aware of the publication.

Literary Publication Deadlines

School literary publications are published less frequently than school newspapers: some are published monthly, some bi-monthly, some tri-monthly, and some only once or twice during the school year. Staff members working on school literary publications should plan to allow the printer at least one month's time to produce the publication after he has received the last piece of copy. This amount of time will, of course, vary depending on the printer, type of material, total number of pages, and printing method to be used. It is always preferable to meet with the printer as early in the school year as possible to establish specific deadlines and publication date.

TYPICAL STAFF ORGANIZATION FOR A SCHOOL LITERARY PUBLICATION

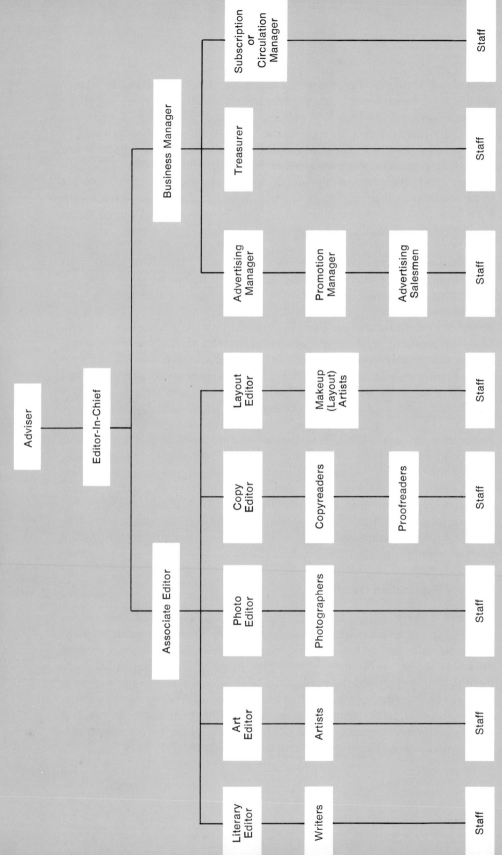

Organization of Editorial Content

The organization of the editorial content of a school's literary publication will have more unity and coherence when an overall theme is used for each issue. For example, one issue might use "Spring" as the general theme for every story, poem, photo, and piece of artwork, and the following issues could use the remaining seasons of the year as their themes. Another type of theme often used is the social commentary theme. This type of theme deals with areas of social concern such as problems of the city, problems of farm communities, or major problems faced by today's youth.

WRITING FOR THE LITERARY PUBLICATION

Usually, the most competent writers on school literary publications are those writers who have already mastered the basic writing assignments discussed in Part Two of this book, "Basic Mass Media Writing Assignments." Ideally, these writers will have served their "apprenticeships" as reporters on the school newspaper. Such great fiction writers as John Steinbeck, Ernest Hemingway, Edwin O'Connor, and Albert Camus began their literary careers as newspaper reporters.

Who are My Readers?

One of the first questions the writer for the school literary publication must ask himself is, "Who are my readers?" Often, the readers of school literary publications are the more serious, mature students. These students are usually avid readers who are dedicated to literary pursuits. Articles for the literary publication must, therefore, be thought-provoking and well-written, thus ensuring a literary publication recognized by its readers for its high quality and literary merit. A literary publication known for its excellence of form and content seldom becomes involved in censorship problems.

Language Usage and Content

Many of the writing suggestions contained in Chapter 11, "Feature Writing," can be applied when writing articles for literary publications. In their writing, literary writers often establish tone, mood, character, and plot, and attempt to involve the reader in an awareness of one or more of the five senses: touch, smell, sight, taste, and hearing. For example, imagine trying to re-create in writing the experience of attending a carnival in terms of sight alone, without including the shouts of the barkers at the concessions, the clatter of the machinery operating the amusements, the music of the merry-go-round, the odors from the food stands and sawdust, the taste of cotton candy, or the feel of the stuffed animal you won. The next time you read a piece of literature that particularly appeals to you, notice how the author has used description to give you the total picture of what he is experiencing.

Appealing to the sense of sight, Richard Harding Davis, reporting in 1914 for the *London Illustrated News,* wrote the following description of the German army entering Brussels.

EXAMPLE:

> For seven hours the army passed in such solid columns that not once might a taxicab or trolley car pass through the city. Like a river of steel it flowed, gray and ghostlike. Then, as dusk came and as thousands of horses' hoofs and thousands of iron boots continued to tramp forward, they struck tiny sparks from the stones, but the horses and the men who beat out the sparks were invisible.

In the following example written in 1937 by Ernest Hemingway, who had been assigned to cover the Spanish Civil War for *The New York Times,* the sounds of war are described.

EXAMPLE:

> MADRID, April 24, 1937—The window of the hotel is open and, as you lie in bed, you hear the firing in the front line seventeen blocks away. There is a rifle fire all night long. The rifles go "tacrong, carong, craang, tacrong," and then a machine gun opens up. It has a bigger caliber and is much louder—"rong, cararing, rong, rong."

Another essential quality to consider when writing for school literary publications is choice of material. Commenting on the value of personal experience as source material, author William Faulkner once said:

> A writer is trying to create believable people in credible, moving situations in the most moving way he can. Obvi-

ously, he must use as one of his tools the environment which he knows.

Personal observation also makes good source material. Student writers should make a habit of taking notes when at the scene of an event that intrigues them. They might later consider using the information contained in these notes as the basis for the next poem, short story, essay, or nonfiction article they write.

To be an accomplished writer for a literary publication, the writer must have an appreciation for the English language. He should work hard at developing his vocabulary. In keeping with the adage, "Use a word three times and it's yours," student writers, when discovering words they can't define, might consider writing the words on a scrap of paper and, when the time is available, looking up the definitions. The student writer should then plan to use these new words in his conversation and writing. Like all writers, literary publication writers must, at all times, be concerned with correct word usage. Mark Twain once said:

> The use of the right word and use of *almost* the right word is like comparing lightning to a lightning bug.

The student writer who listens to lectures on writing and reads all available books on the subject cannot, of course, become a writer until he actually writes. Many student writers who have the opportunity to submit material to their school's literary publications constantly seek out people who will offer constructive criticism. Others enroll in as many writing classes as possible, and some apply for correspondence courses from such institutions as the Famous Writers School. Such courses of instruction help discipline student writers, forcing them to write regularly.

Making Language Work for You

Transition—Often, beginning literary publication writers are not aware of the necessity of building the paragraphs within their articles on the material already presented in preceding paragraphs. The use of transitional devices between sentences and paragraphs can help a writer achieve unity and smoothness in his articles. Fortunately, most of the transitional devices used to lead the reader from one thought to another are natural and simple, and are often used in conversation. Following are some of the most common transitional devices used by literary publication writers:

457

1. Continuing the same subject from one sentence to the next by repeating the same words or by using a synonym.
2. Using a pronoun that refers to a word in the preceding sentence.
3. Using the object of the preceding sentence as the subject of the next sentence, to effect continuation and development of the topic.
4. Making sentences parallel in structure.

Students who hope to become successful writers on school literary publications should attempt to use a number of figures of speech in their writing. Figures of speech help to make a literary article come alive and be more understandable to the reader. The four most common figures of speech are: simile, metaphor, hyperbole, and personification.

Simile—A simile is a comparison (expressed with "like" or "as") of two essentially unlike objects on the basis of a limited similarity. In the Richard Harding Davis selection used earlier, the German army is compared to a river: "Like a river of steel it flowed, gray and ghostlike."

Metaphor—A metaphor is a figure of speech in which a word or phrase literally denoting one kind of object or idea is used in place of another to suggest a likeness or analogy between them. Had Davis wanted to use a metaphor, he could have written: "The army was a river of steel, gray and ghostlike."

Hyperbole—Hyperbole, an even further intensification of the simile, is used to express extreme exaggeration to create an effect. To say a six-inch fish is eight inches is a lie; to call it a yard long is hyperbole.

Personification—Personification is used to attribute human qualities to imaginary or nonhuman creatures, things, or abstractions in order to better explain nonhuman things in familiar terms. "Dawn came dancing over the fields" is an example of personification. The following example, which uses both personification and metaphor, was written by Will Irwin for the *New York Sun* following the San Francisco fire of 1906.

EXAMPLE:

> Old San Francisco is dead. The gayest, lightest-hearted, most pleasure-loving city of this continent, and in many ways the most interesting and romantic, is a horde of huddled refugees living among ruins. It may rebuild; it probably will; but those who have known that peculiar city by the Golden Gate and have caught its Flavor of the Arabian Nights feel that it can never be the same.

The following lead, about the same tragedy, was written by Jack London for *Collier's Magazine*. A comparison of it with the preceding lead will show that without figures of speech many stories (even though written by famous writers) can be dull, lifeless, and boring.

EXAMPLE:

> The earthquake shook down on San Francisco hundreds of thousands of dollars' worth of walls and chimneys. But the conflagration that followed burned up hundreds of millions of dollars' worth of property. There is no estimation within hundreds of millions of the actual damage wrought. Not in history has a modern imperial city been so completely destroyed. San Francisco is gone! Nothing remains of it but memories and a fringe of dwelling houses on its outskirts. Its industrial section is wiped out. The factories and warehouses, the great stories and newspaper buildings, the hotels and the palaces of the nabobs, are all gone. Remains only the fringe of dwelling houses on the outskirts of what was San Francisco.

It has often been said that as a group writers are an unhappy lot because, never being completely satisfied with their manuscripts, they continually seek out phrases and sentences they feel need additional polishing. Ernest Hemingway is said to have rewritten one pivotal sentence at least one hundred times. Asked if writing was easy for him, James Thurber once said:

> For me, it's mostly a question of *rewriting*. It's part of a constant attempt on my part to make the finished version smooth, to make it seem effortless. A story I've been working on was rewritten fifteen complete times.

And, according to William Faulkner, successful writing requires "ninety-nine percent talent, ninety-nine percent discipline, ninety-nine percent work."

Writing Interpretive Literary Articles

Because of the length of time involved between a newsworthy event and the deadline date for the average literary publication, some literary publication editors prefer to use nonfiction, interpretive articles in which timeliness is of minor importance. In the nonfiction, interpretive literary article, something new can be said about an event that has already taken place. The writer of the interpretive article gives an interesting element in the background of the event significance (rather than timeliness) by highlighting it for the reader.

Analogy—Interpretive literary article writers sometimes use analogy. Use of the analogy (comparison) infers that if two or more things are alike in some respects, they will probably be alike in others. For example, to give a better understanding of the atom a writer might write: "The atom has an internal nucleus with a system of electrons traveling around it in much the same way the sun has the planets revolving around it."

Anecdotes, Specific Details, Conflicts, and Case Studies—Interpretive literary article writers might also attempt to arouse reader interest by using such reportial techniques as anecdotes, specific details, conflict, and case studies. An example of the use of a case study in an interpretive article would be an article that documented the events in the life of a school dropout for one year after the dropout left school. In the following interpretive article lead, the writer points out the reason for the results of his baseball team's poor showing.

EXAMPLE:

> The inability to score runs has cost the hardballers dearly this season. Scoring one run or less in 11 of their 17 games, the team racked up a poor 4–13 record. . . .
>
> Dan Fischer
The Plume
Purcell High School
Cincinnati, Ohio

Using such reporting techniques as quotations, anecdotes, and specific incidents and details, the student writer of the following interpretive literary article won a writing award.

EXAMPLE:

When People Think of Circus —

"When people think of circus, the wherefores and the whys of it, they think of all the adjectives proclaiming, what's the size of it? The most amazing melody of merriment and mirth, the circus is the greatest show on earth."

This has been true from the earliest beginnings of the circus and has kept it alive to the present day. Yes, it is alive—at least Mr. Emmett Kelly, Jr. (Clown Prince), and Mr. James Cole, owner-manager of Cole's All-Star Indoor Circus have given me definite no's and distasteful looks when I brought up the term "dying institutions." Ringling Brothers and Barnum & Bailey Circus is just beginning its ninety-fourth consecutive season. Think, if you can, of the millions of people, of the wide-opened mouths, and even of the offended noses that have experienced this spectacle.

It has changed: actually there is an entirely new over-all concept of the circus. Most of the shows have moved indoors, not because of failure, but because of "class and status improvement." Now you can dress up and watch the thrilling acts from comfortable seats, not planks of wood. One other change, a heartbreaker for those who can say "I remember when," is the elimination of the parade. No more beautiful wagons, prancing horses, and huge elephants to watch as they march down the main street to the circus grounds. Reminiscing, Mr. Kelly told us how this has actually hurt the circus. "In some towns, like Fort Wayne, Indiana, where the coliseum is way out of town, the folks don't even know the circus is in town. They used to follow the parade and then stay to see the show, but not any more." Luckily, this sad state of affairs is not true across the country. The greatest portion of our country knows well when the circus is in town and supports it wholeheartedly. Last year, Ringling Brothers grossed more than they ever had before, and the prospects are just as good for this year.

The wages for performers are correspondingly high. The chorines with Ringlings' earn $105 per week. Some of those daring young men on the flying trapeze may earn as much as $5000 per week. Yes, again that is per week, but you have to take into consideration the years of practice and sometimes the months between big dates when they are not paid at all.

The circus families of this generation seem to be staying with it. Even with all the eight-hundred-mile one-night jumps they may have to make between shows, they are tied to the circus with an uncanny bond. Their whole life and work is a family heritage. The families are exceptionally close because they not only live together, they work together. Each person is involved in the success of the act and in the family's livelihood. Even outside family circles, the entire show is clannish. Again quoting Emmett Kelly, Jr., "When I'm with another type of show (ice show, for example), all the people are friendly enough, but you can't help but feel the difference because you aren't one of them. You don't know the same people or you don't share the same experiences. Each type of show has a separate world of its own."

By this time, you may be saying, "How can they stand it, always traveling?" True enough, but their lives are little different from those of a traveling salesman or of a construction worker. Actually, circus people have the advantage because they travel as a unit, in families.

In the back of my mind, I can hear my mother saying, "If you've seen one, you've seen them all," and it brings me back to the defensive position. At this point, I consider all my readers hostile to the cause of spreading interest in the circus, so may I say that my mother is wrong! The actual turnover and change within acts is tremendous. Many of the acts we see, like the one that was in Rochester—The Rosell Troupe of high wire artistes—are imported from other countries to add variety. This particular troupe is from South America: Three actors are from Colombia, one is from Ecuador, and one is from Santo Domingo. Theirs is only one of hundreds of imports. In addition to variety, I have heard other reasons why acts are brought in. One person said that foreign acts are of a better quality, while another person thinks they are imported because actors are able to do more than one act; that is, one group may appear two or three times in the same show. You can see the resulting conflict: for quality you need specialization, not diversity.

In the United States, it is almost impossible to break into the circus from the outside. Naturally, there must be one or two prime exceptions. John Cuneo, one of these exceptions, was born in Chicago. He is the son of a multi-millionaire and is a graduate of Georgetown University. Through a hobby, he became an animal trainer. A statement he made a number of years ago helps to explain the present image of the circus. "There are no big names to capture the public imagination. There is no Marilyn Monroe or Mickey Mantle in the circus." This is why most of us accept the circus with a mediocrity of enthusiasm. Then again, the complacency may only be a part of growing up; no, a part of growing older.

My argument is nearly over, but I have two incidents that have closer appeal. The late Professor George J. Keller was raised in Elcomsburg, New York. His brother now resides in nearby Hilton. Professor Keller was an art professor and dean of students at Columbia and Bucknell Universities, before he turned to lion training. In his mid-life, Professor Keller gave up an established career for one that was risky and dangerous. This alone gives you a little insight into the strength of circus lure or circus "bug."

Another lion trainer has a malady that must be hard to live with. Eddy Kuhn has asthma and is allergic to his cats (lions). To continue working, he must have an inoculation once a week. That is true devotion to one's work!

Perhaps it is circus, perhaps it is the people in it, but something has given the whole of it a rare quality of magic and of longevity. With this, how could it ever die? It will always be the "Greatest Show on Earth"!

Carol Annas
The Spectrum
Nazareth Academy
Rochester, New York

Writing Literary Articles Based on News

Some of the most interesting articles contained in school literary publications are based on news items. Alert editors keep abreast of general news developments beyond the area of regular school activities, often applying a local-interest feature to current news events. After some research and interviewing concerning a power blackout, two student writers presented the following feature. The feature has reader interest, timeliness, and proximity.

Those Cold Suppers by Candlelight — Remember?

Candlelight, cold suppers, and blazing fires on the hearth—that was the order of the day for many caught in the recent blackout. Mercians, along with all other residents of the area, will long be abuzz about what they did when the power failed.

Debby Oravac heard the doorbell ring. As she opened the door the lights went out and she greeted a young boy selling light bulbs.

Mary Ann Gould, working downtown at the time, reports jammed cash registers, elevators stuck between floors, and, in general, mass confusion.

Sue Donovan and her family were determined not to go without a hot dinner. Sue's family enjoyed a perfect meal cooked on the barbeque grill by Sue's father.

Sister Mary Bonaventure found herself on Joseph Avenue during the announced period of looting.

And Mary Beth Meagerty attended Mass in the dark.

The blackout proved to be a source of alarm for Mary Ellen Barrett's mother who almost unintentionally gave conditional baptism to the family's two-week-old baby.

Dorine MacLauchlan works as a cashier at Loblaw's at Garson and Culver. She says she always has liked her job but on that day she suffered stiff muscles in her arms by manually cranking the cash register while people remained to shop.

Mercy volunteers were on the scene at hospitals and rest homes when the lights went out. Maggie O'Dwyer was working at St. Mary's and was forced to trek up the stairs (five flights!) to deliver the patients' trays.

Sue Conradt, who works at the Episcopal Home, helped lead the elderly people by flashlight to their rooms. When she was not helping there, she watched the younger children.

On the other side of the city at St. Ann's Home, Mary Ellen LeVan was serving dinner. The lights dimmed for a few minutes but finally went out. Mary Ellen was asked to help the Sisters in a new project. This project was to lead about 100 ambulatory guests up the stairs from the dining room on the ground floor to their rooms on the sixth, seventh, eighth, and ninth floors. Because of recent heart conditions, each guest had to rest at each landing on chairs provided by the residents of the various floors.

Maureen Dever, along with many others, resolved the problem of what to do in a fairly simple way. She went to bed at 7 p.m.—the earliest she's been in bed since she entered Mercy!

The Quill
Our Lady of Mercy High School
Rochester, New York

Writing Literary Articles with a Fictional Approach

Our era might well come to be labeled "The Age of Writers with a Cause" as more and more writers and novelists reflect their concern for human conditions. Writers such as William Faulkner, John Steinbeck, and Norman Mailer have been able to convincingly express their concern by using the fictional approach. Student writers, very much aware of problems of social concern, often use the fictional approach in their literary presentations.

EXAMPLE:

The Children: The two boys sat on the bank of the river in the shade of the giant oak tree. For a long time neither of them spoke. One twisted a lock of his long reddish-blonde hair. The other pulled up the weeds and tore them into small pieces. He thought of all the times they had sat together under this same tree talking about every subject imaginable.

He thought of all the times they had wrestled and swum and played football, and all the other games they had played. He looked at his friend, wondering what he was thinking, wondering if he, also, could be thinking the same thing.

The first boy's face was wrinkled in deep thought. He felt his friend's stare and looked back. "I don't want you to have to go away," he said.

"I guess we ain't got much choice, though," replied the second.

"But people are so blind. Why can't they understand?"

"Maybe someday they will . . . But until then it's useless to try to force them to believe in somethin' they been taught ain't right," the second boy replied. He threw all the bits of grass he had been tearing up into the river. He stood up and kicked the dirt. The wind picked up the dust and the cloud floated off. "Well, I guess I gotta go."

The first boy stood up, and as he looked at his friend his eyes grew narrow and tears welled up in them.

"Goodbye," he stammered.

"Goodbye," the other boy said quietly and turned and left.

The first boy sat back down and buried his head in his hands. Hot salty tears ran down his face.

"Why?" he pleaded.

"Why can't he be my friend? Why? How come he's black?"

Charlotte Searl
Tam O'Shanter
Lakeland High School
Lakeland, Florida

Writing Literary Reviews

Many school literary publications feature reviews of stage plays, motion picture and television presentations, and books. Literary publication staff members with experience in music, art, or drama are often chosen to write the reviews. Ordinarily, when writing a literary review, the reviewer uses a format that includes in the lead paragraph identifying information about the matter being reviewed, followed by the reviewer's major impression and a brief synopsis. Specific characters or portions of the material being reviewed may then be singled out for special comment. Student reviewers should be aware that reviews, as well as being informative, should be constructive.

Book Reviews—Even though a book review is usually shorter than a review of a play, motion picture, or television presentation, it should still follow a similar format. Book reviews are often preceded by the title of the book, the author's name, the type of book (fiction, nonfiction, bibliography, etc.), the number of pages, and the price. The reviewer's name usually appears at the end of the review. Following is a student example of a book review.

EXAMPLE:

A meaningful book telling of an individual in a collective society, *Anthem*, by Ayn Rand, describes the sin of projecting individuality. The society was one where "I" existed only as a trivial and expendable part of a mighty machine, the whole. People referred to themselves as "We," never "I": for "I" is a strong word. It is a word of vibrant initiative. The unquestioned rule of the society was that each person must be incomplete, totally dependent upon everybody. *Anthem* is particularly intriguing in the era of mass conformity and leisurely individuality.

Elizabeth McLaughlin
Horizons
Mount Saint Mary Seminary
Nashua, New Hampshire

Stage, Motion Picture, and Television Reviews—While members of the student body are often more interested in reading the reviews of stage productions sponsored by their own dramatic clubs, many school literary publications help keep students informed by also featuring reviews of dramatic presentations sponsored by other schools, professional stage plays, and television and motion picture presentations. Stage, motion picture, and television reviews for school literary publications follow the same general format discussed in this Chapter under "Writing Literary Reviews." Following is a student example of a motion picture review.

EXAMPLE:

2001, based on the book by Arthur C. Clarke, is more of an experience than most movies. It is big, haunting, and unique. Only 46 minutes out of 159 have dialogue, but the rest is hardly silent scenery. Scenes of drifting spacecraft are accompanied by a powerful arrangement of *The Blue Danube;* but music is not the only element of the sound. When the first of several mysterious slabs appears, it emits a noise of such intensity that it is actually painful to the viewer's ears. Thus the audience becomes almost a part of what is going on.

The movie starts with the first ape-like men on earth who chase each other from a water hole. When one of the apes discovers that a hand-held bone makes a good weapon, he seems to go berserk and smashes to pieces the skeleton from which he took the bone. This is made an extremely frightening sequence by the heavy sound of drums, the terrifying sight of the ape, occasional shots of only his hairy arm swinging down with the bone, and by the implication of the fact that man's first discovery was a weapon.

Finally, after killing another ape, he throws the bone into the air and it becomes a spacecraft. After a while comes the first dialogue and the introduction of the plot, an almost minor part of *2001*. Another slab is discovered on the moon, put there 4,000,000 years earlier. It also emits a long shriek which seems to be a signal aimed at Jupiter. An expedition is sent there to search for what must be a tremendously advanced civilization. The spacecraft is entirely controlled by Hal, the computer, who seems more human than the astronauts. He eventually goes insane and kills everyone except Keir Dullea, who plays his part excellently, and the viewer is nearly scared out of his seat when an emergency buzzing suddenly starts and the screen flashes red with the news of Hal's malfunction. The deaths of three hibernating astronauts are indicated simply by the levelling off of their life function oscilloscope lines.

Dullea 'kills' Hal, gets to Jupiter by himself, spots another slab, and we are taken for a wild psychedelic ride. This is a sort of transcendental contact with the advanced civilization, since all they do would seem like magic to us.

There are many implications made about man and his developments and the film is somewhat of a picture and sound essay of philosophy on man.

Technically, the film is a fantastic accomplishment. An indication of this is the $750,000 paid for the centrifuge ordered by Kubrick for the spacecraft scenes. The photographic effects are done by completely new developments of Kubrick himself. They create fascinating scenes. *2001* is a great science fiction movie, portraying with great effect the best guesses as to what our technology will be in 33 years. It is also a bitterly humorous comment on what man's scientific development is doing for, and to, man.

Carl Greenberg
The Student's Pen
Pittsfield High School
Pittsfield, Massachusetts

POETRY IN SCHOOL LITERARY PUBLICATIONS

Students who write for school literary publications often discover that the medium of poetry can be one of the most expressive means available for defining their innermost feelings. Many school literary-art oriented publications feature poetry and artwork exclusively. Sometimes these poems, exclusive of their accompanying artwork, are quiet and contemplative in theme, as in the following student example.

EXAMPLE:

This is my country, silver-streaked and shining in the sun.
The sands stir restlessly beneath the breath of the sea.
The surf seeks the shore, crashing against the rocky coast,
  roaring the ocean's command.
This is my country, where the wind blends with the wild
  waters and cries of its freedom.

These are my people, the young, the free,
The people full of hope and love, eager for adventure.
The people who open their eyes and ears, who hear their
  hearts pound to the beat of the surf.
The eagerness of life fills their minds, feeds their souls.
Today they are born to the freedom of youth and tomor-
  row they shall begin the pursuit of maturity and of peace.

Horizons
Mount Saint Mary Seminary
Nashua, New Hampshire

Poetry of Humor and Satire—Poetry containing humor or satire can help attract readers to a school literary publication. In the following student example a clever parody of a nursery rhyme in the poetic style of Carl Sandburg
helps make the poem both timely and effective.

EXAMPLE:

Candle Jumper of the world,
Flame-Leaper, Scorcher of Pants,
Player with Fire and the Nation's Hot Seat;
  Nimble, quick, spry
  Boy of the burned blue jeans;
They tell me you are inconsistent and I answer:
  for I have seen you take a running start
  and sail above the fiery wick.
They tell me you are inconsistent and I answer:
  Yes, it is true I have seen you leap up and
  out and singe your posterior with a frightening
  yelp.
    Approaching,
    Springing,

Soaring,
Screaming,
Proud to be Candle Jumper of the world, Flame-
leaper, Scorcher of Pants, Player with Fire
and the Nation's Hot Seat.

Tam O'Shanter
Lakeland High School
Lakeland, Florida

ILLUSTRATING THE LITERARY PUBLICATION

The artwork contained in school literary publications can serve two purposes: it can be functional (illustrative of the editorial content), or decorative (ornamental and unrelated to the editorial content). In either case, literary publication artwork is usually more creative and artistic than the artwork contained in school newspapers. Many literary publications use abstract photographs and illustrations that attempt to portray the tone, mood, character, or plot of the editorial material being illustrated, and can be said to serve a purpose similar to that served by "mood music"—the portrayal of a mood or creation of a visual image. For example, when you listen to mood music you visualize what the composer is attempting to portray. Because the student artist is faced with a similar situation when abstractly illustrating the editorial content of a literary publication, he must translate the literary writer's words into a visual image that helps the reader create a mental picture of the tone or mood of the article. The student artist must, of course, read and understand the selection before attempting to illustrate it. Often, he will find it helpful to consult with the writer to obtain ideas.

Quality photographs for use in school literary publications are sometimes difficult to obtain. Because student photographers assigned to school yearbooks and newspapers usually have little time left for literary publication assignments, literary publication editors must plan such assignments well ahead of deadlines.

Many photographs taken during the summer prior to the opening of the school year can be adapted for use in literary publications, and different photographic printing techniques, distinctive cropping, and use of high-contrast papers can often enhance the quality of standard photographs (see photographic illustrations on the following page), making them more acceptable for use in literary publications.

The covers for most school literary publications are usually kept simple, and many covers carry only the title of the publication and the school's name. Most school literary publication covers are manufactured from heavy paper stock.

Distinctive photographic techniques that enhance the quality of standard photographs are often utilized in school literary publications.

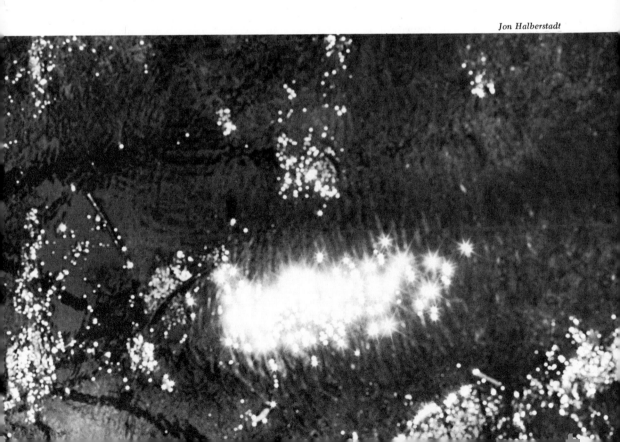

ACTIVITIES

1. Discuss in class the latest issue of your school's literary publication. What type of literary publication is it? Why? Discuss possibilities for improvements. If your school does not have a literary publication, discuss possibilities for producing one. What type of literary publication would it be? How would it be staffed? How often would it be published? Discuss your answers with a proposed adviser.

2. List at least three possible themes for a school literary magazine. Then, in outline form, suggest possible ways for handling each of these themes.

3. Write a two-page article based on all five senses for submission to a literary publication. Exchange your completed article with a fellow student for practice in copy editing.

4. Choose a controversial subject on which to write a brief interpretive literary publication article. Prepare the article so that it contains the four figures of speech described in this chapter. Upon completion of the article, eliminate all of the figures of speech. Compare the two versions. Which version do you prefer? Could the version in which the figures of speech have been eliminated be acceptable as a news story?

5. Choose a well-known story, poem, or nursery rhyme (such as "Jack and Jill") and rewrite it in the style of your favorite fiction writer or poet. Read your rewritten material to your classmates, asking them to determine whose style the finished article reflects.

6. Choose a televised documentary film (well in advance of its scheduled viewing time) that all members of the class can watch. Prepare a review based on the televised show. Choose the best review for submission to your school's literary publication or newspaper.

7. Prepare a brief, two-paragraph review on the last book you read.

8. As art editor for your school literary publication, you have been assigned to have illustrated an article based on a popular song. Using a song of your choice, would you have the article illustrated by an artist, or photographs prepared? Why? What suggestions would you make for artwork or illustrations to accompany the article?

READING

BIRD, GEORGE L., *Modern Article Writing*. Wm. C. Brown, Dubuque, Iowa, 1967.
BOIS, J. SAMUEL, *Explorations in Awareness*. Harper & Row, New York, 1957.

470

BRADBURY, RAY, *Fahrenheit 451*. Ballantine Books, New York, 1964. (PB)

BURACK, ABRAHAM S. (Ed.), *The Writer's Handbook*. Writer, Inc., Boston, 1968.

COWLEY, MALCOLM (Ed.), *Writers at Work: The Paris Review Interviews*, 2 vols. Viking, New York. (PB)

ENGLE, PAUL (Ed.), *On Creative Writing*. Dutton, New York, 1964.

FERGUSON, ROWENA, *Editing the Small Magazine*. Columbia University Press, New York, 1958. (PB)

FLESCH, RUDOLF, *The Art of Readable Writing*. Harper & Row, New York, 1949.

FOX, EDWARD S., *How to Write Stories That Sell*. Writer, Inc., Boston, 1961.

GUNNING, ROBERT, *The Technique of Clear Writing*. McGraw-Hill, New York, 1968.

HAYAKAWA, S. I., *Language in Thought and Action*. Harcourt, Brace & World, New York, 1964.

HILLYER, ROBERT, *First Principles of Verse*. Writer, Inc., Boston, 1950.

——, *In Pursuit of Poetry*. Writer, Inc., Boston, 1960.

McGRAW, ELOISE JARVIS, *Techniques of Fiction Writing*. Writer, Inc., Boston, 1959.

MARILLIER, HENRY C., *University Magazines and Their Makers*. Gale Research Co., Detroit, Mich., 1969.

MODERN LANGUAGE ASSOCIATION, *The Little Magazine and Contemporary Literature*. Modern Language Association, New York, 1966. (PB)

MURPHEY, ROBERT W., *How and Where to Look It Up*. McGraw-Hill, New York, 1958.

NATIONAL COUNCIL OF TEACHERS OF ENGLISH, *The School Literary Magazine*. National Council of Teachers of English, Champaign, Ill., 1966.

NIGGLI, JOSEFINA, *The Pointers on Playwriting*. Writer, Inc., Boston, 1967.

ROOT, ROBERT, *Modern Magazine Editing*. Wm. C. Brown, Dubuque, Iowa, 1966.

WEEKS, EDWARD, *Breaking into Print*. Writer, Inc., Boston, 1962.

WHITTEMORE, REED, *Little Magazines*. University of Minnesota Press, Minneapolis, Minn., 1963. (PB)

WOLSELEY, ROLAND E., *Understanding Magazines*. Iowa State University Press, Ames, Iowa, 1969.

Purple and more bl

The white-edged wa
Were green—like le

Where sunlight glin
From copper to gold

Chapter 21

Producing and Financing
the School Literary Publication

472

ainst the horizon.

gainst the shore

in some dark bower

outer edges

outer glow.

PRODUCING THE LITERARY PUBLICATION

The success of a school literary publication is considered by many to be completely dependent on the quality of the publication's editorial content. Many literary publication staff members, however, believe that because production techniques play a particularly vital role in a literary publication's visual appeal, the production aspects can often be considered of equal importance to, if not more important than, the literary content. The maxim "mere excellence of content is not enough to lure the reader to a publication," is, therefore, a basic principle that many literary publication editors choose to abide by. All of the production techniques used in the planning, copy editing, designing, and laying out of pages for a school literary publication have a major effect on the publication's overall success. Because the literary publication has no traditional format, the role that production techniques play in contributing to its success is, in many cases, more important than a similar role played in the production of other school publications.

Every piece of written material and illustrative artwork contained in the literary publication is, in effect, competing with every other feature: each feature is competing for reader interest—each one attempting to not only halt the reader as he glances through the pages, but to hold his attention until he has read the feature in its entirety.

COPY EDITING THE LITERARY PUBLICATION

Before being released for publication, all of the materials scheduled to be printed in a school literary publication must be copy edited and proofread by procedures similar to those discussed in the newspaper and yearbook chapters of this book. Students assigned the tasks of copy editing and proofreading on a school literary publication must be painstaking in their efforts and, more often than on school newspapers and yearbooks, must consult with the writers of articles for verification of suggested changes. Often, writers of literary articles use seemingly incorrect grammatical and structural forms for effect, and the copy editor, if not aware of that intended effect, might easily destroy the purpose of the article. For example, the first chapter of William Faulkner's *The Sound and the Fury*, in order to represent the thoughts of a mentally retarded person, consists mostly of sentence fragments. (In the final analysis, the retarded person is revealed as seemingly more sane than most of the supposedly sane persons in the story.) Had a copy editor corrected the fragments, Faulkner's characterization would have been destroyed.

Following Style

"Don't change anything unless you have checked thoroughly and are certain the original will be improved" is a rule many copy editors would do well to follow. The literary publication copy editor is concerned with making editorial material consistent and correct, and he often applies conventional rules of usage, spelling, punctuation, sentence structure, and paragraph organization to the copy he edits. He is aware, however, that because our language is constantly changing, language rules can only approximate the rules the majority of educated persons seem to be observing in their speech and writing at a given time.

Preparing a Style Guide—In setting up a style guide (or style sheet) for the school literary publication, the copy editor must be constantly aware that the goal of the literary writer (like the goal of the speaker) is to be understood. Rules, if they are to be useful, must allow for the variations of formal and informal usage in writing, and the appropriateness of one usage over another will depend, of course, on the occasion. Because our language is used in many different ways, with none of these ways being always right or wrong, copy editors preparing a style guide for a literary publication should make allowances for such language differences, taking into consideration that the style used to convey the purpose of any literary article will vary in standard usage (from formal to informal) depending on the writer and his intent. An editor once pointed out to Winston Churchill that the then Prime Minister of Great Britain had ended a sentence with a preposition. To have rewritten the sentence would have resulted in a stilted construction, and to show the ridiculousness of such a rigid rule of usage Churchill objected to the suggested editorial change in his sentence by indignantly retorting to the editor: "That is something up with which I will not put."

Mechanical Requirements—Some school literary publications have specific mechanical requirements for the handling of editorial materials that copy editors must be aware of. Such requirements should also be contained in the publication's style guide. If, for example, all poems are to be set in italics and the heads of fiction articles are to be set in a larger type face, the copy editor, having consulted the style guide, should indicate such requirements on the manuscript. Once any material has been set in type it should not be changed unless absolutely necessary, and then only if the publication is prepared to pay the compositor extra for alterations. The standard copy-editing symbols used by many school literary publications are contained in Appendix X at the end of this book, and an example of typed manuscript containing copy-editing markings is shown on page 375 of Chapter 17, "Producing and Financing the School Newspaper."

Marking Copy

After the copy has been edited, it must be marked for the printer so that he will know which kinds and sizes of type to use, and to ensure that it will fit the space planned for it on the layouts. Type is measured in units called points. One point is equivalent to 1/72 of an inch. Some of the standard type sizes used for the body type (not for headlines) in school literary publications are as follows:

This line is printed in 8-point type.
This line is printed in 9-point type.
This line is printed in 10-point type.
This line is printed in 11-point type.
This line is printed in 12-point type.

There are many different "families," or kinds, of type faces. The type face for the body type on this page is Caledonia. Most type faces can be set in roman (as is the body type on this page), *italics*, or **boldface**. Some of the type faces most commonly used for school literary publications are as follows:

This line is printed in 10-point Caslon (roman).

This line is printed in 10-point Caledonia (italic).

This line is printed in 10-point Century Schoolbook (boldface).

This line is printed in 10-point Granjon (roman).

This line is printed in 10-point Times Roman (italic).

This line is printed in 10-point Spartan Light (roman).

The leading (space between lines) and the width the copy is to be set at must also be marked. The leading (pronounced leding), like type, is measured in points. The leading between the lines of body type on this page is two points. The type size of the Caledonia face used for the body type on this page is ten points. Ten-point type with two points of leading between the lines is called "ten on twelve."

After marking the point size and leading for all of the type, the width the type is to be set at must be marked. The width of printed material is measured in units called picas. One pica consists of 12 points and is 1/6 of an inch. One inch contains 12 picas, or 72 points. The illustration on this page shows a pica ruler, a measuring device used by printers and copy editors to determine printing measures.

After marking the manuscript for point size, leading, type face, and the width the material is to be set at, all headlines and captions must be marked for size and type faces to be used. It is also necessary to mark copy for italics and boldface. These markings are shown in Appendix X.

Fitting the Copy

Copy editors must know the amount of copy needed to fill each page and the approximate length each story will run once it has been set in type. The length (or column depth) a story will require when set in type depends on the following three factors:

1. The size of type the story is to be set in.
2. The column width.
3. The amount of leading (space) between the lines.

While there are many complicated methods for computing lengths of material, the most common method used by literary publication copy editors can be called the "typed-measure" method. To determine the column

476

depth typed material will take when set in print using the "typed-measure" method, find, from a previous issue of your literary publication, an article set in the same type size, type face, and column width desired. Mark off one inch of printed copy. Then, setting the typewriter margins just as they were set when the manuscript was typed, retype the printed sentences contained in the one-inch space. The resulting number of lines will indicate the number of typed lines needed to fill a printed, one-inch deep space. Next, to find how many inches the entire story will run, divide the number of lines in one inch of printed copy into the total number of typed lines contained in the manuscript. For example, if you find that five lines of typed copy equal one inch of printed copy when set in 10-point type, leaded two points between lines at a two-and-one-half inch column width, and the manuscript contains 40 typewritten lines, the printed story will be eight inches in depth.

Writing Headlines

In most literary magazines the author will title his article or poem. If not, this must be done by the copy editor who should try to answer the question: "What is this story about?" Titles should have something interesting to say, or to suggest, about the story and should, when possible, relate to something the reader recognizes as his concern. Copy editors, in order to capture reader interest, often write imaginative and provocative titles. The title, however, should not promise something that is not fulfilled by the content of the story. Modern trends are away from flowery titles and from ones that aren't relevant to the content of the story. See Chapter 17, "Producing and Financing the School Newspaper," for useful suggestions on the writing and copyfitting of headlines.

Handling Artwork

Artwork for the school literary publication, often more artistic in nature than the artwork contained in school newspapers and magazines, must be handled with care. All artwork (photos and illustrations) must be identified both on the layout and on the artwork itself. This is of particular importance with literary publication artwork because much of it, being interpretive and decorative in nature, does not have identifying captions. Photo essays are often used in school literary publications of the literary-art oriented type, and often contain one overall caption for all of the artwork or photos on a two-page spread. Crop marks for artwork are made on the fronts of the illustrative material, and descriptive, locational, and identifying markings are usually made on the backs. The following illustration is an example of a two-page photo essay layout having one overall caption.

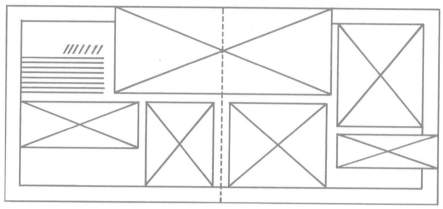

Layout for a two-page photo essay with one overall caption.

Unity, Coherence, and Emphasis

Unity, coherence, and emphasis—the three elements of major importance in writing and producing the school yearbook—are of equal importance in producing the school literary publication. In producing the literary publication, unity can be achieved by use of a theme and consistent style for layouts. Coherence can be achieved with balance (see Chapter 19, "Producing and Financing the School Yearbook"), and emphasis obtained by attracting attention to the most important element on the page by locating that element in a position of major importance. While both formal and informal balance are used when laying out pages for school literary publications, the trend is more toward use of informal balance.

Literary Publication Covers

Many school literary publications use intriguing artwork on their covers while others use only the name of the publication. Some schools, unable to afford the production costs involved in printing, have only the cover printed commercially and the inner content mimeographed by staff members. In either case, the cover for the literary publication should be in good taste and representative of the content, and could reflect the dominant theme of the issue. As with school yearbooks the three basic types of covers are: padded, hard, and paper. The majority of schools use paper, the least-expensive type. Paper covers, good only for publications containing 100 pages or less, are usually manufactured from a durable, heavy-weight stock.

LITERARY PUBLICATION PRINTING METHODS

Because of the high costs involved in printing, many schools have avoided establishing their own literary publications. Offset and letterpress printers often charge as much as $1 a copy to print a 24-page literary magazine, including illustrations. Such high production costs must then be reflected in the publication's price, making the sales price beyond the means of the average student. However, such schools should consider other printing methods, mainly because the end result—a medium for the publishing of student work —is far more important than a quality printing job. Although many school literary publications are printed by the photo-offset and letterpress methods discussed in Chapter 19, "Producing and Financing the School Yearbook," the majority are printed by other, less expensive, processes.

Mimeographed Publications

Many school literary publications are produced by mimeograph (see description of this process in Chapter 17, "Producing and Financing the School Newspaper"). In mimeographing, care must be taken of the stencil, especially when artwork and titles are being done. Typewriter keys must be kept clean and the margins carefully set when using this process. Plastic guides are available for use in lettering-in titles. A major drawback in using the mimeograph to produce school literary publications is that photographs reproduce poorly and lose their quality on electronic stencils. To combine photographs with mimeograph, some mimeographed newspapers send their photographs and a supply of paper to an engraver who prints the photos on the paper in the locations specified. Then the stenciled copy is run off on the paper with the photographs. The illustration on page 480 is an example of a page combining a photograph with mimeographed copy.

Low-cost Printing Methods

Editors and advisers of school literary publications often consider having their publications printed by one of the many new, relatively inexpensive offset methods. Small, "do-it-yourself" offset presses cost under one thousand dollars, and the plates for these presses cost only slightly more than mimeograph stencils. For this reason, a number of schools have purchased these presses and do a great variety of work with them. Recent statistics show that some 150,000 of these presses are now in use in schools, with about 12,000 more being added each year. In addition to their low initial cost, these

Alison Whitelaw

MY LOVE STILL PUPPY YOUNG

she came to me tonight
hair still damp with angry weather
and eyes of a nut shell tree
that saw much more than words.

i laughed a rainbow as she sipped
the red wine of forgotten grapes
and clothed my eyes with winding hair
as i looked upsidedownedly at her chin.

Ah! such wonders are to be found
in chins and hair. . . .

i went to her tonight,
my love still puppyyoung
from playing on swings and slides
of my days in sawdust playgrounds

she smiled a birthday smile
at me, as my harmonica played candlelight
in the pale room where we lay
with the rain   outside

we saw love for the first time
tonight, and we smiled at each other's love
in mother baby smiles. at the darkness
we smiled. and at nothing, nothing at all

          we smiled

                    Randy Love

living electric fairytale
reality
dissolves on your tongue. . . .
mind's prism candle melts
filling hollow bodies up
overflowing -
oceans of liquid dreams
spill rainbow
waterf
     a
     l
     l
     s

can you swim?

          Lisa Kampmeyer
                    Orpheus
          Redwood High School
          Larkspur, California

Many literary publications combine photographs with mimeographed copy.

480

presses are comparatively inexpensive to maintain and are also valuable because they can reproduce color and photographs. To set the type for these presses, an electric typewriter can be used to retype the manuscript copy onto presensitized paper. A press plate is made by placing the presensitized paper onto an aluminum plate the size of the literary publication's page and using a chemical for development in much the same way that a photographer develops his negatives. For less than one dollar a plate, any offset printer can then strip in the photographs. Because of the simplified operation of presses of this type, students find them easy to handle. These offset presses can be equipped with attachments for perforating, numbering, embossing, and printing on two sides of the paper.

In addition to aluminum printing plates, there are direct-image and photo-direct image plates. With the direct-image method, direct-image masters are prepared by typing, drawing, or lettering directly onto a paper master. Special ribbons, pencils, and inks are used. The most recent development, the photo-direct image plate, utilizes a special silver emulsion on a polyethylene-coated base in a process by which the film actually becomes the plate itself. In this process the image is photographed with a special camera and the plate is processed in about 30 seconds. The photo-direct method is adaptable to printing up to 10,000 copies. For other low-cost printing methods to consider when deciding how to print school literary publications, see Chapter 17, "Producing and Financing the School Newspaper."

FINANCING SCHOOL LITERARY PUBLICATIONS

Although the business functions on school literary publications are usually much smaller operations than on school newspapers and yearbooks, they are, nonetheless, important operations.

Probably one of the most frequent questions asked of literary publication editors-in-chief is, "Why doesn't your magazine come out more often?" The most frequent answer is that there usually just isn't enough money in the school's printing budget.

The literary publication business manager's job is similar to the job of his counterpart on the school yearbook or newspaper. The business manager must prepare a budget for each issue, and an overall budget for the year. The business manager supervises the advertising, circulation, and promotion departments to make sure that his publication remains profitable. Literary publication income is derived from advertising, patrons, and from individual sales, while the major expenses are from printing, supplies, and miscellaneous office and art supplies.

Advertising

As with the newspaper and yearbook, literary publication advertising representatives must contact the various merchants in their communities and attempt to sell them advertising space. Some schools also solicit contributions from patrons and alumni, and others offer a combined advertising rate for advertisers who wish their ads to appear in more than one school publication.

Depending upon the printing expenses and the sales price of the publication, the amount of advertising will, of course, vary. To be profitable, the amount of advertising space should be approximately 50 percent of the total number of pages in the publication.

Circulation

Distribution representatives should be assigned to specific areas throughout the school. These student representatives should familiarize themselves with the content of each issue and should be able to present a convincing sales talk. For example, if a distribution representative knows that a particular student is interested in sports, and the literary publication contains a sports story, the representative should mention the article to the student. Tables displaying copies of the publication might be set up in the main corridors of the school so that students could have ready access to purchasing the literary publication.

Promotion

Staff members in the Promotion Department should see to it that their promotion campaigns do not overlap campaigns sponsored by the school yearbook and newspaper.

About a week prior to the literary publication's printing, posters advertising the publication might be placed in prominent places throughout the school. Major stories could be featured on these posters. The school newspaper can also be used to publicize the literary publication and, in addition to advertising it, the newspaper can present pictures of the literary publication's cover, interviews with the editor of the publication, and feature stories about the publication's content.

ACTIVITIES

1. Which do you think is more important to the success of each of the types of school literary publications listed under *a* to *c*: the editorial content, or the production techniques that enhance the publication's visual appeal? Explain your reasoning.

    a. Literary-art oriented.

    b. Combination literary magazine-newspaper.

    c. Yearbook supplement.

2. From a recent issue of a consumer magazine, approximate the percentages of advertising and editorial content. Explain why these percentages help to ensure the publication's financial success. What, usually, is the minimum advertising percentage necessary to ensure a reasonably profitable school literary publication?

3. Plan and lay out a two page spread for an 8½ x 11-inch literary publication using the following elements:

    a. A seven-inch wide headline.

    b. Two photographs (one measuring 7″ x 7″, the other 6½″ x 4″).

    c. A feature article set 18 picas wide (3″) and 10″ deep.

4. What three factors do you need to know in order to determine the amount of space that copy will take when set in type?

5. Count the number of lines on three pages of typewritten copy. Using the procedure explained in this chapter under "Fitting the Copy," estimate how many inches of printed space the typed material will fill when set in the same type face, size, and column width as the body type in this book.

6. Suggest five possible literary publication illustrations for a humorous feature that informs female students about the latest fashion trends.

7. For a layout in which you have used informal balance, how would you achieve unity, coherence, and emphasis?

8. Explain the differences between editorial and mechanical requirements as contained in a literary publication's style guide.

9. Prepare a brief, one-page editorial style guide for a proposed literary publication. Include such items as spelling, punctuation, and capitalization. Give samples for each item you include. For example: Spelling—compound words are to be spelled as one word (teenager, percent). Punctuation—hyphenate unit modifiers (a half-baked cake). Capitalization—use capital letters to begin a quoted sentence used with an explainer (He said, "The material is inside.").

10. Prepare a brief mechanical style guide for a proposed literary publication. Include information that explains how material will be set. For example: Poems—all titles for poems will be set in boldface, flush left on the page. All bylines for poems will be set in italics, flush right on the page, etc.

READING

ARNOLD, EDMUND C., *Ink on Paper*. Harper & Row, New York, 1963.

BIGGS, JOHN, *Basic Typography*. Watson-Guptil Publications, New York, 1969.

BURT, SIR CYRIL, *A Psychological Study of Typography*. Cambridge University Press, New York, 1959.

CLEETON, G. U., AND C. W. PITKIN, *General Printing*. Taplinger Publishing Co., New York, 1958.

GAMBLE, CHARLES W., *Modern Illustration Processes*. Pitman, New York, 1947.

GOGOLI, JOHN E., *Photo-Offset Fundamentals*. Taplinger Publishing Co., New York, 1967.

HANSON, GLENN G., *How to Take the Fits Out of Copyfitting*. Mul-T-Rul Co., Fort Morgan, Colo., 1967.

HOLDER, ROBERT, *A Complete Guide to Successful School Publications*. Prentice-Hall, Englewood Cliffs, N.J., 1964.

JONES, HERBERT, *Type in Action*. Boston Book & Art Shop, Boston.

KARNER, ERWIN F., AND C. M. CORDELL, *Successful School Publications*. J. Weston Walch, Portland, Me., 1959. (PB)

LASKY, JOSEPH, *Proofreading and Copy Preparation: A Textbook for the Graphic Arts Industry*. Mentor Press, New York, 1954.

LATIMER, H. C., *Survey of Lithography*. Graphic Arts Technical Foundation, Pittsburgh, Pa., 1954.

LEE, MARSHALL, *Bookmaking*. Bowker, New York, 1965.

LIEBERMAN, J. BENJAMIN, *Types of Type Faces and How to Recognize Them*. Sterling, New York, 1967.

MAGAZINE PUBLISHERS ASSOCIATION, *Profitable Difference*. Magazine Publishers Association, New York.

McCLURE, LESLIE W., AND PAUL C. FULTON, *Advertising in the Printed Media*. Macmillan, New York, 1964.

ROBERTS, RAYMOND, *Typographic Design*. John de Graff, Tuckahoe, New York, 1967.

SCHWAB, VICTOR O., *How to Write a Good Advertisement*. Harper & Row, New York, 1962.

SKILLIN, MARJORIE, ET AL, *Words into Type*. Appleton-Century-Crofts, New York, 1964.

STRAUSS, VICTOR, *The Printing Industry*. Bowker, New York, 1967.

TINKER, MILES A., *Legibility of Print*. Iowa State University Press, Ames, Iowa, 1962.

WEINER, J., AND L. ROTH, *Paper and Its Relation to Printing*. Institute of Paper Chemistry, Appleton, Wis., 1969.

APPENDIX I

IMPORTANT DATES AND EVENTS IN AMERICAN JOURNALISM

1638 Printing press built in Cambridge, Massachusetts Bay Colony.

1690 First paper mill built in Germantown, Pennsylvania.

1690 First American newspaper, *Publick Occurrences Both Forreign and Domestick*. published by Benjamin Harris in Boston. It lasted only one issue.

1704 John Campbell established first continuously published American newspaper, the *Boston News-Letter*.

1732 First foreign language newspaper, *Philadelphia Zeitung*, published.

1735 John Peter Zenger, editor and publisher of *New York Weekly Journal* tried for libel and acquitted in first case establishing freedom of the press from censorship when facts reported are accurate.

1741 First two American magazines, *American Magazine* and *General Magazine*, published in Philadelphia, Pennsylvania.

1745 First attempt at stereotype printing made in Philadelphia, Pennsylvania.

1783 *Pennsylvania Evening Post* changed from a tri-weekly to a daily, thus becoming first daily newspaper in America.

1784 *Pennsylvania Packet and Daily Advertising* became first successful daily newspaper.

1786 First newspaper west of the Appalachians, the *Pittsburgh Gazette*, founded.

1791 Freedom of the press established by First Amendment.

1798 Lithographic printing rediscovered.

1800 Invention of Fourdrinier machine which made paper in continuous web.

1800 Use of streotyping in newspaper production.

1814 Development of the steam-driven press.

1825 Cylinder press, invented in Germany, used by *New York Daily Advertiser*, thus making possible mass-circulation dailies.

1827 First Negro newspaper, *Freedom's Journal*, published in New York.

1833 Successful penny newspaper, *New York Sun*, published. It stressed timeliness, local news, and human interest stories, and opened the way for mass-circulation dailies.

1835 James Gordon Bennett founded *New York Herald*, first newspaper to print Wall Street news (1835), establish foreign correspondents, and make use of the telegraph for news transmission (1846).

1839 Daguerre developed practical method of photography (daguerrotype).

1841 Horace Greeley founded *New York Tribune*, established to promote social reform and education of the masses.

1844 Morse transmitted first telegraph message.

1845 Rotary press using several rotating cylinders instead of the flat platen or the single cylinder developed by Richard Hoe.

1846 Manufacture of newsprint paper from woodpulp, first developed in Germany, introduced in America.

1848 *New York Associated Press* formed, first modern press association in America.

1850 *Harper's New Monthly Magazine* published, creating market for general-circulation magazines.

1850 International Typographers Union (ITU) organized.

1861 Transcontinental messages relayed by telegraph.

1861 Stereotypes introduced in newspaper printing.

1865 Mechanical device for feeding web into rotary press developed.

1866 Successful transatlantic cable laid.

1867 First practical typewriter perfected.

1868 Rotary press capable of printing both sides of web introduced into newspaper production.

1869 Washington and Lee University instituted first on-the-job educational program for journalists.

1873 Illustrated daily newspaper, *New York Daily Graphic*, published.

1876 Bell transmitted first telephone message.

1879 University of Missouri offered first course in journalism.

1879 Scripps Family formed first modern newspaper chain.

1880 First half-tone appeared in *New York Daily Graphic*.

1881 Offset printing press designed.

1881 Commercial long-distance telephone line opened.

1886 Mergenthaler Linotype machine, patented by Mergenthaler in 1885, used by *New York Tribune*.

1886 Frederick Ives perfected half-tone, thus making possible printing of photographs in newspapers.

1887 American Newspaper Publishers Association formed.

1893 First color illustrations printed in newspapers.

1893 University of Pennsylvania instituted first complete curriculum in journalism.

1894 Thomas A. Edison introduced motion pictures to public.

1896 Guglielmo Marconi transmitted radio signals over extended distance.

1900 *New York World* appeared as tabloid newspaper, emphasizing pictorial, concise, and lively presentation of news in five-column format.

1900 R. A. Fessenden transmitted human voice by radio.

1903 First motion picture which told story, *The Great Train Robbery*, made.

1904 Lithography applied to offset printing.

1904 Arthur Korn developed and transmitted messages via radio facsimile.

1905 Radio facsimile patented in America.

1907 E. W. Scripps began *United Press Association* as Scripps news-gathering service.

1908 Organized school of journalism started at the University of Missouri.

1912 Columbia University instituted graduate school of journalism.

1915 Transcontinental telephone service opened between San Francisco and New York.

1915 First modern feature film, *The Birth of a Nation*, produced.

1917 First Pulitzer Prizes awarded.

1919 Woodrow Wilson became first president heard on radio.

1920 First regular commercial radio broadcasts made by WWJ, Detroit, and KDKA, Pittsburgh.

1921 National Scholastic Press Association founded.

1922 Photograph transmitted by facsimile across Atlantic Ocean.

1922 American Society of Newspaper Editors (ASNE) formed.

1923 *Time* started new fashion in news magazines.

1923 NBC became first radio network. CBS began in 1927, and MBS in 1934.

1923 American Society of Newspaper Editors adopted the Canons of Journalism.

1924 Columbia Scholastic Press Association organized.

1926 Quill and Scroll honor society formed.

1927 Experimental TV program transmitted between New York and Washington.

1927 Transatlantic radio-telephone service begun between London and New York.

1927 *The Jazz Singer* became first feature-length talking picture.

1928 Teletypesetter perfected, enabling Linotype machines to set type directly from perforated tape.

1928 Television programming begun by WGY, Schenectady, New York.

1931 Catholic School Press Association organized.

1933 Edwin H. Armstrong built first FM radio station.

1933 American Newspaper Guild organized.

1934 Federal Communications Commission (FCC) began operations.

1935 *Associated Press* wirephoto network established.

1936 *Life* started new trend in picture magazines.

1937 National Association of Broadcasters (NAB) promulgated radio broadcasting code.

1937 Radio facsimile newspaper transmitted by KSTB, St. Paul, Minnesota.

1939 Franklin D. Roosevelt became first president seen on television.

1940 RCA and CBS demonstrated experimental color television.

1941 Commercial television authorized by FCC.

1945 Ultra-High frequency channels made available for television.

1945 Color photograph transmitted via facsimile.

1947 Transistor developed.

1948 High-speed facsimile transmission demonstrated by transmitting Margaret Mitchell's entire novel of 457,000 words, *Gone with the Wind*, a distance of three miles in two minutes and twenty-one seconds.

1948 Xerography printing developed.

1949 Successful commercial photographic typesetting machine, *Fotosetter*, employed in newspaper production.

1950 Community antenna television (CATV) introduced.

1951 CBS introduced limited color broadcasting.

1951 Commercial electronic computer, UNIVAC, produced.

1951 First transcontinental live telecast.

1952 National Association of Broadcasters introduced broadcasting code for television.

1952 Federal Communications Commission made channels available for non-commercial television.

1953 KUHT, Houston, became first television station to broadcast educational programming.

1953 First color television program broadcast.

1955 Television tape recording introduced.

1955 Alabama established first state educational television network.

1957 First artificial satellite launched.

1960 Functional laser beam developed.

1961 Laser beam developed for use in communications.

1962 WHCT, Hartford, began first pay-TV programming.

1962 Television program relayed via space satellite.

1965 Pictures of moon are telecast live from U.S. spacecraft.

1967 Public Broadcasting Act passed, furthering non-commercial television broadcasting.

1967 Facsimile transmission sent via satellite from London, England to San Juan, Puerto Rico.

1968 Computer used to edit length of news stories.

1968 Increased application of automation and computerized technology to printing.

1969 Laser beam used in facsimile transmission, increasing clarity and speed of transmitted photographs.

1969 Pictures of moon, from the moon, are telecast live to home viewers.

APPENDIX II

CODE OF ETHICS, OR CANONS OF JOURNALISM—

American Society of Newspaper Editors

The primary function of newspapers is to communicate to the human race what its members do, feel, and think. Journalism, therefore, demands of its practitioners the widest range of intelligence, or knowledge, and of experience, as well as natural and trained powers of observation and reasoning. To its opportunities as a chronicle are indissolubly linked its obligations as teacher and interpreter.

To the end of finding some means of codifying sound practice and just aspirations of American journalism, these canons are set forth:

I

Responsibility—The right of a newspaper to attract and hold readers is restricted by nothing but considerations of public welfare. The use a newspaper makes of the share of public attention it gains serves to determine its sense of responsibility, which it shares with every member of its staff. A journalist who uses his power for any selfish or otherwise unworthy purpose is faithless to a high trust.

II

Freedom of the Press—Freedom of the press is to be guarded as a vital right of mankind. It is the unquestionable right to discuss whatever is not explicitly forbidden by law, including the wisdom of any restrictive statute.

III

Independence—Freedom from all obligations except that of fidelity to the public interest is vital.
1. Promotion of any private interest contrary to the general welfare, for whatever reason, is not compatible with honest journalism. So-called news

communications from private sources should not be published without public notice of their source or else substantiation of their claims to value as news, both in form and substance.

2. Partisanship, in editorial comment which knowingly departs from the truth, does violence to the best spirit of American journalism; in the news columns it is subversive of a fundamental principle of the profession.

IV

Sincerity, Truthfulness, Accuracy—Good faith with the reader is the foundation of all journalism worthy of the name.

1. By every consideration of good faith a newspaper is constrained to be truthful. It is not to be excused for lack of thoroughness or accuracy within its control, or failure to obtain command of these essential qualities.

2. Headlines should be fully warranted by the contents of the articles which they surmount.

V

Impartiality—Sound practice makes clear distinction between news reports and expressions of opinion. News reports should be free from opinion or bias of any kind.

1. This rule does not apply to so-called special articles unmistakably devoted to advocacy or characterized by a signature authorizing the writer's own conclusions and interpretation.

VI

Fair Play—A newspaper should not publish unofficial charges affecting reputation or moral character without opportunity given to the accused to be heard; right practice demands the giving of such opportunity in all cases of serious accusation outside judicial proceedings.

1. A newspaper should not invade private rights or feelings without sure warrant of public right as distinguished from public curiosity.

2. It is the privilege, as it is the duty, of a newspaper to make prompt and complete correction of its own serious mistakes of fact or opinion, whatever their origin.

Decency—A newspaper cannot escape conviction of insincerity if while professing high moral purpose it supplies incentives to base conduct, such as are to be found in details of crime and vice, publication of which is not demonstrably for the general good. Lacking authority to enforce its canons the journalism here represented can but express the hope that deliberate pandering to vicious instincts will encounter effective public disapproval or yield to the influence of a preponderant professional condemnation.

APPENDIX III

THE ASSOCIATED PRESS MANAGING EDITORS (APME) CRITERIA FOR A GOOD NEWSPAPER

A good newspaper prints the important news and provides information, comment, and guidance which are most useful to its readers.

It reports fully and explains the meaning of local, national, and international events which are of major significance in its own community. Its editorial comment provides an informed opinion on matters of vital concern to its readers.

By reflecting the total image of its own community in its news coverage and by providing wise counsel in its editorials, a good newspaper becomes a public conscience. It also must be lively, imaginative, and original; it must have a sense of humor, and the power to arouse keen interest.

To implement these principles of good editing requires a skilled staff, an attractive format, adequate space for news and comment, and a sound business foundation.

The staff must possess the professional pride and competence necessary to breathe life and meaning into the daily record of history. Good writing must be combined with an effective typographical display of copy and pictures to capture the full drama and excitement of the day's news. Good printing is essential.

News and comment of most immediate interest and importance to the local community shall have priority for the available space, which will depend on the size and resources of the newspaper.

To assure a financially strong and independent publication, and one that is competitive with other media, a good newspaper must maintain effective circulation, advertising, and promotion departments.

Criteria of a Good Newspaper

A good newspaper may judge its own performance—and be judged—by the criteria which follow:

Accuracy—The newspaper shall:
1. Exert maximum effort to print the truth in all news statements.
2. Strive for completeness and objectivity.
3. Guard against carelessness, bias or distortion by either emphasis or omission.

Responsibility—The newspaper shall:
1. Use mature and considered judgment in the public interest at all times.
2. Select, edit, and display news on the basis of the significance and its genuine usefulness to the public.
3. Edit news affecting public morals with candor and good taste and avoid an imbalance of sensational, preponderantly negative, or merely trivial news.
4. Accent when possible a reasonable amount of news which illustrates the values of compassion, self-sacrifice, heroism, good citizenship, and patriotism.
5. Clearly define sources of news, and tell the reader when competent sources cannot be identified.
6. Respect rights of privacy.
7. Instruct its staff members to conduct themselves with dignity and decorum.

Integrity—The newspaper shall:
1. Maintain vigorous standards of honesty and fair play in the selection and editing of its contents as well as in all relations with news sources and the public.
2. Deal dispassionately with controversial subjects and treat disputed issues with impartiality.
3. Practice humility and tolerance in the face of honest conflicting opinions or disagreement.
4. Provide a forum for the exchange of pertinent comment and criticism, especially if it is in conflict with the newspaper's editorial point of view.
5. Label its own editorial views or expressions of opinion.

Leadership—The newspaper shall:
1. Act with courage in serving the public.
2. Stimulate and vigorously support public officials, private groups, and individuals in crusades and campaigns to increase the good works and eliminate the bad in the community.

3. Help to protect all rights and privileges guaranteed by law.

4. Serve as a constructive critic of government at all levels, providing leadership for necessary reforms or innovations, and exposing any misfeasance in office, or any misuse of public power.

5. Oppose demagogues and other selfish and unwholesome interests regardless of their size or influence.

Guide for a Good Newspaper

A good newspaper should be guided in the publication of all material by a concern for truth, the hallmark of freedom, by a concern for human decency and human betterment, and by a respect for the accepted standards of its own community.

APPENDIX IV

JOURNALISM SCHOOLS ACCREDITED BY THE AMERICAN COUNCIL ON EDUCATION FOR JOURNALISM (ACEJ)

UNIVERSITY OF ARIZONA
Tucson, Arizona 85721
Department of Journalism

BOSTON UNIVERSITY
Boston, Massachusetts 02215
School of Public Communication

UNIVERSITY OF COLORADO
Boulder, Colorado 80302
School of Journalism

COLUMBIA UNIVERSITY
New York, New York 10027
Graduate School of Journalism

UNIVERSITY OF FLORIDA
Gainesville, Florida 32601
School of Journalism and Communications

FRESNO STATE COLLEGE
Fresno, California 93726
Department of Journalism

UNIVERSITY OF GEORGIA
Athens, Georgia 30601
Grady School of Journalism

UNIVERSITY OF HOUSTON
Houston, Texas 77004
Department of Communications

UNIVERSITY OF ILLINOIS
Urbana, Illinois 61801
College of Journalism and Communications

INDIANA UNIVERSITY
Bloomington, Indiana 47401
Department of Journalism

IOWA STATE UNIVERSITY OF AGRI-
CULTURE AND MECHANIC ARTS
Ames, Iowa 50010
Depart. of Technical Journalism

UNIVERSITY OF IOWA
Iowa City, Iowa 52240
School of Journalism

KANSAS STATE UNIVERSITY OF AGRICUL-
TURE AND APPLIED SCIENCE
Manhattan, Kansas 66502
Depart. of Technical Journalism

UNIVERSITY OF KANSAS
Lawrence, Kansas 66044
William Allen White School of
Journalism

KENT STATE UNIVERSITY
Kent, Ohio 44240
School of Journalism

UNIVERSITY OF KENTUCKY
Lexington, Kentucky 40506
School of Communications

LOUISIANA STATE UNIVERSITY AND AGRI-
CULTURAL AND MECHANICAL
COLLEGE
University Station, Baton Rouge,
Louisiana 70803
School of Journalism

MARQUETTE UNIVERSITY
Milwaukee, Wisconsin 53233
College of Journalism

UNIVERSITY OF MARYLAND
College Park, Maryland 20740
Department of Journalism

UNIVERSITY OF MICHIGAN
Ann Arbor, Michigan 48104
Department of Journalism

MICHIGAN STATE UNIVERSITY
East Lansing, Michigan 48823
College of Communication, Arts

UNIVERSITY OF MINNESOTA
Minneapolis, Minnesota 55455
School of Journalism and Mass
Communications

UNIVERSITY OF MISSOURI
Columbia, Missouri 65201
School of Journalism

UNIVERSITY OF MONTANA
Missoula, Montana 59801
School of Journalism

UNIVERSITY OF NEBRASKA
Lincoln, Nebraska 68508
School of Journalism

UNIVERSITY OF NEW MEXICO
Albuquerque, New Mexico 87106
Department of Journalism

UNIVERSITY OF NORTH CAROLINA
Chapel Hill, North Carolina
27514
School of Journalism

NORTH TEXAS STATE UNIVERSITY
Denton, Texas 76203
Department of Journalism

NORTHWESTERN UNIVERSITY
Evanston, Illinois 60201
Medill School of Journalism

OHIO STATE UNIVERSITY
Columbus, Ohio 43210
School of Journalism

OHIO UNIVERSITY
Athens, Ohio 45701
School of Journalism

OKLAHOMA STATE UNIVERSITY
Stillwater, Oklahoma 74075
School of Journalism

UNIVERSITY OF OKLAHOMA
Norman, Oklahoma 73069
H. H. Herbert School of Journal-
ism

UNIVERSITY OF OREGON
Eugene, Oregon 97403
School of Journalism

PENNSYLVANIA STATE UNIVERSITY
University Park, Pennsylvania
16802
School of Journalism

RUTGERS, THE STATE UNIVERSITY
New Brunswick, New Jersey
08903
School of Journalism

SAN FERNANDO VALLEY STATE COLLEGE
Northridge, California 91324
Department of Journalism

494

SAN FRANCISCO STATE COLLEGE
San Francisco, California 94132
Department of Journalism
SAN JOSE STATE COLLEGE
San Jose, California 95114
Department of Journalism and
Advertising
UNIVERSITY OF SOUTH CAROLINA
Columbia, South Carolina 29208
School of Journalism
SOUTH DAKOTA STATE UNIVERSITY
Brookings, South Dakota 57006
Department of Printing and Jour-
nalism
SOUTHERN ILLINOIS UNIVERSITY
Edwardsville, Illinois 62901
Department of Journalism
UNIVERSITY OF SOUTHERN CALIFORNIA
Los Angeles, California 90007
School of Journalism
STANFORD UNIVERSITY
Stanford, California 94305
Department of Communication
SYRACUSE UNIVERSITY
Syracuse, New York 13210
Newhouse Communications Cen-
ter, School of Journalism
TEMPLE UNIVERSITY
Philadelphia, Pennsylvania 19122
School of Communications and
Theatre

UNIVERSITY OF TENNESSEE
Knoxville, Tennessee 37916
School of Journalism
TEXAS A&M UNIVERSITY
College Station, Texas 77843
Department of Journalism
UNIVERSITY OF TEXAS
Austin, Texas 78712
School of Communication
TEXAS CHRISTIAN UNIVERSITY
Fort Worth, Texas 76129
Department of Journalism
TEXAS TECHNOLOGICAL COLLEGE
Lubbock, Texas 79409
Department of Journalism
UNIVERSITY OF UTAH
Salt Lake City, Utah 84112
Department of Journalism
UNIVERSITY OF WASHINGTON
Seattle, Washington 98105
School of Communications
WASHINGTON AND LEE UNIVERSITY
Lexington, Virginia 24450
Lee Memorial Journalism Foun-
dation
WEST VIRGINIA UNIVERSITY
Morgantown, W. Virginia 26506
School of Journalism
UNIVERSITY OF WISCONSIN
Madison, Wisconsin 53706
School of Journalism

APPENDIX V

IMPORTANT AND INFLUENTIAL AMERICAN NEWSPAPERS

Akron Beacon Journal
Atlanta Constitution
Baltimore Sun
Boston Globe

Boston Herald Traveler
Buffalo News
Chicago News
Chicago Sun-Times

Chicago Tribune	Minneapolis Star
Cleveland Press	Minneapolis Tribune
Christian Science Monitor	National Observer
Dallas Times Herald	The New York Times
Denver Post	Pittsburgh Press
Des Moines Register	Providence Journal
Detroit Free Press	San Francisco Chronicle
Detroit News	St. Louis Globe-Democrat
Kansas City Star	St. Louis Post-Dispatch
Los Angeles Times	Toledo Blade
Louisville Courier-Journal	The Wall Street Journal
Miami Herald	Washington Post
Milwaukee Journal	Washington Star

APPENDIX VI

PREAMBLE TO THE TELEVISION CODE OF THE NATIONAL ASSOCIATION OF BROADCASTERS

Television is seen and heard in every type of American home. These homes include children and adults of all ages, embrace all races and all varieties of religious faith, and reach those of every educational background. It is the responsibility of television to bear constantly in mind that the audience is primarily a home audience, and consequently that television's relationship to the viewers is that between guest and host.

The revenues from advertising support the free, competitive American system of telecasting, and make available to the eyes and ears of the American people the finest programs of information, education, culture, and entertainment. By law the television broadcaster is responsible for the programming of his station. He is, however, obligated to bring his positive responsibility for excellence and good taste in programming to bear upon all who have a hand in the production of programs, including networks, sponsors, producers of film and of live programs, advertising agencies, and talent agencies.

The American businesses which utilize television for conveying their advertising messages to the home by pictures with sound, seen free-of-charge on the home screen, are reminded that their responsibilities are not limited to the sale of goods and the creation of a favorable attitude toward the sponsor by the presentation of entertainment. They include, as well, responsibility for utilizing television to bring the best programs, regardless of kind, into American homes.

Television and all who participate in it are jointly accountable to the American public for respect for the special needs of children, for community responsibility, for the advancement of education and culture, for the acceptability of the program materials chosen, for decency and decorum in production, and for propriety in advertising. This responsibility cannot be discharged by any given group of programs, but can be discharged only through the highest standards of respect for the American home, applied to every moment of every program presented by television.

In order that television programming may best serve the public interest, viewers should be encouraged to make their criticisms and positive suggestions known to the television broadcasters. Parents in particular should be urged to see to it that out of the richness of television fare, the best programs are brought to the attention of their children.

APPENDIX   VII

THE RADIO BROADCASTER'S CREED

We believe:

That Radio Broadcasting in the United States of America is a living symbol of democracy; a significant and necessary instrument for maintaining freedom of expression, as established by the First Amendment to the Constitution of the United States;

That its influence in the arts, in science, in education, in commerce, and upon the public welfare is of such magnitude that the only proper measure of its responsibility is the common good of the whole people;

That it is our obligation to serve the people in such manner as to reflect credit upon our profession and to encourage aspiration toward a better estate for all mankind; by making available to every person in America such programs as will perpetuate the traditional leadership of the United States in all phases of the broadcasting art;

That we should make full and ingenious use of man's store of knowledge, his talents, and his skills and exercise critical and discerning judgment concerning all broadcasting operations to the end that we may, intelligently and sympathetically:

> Observe the proprieties and customs of civilized society;
>
> Respect the rights and sensitivities of all people;
>
> Honor the sanctity of marriage and the home;
>
> Protect and uphold the dignity and brotherhood of all mankind;
>
> Enrich the daily life of the people through the factual reporting and analysis of news, and through programs of education, entertainment, and information.
>
> Provide for the fair discussion of matters of general public concern; engage in works directed toward the common good; and volunteer our aid and comfort in times of stress and emergency;
>
> Contribute to the economic welfare of all by expanding the channels of trade, by encouraging the development and conservation of natural resources, and by bringing together the buyer and seller through the broadcasting of information pertaining to goods and services.

APPENDIX VIII

THE PRODUCTION CODE OF THE
MOTION PICTURE ASSOCIATION OF AMERICA, INC.

Motion picture producers recognize the high trust and confidence which have been placed in them by the people of the world and which have made motion pictures a universal form of entertainment.

They recognize their responsibility to the public because of this trust and because entertainment and art are important influences in the life of a nation.

Hence, though regarding motion pictures primarily as entertainment without any explicit purpose of teaching or propaganda, they know that the motion picture within its own field of entertainment may be directly responsible for spiritual or moral progress, for higher types of social life, and for much correct thinking.

On their part, they ask from the public and from public leaders a sympathetic understanding of the problems inherent in motion picture production and a spirit of cooperation that will allow the opportunity necessary to bring the motion picture to a still higher level of wholesome entertainment for all concerned.

General Principles

1. No picture shall be produced which will lower the moral standards of those who see it. Hence the sympathy of the audience shall never be thrown to the side of crime, wrong-doing, evil, or sin.
2. Correct standards of life, subject only to the requirements of drama and entertainment, shall be presented.
3. Law—divine, natural or human—shall not be ridiculed, nor shall sympathy be created for its violation.

APPENDIX IX

PROOFREADING SYMBOLS

In the pages that follow, each black dot (•) preceding a function indicates that the marginal or internal symbol is used in manuscript editing as well as in marking proof.

General Corrections

Function	Marginal Symbol	Internal Symbol	Example
Delete	*(delete mark)*	/ or —	Good*e* design is functional.
Delete & Close up	*(delete & close up mark)*	*(close up mark)* or *(tie)*	Good design is functional.
• Paragraph	¶ or *(pilcrow)*	∧	Good design is functional. Ice cream melts in hot weather.
• No paragraph	no ¶	⌐ or *(run-on)*	no ¶ Functional color is one element of good design. It is used to graphically illustrate a pertinent point in the text.

499

Function	Marginal Symbol	Internal Symbol	Example
• Spell out	*sp*	◯	Supplementary publications for textbooks must be available before *sp* ⟨Sept⟩ and as early as possible.
• Stet (let it stand)	*stet*	. . . .	Good design is func~~tional.~~
• Underscore	*u/s*	——	Good design is functional.
Designation of a compositor's error	⟨P.E.⟩)show correction)	0 or — or ∧ or /	⟨P.E.⟩ Good⌿e design is functio⌿onal.

Punctuation and Special Character Corrections

Function	Marginal Symbol	Internal Symbol	Example
Period or decimal point (.)	⊙	∧ or /	⊙/. Good design is functional⌿ ⊙/ 17 + 4.2 = 5.9
Colon (:)	⊙	∧ or /	⊙ Describe these terms⌿ pica, point, spacing and leading.
Semicolon (;)	⟨;⟩	∧ or /	Publishing generally involves four major phases: the authoring and editing ⟨;⟩ of a manuscript⌿ the trans-

Function	Marginal Symbol	Internal Symbol		Example
			⑤	formation of the manu-script into graphically pleasing forms/ the plating, printing and binding of the book; and the distribution and sale of the book.
Hyphen (-)	=	∧ or /	=	A print bind order must be set for each new publi-cation based on sales office estimates and related pub-lications.
Comma (,)	⸜		⸜/⸜/	Sharp clean and neat marking of proofs con-tributes to production effi-ciency lower costs and greater accuracy.
• En dash (–)	$\frac{/}{N}$	∧ or /	$\frac{/}{N}$	The 1967/ 1968 football season is underway.
• Em dash (—)	$\frac{/}{M}$	∧ or /	$\frac{/}{M}$	Have the student write seven biographies. three reviews. one thesis.
Quotation mark, single (' ') or double (" ")	⌄ or ⌄; ⌄⌄ or ⌄⌄	∧ or /	⌄⌄ ⌄⌄	Good design is functional,
Exclamation mark (!)	/̣	∧ or /	/̣	We got the award
Interrogation mark (?)	?̣	∧ or /		Did we get the award.

Function	Marginal Symbol	Internal Symbol	Example
Parentheses ( )	(or)	∧ or /	Publication planning in-cluding supplementary titles promotes basic un-derstanding at the time for budget appropriation.
Brackets [ ]	[or]	∧ or /	The Fifty Books of the Year, AIGA, is one of the exclusive design award shows.
Virgule (slash) (/)	shill	∧ or /	The designer's choice was limited to 10 point shill and or 12 point of a sans serif family.

Typeface Corrections

Function	Marginal Symbol	Internal Symbol	Example
Wrong font	wf	/	wf Good design is functional.
Broken or smashed type	X	/ or —	X Good design is functional.
Invert	⌒	/ or —	⌒ Good design is functional.
Change to Roman basal weight type	Rom	◯	Rom Good design is functional.
Change to Italic basal weight type	ital	◯	ital Good design is functional.

Function	Marginal Symbol	Internal Symbol	Example
Change to Roman boldface type	*Rom bf*	⬯	*Rom bf* (Good design) is functional.
Change to Italic boldface type	*ital bf*	⬯	*ital bf* (Good design) is functional.
• Set in Roman basal weight capitals	*caps*	═	*caps* Good design is functional.
• Set in Roman basal weight lower case	*lc*	/////////	*lc* GOOD DESIGN is functional.
• Set in Roman basal weight capitals and lower case	*cap + lc*	≡ and /// as required	*c + lc* good design is FUNCTIONAL.
• Set in Roman basal weight small capitals	*s. c.*	══	*s.c.* good design is functional.
Set in Roman basal weight capitals and small capitals	*caps + s.c.*	≡ and ═ as required	*caps / s.c.* Good design is functional.
• Set in Italic basal weight capitals	*ital caps*	≡	*ital caps* Good design is functional.
• Set in Italic basal weight lower case	*ital.*	—	*ital* Good design is functional.
• Set in Italic basal weight capitals and lower case	*ital c + lc*	≡	*ital caps + lc* Good design is functional.
Set in Roman boldface capitals	*bf caps*	∼∼∼	*bf caps* Good design is functional.
Set in Roman boldface lower case	*bf*	∼∼∼	*bf* Good design is functional.

503

Spacing, Leading, and Positioning Corrections

Function	Marginal Symbol	Internal Symbol	Example
Less space (reduce space)	⌣	⌣	⌣ Good design is functional.
Close up (delete all space)	⌒	⌒	⌒ The title was set in italic bold face capitals.
Space	#	∧ or /	# Gooddesign is functional.
Equal spacing (space evenly)	eq. #	∧ ∧ ∧	eq.# Gooddesign ∧ is functional.
• Transpose (transfer)	tr	⊃ or ⊓ or ⊂	tr functional Good design is.
Horizontal alignment	=	=	=/= Good design is functional.
• Vertical alignment	//	//	// Good design is functional, simple and practical
• Horizontal move of type to the right	⊐	⊐	⊐ DESIGN
• Horizontal move of type to the left	⊏	⊏	⊏ DESIGN
• Vertical move of type towards head	⌐ ¬	⌐ ¬	⌐ DESIGN
• Vertical move of type towards foot	∟ ⌟	∟ ⌟	∟ DESIGN
• Center vertically	⊔ ⊓	⊔ ⊓	⊔ ⊓ GOOD DESIGN IS FUNCTIONAL
• Center horizontally	⊐ ⊏	⊐ ⊏	⊐ ⊏ ⊐DESIGN⊏

APPENDIX X

COPYREADING SYMBOLS

Marked Copy	Meaning	Set Copy
N.Y.	Spell out.	New York
6	Spell out number.	Six
Doctor	Abbreviate	Dr.
Fifty	Write in numerals	50
adress Letter (the)	Insert a letter or word.	address the letter
walks	Delete letter.	walk
acknowledgement	Delete letter and close up.	acknowledgment
book shelf	Close up space.	bookshelf
bookreview	Separate elements.	book review
centre	Transpose letters.	center
park baseball	Transpose words.	baseball park
Lim Polymer	Spell as is.	Lim Polymer
the daily newspaper	Delete word and close up.	the newspaper
Dr	Add period.	Dr.
Detroit Mich.	Add Comma.	Detroit, Mich.
James house	Add apostrophe.	James' house
Four score and . . .	Add quotes.	"Four score and . . ."
boston	Capitalize.	Boston
Presidential race	Change to lower case.	presidential race
Scholastic Press	Print in Small Caps.	SCHOLASTIC PRESS
The New York Times	Italicize.	*The New York Times*
The Editor-in-Chief	Set in bold face.	**The Editor-in-Chief**
The Editor in Chief =/	Insert hyphen.	The Editor-in-Chief
¶ Advertising is growing.	Indent for paragraph.	Advertising is growing.
no ¶ New agencies open . . .	No paragraph.	New agencies open . . .
. . . salesman. Executives are . . .	Bring two sentences together.	. . . salesman. Executives are . . .

GLOSSARY OF TERMS

A

Account executive (*Account representative*): member of an advertising agency (or department) responsible for the supervision and management of an advertising client's account.

Action-line column: a newspaper (or magazine) column that receives and investigates readers' questions and complaints, often suggesting solutions.

Advance story: a story that informs the reader about a future event.

Advertisement: a message which has as its goal the transaction of business between a consumer and a supplier.

Advertising agency: a business firm that gives advertising advice and services to clients.

Advertising beat sheet: a listing of advertising salesmen and of potential advertisers the salesmen have been assigned to contact.

Advertising contract: written agreement between a customer and an advertising medium or agency concerning advertising space or time.

Affiliate: member of a major national radio or television network system.

Agate: 5½-point type usually used for classified newspaper advertisements.

Anchor story (*bottom anchor story*): story or article, located near the bottom of a page, having enough importance to achieve visual balance in page layout.

Art: photographs or illustrations to be included in an advertisement or in printed material.

Assignment: instructions to a reporter or photographer for covering a specific event.

Assignment sheet: listing of news coverage assignments for reporters and photographers, usually kept by managing editor or news editor.

Astonisher (See *Kicker*).

Audio-visual writer: writer for radio (audio) or television (audio-visual) mediums.

Audit Bureau of Circulation: a business agency that monitors and verifies circulation figures of publications, making such information available to clients.

B

Background story: often presented as a sidebar story, supplying the additional background information not contained in a straight news account.

Bank (See *Deck*).

Banner (*Streamer*): headline that extends across the full width of a page.

Beat (*Run*): place or source of news covered regularly by reporters.

Bias: prejudice; opinion of a writer that, when injected into newswriting, destroys the writing's objectivity.

Biased news (See *Slanted*).

Billing copy (*Tear sheet*): printed copy of a page or that part of a page containing an advertisement, usually sent to advertiser with bill as proof of publication.

Bleed: any artwork or photo that extends over the edge of the trimmed page.

Blurb (See *Filler*).

Body: all of a news story following the lead.

Body copy (See *Copy*).

Body type: type, usually 8-point, in which news stories are set (except heads).

Boil down: to reduce a story in size.

Boilerplate (See *Filler*).

Boldface type: type that prints heavier and blacker than regular type. (Used for emphasis.)

Border (*Box*): metal strips used to box stories, ads, etc.

Break: point in a column at which a story is divided, to be continued in another column or page.

Broadcast: any informative or entertaining presentation made public by means of radio or television.

Buried lead: most important fact in the story, not contained in the opening.

C

Cable television (See *CATV*).

Candid photo: unposed photographs in which subjects are photographed while acting naturally or spontaneously.

Canned material: written or photographed material (usually feature) prepared by news syndicates and sold to members of the mass media.

Canopy head: headline having a main line of three or more columns in width, with following decks on extreme right and left.

Caps (*Upper case*): capital letters.

Caps and small caps (also *c & sc*): type matter set in small capital letters, except for first letters of prominent words which are set in regular capitals.

Caption (*Cutline, Legend*): descriptive, explanatory material appearing in type above, below, or beside a picture.

Caster: a machine for making type.

Catholic School Press Association: scholastic press association offering services to Catholic high schools and colleges (C.S.P.A., Marquette University, 552 North 13th Street, Milwaukee, Wisconsin 53233).

CATV (Community Antenna Television): television piped into areas and communities by means of cable television antennas (usually paid for by consumers).

Censorship: control (usually government or religious) over the communications media in order to prevent certain types of material from being published.

Chain newspapers: groups of newspapers published under the control of one man or organization.

Character: one figure, letter, number, sign, or symbol in a given type face.

Chase: metal frame used to hold a page of type as it is run off on a flatbed press or before it is stereotyped.

Chronological story: story that presents details in the order that they occurred.

Circulation: average total number of copies of a publication distributed per issue; also, the process of distributing a publication.

Circulation manager: person assigned the overall reponsibility for distributing a publication.

City editor: person assigned to supervise the gathering and preparation of news of the community in which the newspaper is published.

Classified ad: an advertisement for goods or services, usually set in 5½ point type that appears in the newspaper's classified advertising section.

Classified advertising manager: person assigned the overall responsibility for that section of a newspaper containing classified advertisements.

Cliché: expression that has become trite from overuse.

Clipping service: service set up to cut out and supply materials from many printed sources on any given subject.

Coaxial cable: cable consisting of a tube of electrically conducting material surrounding a central conductor, used to transmit telephone, telegraph, and television signals of high frequency.

Code of ethics: set of principles or standards that determines proper conduct or practice.

Cold type: type used in offset lithography (usually produced by IBM Typewriter, Varityper, or Justowriter).

Collate: to put together in specified or chronological order.

Color shot: photograph (or television shot) in color; or a black and white feature picture.

Column: timely and periodically produced presentation of editorial material, giving expression to the writer's own opinion; also, a vertical row of type on a printed page.

Column rule: strips of metal used to produce the vertical rules that divide printed columns on a page.

Combination head: headline that extends across two or more related stories.

Communications satellite: man-made object or vehicle containing transmission apparatus, intended to orbit the earth receiving and relaying high-speed transmissions.

Community service program (See *Public affairs program*).

Composing room: that part of a printing shop's (or plant's) production department where copy is set into type.

Composite: several parts combined to make a whole; as, a photographic composite in which several negatives are combined to be printed as one photograph.

Composite news story: news story with more than one main idea or thought; news story combining several stories into one.

Composition: photographic arrangement of subjects to produce an eye-catching, visually pleasing effect.

Continuous tone: photographic image which has not been screened and contains shade tones from black to white.

Copy: any written material ready to be set in type; any photograph or illustration to be made into an engraving.

Copy appeal: ability of copy to catch the reader's eye and hold the reader's interest.

Copy blocks: segments of copy used in making up page layouts.

Copy desk: table or desk at which copyreaders work, usually semicircular in shape.

Copyfitting: adjusting or rewriting copy to make it fit alloted space.

Copyholder: person assigned to follow and read aloud original copy while the proofreader checks for errors.

Copyreader: person assigned to correct and improve copy submitted by writers and reporters.

Copyright: author's or artist's right to control publication of his original material.

Copywriter: person assigned to write copy, usually for advertisements (advertising copywriter).

Corantos: first English newspapers of significance, appearing in the 1620's.

Coverage: obtaining of all available information and facts connected with a news event or story.

Credibility gap: term coined during Johnson administration concerning believability of government-emanated information as reported in the mass media.

Credit line: line of print stating the author's name or source of a story or picture.

Cropper's L's: L-shaped pieces of cardboard used to show how cropping will affect an illustration.

Cropping: marking an illustration or photograph to eliminate unwanted details, and indicating for the printer or engraver the part to be used.

Crossline: centered headline deck made up of a single line of type running across a column, not necessarily full-column width.

Crusading newspaper: newspaper that conducts special campaigns to promote worthy causes, or to expose unlawful or immoral conditions.

C.S.P.A.: scholastic press association offering services to school publications (Columbia Scholastic Press Association, Columbia University, Box 11, Low Memorial Library, New York, N.Y. 10027).

Cut: general term for a halftone, electrotype, stereotype, zinc etching, or any kind of engraving; also, to reduce the length of a story.

Cutline (See *Caption*).

Cut-off rule: printed horizontal rule used to separate stories, advertisements, and other typographical units, usually running from column rule to column rule.

Cut-off test: test applied to news stories to determine if last paragraphs contain essential facts, thus allowing makeup man to delete from end of story when necessary.

D

Dateline: line of type giving date of publication, usually appearing below the nameplate.

Deadline: time limit applied to all copy to be sent to printer.

Deck (*Bank*): secondary headline placed under the main headline; also, table on which typeset copy is stored for future use.

Delete: printer's term for remove or take out.

Desk man: sub-editor of a section or

department; also a reporter or editor assigned to receive news by telephone.

Disc jockey: person employed by network or local radio stations to play records for broadcast, and to sometimes announce news and advertisements.

Display: use of copy, pictures, or headlines in a way designed to make them easy to locate and read.

Display ad: large-size advertisement placed in prominent location in a publication.

Display type: large or decorative type used for headlines, titles, or advertising (not body type).

Diurnals: oldest-known regularly published accounts of daily news developed from accounts of English Parliamentary proceedings in 1641.

Division page (yearbook): a page or pages used to separate the major sections in the yearbook.

Documentary: a presentation (filmed or written) providing factual or substantial support for the statements and information contained therein.

Double truck: two facing pages laid out and made up as one double-width page.

Down style: newspaper style for type that capitalizes initial letters of as few words as possible.

Draft: (as in rough draft or first draft) initial manuscript or copy preparation before copyreading and final typing.

Dummy: sketch or layout of the way a page will look, showing makeup man where each makeup element is to be located; also, a blank page or blank book used for planning something to be published.

Duotone: photograph printed in black and one other color.

Duplicated newspaper: newspaper produced by machines using stencils, such as mimeograph.

E

Ear: type composition or design, usually boxed, placed in upper corner of page (to left or right of nameplate).

Editing: checking copy to ensure suitability for publication.

Edition: one issue of a publication.

Editor: person in charge of putting out a publication or section of a publication.

Editorial: type of journalistic writing which interprets the news, often reflecting the writer's or publication's opinions, beliefs, or policy.

Editorial policy: statement of a publication's goal or purpose; a given publication's official attitude toward debatable topics in the news; a principle followed by a publication in its news presentations.

Editorialize: to inject opinion into straight news presentations.

Education editor: editor assigned to supervise that section of a publication dealing with educational matters.

Educational television: noncommercial or "public" television used (usually on closed-circuit systems) to present educational materials.

Element of news (See *News element*).

Em: unit for measuring a quantity of type, square in shape, with each dimension being the same as the type size it represents; the horizontal space in body type is equal in width to the space occupied by the letter m.

En: one-half em.

Endmark: mark written or typed at the end of copy to notify the printer that the story is complete.

Engraving: metal or plastic plates that reproduce illustrations or photos.

Etch: removal of parts of a metallic plate by acid.

Ethnic newspaper (or publication): newspaper or publication that presents news and information of interest to a specific ethnic group.

Exchange editor: editor assigned the responsibility for the reciprocal exchange of his publication for other publications, who usually brings to the attention of other staff members items of note or concern contained in the publications received in the exchange.

Exchange publications: publications exchanged reciprocally, usually between schools.

Expository feature story: feature story that explains some topic of news value, emphasizing the *why* and *how* of the event.

Exposure meter: instrument by which photographers determine correct light exposure.

Extra: special edition of a newspaper.

F

Facing page: opposite page.

Facsimile: process by which printed matter and pictures are electronically transmitted.

Fast film: specially manufactured camera film prepared to allow picture-taking with short exposures.

Feature: news story, written informally, providing information and entertainment.

F.C.C.: Federal Communications Commission—agency of the federal government responsible for licensing and supervising broadcasters.

Filler (*Boilerplate, Liner*): extra informational material, usually short in length, that can be used at any time, prepared to help fill columns and to relieve monotony of solid columns of type; often supplied by syndicates.

Film holder: device for holding cut film in back of camera.

Five "W's" and the "H": the who, what, when, where, why, and how that constitute the basis for news stories.

Flag: nameplate appearing on page one.

Flat-bed press: printing press on which type rests on a flat surface; printing is accomplished by rolling flat pieces of paper across the type.

Flat lighting: results of too much artificial light thrown directly onto subject being photographed.

Flat rate (advertising): fixed advertising rate based on established price per column inch or agate line.

Floating nameplate: publications nameplate, which may appear in different position from issue to issue.

Flush: body type set even with margins.

Flush head: a headline unit having all lines flush with the left-hand rule or margin.

Focus: sharp image obtained by adjusting the distance between camera lens and film, or lens and plate.

Fold: imaginary horizontal line across the center of a newspaper page.

Folio: page number; sheet of paper folded once; book made up from large sheets of paper folded once.

Font: complete set of type of one size and style, including complete alphabets in capitals and lower case letters plus numerals and special symbols.

Foreign correspondent: newsman assigned to cover news from areas outside continental limits of the United States.

Form: type composition made up into a specified arrangement and locked into a metal frame (or chase) for printing or stereotyping.

Formal style: composition (writing) that strictly follows traditional rules of grammar and usage.

Format: plan for shape, size, and make-up of a piece of printing or publication.

Freelance writer: writer having no direct affiliation with any one given publication, thus enabling him to supply materials to several publications.

Free press: a press that is not censored except by itself, that reports the truth as it sees it.

Future book: date book listing story possibilities of future events (usually maintained by city editor).

G

Galley: long, narrow metal or wood tray used to hold type before it is placed in chase.

Galley proof: printed impression or proof of the type contained in galleys, usually printed on long, narrow strips of paper.

Gang: assembling of all similar materials into a single unit or group, for economy.

Ghost writer: writer assigned to write materials for someone else.

Giveaway: commercial publication, distributed free, having little editorial content and much advertising.

Gothic type: sans-serif type faces characterized by unslanted, straight up and down strokes.

Graflex: type of press camera used by news photographers.

Ground-glass plate: plate of glass on some cameras that reflects what will be contained in the picture.

Guideline: printer's instructions, usually written in capital letters above a story.

Gutter: space in a form that produces the inside margins of printed pages.

H

Halftone: cut made from a photograph; engraving that reproduces photographs, made by photographing the original photograph or picture through a fine screen to break the image down into a series (or pattern) of dots.

Hanging indentation: headline deck with first line running from column margin to column margin, and succeeding lines indented at left.

Hard news: non-feature and straight news.

Headline schedule: listing of examples of type faces used regularly for a publication's headlines.

Head-shot: photograph (portrait) showing only head and shoulders of subject.

Highlights: those parts of a photograph or picture appearing white or close to white; also, major points in a news story or feature.

Hold copy: materials, already set in type but not included in a publication, held for use in future printings.

Horizontal makeup: makeup style using headlines, cuts, and stories that extend across two or more columns.

Hot type: type used in letterpress composing, made from metal slugs.

House ad: advertisement in a publication advertising that publication, such as subscription information, feature highlights, etc.

House organ (*Company publication, House publication*): publication, produced by or for a company, organization, etc., containing news and information of interest to employees or members of that company or organization.

HTK (or *HTC*): abbreviation for printer's spelling of *Head to Kum;* incomplete copy awaiting headline.

Human interest: news element designed to stimulate the reader's feelings and emotions by presenting entertaining, interesting news about people and their actions.

512

I

Immediacy: news element stressing timeliness and freshness of reporting.

Impression: pressure of type, plate, or blanket in contact with paper.

Impulse item: non-essential product marketed by advertisers.

In-depth (coverage, reporting): news presentation emphasizing background, causes, and consequences of events.

Index: alphabetical listing of the contents of a publication.

Interest group (*special-interest group*): organized individuals using mass media to further their ideas, prestige, and power.

Interpretive journalism: type of journalism in which complex matters are explained and clarified.

Inverted pyramid head: headline in which the lines taper to the bottom, giving the appearance of an upside-down pyramid.

Inverted pyramid structure (or paragraph): newspaper writing style arranging information in order of descending news value.

J

Journalism: all of the activities involved in the gathering, organizing, presenting, and publishing of news.

Journalist: individual connected with gathering, organizing, presenting, and publishing news.

Jump head: line of type preceding continuation of a story that helps identify that story.

Jump line: line of type indicating where a story is continued to, or where a story has been continued from.

Justification: making all lines of type in a column exactly the same width.

Justified column (or margin): set type which always fills the line, thus creating uniform margins.

Justowriter: cold type, tape-controlled composing machine that automatically types and justifies a line of copy.

K

Kicker (*Astonisher, Read-in, Tagline, Whiplash*): short headline above or below main head, usually set in smaller-size type than main head.

Kill: to prevent or prohibit the printing or setting of copy.

Kinetoscope: machine invented by Edison for showing motion pictures.

L

Laser: device used for focussing, harnessing, and amplifying light energy.

Layout (See *Dummy*): finished plan for printed page, showing position and placement of all headlines, copy, photographs, illustrations, and advertisements.

Layout editor: individual responsible for planning the location of all items to be printed.

Lead (pronounced *leed*): first section of news story that introduces or summarizes a news event, usually contained in one paragraph.

Lead (pronounced *led*): thin strip of metal used between lines of type to separate and space them vertically.

Legend (See *Caption*).

Letter of query: letter written by free-lance writers to magazine editors, providing details of proposed article.

Letterpress: printing method by which the ink is transferred from the raised surfaces of the printing plate directly onto the paper.

Libel: written statement that impugns and oppugns a person's character.

Light meter: light-sensitive instrument used for measuring light available for photographing.

Liner (See *Filler*).

Line cut: engraving made from a drawing rendered in solid black on a white background.

Linotype: hot-metal, typecasting machine which casts a line of type on one piece of metal.

Lithographer: person who prepares an offset plate for printing.

Lithography: process of printing from a plane surface which accepts ink only on the design to be reproduced.

Live coverage: radio and television broadcasting of events simultaneously with their occurrence.

Lock-up: finished form of page, containing all engravings, type, and headlines, ready to be stereotyped.

Log (radio, tv): list of all sales, programming, and engineering activities to be forwarded to FCC for review.

Logo (*Logotype*): unique design of cast type used for identifying the name or trademark of a product.

Long-shot (*Establishing shot*): first shot taken by a motion-picture photographer when panning his subject.

M

Magazine newspaper supplement: magazine-style publications prepared for weekend newspapers.

Make-up: arrangement of engravings, type, and headlines on a page.

Managing editor: supervisor of all news-gathering operations on a newspaper.

Marketing research: systematic investigation of consumer needs, attitudes, and habits, usually conducted by an advertising agency.

Mass communication: dissemination of information to large numbers of people.

Mass media: any means of disseminating information or entertainment to large groups of people.

Masthead: statement of ownership and other related facts concerning a publication.

Mat (*Matrix*): mold made by pressing type form against receptive surface; in stereotyping, the paper mold used in printing newspapers.

Measure: width of type, usually expressed in picas.

Mechanical department: division of a newspaper responsible for composition, printing, and production.

Media director: a member of an advertising agency who determines the media an advertisement is to appear in (a decision usually based on which media will give the best return for the most reasonable investment).

Medium: instrument or means for transmitting message between sender and receiver.

Message: words, pictures, or signs exchanged between sender and receiver.

Monotype: machine for setting individual characters of type.

Montage: several photographs or illustrations combined to produce one overall photograph or illustration.

More: used at end of page of copy to indicate story is continued.

Morgue: library of files containing background information.

Muckraking: type of journalism dedicated to sensationally exposing problems and wrong-doing.

N

Nameplate: publication's title, usually appearing near the top of the front page or front cover.

National advertising manager: newspaper employee who supervises sales and placement of advertisements for nationally known products.

Network: group of radio or television stations which broadcast the same programs.

News: timely information about events that have occurred, are occurring, or will occur.

Newsbook: early forerunner of modern newspaper.

Newscast: any informative presentation (news program, documentary, etc.) made public by means of radio or television.

Newscaster: television or radio announcer who broadcasts news.

News director: individual in charge of the assigning and editing of news stories for the electronic media.

News editor (*Telegraph editor*): journalist who selects wire-service stories for newspaper publication.

News element: one of several qualities that attract reader interest to news presentations.

News interpreter: broadcast commentator who analyzes and interprets news events.

News leak: off-the-record information given to reporters.

Newsprint: inexpensive grade of paper used for printing newspapers.

News release (*Press release, Publicity release*): written information distributed to reporters by news source.

News source: reliable individual or group which supplies information to newsmen.

News story: factual report of news event.

Novelty lead: general term applied to any of several ways for writing an opening paragraph for news stories and feature articles.

N.S.P.A.: scholastic press association offering services to school publications (National Scholastic Press Association, 18 Journalism Building, University of Minnesota, Minneapolis, Minnesota 55455).

N.S.Y.A.: scholastic press association offering services to school publications (National School Yearbook Association, Post Office Box 17344, Memphis, Tennessee 38117).

O

Obituary: news story about a death.

Offset: method of printing from a flat plate.

Outline cut: engraving bordered by fine lines on all sides.

Over-banner: banner headline appearing above name of publication.

Overlay: sheet of transparent paper, placed over an illustration, containing instructions for engraver.

Overset: set type not used in a particular edition.

P

Phototypesetting: Method for setting type photographically.

Pica: 1/6-inch unit used to measure the size of type.

Pied type: type that is scrambled.

Platen press: flat-bed press used for letterpress plates.

Point: 1/72-inch unit used to measure the size of type.

Policy: editorial views and opinions of a publication.

Positive: photographic image which corresponds to original copy (the reverse of negative).

Proximity: news element having information about familiar people, places, or situations.

Public affairs programs: programs, in the public interest, prepared by radio and television stations.

Pulp magazine: inexpensively produced magazine, often presenting sensational articles.

Pyramided ads: advertisements bulked together on a page to resemble structure of a pyramid, so that each ad will be adjacent to news copy.

Q

Quill and Scroll: International honor society of journalism for high schools (School of Journalism, State University of Iowa, Iowa City, Iowa 52240).

R

Reproduction proof (*Repro*): proof (usually on quality stock) of final copy from which offset plates are made.

Rotary press: cylinder press used mainly by large newspapers for printing letterpress plates.

Running foot: line of type appearing at bottom of inside pages, giving name, date, and page number.

Running head: line of type appearing at top of inside pages, giving name, date, and page number.

S

Section editor: editor in charge of a particular section of a yearbook or literary publication.

Sensationalism: practice of selecting and treating news in a manner calculated to arouse emotional response.

Silhouette halftone: halftone in which all of the background material is deleted in order to emphasize only the main subject in the picture.

Slander: false charges made verbally, or verbal misrepresentations, that defame or damage a person's character.

Slanted news: news presentations written to reflect an opinion (usually the writer's opinion or the opinion of the medium the material is written for).

Sliding scale of rates: advertising rates that vary according to size, type, and location of advertisement.

Slug: metal bar on which linotype is set.

Spot news: timely news, usually occurring unexpectedly.

Stencil: type of printing plate used on mimeograph machines.

Stereotype: duplicate of a letterpress printing plate.

Stet: printer's term for "leave in" or "let stand."

Stripping: placement of negatives (or positives) in their planned position on a flat before platemaking.

Subhead: small headline within a story, inserted to indicate a subdivision within the story.

Subsidized newspaper: newspaper that is not self-supporting and must depend upon extra financial aid.

Summary lead: opening paragraph of a news story that presents the key facts of the story.

Syndicate: company, organization, or agency that buys and sells newsworthy materials to be used by members of the print media.

T

Theme: general idea expressed throughout a publication's copy and illustrations.

Tombstone: two or more headlines of same size and style, placed next to each other on same page.

Type block: page area, exclusive of margins, on which type and illustrations normally appear.

Typo: typographical error made either in typing or setting of copy.

U

Upper and lower case: type set with first letters of important words capitalized, remaining letters appearing in lower case.

Upper case: capital letters.

Up style: newspaper style in which all initial letters of important words are capitalized for emphasis.

V

Varitype: cold-type composing machine that utilizes a wide variety of type sizes, capable of justifying lines of copy.

Vignette: halftone made so that printed image fades off into white at edges.

W

Web press: term applied to high-speed printing presses that print on a continuous sheet of paper.

Widow: less than a line of type appearing by itself on the top of a page.

Wire service: news-gathering organization that obtains and services news for members of the mass media of communication. *United Press International* (UPI) and the *Associated Press* (AP) are this country's largest wire services; *Reuters* is Great Britain's.

XYZ

Yellow journalism: unethical, sensational news reporting.

Zinc etching: engraving of a line drawing made in zinc.

Index

B C D E F G H   07654321

PRINTED IN THE UNITED STATES OF AMERICA